THE THEORY AND PRACTICE OF COUNSELLING

THE THEORY AND PRACTICE OF COUNSELLING

2nd Edition

Richard Nelson-Jones

CASSELL

Cassell

Wellington House	PO Box 605
125 Strand	Herndon
London WC2R 0BB	VA 20172

First edition published by Holt, Rinehart and Winston Ltd

Reprinted 1996, 1997

British Library Cataloguing-in-Publication Data
A catalogue record for this book is available from the British Library.

ISBN 0-304-33135-X (hardback)
    0-304-33137-6 (paperback)

Typeset by Litho Link Ltd, Welshpool, Powys, Wales
Printed and bound in Great Britain by
Redwood Books, Trowbridge, Wiltshire

Contents

PART THREE EXISTENTIAL

Preface

Welcome

Welcome to the second edition of *The Theory and Practice of Counselling*. In this textbook I aim to provide you with clear, concise, easily accessible overviews of the major concepts and practices of some of the main theoretical approaches influencing contemporary human service providers. All people who counsel operate from theoretical frameworks about how clients become the way they are, how they maintain their problems, and how they can be helped to change. In this book I systematically present different theoretical approaches to help you become more aware not only of *how* you might counsel, but of the underlying reasons *why* you might choose to counsel in that way. In addition, this book encourages you to gain a greater understanding of your own behaviour. Counselling theories may be viewed as theories of human development or of personality. Their relevance extends beyond clients and counsellors to people in general, including you!

Intended readership

I intend this book as a basic textbook for undergraduate and postgraduate counselling theory courses in counsellor education, psychology, social work, nursing, personnel management, career development, pastoral care, welfare, teacher training and other areas of human service education. Also, I see this book as a text for counselling courses run by voluntary agencies. In addition, I intend the book as a user-friendly introduction to personality theory for undergraduate students in the behavioural and social sciences. I hope the book's applied academic emphasis appeals to many of these students and their lecturers.

Contents

The book consists of seven sections, aiming to give a selective yet comprehensive coverage of counselling theory and practice. The first section contains an introductory chapter that reviews some different ways of viewing counselling and what counselling theories set out to achieve. The second section consists of a chapter each on four theoretical approaches that might broadly be called humanistic. The approaches are Rogers' person-centred counselling, Perls' gestalt counselling, Berne's transactional analysis and Glasser's reality counselling. The third section presents two chapters representing important contemporary existential approaches to counselling: namely, Yalom and May's existential counselling and Frankl's logotherapy. For both its historic and present influence on counselling, the book's fourth section presents a chapter on the theory and practice of Freud's psychoanalysis.

In the fifth section, I focus on traditional behavioural theory and practice. The chapter on behavioural theory reviews the contributions of Pavlov, Watson, Skinner, Wolpe and Eysenck. The chapter on behavioural practice reviews interventions based on behavioural theory: for example, systematic desensitization and reinforcement methods. The sixth section on cognitive and cognitive-behavioural counselling starts with a chapter on Bandura's social cognitive theory, which questions the exclusive focus on observable behaviour by traditional behaviourists. The next two chapters present Ellis' rational emotive behaviour counselling and Beck's cognitive counselling. The seventh and final section of the book looks at two different approaches to working with the theory and practice of more than one approach: Lazarus' 'technically-eclectic' multimodal counselling and my own 'integrative' lifeskills counselling.

The main focus of the book is on counselling individuals. Consequently, there are no chapters on family counselling or group counselling, each of which might merit a separate book. Also, despite their importance, I have not included chapters that focus on special areas of counselling: for instance, career, multicultural or feminist counselling.

I have refrained from evaluating the different counselling approaches at the end of each chapter for three reasons: first, to avoid seeming to criticize theorists whom I asked for help in presenting their approaches accurately; second, to allow you to form your own opinions after reading and working with the material in the chapter; and, third, because I present my own ideas in the book's final chapter.

For those of you familiar with the book's first edition, the main changes in the new edition are: using the word 'counselling' rather than the term 'counselling psychology' in the title; the addition of chapters on gestalt, existential, logotherapy, cognitive and lifeskills counselling as well as on social cognitive theory; reviewing the theory and practice of each approach in the same chapter rather than dividing the book into two separate theory and practice parts; omitting material on group counselling and psychological education; and not focusing on special areas of counselling, for instance relationship concerns.

Features

I draw your attention to the following features of the book.

- *Authoritative.* I have striven to provide up-to-date and accurate presentations of each theoretical approach. For instance, when preparing the book, I contacted living theorists for their most recent material. In addition, I gave theorists the opportunity to preview chapters on their work and to suggest alterations.

- *Thorough and clear presentation.* Most chapters follow a standard format of subheadings that helps to ensure that the approach is thoroughly and clearly presented; namely, preview, introduction, assumptions, acquisition, maintenance, practice, chapter review and self-referent questions, annotated bibliography, and further references. This standard format assists you both in learning and in critically analysing the different theories.

- *Simple English.* I have tried to use simple, accessible English, while remaining sensitive to the distinctive terms and concepts used by different theorists.

- *Aids to comprehension and revision.* To learn a counselling theory properly, you need to understand its concepts. Each chapter ends with questions that help you review your knowledge of concepts. Both the chapter review questions and the summaries at the start of chapters are designed to help you to revise the material for term papers and tests.

- *Personal growth focus.* In addition to chapter review questions, each chapter ends with self-referent questions. These self-referent questions allow you to learn about the theory, and possibly to develop as a person, by applying to yourself concepts and interventions discussed in the chapter.

- *Help with further reading.* You are encouraged to use chapters in this book as stepping stones to reading primary sources. Each chapter ends with an annotated bibliography of some main additional reading suggestions as well as a fuller listing of further references.

Acknowledgements

I acknowledge with gratitude and admiration the distinctive contributions to the theory and practice of counselling of all people whose work this book presents. I thank the following theorists for providing material for the book: Albert Bandura, Aaron Beck, Albert Ellis, Arnold Lazarus and Irvin Yalom. While accepting full responsibility for the final outcome, I am grateful to the following people for providing feedback on drafts of chapters: Albert Bandura, Andrew Butler (for Aaron Beck), Marjorie Dempster (for William Glasser), Windy Dryden, Albert Ellis, Arnold Lazarus, Ian Stewart, Brian Thorne, Marjorie Weishaar, Franz Vesely (for Viktor Frankl) and Petruska Clarkson.

I thank my editor at Cassell, Naomi Roth, for commissioning the book, helping me improve its quality, and for her continuing encouragement and support of my writing endeavours.

Last, but not least, I thank all readers of *The Theory and Practice of Counselling* for your interest and indulgence. I hope that you find working with the book to be a very rewarding experience.

Richard Nelson-Jones

PART ONE

Introduction

ONE
Introduction

PREVIEW

- *Counselling may be viewed as a special kind of helping relationship, as a repertoire of interventions, as a psychological process, or in terms of its goals, its clienteles, and the people who counsel. No really valid distinctions can be drawn between counselling and psychotherapy.*

- *A theory is the formulation of the underlying principles of certain observed phenomena which have been verified to some extent. Three of the main functions of counselling theories are: providing conceptual frameworks, providing languages, and generating research.*

- *Sources of counselling theory include: historical and cultural contexts; theorists' personal histories, personalities, interest in writing and communicating ideas, and professional experiences and frustrations; research; the influence of other theorists; and insights from disciplines other than psychology.*

- *Counselling theories can be used for good or ill. Potential limitations of counselling theories include: restriction of focus, counsellor rigidity, unethical selling, depowering clients, and supporting the status quo.*

- *In addition to working with this book, you can learn about counselling theories by: applying them to yourself; reading primary sources, secondary sources and case studies; watching and listening to audio-visual material; attending training courses and workshops; and undergoing supervision and personal counselling by skilled practitioners.*

WHAT IS COUNSELLING?

The term 'counselling' is used in a number of ways. For instance, counselling may be viewed: as a special kind of *helping relationship;* as a *repertoire of interventions;* as a *psychological process;* or in terms of either its *goals,* or the *people who counsel,* or its *relationship to psychotherapy.* I discuss each in turn.

Counselling as a helping relationship

Virtually all counsellors agree that a good helping relationship is necessary to be effective with clients. Some counsellors regard the helping relationship as not only necessary but sufficient for constructive changes to occur in clients (Rogers, 1957). One way to define counselling involves stipulating central qualities of good helping relationships. Suffice it for now to say that these counsellor-offered qualities, sometimes called the 'core conditions', are empathic understanding, respect for clients' potentials to lead their own lives, and congruence or genuineness. Terms like 'active listening' and 'rewarding listening' are other ways of expressing the central skills of the basic helping relationship. Those viewing counselling predominantly as a helping relationship tend to be adherents of the theory and practice of person-centred counselling.

Counselling as a repertoire of interventions

Most counsellors would regard the helping relationship as neither sufficient nor sufficiently expeditious for constructive client changes to occur. Consequently, they require a set of interventions in addition to the helping relationship. Alternative terms for interventions are counselling methods or helping strategies. Counsellors who have a repertoire of interventions need to address questions of which interventions to use, with which clients, and with what probability of success? Counsellors' repertoires of interventions reflect their theoretical orientations: for instance, psychoanalytic counsellors use psychoanalytic interventions, rational-emotive behaviour counsellors use rational emotive behaviour interventions, and gestalt counsellors use gestalt interventions. Some counsellors are eclectic and use interventions derived from a variety of theoretical positions. Corsini goes even further and writes: 'I have come to believe that what counts in psychotherapy is *who* does it and *how* and to *whom* it is done: the *whohowwhom* factor.' (Corsini, 1989, p. 10). He suggests that counsellor personality and counsellor-client match are also important along with specific interventions.

Counselling as a psychological process

In this book the word counselling is used as a shorthand version of the term psychological counselling. Whether viewed either as a helping relationship characterized by the core conditions or as a repertoire of interventions derived from different theoretical positions, counselling is a psychological process. Reasons for the fundamental association between psychology and counselling include the following. First, the *goals* of counselling have a mind component in them. In varying degrees, all counselling approaches focus on altering how people feel, think and act so that they may live their lives more effectively. Second, the *process* of counselling is psychological. Counselling is not static, but involves movement between and within the minds of both counsellors and clients. In addition, much of the process of counselling transpires within clients' minds between sessions and when clients help themselves after counselling ends. Third, the underlying *theories* from which counselling goals and interventions are derived are psychological. Many of the leading counselling theorists have been psychologists: Rogers and Ellis are prime examples. Most of the other leading theorists have been psychiatrists: for instance, Beck and Berne. Fourth, psychological *research* contributes both to creating counselling theories and to evaluating counselling processes and outcomes.

Goals for counselling

Counsellors may have different goals with different clients, for instance assisting them to: heal past emotional deprivations, manage current problems, handle transitions, make decisions, manage crises, and develop specific lifeskills. Sometimes goals for counselling are divided between remedial goals and growth or developmental goals. The dividing line between remedying weaknesses and developing strengths is unclear. Also, attaining both remedial and developmental goals can serve preventive functions. Though much counselling is remedial, its main focus is on the developmental tasks of the vast majority of ordinary people rather than on the needs of the more severely disturbed minority.

Developmental tasks are tasks which people face at various stages of their lifespan: for instance, becoming independent, finding a partner, raising children, and adjusting to old age. Attaining developmental tasks involves both containing negative qualities and fostering positive qualities. Counselling's major focus is on psychological wellness or on positive mental health (Jahoda, 1958). Maslow's description of the characteristics of self-actualizing people represents an attempt to state goals positively in development rather than remedial terms (Maslow, 1970). His self-actualizing characteristics include: creativity, autonomy, social interest, and problem centredness.

Whatever the theoretical position, counselling goals emphasize increasing clients' personal responsibility for creating and making their lives. Clients need to make choices that enable them to feel, think and act effectively. They require the capacity to experience and express feelings, think rationally and to take effective actions to attain their goals. Clients are continually making choices. As Maslow observed: 'To make the growth choice instead of the fear choice a dozen times a day is to move a dozen times a day towards self-actualization' (Maslow, 1971, p. 47). Counsellors tend to be most effective when they enable clients to help themselves when counselling ends. Thus the ultimate goal of counselling is self-helping so that clients become their own best counsellors.

Who counsels?

A vast range of people counsel. The following are four categories of people who might view themselves as using counselling knowledge and skills, but not necessarily as counsellors. First, there are *helping service professionals*. Such people include counsellors, counselling psychologists, career officers, social workers and psychiatrists.

Second, there are *voluntary counsellors* trained in helping skills. These people may work in settings such as marriage guidance councils, young people's counselling services, and numerous voluntary agencies. Third, there are many *people using counselling skills as part of their jobs:* for instance, welfare workers, nurses, teachers, supervisors, clergy, doctors and trade union officials. Fourth, there are *informal counsellors* in daily relationships. Everyone has opportunities to assist others to develop their potentials be they marital partners, work colleagues, children, or friends.

Counselling and psychotherapy

Attempts to differentiate between counselling and psychotherapy are never wholly successful. Both counselling and psychotherapy represent diverse rather than uniform knowledge and activities. It is more accurate to think of counselling approaches and psychological therapies. Both claim to be based on 'informed and planful application of techniques derived from established psychological principles' (Meltzoff & Kornreich, 1970, p. 6). Attempts to distinguish counselling and psychotherapy include: psychotherapy focuses on personality change of some sort while counselling focuses on helping people use existing resources for coping with life better (Tyler, 1961); they are the same qualitatively, but differ only quantitively in that therapists listen more and engage in less informing, advising and explaining than counsellors (Corsini, 1989); and psychotherapy deals with more severe disturbance and is a more medical term than counselling. Both counselling and psychotherapy use the same theoretical models and 'stress the need to value the client as a person, to listen sympathetically and to hear what is communicated, and to foster the capacity for self-help and responsibility' (BPS Division of Clinical Psychology, 1979, p. 6).

Many psychologists, such as Truax and Carkhuff (1967), Corey (1993) and Patterson (1974, 1986), use the terms counselling and psychotherapy interchangeably and Patterson concludes that there are no essential differences upon which agreement can be found. I agree that there is a considerable overlap between counselling and psychotherapy. Nevertheless, throughout this book I use the terms counselling and counsellor in preference to therapy and therapist. This is partly for the sake of consistency and partly because I regard counselling as a less elite term than therapist.

WHAT IS A COUNSELLING THEORY?
What is a theory?

Hall and Lindzey write: 'A theory is an unsubstantiated hypothesis or speculation concerning reality which is not yet definitely known to be so. When the theory is confirmed it becomes a fact' (Hall & Lindzey, 1970, p. 10). These authors make the division between theory and fact too rigid. Rather a theory is a formulation of the underlying principles of certain observed phenomena which have been verified to some extent. A criterion of the power of a theory is the extent to which it generates predictions which are confirmed when relevant empirical data are collected. The more a theory receives confirmation or verification, the more accurate it is. Facts strengthen rather than replace theories.

Theories consist of a set of stated assumptions and concepts, ideally related to each other and internally consistent. A theory's assumptions and concepts should form a meaningful framework sufficient to encompass the phenomena that the theory seeks to describe and explain. In addition, a theory's assumptions and concepts allow the formation of hypotheses to test its validity. Furthermore, a theory may lead to the expansion of knowledge through suggesting and stimulating observation of relationships between events previously unobserved.

Functions of counselling theories

What do counselling theories do? Why are they useful? Counsellors cannot avoid being counselling theorists. All make assumptions about how clients become the way they are and about change. Three of the main functions of counselling theories are providing conceptual frameworks, providing languages, and generating research.

Theories as conceptual frameworks

Counsellors are decision makers. They continually make choices about how to think about clients' behaviour, how to treat them, and how to respond on a moment-by-moment basis during counselling sessions. Theories provide counsellors with concepts which allow them to think systematically about human development and counselling practice.

Counselling theories may be viewed as possessing four main elements if they are to be stated adequately. These elements are: (1) a statement of the basic *assumptions* underlying the theory; (2) an explanation of the *acquisition* of helpful and unhelpful behaviour; (3) an explanation of the *maintenance* and perpetuation of helpful and unhelpful behaviour; (4) an explanation of how to help clients *change* their behaviour and *consolidate* their gains when counselling ends. Figure 1.1 shows how counselling theories can be viewed as containing a model of human development and a model of practice.

When reading about the different counselling theories, you may observe that many if not most have significant gaps in their conceptual frameworks. They are partial rather

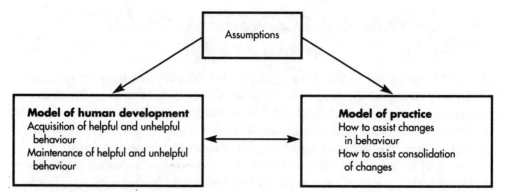

Figure 1.1 Diagrammatic representation of the elements of a theory and their interrelationships.

than complete or comprehensive theories. Arguably, some of the missing concepts in the theories are implicit rather than explicit. Also, theorists select for more thorough treatment those elements of a theory that they consider important. For instance, Ellis's rational emotive behaviour theory has a wider variety of explanatory concepts concerning how behaviour is maintained than how it is initially acquired.

Allport (1962) has suggested that however excellent the natural eyesight of counsellors may be, they always look at their clients through professional spectacles, with three lenses being worthy of special scrutiny. These are (a) persons seen as reactive beings, as in behaviourism; (b) persons seen as reactive beings in depth, as in psychoanalysis; and (c) persons seen as beings-in-process-of-becoming, which covers trends that might now be labelled humanistic-existential psychology. Some 30 years later, Allport's three lenses require supplementing by cognitive and cognitive-behavioural counselling lenses. In addition, an increasing number of counsellors find single lenses to be too restrictive and regard themselves as either integrative, putting together various theoretical parts into a consistent and meaningful whole, or eclectic, drawing from different theories in response to the demands of practice (Garfield, 1982; Zook & Walton, 1989).

Theories as languages

Another function of theories is similar to that provided by languages. Languages are vocabularies and linguistic symbols that allow communication about phenomena. Like the major spoken languages of English, French, Spanish and Mandarin Chinese, the different theorists develop languages for the phenomena they wish to describe: for instance, behavioural, psychoanalytic or person-centred languages. Language can both unite and divide. It can encourage communication between people who speak the same language, but discourage communication when they do not. Each theoretical position has concepts described in unique language. However, the uniqueness of the language may mask common elements among theories: for example, the concept of conditions of worth in person-centred counselling is similar to the concept of super-ego in psychoanalysis, though you would not know this from the language!

The counselling process is a series of conversations requiring languages. In any counselling contact there are at least four kinds of conversations going on: namely, counsellor and client inner and outer speech (Nelson-Jones, 1986). All counsellors who operate out of explicit theoretical frameworks are likely to talk to themselves about clients in the language of that framework. In varying degrees their counselling practice will match their language. Counsellors do not always act according to how they think. Also, in varying degrees counsellors share their theoretical language with clients. For example, unlike in transactional analysis, the language in which person-centred theory is expressed tends not to be shared with clients. Instead, person-centred counsellors try to reflect and match clients' outer speech.

Clients are also theorists, though usually without the sophistication of their counsellors. Approaches like rational emotive behaviour counselling and lifeskills counselling actively try to influence the language with which clients converse with themselves to become more functional. In a sense, the language of counsellors is being exported to clients so that they can better help themselves once counselling ends. These approaches educate clients to converse with themselves like either rational-emotive or lifeskills theorists.

Theories as sets of research hypotheses

The social psychologist Kurt Lewin is reported to have said that 'nothing is more practical than a good theory'. Paraphrasing him, perhaps 'nothing is more scientific than a good theory'. Theories can be both based on and drive research. For example, behavioural theory is based both on animal research – involving pigeons, rats, dogs and cats – and on human research. In addition, behavioural theory has led to counselling process and outcome research that tests the validity of behavioural interventions. Theories can also generate research 'by suggesting general ideas or by arousing disbelief and resistance'(Hall & Lindzey, 1985, p. 7). For example Freud's psychoanalytic theory was as important for opening up 'broad new paths of investigation' as for generating 'specific, testable propositions' (p. 7).

Counselling is a complex process involving counsellor, client and contextual variables in addition to what interventions counsellors use and how well they use them. Corsini (1989) views psychotherapy as an art based on science and suggests that there can be no simple measures for so complex an activity. Corsini's comments do not invalidate the usefulness of theory driven counselling research. Rather they suggest that great care need be taken over research designs and that researchers need beware of over-interpreting their findings.

Theories provide counsellors with frameworks within which to make predictive hypotheses. Whether acknowledging it or not, all counsellors are practitioner-researchers. Counsellors make hypotheses every time they decide how to work with specific clients and how to respond to what clients say. Clients are also practitioner-researchers who make predictions about how best to lead their lives. If valid counselling theories are transmitted to clients, this may increase the accuracy with which they can predict the consequences of their behaviours and, hence, gain more control over their lives.

Sources of counselling theory

Whence do counselling theories come? Following are some suggestions.

• *Historical and cultural contexts.* Theories do not incubate and emerge in vacuums. Theorists are influenced by the historical and cultural contexts in which they live. For example, the prevalence of sexual repression in turn of the century Austria influenced Freud to develop a theoretical position in which unacknowledged sexuality plays a large part. Another example is that, during the first half of the twentieth century, parents tended to dominate their families more than they do now. Carl Rogers was brought up in the first quarter of the century. His person-centred counselling reflects the need for individuals to have nurturing and accepting relationships within which to work through the effects of judgemental family upbringings so that they can 'become persons' (Rogers, 1961, 1980). Whereas Rogers reacted against certainty, the popularity of existential counselling in the latter part of this century partly represents a reaction to the structurelessness of much of modern society (Yalom, 1980). Old certainties provided by institutions like family and church no longer exist to the same extent and many people are faced with a more obvious need to create their own meaning.

Culture also plays a part in influencing theory. For example, ideas of desirable behaviour differ greatly between Western and Eastern cultures. Western counselling theories reflect a value on individualism that people from Eastern cultures, with their greater emphasis on group harmony, may find uncongenial (Ho, 1985).

• *Personal history.* Some counselling theorists seem motivated to design theories that will help not just clients, but themselves. Freud's self-analysis played a major role in providing insights for his main work *The Interpretation of Dreams* (Freud, 1976; Jones, 1963). Frankl's logotherapy stems from his youthful despair over the apparent meaninglessness of life (Frankl, 1988).

Rogers observes of his upbringing: 'I knew my parents loved me, but it would never have occurred to me to share with them any of my personal or private thoughts or feelings, because I knew these would have been judged and found wanting' (Rogers, 1980, p. 28). Rogers' person-centred counsellor has the empathy and non-possessive warmth that Rogers found missing in his parents and needed for his own growth.

In 1993 I attended a talk by Albert Ellis in which he recounted how, in his late teens, he regularly went to the Bronx Botanic Gardens in New York and forced himself to sit next to women on park benches and strike up conversations with them so that he could learn to control his shyness and build his relating skills. Here, early in life, Ellis was trying to think and behave more rationally in one of his problem areas. My lifeskills counselling approach reflects my own struggles and attempts to develop and maintain lifeskills strengths rather than skills weaknesses (Nelson-Jones, 1992, 1993).

• *Personality.* Another possibility is that counselling theorists not only design theories to help with their own problems, but also to reflect their personalities. For instance, Corsini observes that Freud's psychoanalysis, in which the analyst sits behind a client reclining on a couch and listens intently to what he or she says, reflected Freud's own shy and bookish personality (Corsini, 1956, 1989). Corsini knew Rogers both personally, as a client and student, and socially. He observes that Rogers and his system were identical. Though Rogers was not without his share of aggression and ambition, his person-centred counselling appears to have reflected his gentle and sensitive personal style. On the other hand, theorists like Ellis and Perls seem far more comfortable challenging clients' irrational ideas and smoke-screens, a characteristic they may possess in both their private and professional lives.

Counselling theorists possess similar as well as different personality characteristics. A common characteristic is that they are creative thinkers who are prepared to challenge existing ways of working. Also, many theorists possess high energy levels.

• *Interest in writing and communicating ideas.* As well as a talent for theorizing, theorists need the ability to write passably well in order to get published. When researching the biographical sketches for this book, I was struck by how many of the theorists early in their lives showed an interest in writing. In his teens, Lazarus helped edit a body-building magazine. Beck was editor of his high school newspaper and an undergraduate

English major. Skinner majored in English and planned to become a writer. Ellis too envisaged a writing career and wrote reams in his quest to become the Great American Novelist. May's main interest at college was English literature. Berne studied English along with psychology and pre-medicine as a undergraduate and his mother was a journalist. Later in their lives at least two theorists, Skinner and Yalom, branched out to write novels (Skinner, 1948; Yalom, 1991).

An ambition to communicate distinctive ideas, become known and, possibly, reap the financial rewards of successful authorship may also fuel theorists' productivity. However, readers should be circumspect about attributing commercial motives to theorists. For over 30 years Ellis has donated all his royalty, client and workshop income to the Institute for Rational-Emotive Therapy.

All theorists think they have something of value to offer and want to share it. For instance, throughout his professional life Rogers was very concerned with making an impact on others. Though motivation is complex, probably altruism, social interest and enjoyment also contribute to theorists' willingness to generate and share ideas.

• *Professional experiences and frustrations.* Though behavioural theory owes much to experimental psychology, for the most part the major counselling theories emanate from people who were practitioners as well as scholars. Frustration, creative insights, clinical experimentation and careful observation can each contribute to developing a counselling theory. Beck, Berne, Ellis and Perls were trained in psychoanalysis. Their negative experiences in practising psychoanalysis challenged them to develop their own positions. Each used their work with clients to develop and experiment with different ways of helping them. Reality counselling stems from Glasser's disillusionment with the psychoanalytic psychology to which he was exposed during his training and from observing many analytic teachers not practising what they taught.

Lazarus was stimulated to develop his multimodal counselling approach as a reaction to the restrictiveness of traditional behaviour therapy. Rogers developed his person-centred approach from discovering the limitations of existing ways of working. He recalls that, when in the 1930s he worked at the Rochester Child Study Department (later renamed the Child Guidance Centre), he obtained far better results with clients from listening to them than from diagnostic understanding and advice (Rogers, 1980).

• *Research.* Research can influence both the initial development of theory and test its usefulness. Behavioural counselling theory is based on experimental research: for instance, Pavlov's classical conditioning is based on experiments with dogs; Skinner's operant conditioning on experiments with pigeons and rats; and Wolpe's counter-conditioning by reciprocal inhibition on experiments with cats. Counselling theory is also based on counselling interview or clinical research. Counselling theorists are practitioner-researchers generating and testing hypotheses in their counselling practice. Thus professional experience is one form of interview research. Counselling theorists differ in the extent to which they either engage in or generate more formal interview research. On the one hand, approaches like cognitive counselling, rational-emotive counselling, person-centred counselling and behavioural counselling are heavily researched. On the other hand, there is a paucity of research into approaches like transactional analysis, gestalt counselling, existential counselling and reality counselling.

• *Other theorists.* Theorists are influenced by other theorists, both past and current. For example, Yalom and May's version of existential counselling, Berne's transactional analysis and Perls' gestalt counselling are each influenced by psychoanalysis. Beck (Beck & Weishaar, 1989) acknowledges that the theoretical underpinnings of his cognitive counselling are derived from the phenomenal, structural and depth, and cognitive approaches to psychology. An integrative approach like lifeskills counselling (Nelson-Jones, 1992, 1993) draws from numerous theorists, such as Rogers, Ellis, Beck, Bandura, and Yalom and May, to mention but a few.

• *Other disciplines.* Other disciplines influence how counselling theory develops. Freud's view of the person probably owes much to his medical background: for instance, his instinct theory. Ellis (1989) acknowledges his debt to the Stoic philosophers, particularly Epictetus and Marcus Aurelius. Frankl's logotherapy is enlightened by theology. Other disciplines which contribute to counselling theory include sociology, anthropology, politics and social psychology.

Limitations of counselling theory

All counselling theories should carry the psychological equivalent of health warnings. They can be used for ill as well as for good. Following are some potential disadvantages of theories.

• *Restriction of focus.* A criticism of many counselling theories is that they present partial truths as whole truths. Rogers may be viewed as an example of this tendency to overgeneralize. He posits a unitary diagnosis of all clients' problems, namely that they are out of touch with their actualizing tendencies, and sees the helping relationship as necessary and sufficient in all instances (Rogers, 1957). The traditional behaviourists pay insufficient attention to thoughts and feelings. Ellis focuses on irrational beliefs at risk of paying insufficient attention to other aspects of thinking, for instance perceiving accurately or using coping self-talk. Freud emphasizes uncovering unconscious material through the analysis of dreams, but says little about developing specific effective behaviours to deal with everyday problems. The trend to eclecticism among practitioners attests to this negative aspect of the major theories (Garfield, 1982; Zook & Walton, 1989).

• *Counsellor rigidity.* A function of theory is that it meets insecure counsellors' need for certainty. A beneficial side-effect of theoretical faith may be that it provides counsellors with confidence that gets transmitted to clients. However, such confidence may be misplaced. Many counsellors suffer from 'delusions of certainty' and a 'hardening of the categories' (Hubble & O'Hanlon, 1992, p. 26). Blocher (1987) sees many counsellors as taking boy scout loyalty oaths to pseudotheories. Other terms for this are true believerism and *rigor psychologicus*. Instead of acting as effective practitioner-researchers who test their theoretical hypotheses, such counsellors allow theory to interfere with the accuracy with which they assess and treat clients.

This tendency to theoretical rigidity is heightened by the development of theoretical schools. On the positive side, such schools can foster useful research and training. On the negative side, counselling schools can turn into self-congratulatory status systems that reinforce rigidity. Preferment goes to those that toe the line rather than those too interested in theoretical breadth. The different languages of theoretical schools can disguise similarities between them. In addition, language differences can lead to people only talking to those speaking the same language rather than to a broader sharing of knowledge and experience.

• *Unethical selling.* At worst, the development of theoretical schools can lead to an unethical approach to selling counselling services. Counselling certainties replace the struggle to offer valid psychological services. Practitioners of varying levels of training aim to market theoretical approaches for their own financial gain. The public requires protection in such instances. However, sometimes such abuses can be difficult to prevent and prove.

• *Depowering clients.* Some theories may lead to pathologizing clients by focusing more on what is wrong rather than on what is right. In addition, theories can make clients' problems out to be more severe than they are. For instance, psychoanalysts can view learned ineffective behaviour as symptomatic of deeper underlying conflicts. Also, if clients give negative feedback to analysts they can be labelled as resisting and acting out their negative transferences rather than having their feedback taken seriously.

The language of theories can create a power imbalance between counsellors and clients. Counsellors who think in a special theoretical language that they do not share can put themselves in superior-inferior relationships with clients. Furthermore, the language of some theories does little to empower clients once they leave counselling. Ideally, the language of counselling is that of self-helping. Clients unable to articulate what to think and do when faced with problems after counselling are less likely to maintain gains than clients who can instruct themselves appropriately.

• *Supporting the status quo.* Counselling theories can contain many assumptions about how people should behave and about the causes of their behaviour. For example, possibly all counselling theories in this book insufficiently take into account cultural differences. Instead, theorists present their ideas as more culture-universal and less culture-specific than they really are. In addition, counselling theories focus on individuals, couples and families, and can ignore or underestimate how much socio-environmental conditions like poverty, poor housing and racial discrimination may contribute to explaining ineffective behaviour. Though feminist and gender-aware theorizing is attempting to redress the balance, most counselling theories insufficiently take into account the influence of sex-role conditioning. Also, counselling theories assume heterosexuality and insufficiently take into account the needs of gay, lesbian and bisexual clients.

HOW TO LEARN ABOUT COUNSELLING THEORIES

Everyone who counsels is a counselling theorist. How can you make yourself a better counselling theorist and hence a more effective counsellor? Following are some suggestions.

• *Work with this book.* Though based on the writings of the original theorists, this book is a secondary source. Nevertheless, it should provide you with a faithful overview of the main counselling theories. To understand any theory you need to master its basic concepts. It is insufficient just to read about them. You will need actively to work on understanding and memorizing them. At the end of each theory chapter I provide review and revision questions that test your knowledge of basic concepts.

• *Apply the theories to yourself.* Applying the different theories to your own life is one way to make learning them more interesting. What do the theories say that seems applicable to you and why? Another way to understand the theories is to think about how applicable they are to past, present or future clients. What in different theories might prove useful in your practical work and why? Also, you can compare and contrast different theories in an attempt to critically evaluate their strengths and weaknesses. Still a further way to learn about the theories is to try to develop a theoretical position of your own. For more than twenty years I have asked students in my counselling theories classes to write a paper that presents their current thinking about the theory and practice of their counselling work. The final chapter of this book on lifeskills counselling represents my attempt to answer the question I've asked students.

• *Read primary sources.* Primary sources are books and articles written by the theorists themselves. Ultimately, there is no substitute for reading primary sources. You will get a much broader and deeper impression of the different theories if you read widely the works of their originators. After describing the work of each theorist, I provide a brief annotated bibliography plus other primary source references.

• *Read other secondary sources.* You can read other secondary sources beyond this book. Some secondary sources are counselling and psychotherapy textbooks. For instance, *Current Psychotherapies* is an edited book containing a mixture of primary and secondary sources (Corsini & Wedding, 1989). Single author textbooks include Corey's (1993) *Theory and Practice of Counseling and Psychotherapy* and Patterson's (1986) *Theories of Counseling and Psychotherapy.* Hall and Lindzey's (1985) *Introduction to Theories of Personality* reviews many major counselling theories, among others. All major counselling approaches beget many secondary source books, of which Hall's (1954) *A Primer of Freudian Psychology* is a good example.

• *Read case studies.* You can also learn about how the different counselling theories are applied by reading case studies. Sources of case studies are Wedding and Corsini's (1989) edited book *Case Studies in Psychotherapy* and Corey's (1991) *Case Approach to Counseling and Psychotherapy.*

• *Watch and listen to audio–visual material.* You can obtain a further insight into the different theorists by watching films and videotapes and listening to audiocassettes of them discussing their theories and working with clients. For instance, audio–visual material is available for theorists like Beck, Ellis, Frankl, Lazarus, Perls and Rogers.

• *Attend training courses and workshops.* I assume that if you are reading this book you are probably already a member of a counselling theory class. You may expand your knowledge and skills in the different theories by attending training courses and workshops run by competent adherents of the different approaches. Broad counselling theory courses are likely to be limited in presenting different approaches both by time constraints and by lecturer preferences. You may get a much more thorough introduction to any single approach if you attend workshops and courses run by specialists in it.

• *Undergo supervision.* A good way to learn about the theory and practice of a counselling approach is to be supervised by a practitioner skilled in it. For instance, you can learn one approach thoroughly and then seek to broaden how you work by obtaining supervision from practitioners of different approaches.

• *Undergo personal counselling.* If a counselling approach particularly appeals to you, one way to learn about its practice is to become a client of a skilled practitioner in the approach. For some approaches, for instance psychoanalysis, a training analysis is an integral part of learning the approach.

CHAPTER REVIEW AND SELF-REFERENT QUESTIONS

Chapter review questions

1. What is counselling?
2. How does counselling differ from psychotherapy?
3. What is a theory?
4. What are the functions of counselling theories?
5. What are the sources for counselling theories?
6. What is the relationship between counselling theory and counselling research?
7. What are the limitations or disadvantages of counselling theories?

Self-referent questions

1. Describe your present preferences regarding counselling theory.
2. How can you best learn about counselling theories?
3. How can you best develop a theoretical position to guide your counselling practice?

Annotated bibliography

Corsini, R.J. & Wedding, D. (Eds.) (1989). *Current Psychotherapies* (4th ed.). Itasca, IL: Peacock. This book is a mixture of primary and secondary sources. Chapters on person-centred, rational-emotive, cognitive, existential, and multi-modal therapies are written by their originators, sometimes with co-authors. Secondary source chapters review psychoanalytic, Adlerian, behaviour, transactional analysis, and family therapy. A final chapter reviews Asian psychotherapies, psychodrama, and bioenergetic analysis.

Corey, G. (1993). *Theory and Practice of Counseling and Psychotherapy* (4th ed.). Pacific Grove, CA: Brooks/Cole. This book surveys the major concepts and practices of contemporary therapeutic systems and addresses some ethical and professional issues on counselling practice. The therapies reviewed are: psychoanalytic, Adlerian, existential, person-centred, gestalt, transactional analysis, behaviour, rational-emotive and other cognitive behaviour approaches, and reality therapy.

Hall, C.S. & Lindzey, G. (1985). *Introduction to Theories of Personality*. New York: Wiley. This book is intended to make the authors' well-established text *Theories of Personality* (first edition, 1957) more accessible to beginning psychology students. Though many major theories of counselling are covered, notable exceptions include cognitive, gestalt, rational-emotive and transactional theories. The book is very strong in presenting the ideas of Freud, Jung and the neo-Freudians.

Further references

Allport, G.W. (1962). Psychological models for guidance. *Harvard Educational Review, 32,* 373–81.

Beck, A.T. & Weishaar, M.E. (1989). Cognitive therapy. In R.J. Corsini & D. Wedding (Eds). *Current Psychotherapies* (4th ed., pp. 285–320). Itasca, IL: Peacock.

Blocher, D. (1987). On the uses and misuses of the term *theory*. *Journal of Counseling and Development, 66,* 67–8.

Corey, G. (1991). *Case Approach to Counseling and Psychotherapy*. Pacific Grove, CA: Brooks/Cole.

Corsini, R.J. (1956). Freud, Rogers and Moreno. *Group Psychotherapy, 9,* 274–81.

Corsini, R.J. (1989). Introduction. In R.J. Corsini & D. Wedding (Eds.). *Current Psychotherapies* (4th ed., pp. 1–16). Itasca, IL: Peacock.

Division of Clinical Psychology (1979). *Report of the Working Party on the Psychological Therapies*. Leicester: British Psychological Society.

Ellis, A. (1989). Rational-emotive therapy. In R.J. Corsini & D. Wedding (Eds.). *Current Psychotherapies* (4th ed., pp. 197–238). Itasca, IL: Peacock.

Frankl, V.E. (1988). *The Will to Meaning: Foundations and Applications of Logotherapy*. New York: Meridian.

Freud, S. (1976). *The Interpretation of Dreams*. Harmondsworth: Penguin. Original edition, 1900.

Garfield, S.L. (1982). Eclecticism and integration in psychotherapy. *Behavior Therapy, 13,* 610–23.

Hall, C.S. (1954). *A Primer of Freudian Psychology*. New York: Mentor.

Hall, C.S. & Lindzey, G. (1970). *Theories of Personality*. New York: Wiley.

Ho, D.Y.F. (1985). Cultural values and professional issues in clinical psychology: Implications from the Hong Kong experience. *American Psychologist, 40,* 1212–18.

Hubble, M.A. & O'Hanlon, W.H. (1992). Theory countertransference. *Dulwich Centre Newsletter, 1,* 25–30.

Jahoda, M. (1958). *Current Concepts of Positive Mental Health*. New York: Basic Books.

Jones, E. (1963). *The Life and Work of Sigmund Freud*. New York: Anchor Books.

Maslow, A.H. (1970). Self-actualizing people: A study of psychological health. In Maslow, A.H., *Motivation and Personality* (2nd ed., pp.149–80). New York: Harper & Row.

Maslow, A.H. (1971). *The Farther Reaches of Human Nature*. Harmondsworth: Penguin.

Meltzoff, J. & Kornreich, M. (1970). *Research in Psychotherapy*. New York: Atherton.

Nelson-Jones, R. (1986). Toward a people centred language for counselling psychology. *The Australian Counselling Psychologist, 2,* 18–23.

Nelson-Jones, R. (1992). *Lifeskills Helping: A textbook of Practical Counselling and Helping Skills*. Sydney: Holt, Rinehart and Winston.

Nelson-Jones, R. (1993). *Practical Counselling and Helping Skills: How to Use the Lifeskills Helping Model* (3rd ed.). London: Cassell.

Patterson, C.H. (1974). *Relationship Counseling and Psychotherapy*. New York: Harper & Row.

Patterson, C.H. (1986). *Theories of Counseling and Psychotherapy* (4th ed.). New York: Harper & Row.

Rogers, C.R. (1957). The necessary and sufficient conditions of therapeutic personality change. *Journal of Consulting Psychology, 21,* 95–104.

Rogers, C.R. (1961). *On Becoming a Person.* Boston, MA: Houghton Mifflin.

Rogers, C.R. (1980). *A Way of Being.* Boston, MA: Houghton Mifflin.

Skinner, B.F. (1948). *Walden Two.* New York: Macmillan.

Truax, C.B. & Carkhuff, R.R. (1967). *Toward Effective Counselling and Psychotherapy.* Chicago, IL: Aldine.

Tyler, L. (1961). *The Work of the Counselor* (2nd ed.). New York: Appleton-Century-Crofts.

Wedding, D. & Corsini, R.J. (Eds.) (1989). *Case Studies in Psychotherapy.* Itasca, IL: Peacock.

Yalom, I.D. (1980). *Existential Psychotherapy.* New York: Basic Books.

Yalom, I.D. (1991). *When Nietzsche Wept.* New York: Basic Books/Harper.

Zook, A. & Walton, J.M. (1989). Theoretical orientations and work settings of clinical and counseling psychologists: A current perspective. *Professional Psychology: Research and Practice, 20,* 23–31.

PART TWO

Humanistic

TWO

Person-Centred Counselling

PREVIEW

- *Person-centred or client-centred theory emphasizes the importance of people's subjective self-concept, which consists of the ways in which they perceive and define themselves.*

- *The actualizing tendency inherent in the organism to maintain and enhance itself is people's single motivating drive.*

- *Very early on in life humans start developing a self-concept. Many of the self-conceptions which form the self-concept are likely to be based on the organism's own valuing process. However, other self-conceptions reflect internalized conditions of worth or the values of others treated as if they were based on the organism's own valuing process. Thus a conflict arises between the actualizing tendency and the self-concept, which is a subsystem of the actualizing tendency, in that conditions of worth impede accurate perception of both inner and outer experiences.*

- *Subception is the mechanism by which the organism discriminates experience at variance with the self-concept. Depending on the degree of threat inherent in the experience, the organism may defend its self-concept by denying the experience or distorting its perception. People are psychologically well to the extent that their self-concepts allow them to perceive all their significant sensory and visceral experiences.*

- *Rogers' and Maslow's goals for counselling and living are reviewed, and six key characteristics of the self-concepts of fully functioning or self-actualizing persons are identified, namely, openness to experience, rationality, personal responsibility, self-regard, capacity for good personal relations, and ethical living.*

- *The practice of person-centred counselling emphasizes the quality of the interpersonal relationship. Its central assumption is that if counsellors provide clients with certain attitudinal conditions then constructive personality change will occur. There is no assessment. The person-centred counsellor provides to all clients the same attitudinal conditions of congruence, unconditional positive regard and empathy.*

- *The impact of these conditions on clients leads them to possess more congruence, self-regard and empathy. In short, clients are in the process of becoming persons and regulating their own lives.*

INTRODUCTION

On 11 December, 1940, Carl Rogers gave a presentation at the University of Minnesota entitled 'Some newer concepts in psychotherapy'. This 'is the single event most often identified with the birth of client-centred therapy' (Raskin & Rogers, 1989, p. 162). In 1974, Rogers and his colleagues changed the name from 'client-centred' to 'person-centred'. They believed that the new name would more adequately describe the human values and the mutuality underlying their approach and would apply to contexts other than counselling and psychotherapy. However, Thorne observes: 'Rogers never completely jettisoned the term client-centred therapy. He uses client-centred and person-centred interchangeably when talking about counselling and psychotherapy but *always* employs the term 'the person-centred approach' when referring to activities outside the one-to-one therapy situation' (B. Thorne, personal communication, 15 March 1994).

The central hypothesis of the person-centred approach is that every person has within himself or herself 'vast resources for self-understanding, for altering his or her self-concept, attitudes, and self-directed behaviour – and that these resources can be tapped only if a definable climate of facilitative psychological attitudes can be provided' (Rogers, 1986, p. 197). Empathy, congruence and unconditional positive regard are the three counsellor-offered faciliative conditions that Rogers regarded as necessary and sufficient for therapeutic change (Rogers, 1957; Raskin & Rogers, 1989).

This chapter is drawn mainly from Rogers' writings. However, he encouraged colleagues and associates to develop it and, consequently, regarded his theory as a group enterprise (Rogers, 1959). In addition, Rogers was influenced by psychologists like Combs, Snygg and Maslow. I refer to their work where it appears to add to or clarify Rogers' own contribution.

Carl Rogers

Carl Ransom Rogers (1902–87) was an American born in Illinois, the fourth of six children. His father was a civil engineer and contractor who had a construction business. A rather sickly boy, he lived his childhood in a close-knit family in which hard work and a highly conservative, almost fundamentalist, Protestant Christianity were equally revered. When Rogers was 12 his parents bought a farm, and this became the family home. Rogers regarded his parents as masters of the art of subtle, loving control. He shared little of his private thoughts and feelings with them because he knew these would have been judged and found wanting. Until Rogers went to college he was a loner who read incessantly and who adopted his parents' attitude towards the outside world, summed up in the statement: 'Other persons behave in dubious ways which we do not approve in our family' (Rogers, 1980, p. 28). Such dubious ways included playing cards, going to the cinema, smoking, dancing, drinking and engaging in other even less mentionable activities. He was socially incompetent in other than superficial contacts and, while at high school, had only two dates with girls. He relates that his fantasies during this period were bizarre and would probably have been classified as schizoid by a psychological diagnostician.

Rogers entered the University of Wisconsin to study agriculture, but later changed to history, feeling that this would be a better preparation for his emerging professional goal of becoming a minister of religion. His first real experience of fellowship was in a group there who met in a YMCA class. When he was 20, Rogers went to China for an international World Student Christian Federation Conference and, for the first time, emancipated himself from the religious thinking of his parents, an essential step towards becoming an independent person. Also, at about this time Rogers fell in love, and, on completing college, married Helen, who was an artist. The marriage lasted until she died in 1979.

In 1924 Rogers went to Union Theological Seminary, but after two years he moved to Teachers College, Columbia University, where he was exposed to the instrumentalist philosophy of John Dewey, the highly statistical and Thorndikean behavioural approaches of Teachers College, and the Freudian orientation of the Institute for Child Guidance where he had an internship. Along with his formal learning he was starting to understand relationships with others better, and he was beginning to realize that, in close relationships, the elements that 'cannot' be shared are those that are the most important and rewarding to share.

Rogers received his MA from Columbia University in 1928 and then spent 12 years in a community child guidance clinic in Rochester, New York. In 1931 he received his PhD from Columbia University, and in 1939 he published his first book, *The Clinical Treatment of the Problem Child*. During this period Rogers felt that he was becoming more competent as a therapist, not least because his experience with clients was providing him with valuable learning and insights which contributed to a shift from diagnosis to listening. Furthermore, such a relationship approach met his own needs, since, stemming from his early loneliness, the counselling interview was a socially approved way of getting really close to people without the pains and longer time-span of the friendship process outside therapy.

In 1940 Rogers accepted a position as a professor of psychology at Ohio State University and two years later published *Counseling and Psychotherapy*, the contents of which were derived primarily from his work as a counsellor rather than as an academic psychologist. After initial poor sales, the book became well-known because it offered a way to work with veterans returning from the Second World War. From 1945 to 1957 Rogers was professor of psychology and executive secretary of the university counselling centre at the University of Chicago, where non-directive, or client-centred therapy, as it came to be called, was further developed and researched.

In 1957 Rogers was appointed professor of psychology and psychiatry at the University of Wisconsin, where he examined the impact of the client-centred approach on hospitalized schizophrenics. From 1962–3 he was a fellow at the Center for

Advanced Study in the Behavioral Sciences at Stanford University. In 1964 he went to the Western Behavioral Sciences Institute at La Jolla, California, as a resident fellow. Then, in 1968, with some colleagues, he formed the Center for Studies of the Person at La Jolla, where he was a resident fellow until his death. During the latter part of his career Rogers developed a great interest in the application of person-centred ideas to group work, community change, and preventing nuclear, planetary suicide.

Although the years since 1940 were very successful for Rogers and his ideas, they also contained professional and personal struggles. Two professional struggles were those with psychiatry and with behavioural psychology. Rogers fought for psychologists, as contrasted with psychiatrists, to be allowed to practise psychotherapy and to have administrative responsibility over 'mental health' work. Also, he constantly highlighted the philosophical and practical issues involved in a humanistic or person-centred as against a behavioural view of human beings. On a more person level, Rogers continued struggling to become a more real, open and growing person. Furthermore, he had some personal crises and difficulties to handle. During his Chicago period, with counselling help, he worked through a crisis arising from a 'badly bungled therapeutic relationship' (Rogers, 1980, p. 39) with a 'particularly demanding and highly disturbed female client' (Thorne, 1992). In the 1970s, he faced the strain of his wife's long terminal illness. Towards the end of his life Rogers was increasingly aware of his 'capacity for love, my sensuality, my sexuality' (Rogers, 1980, p. 96). Also, having earlier firmly rejected his Christian past, Rogers now realized he had underestimated the mystical or spiritual dimension in life.

Rogers was a committed researcher and pioneered the use of tape-recorders to study counselling processes. In 1956 he received the American Psychological Association's Award for Distinguished Scientific Contributions. Rogers was also an author with a deep commitment to clear and cogent communication. In fact, he sees the theme of his life 'as having been built around the desire for clarity of communication, with all its ramifying results' (Rogers, 1980, p. 66). As well as those already mentioned, his books include: *Client-centered Therapy; On Becoming a Person; Freedom to Learn; Encounter Groups; Becoming Partners; Marriage and its Alternatives; Carl Rogers on Personal Power;* and *A Way of Being.* A chronological bibliography of Rogers' books and articles published in the period 1930–80 is printed at the end of *A Way of Being.*

Rogers was influenced by his own early emotional deprivations to design a counselling approach to overcome their effects and hence to meet his own companionship and growth needs. Other sources of learning included his clients and the stimulus provided by younger colleagues. Rogers claimed that serendipity or 'the faculty of making fortunate and unexpected discoveries by accident' had also been important (Rogers, 1980, p. 64). Rogers enjoyed gardening and finding the right conditions for plants to grow. As with plants, so with people. While regarding the following saying from Lao-Tse as an oversimplification, Rogers feels that it sums up many of his deeper beliefs about human growth.

> If I keep from meddling with people, they take care of themselves.
> If I keep from commanding people, they behave themselves.

If I keep from preaching at people, they improve
themselves.
If I keep from imposing on people, they become
themselves.

ASSUMPTIONS

In 1951 Rogers presented his theory of personality and behaviour as the final chapter
of *Client-centered Therapy*. Eight years later, in an edited publication entitled
Psychology: A Study of Science, he presented an updated version which he regarded as
his major and most rigorous theoretical statement and 'the most thoroughly ignored of
anything I have written' (Rogers, 1980, p. 60). Later, with collaborators (for instance,
Meador & Rogers, 1979; Raskin & Rogers, 1989), Rogers restated his theory, but he did
not alter it. Rogers thought that this and any theory should be a stimulus for further
creative thinking rather than a dogma of truth.

Perceptual or subjective frame of reference

Combs and Snygg (1959) state that, broadly speaking, behaviour may be observed from
either the point of view of outsiders or the point of view of the behavers themselves. It
is sometimes stated that the former is viewing behaviour from the external frame of
reference while the latter is viewing behaviour from the internal, subjective or
perceptual frame of reference. Rogers writes of his fundamental belief in the subjective,
observing that 'Man lives essentially in his own personal and subjective world, and even
his most objective functioning, in science, mathematics, and the like, is the result of
subjective purpose and subjective choice' (Rogers, 1959, p. 191). It is this emphasis on
the subjective, perceptual view of clients which has led to the term 'client-centred'. The
perceptions of clients are viewed as their versions of reality.

Later, Rogers was again to stress that the only reality people can possibly know is
the world which they individually perceive and experience at this moment. The notion
that there is a 'real world', the definition of which can be agreed upon by everyone, is a
luxury that the human race cannot afford, since it leads to false beliefs, like faith in
technology, which have brought our species to the brink of annihilation. His alternative
hypothesis is that there are as many realities as there are people. Furthermore, people
are increasingly 'inwardly and organismically rejecting the view of one single, culture-
approved reality' (Rogers, 1980, p. 26).

Actualizing tendency

Rogers considered there to be a formative tendency at work in the universe. This
formative tendency is 'the ever operating trend toward increased order and interrelated
complexity evident at both the inorganic and the organic level. The universe is always
building and creating as well as deteriorating.' (Rogers, 1980, p. 126).

The actualizing tendency is the single basic motivating drive. It is an active process
representing the inherent tendency of the organism to develop its capacities in the
direction of maintaining, enhancing and reproducing itself. The actualizing tendency

is operative at all times in all organisms and is the distinguishing feature of whether a given organism is alive or dead. The organism is always up to something. In addition, the actualizing tendency involves a development towards the differentiation of organs and functions.

Rogers observes, from his experiences with individual and group counselling and from his attempts to provide students in classes with 'freedom to learn', that 'the most impressive fact about the individual human being seems to be the directional tendency toward wholeness, toward actualization of potentialities' (Rogers, 1977, p. 240). Furthermore, he cited support for the actualizing tendency both in his observations of the natural world, for instance the behaviour of seaweed and of children learning to walk, and in empirical research, be it on sea urchins, rats, human infants or brain-damaged war veterans. The cornerstone of both Rogers' therapeutic and his political thinking was that, because of their actualizing tendency, people move towards self-regulation and their own enhancement and away from control by external forces.

The actualizing tendency is basically positive. It represents Rogers' trust in the wisdom of the organism, 'a trust in a constructive directional flow toward the realization of each individual's full potential' (Raskin & Rogers, 1989, p. 155). People have the capacity to guide, regulate, and control themselves, provided certain definable conditions exist. The person-centred approach posits a unitary diagnosis that all psychological difficulties are caused by blockages to this actualizing tendency and, consequently, the task of counselling is to release further this fundamentally good motivating drive. Maslow (1970) reiterates this assessment of people's basic nature when he writes that the human being does seem to have instinct remnants and that clinical and other evidence suggests that those weak instinctoid tendencies are good, desirable and worth saving.

Often, however, people appear to have two motivational systems, their organismic actualizing tendency and their conscious self. Maslow (1962) writes of the basic conflict in humans between defensive forces and growth trends and observes that the actualizing tendency may involve both deficiency and growth motivations. However, given a certain emotional environment, growth motivations will become increasingly strong.

Organismic valuing process

The concept of an organismic valuing process is central to the idea of a real or true and unique self. A person's organismic valuing process relates to the continuous weighing of experience and the placing of values on that experience in terms of its ability to satisfy the actualizing tendency. For instance, the behaviour of infants indicates that they prefer those experiences, such as curiosity and security, which maintain and enhance their organism and reject those, such as pain and hunger, which do not. This weighing of experience is an organismic rather than a conscious symbolic process. The source of the valuing process or values placed on the various experiences clearly seems to be located in the infants, who react to their own sensory and visceral evidence. As people grow older, their valuing process is effective in helping them to achieve self-actualizing to the degree that they are able to be aware of and perceive the experiencing which is going on within themselves.

Experience and experiencing

Rogers uses the term 'sensory and visceral experience' in a psychological rather than a physiological sense. Perhaps another way of stating sensory and visceral experience is the undergoing of facts and events, which are potentially available to conscious awareness, by the organism's sensory and visceral equipment. People may be unaware of much of their experiencing. For instance, when sitting, you may not be aware of the sensation on your buttocks until your attention is drawn to it. Another example is that you may not be aware of the physiological aspects of hunger because you are so fascinated by work or play. However, this experience is potentially available to conscious awareness. The total range of experience at any given moment may be called the 'experiential', 'perceptual' or 'phenomenal' field. Rogers stressed that physiological events such as neuron discharges or changes in blood sugar are not included in his psychological definition of experience.

The verb experiencing means that the organism is receiving the impact of any sensory or visceral experiences that happen at the moment. Experiencing a feeling includes receiving both the emotional content and the personal meaning or cognitive content 'as they are experienced inseparably in the moment' (Rogers, 1959, p. 198). Experiencing a feeling fully means that experiencing, awareness and expression of the feeling are all congruent.

Perception and awareness

Perception and awareness are virtually synonymous in person-centred theory. When an experience is perceived, this means that it is in conscious awareness, however dimly, though it need not be expressed in verbal symbols. Another way of stating this is that 'perceiving' is 'becoming aware of stimuli or experiences'. Rogers viewed all perception and awareness as transactional in nature, being a construction from past experience and a hypothesis or prediction of the future. Perception or awareness may or may not correspond with experience or 'reality'. When an experience is symbolized accurately in awareness, this means that the hypothesis implicit in the awareness will be borne out if tested by acting on it. Many experiences may not be symbolized accurately in awareness because of defensive denials and distortions. Other experiences, such as buttocks sitting on a chair, may not be perceived, since they may be unimportant to the actualizing tendency.

Awareness, or conscious attention, is one of the latest evolutionary developments of the human species. One way in which Rogers regarded it was as 'a tiny peak of awareness, of symbolizing capacity, topping a vast pyramid of non-conscious organismic functioning' (Rogers, 1977, p. 244). Figure 2.1 attempts to illustrate this. When a person is functioning well, awareness is a reflection of part of the flow of the organism at that moment. However, all too often people are not functioning well, and organismically they are moving in one direction while their aware or conscious lives are struggling in another.

ACQUISITION

Person-centred theory may become clearer to the reader by maintaining a distinction between self and self-concept. The self may be viewed as the real, underlying,

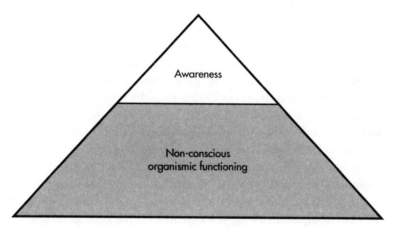

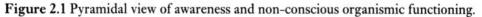

Figure 2.1 Pyramidal view of awareness and non-conscious organismic functioning.

organismic self expressed in popular sayings such as 'To thine own self be true' and 'To be that self which one truly is'. People's self-concepts are their perceptions of themselves, which do not always correspond with their own experiencing or organismic selves. Thus, ideally the actualizing tendency refers to self-actualizing where aspects of self and of self-concept are synonymous or congruent. However, where self and self-concept are incongruent, the desire to actualize the self-concept may work against the deeper need to actualize the organismic self. In Rogers' writings, the above distinction is always implicit, if not always explicit.

Early development of self-concept

The self-concept is the self as perceived, or what a person refers to as 'I' or 'me'. Initially, the self-concept may be made up largely of self-experiences, events in the phenomenal field discriminated by the individual as 'I', 'me', or 'self', even though in a pre-verbal way. For instance, infants who discover their toes may incorporate the fact that they have toes into their self-concept. Also, infants who are hungry may incorporate into their self-concepts the fact that they negatively value hunger. As young people interact with the environment, more and more experience may become symbolized in awareness as self-experience. Not least through interaction with significant others who treat them as a separate self, they develop a self-concept which includes both their perceptions about themselves and the varying positive and negative values attached to these self-perceptions.

Conditions of worth

A need for positive regard from others is a learned need developed in early infancy. Positive regard as used here means experiencing oneself as making a positive difference in the experiential field of another. It is likely that on many occasions young people's behaviour and experiencing of their behaviour will coincide with positive regard from others and hence meet their need for positive regard. For instance, smiling at parents may reflect a pleasurable experience as well as generating positive regard.

However, on other occasions, young people may feel that their experiencing conflicts with their need for positive regard from significant others. Rogers gives the example of the child who experiences satisfaction at hitting his baby brother, but who experiences the words and actions of his parents as saying 'You are bad, the behaviour is bad, and you are not loved or lovable when you behave this way'. An outcome of this may be that the child does not acknowledge the pleasurable value of hitting his baby brother emanating from his own experience, but comes to place a negative value on the experience because of the attitudes held by his parents and his need for positive regard. Thus, instead of an accurate symbolization of the experience, such as 'While I experience the behaviour as satisfying, my parents experience it as unsatisfying', may come a distorted symbolization, such as 'I perceive this behaviour as unsatisfying' (Rogers, 1951, p. 500). Such values, which are based on others' evaluations rather than on the individual's own organismic valuing process, are called conditions of worth. Conditions of worth are prevalent because all too often 'individuals are culturally conditioned, rewarded, reinforced, for behaviors that are in fact perversions of the natural directions of the unitary actualizing tendency' (Rogers, 1977, p. 247).

The concept of conditions of worth is important because it means that people develop a second valuing process. The first is the organismic valuing process which truly reflects the actualizing tendency. The second is a conditions of worth process, based on the internalization or 'introjection' of others' evaluations, which does not truly reflect the actualizing tendency but serves to impede it. However, people possess a false awareness in regard to this second valuing process, since they feel that decisions based on it are in fact based on their organismic valuing process. Thus experiences may be sought or avoided to meet false rather than real needs.

Family life

The adequacy of the self-concepts of parents affects the ways in which they relate to their children. Gordon, a contributor to Rogers' 1951 book *Client-centered Therapy*, has emphasized that the level of self-acceptance or self-regard of parents may be related to their degree of acceptance of the behaviour of their children, though this is not something which is static. Figure 2.2 is a representataion, albeit oversimplified, of the possible effects of parents on their children. Rogers observed that parents are able to feel unconditional positive regard for a child only to the extent that they experience unconditional self-regard. By 'unconditional positive regard' Rogers meant prizing a child even though the parent may not value equally all of his or her behaviours. The greater the degree of unconditional positive regard that parents experience towards the child, the fewer the conditions of worth in the child and the higher the level of its psychological adjustment. Put simply, high-functioning parents create the conditions for the development of high-functioning children. In 1970 Gordon published *Parent Effectiveness Training*, based on Rogerian principles. This book attempts to teach parents how to listen to and talk with their children, thus helping the attitude of prizing to be communicated to them.

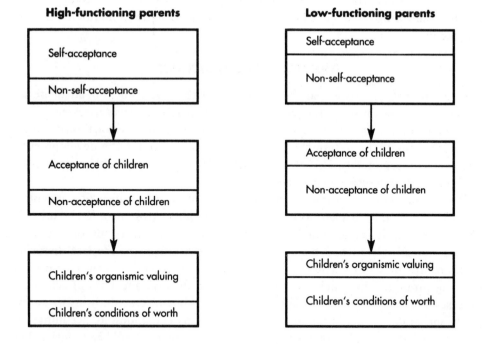

Figure 2.2 Degree of self-acceptance of parents in relation to their acceptance of their children and to the extent of conditions of worth in their children's self-concepts.

Effect of conditions of worth on self-concept

People differ in the degree to which they internalize conditions of worth depending not only on the degree of unconditional positive regard they are offered by significant others, but also on the degree of empathic understanding and congruence shown to them. In addition, the extent of their need for positive regard influences their vulnerability to introjecting conditions of worth. For some, their self-concepts will develop so as to allow much of their experience to be accurately perceived. However, even the most fortunate are likely to internalize some conditions of worth, and the less fortunate are fated to internalize many.

Some common examples of conditions of worth are: 'Achievement is very important and I am less of a person if I do not achieve', 'Making money is very important and, if I do not make much money, then I am a failure', and 'Sexual fantasies and behaviours are mostly bad and I should not like myself for having them'. Thus conditions of worth entail not only internalized evaluations of how people should be, but also internalized evaluations about how they should feel about themselves if they perceive that they are not the way they should be. Rogers believed that it is common for most people to have their values largely introjected, held as fixed concepts and rarely examined or tested. Thus, not only are they estranged from their experiencing, but their level of self-regard is lowered and they are unable to prize themselves fully. Furthermore, by internalizing conditions of worth, they have internalized a process by which they come to be the agents of lowering their own level of self-regard or, more colloquially, of 'self-oppression'.

Marriage and education

The person-centred view is that the conditions for the development of adequate self-concepts and those for the reintegration of inadequate self-concepts are essentially the same. Both contain the characteristics of good and loving interpersonal relationships. Implicit in this is the notion that significant experiences for the development of adequate and, regrettably, also of inadequate self-concepts are neither restricted to childhood and adolescence nor to family life.

Rogers saw contributions to the development of adequate self-concepts as potentially available in many other human situations. Most people are less self-actualizing than desirable because they are cluttered up with conditions of worth. Rogers increasingly turned his attentions to the problems of the less disturbed. Relationships between partners, whether marital or otherwise, can have growth-inducing properties in which conditions of worth dissolve and level of self-regard increases. In *Becoming Partners*, Rogers (1973) gave a moving case study involving Joe's steady and healing concern for and trust in Irene's potential, despite her initial self-conception that 'I don't let you see this little, black, rotten, ugly ball I have buried down inside that's really me, that's unlovable and unacceptable' (Rogers, 1973, p. 100).

Rogers also turned his attention to the under-realized potential of educational institutions for creating emotional climates for the development of healthy self-concepts. He particularly favoured significant experiential learning which was self-initiated and reflected the concerns of students rather than those of teachers or administrators. In addition, he focused on the politics of interpersonal and intergroup relationships and saw his faith in the actualizing tendency as indicating a more democratic sharing of power and control.

MAINTENANCE

For working counsellors the question is not so much how clients become the way they are as what currently causes them to maintain behaviour which does not meet their real needs. The concept of maintenance, or of how maladjusted behaviour and perceptions are perpetuated, often in the face of conflicting evidence, is critical to a full understanding of person-centred theory and practice. Person-centred theory may be viewed as a theory of human information processing or of the processing of experiences into perceptions. This is a process in which, especially for those who are disturbed, conditions of worth play a large part.

Processing of experience

Rogers observed that when experiences occur in people's lives there are four possible outcomes. First, like the sensation of sitting, they may be ignored. Second, they may be accurately perceived and organized into some relationship with the self-concept either because they meet a need of the self or because they are consistent with the self-concept and thus reinforce it. Third, their perception may be distorted in such a way as to resolve the conflict between self-concept and experiencing. For instance, students with low academic self-concepts may receive some positive feedback about their essays and perceive 'The teacher did not read it properly', or 'The teacher must have low standards'. Fourth, the experiences may be denied or not perceived at all. For example, people may have had their self-concepts deeply influenced by strict moral upbringings and thus be unable to perceive their cravings for sexual satisfaction.

Figure 2.3 represents the processing of experience by low-functioning and high-functioning people. Previously I mentioned that people have two valuing processes, their own organismic valuing process and an internalized process based on conditions of worth. Low-functioning people are out of touch with their own valuing process for large areas of their experiencing. In these areas their self-concepts are based on conditions of worth which cause them to distort and deny much of their experiencing. On the other hand, high-functioning people have fewer conditions of worth and thus are able to perceive most of their experiences accurately.

Both high-functioning and low-functioning people are motivated by the actualizing tendency. In addition, they possess a general tendency towards self-actualization, or actualization of that portion of the organism's experience symbolized in the self. The self-concepts of high-functioning people allow them to perceive most significant

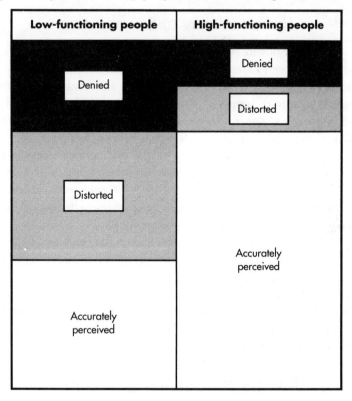

Figure 2.3 Representation of processing of experience by low-functioning and high-functioning people.

sensory and visceral experiences, and thus their self-actualizing entails no significant blockages to their actualizing tendency. However, with low-functioning people a split occurs and 'the general tendency to actualize the organism may work at cross purposes with the subsystem of that motive, the tendency to actualize the self' (Rogers, 1959, p. 197). Low-functioning people engage in a process of self-actualizing insufficiently based on their organism's own valuing process. Consequently, while high-functioning people are able to interact with others and their environments on the basis of largely realistic information, low-functioning people do not have that capacity to any great extent.

Incongruence between self-concept and experience

When experiences are accurately symbolized and included in the self-concept, there is a state of congruence between self-concept and experience or, stated another way, between the self-concept and the organismic self. When, however, experience is denied and distorted, there exists a state of incongruence between self-concept and experience. This state of incongruence may exist where experiences are positive as well as where they are negative. Counselling clients tend to have low self-concepts and frequently deny and distort positive feedback from outside as well as inhibit positive feelings from within.

Threat, anxiety and subception

Rogers uses the concept of subception or pre-perception to explain the mechanism by which sensory and visceral experiences relevant to the actualizing tendency may be denied or inaccurately perceived. He quotes McCleary and Lazarus's finding that 'Even when a subject is unable to report a visual discrimination he is still able to make a stimulus discrimination at some level below that required for conscious recognition' (1949, p. 178). Subception involves a filtering of experience in such a way that experiences contradictory and threatening to the self-concept may be excluded or altered. Thus the organism may discriminate the meaning of an experience without using the higher nerve centres involved in conscious awareness or perception. The process of subception is the mechanism of defence of the self-concept in response to threats to its current structure or set of self-conceptions.

Anxiety is a state of uneasiness or tension which is the response of the organism to the 'subception' that a discrepancy or incongruence between self-concept and experience may enter perception or awareness, thus forcing a change in the currently prevailing self-concept. The term 'intensionality' is used to describe characteristics of the individual who is in a defensive state. Intensional reactions include seeing experience in absolute and rigid terms, overgeneralization, confusing facts and evaluation, and relying on abstrations rather than on reality testing.

Breakdown and disorganization

This section relates to serious disturbance. The self-concepts of very low-functioning people block their accurate perception of large areas of their significant sensory and visceral experience. If, however, a situation develops in which a significant experience occurs suddenly, or very obviously, in an area of high incongruence, the process of defence may be unable to operate successfully. Thus, not only may anxiety be experienced to the extent to which the self-concept is threatened, but, with the process of defence being unsuccessful, the experience may be accurately symbolized in awareness. People are brought face to face with more of their denied experiences than they can handle, with an ensuing state of disorganization and the possibility of a psychotic breakdown. Rogers mentioned that he had known psychotic breakdowns to occur when people sought 'therapy' from many different sources simultaneously and also when clients were prematurely faced with material revealed under the influence of sodium pentathol. Once acute psychotic behaviours have been exhibited, the defensive processes may work to protect people against the pain and anxiety generated by the perception of the incongruence.

Importance of self-concept

A person's self-concept, especially certain self-perceptions which are viewed as central, has been demonstrated to be fundamental to understanding how psychological maladjustment is maintained. The self-concept is so important to people because it is the constellation of the perceptions about themselves and, as such, the means by which they interact with life in such a way as to meet their needs. Effective self-concepts allow people to perceive their experiences realistically, whether they originate within their organisms or in their environments; in other words, such self-concepts allow them open access to their experiences.

Ineffective self-concepts may be maintained tenaciously for a number of reasons. First, as with the effective self-concepts, ineffective self-concepts are perceived as the means of need gratification and the source of personal adequacy. Second, ineffective self-concepts contain within them many conditions of worth which may have been functional at one stage of people's lives, but which have outgrown any usefulness they once possessed. Nevertheless, because they originate from people's need for positive regard, they may be deeply embedded in the structure of their self-concepts as a kind of 'emotional baggage'. Third, the more deeply embedded such conditions of worth have become the more tenaciously they are maintained, since to alter them would involve the anxiety of perceiving the incongruence between these self-perceptions and experiencing. Fourth, the conditions of worth have the effect of lowering people's sense of worth and thus making it less likely that they will have the confidence to acknowledge and face their areas of incongruence. There is a threshold area for both high-functioning and low-functioning people in which they may be able to assimilate incongruent perceptions into their self-concepts. This threshold area appears to be narrower and more tightly defined for low-functioning people.

Characteristics of self-concept

Since the idea of self-concept, sometimes expressed as 'self-structure', 'perceived self', 'phenomenal self', or just 'self', is so fundamental to person-centred theory, I briefly review some of its characteristics.

• *Content areas.* People's self-concepts are unique complexes of many different self-conceptions which constitute their way of describing and distinguishing themselves. Some content areas of people's self-concepts include: bodily, social, sexual, feelings and emotions, tastes and preferences, work, recreation, intellectual, and philosophy and values. People vary in the importance they attach to these various areas and also in the kinds of self-conceptions they have in them. For instance, the shape of one's nose may be felt as important by one person while another may be scarcely aware of it. The self-concept may be described in self-referent statements such as 'I am a good carpenter', 'I like ice-cream' and 'Meeting new people makes me nervous'.

• *Structure or process.* The self-concept may be viewed as a structure made up of different self-conceptions related to each other in various ways. Also, the self-concept is the means or process by which people interact with the environment and by which they ignore, deny, distort or accurately perceive experience.

• *Central-peripheral.* Combs and Snygg (1959) distinguish between the phenomenal self, the organization or pattern of all those aspects which people refer to as 'I' or 'me', and the self-concept, those perceptions about self which are most vital to people themselves and which may be regarded as their very essence. For all people, some self-conceptions are much more central than others, and everyone has their unique way of ordering self-conceptions as central or peripheral, even though this is often more implicit than explicit.

• *Congruence-incongruence.* Many self-conceptions may match the reality of people's experiencing, in which case there is congruence between self-conception and experience. Other self-conceptions may be different in varying degrees from the reality of their experiencing, in which case a state of incongruence exists.

• *Conditions of worth.* Incongruence implies that a self-conception is based on a condition of worth rather than on the organism's own valuing process. For example, an incongruent self-conception for a person may be 'I want to be a doctor', whereas a congruent self-conception may be 'I want to be an artist'. Being a doctor may be based on values internalized from parents, whereas being an artist represents the organism's own valuing process.

• *Subception and defence.* This is an area of self-concept as a process. Experiences may be denied or distorted by the process of subception. This process defends existing self-conceptions by preventing the person from perceiving incongruence and hence possibly changing both self-conceptions and behaviour.

• *Intensionality-extensionality.* Intensionality describes characteristics of a self-concept in a defensive state, for example rigidity and absence of adequate reality testing. Extensionality describes characteristics of a mature self-concept, such as seeing experience in limited, differentiated terms and testing inferences and abstractions against reality.

• *Level of self-regard.* Another way of expressing 'level of self-regard' is 'the degree to which individuals prize themselves'. Rogers stated that when people's self-concepts were such that no self-experience could be discriminated as more or less worthy of positive regard than any other, then they were experiencing unconditional positive self-regard. 'Level of self-acceptance' is another way of stating 'level of self-regard'.

• *Real-ideal.* Whereas real self-conceptions represent my perceptions of how I am, ideal self-conceptions represent my conceptions of how I would most like to be. Both real and ideal self-conceptions form parts of people's self-concept complex.

Table 2.1 Rogers' and Maslow's goals for counselling and for living

Rogers	Maslow	Rogers
Overall goal	*Overall goal*	*Overall goal*
The fully functioning (mature) person	The self-actualizing (psychologically healthy) person	The person of tomorrow
Qualities	*Qualities*	*Qualities*
Open to experience and able to perceive realistically	Superior perception of reality	Openness to the world, both inner and outer
Rational and not defensive	Increased acceptance of self, of others and of nature	Desire for authenticity
Engaged in existential process of living		Scepticism regarding science and technology
Trusts in organismic valuing process	Increased spontaneity, simplicity and naturalness	Desire for wholeness as a human being
Construes experience in extensional manner	Increase in problem-centring	The wish for intimacy
Accepts responsibility for being different from others	Increased detachment and desire for privacy	Process persons
		Caring for others
Accepts responsibility for own behaviour	Increased autonomy and resistance to enculturation	Attitude of closeness towards nature
Relates creatively to the environment	Greater freshness of appreciation	Anti-institutional
Accepts others as unique individuals	More frequent peak experiences	Trusts of the authority within
Prizes himself	Increased identification with human species	Material things unimportant
Prizes others		A yearning for the spiritual
Relates openly and freely on the basis of immediate experiencing	Deeper, more profound inter-personal relations	
Communicates rich self-awareness when desired	More democratic character structure	
	Greatly increased creativeness	
	Superior ability to discriminate ethical values	

PRACTICE
Goals

Person-centred goals are the same for clients, for counsellors and for everyone. Statements of such goals include those by Rogers (1959, 1961), Walker, Rablen and Rogers (1960), Maslow (1962, 1970) and Combs and Snygg (1959). Rogers also made a later statement on the qualities of the person of tomorrow who can live in a vastly changed world (Rogers, 1980). He considered that a 'paradigm shift' was taking place from old to new ways of conceptualizing the person.

Table 2.1 illustrates Rogers' and Maslow's goals for counselling and for living as well as Rogers' conceptualization of the person of tomorrow. Although Rogers writes about the fully functioning person and the person of tomorrow, Maslow about self-actualizing, and Combs and Snygg about adequate persons, there are a number of common themes in their descriptions.

• *Openness to experience.* A self-concept which allows all significant sensory and visceral experiences to be perceived is the basis for effective functioning. Rogers frequently used the term 'openness to experience' to describe the capacity for realistic perception and observed that 'There is no need for the mechanism of "subception" whereby the organism is forewarned of experiences threatening to the self' (Rogers, 1959, p. 206). Openness to experience makes for more efficient behaviour in that people have a wider perceptual field and are able to behave more often from choice than from necessity. Openness to experience may also increase the possibility of spontaneity and creativity, since people are less bound by the strait-jacket of conditions of worth. In other words, openness to experience enables people to engage in an existential process of living where they are alive, able to handle change, and alert to the range of their choices for creating their lives.

• *Rationality.* A feature of openness to experience is that it allows for rationality. When people are in touch with their actualizing tendency their behaviour is likely to be rational in terms of maintaining and enhancing their organism. Maslow (1970) observed that neurotics were not emotionally sick; they were cognitively *wrong*. Rogers thought it tragic that most people's defences kept them out of touch with how rational they could be. What was earlier described as extensionality rather than intensionality is a characteristic of this rationality.

• *Personal responsibility.* The term 'personal responsibility' refers to people taking responsibility *for* their self-actualizing and not just feeling responsible to others. This covers Rogers' ideas of individuals' trust in their organismic valuing process, trust of the authority within, acceptance of responsibility for their own behaviour, and also acceptance of responsibility for being different from others. It also incorporates Maslow's idea of increased autonomy and resistance to enculturation. Personally responsible people, within the existential parameters of death and destiny, are capable of taking control of their lives and of self-actualizing. The person-centred philosophy in many aspects is one of self-control, self-help and personal power, hopefully within the context of caring relationships. Acknowledgement of personal responsibility is a central part of the self-concepts of effective people.

• *Self-regard.* Self-regard is another important part of the self-concepts of effective people. One way of expressing this is that a person possesses a high degree of unconditional self-regard, or self-acceptance. It is a self-regard based on their organismic valuing process rather than on the praise and needs of others. People with a high degree of unconditional self-regard will prize themselves, even though they may not prize all their behaviours and attributes. Combs and Snygg (1959) observed that it was not only the number but the importance of the positive self-conceptions that defines the adequate personality. Perhaps self-acceptance is a more fundamental way of stating the desired quality, since positive self-conceptions or evaluations may reflect conditions of worth which impede realistic perception.

• *Capacity for good personal relations.* Self-acceptance means that people are less likely to be defensive and hence more likely to accept others. Good personal relations incorporate Rogers' notions of accepting others as unique individuals, prizing others, relating openly and freely to them on the basis of immediate experiencing, and having the capacity, when appropriate, to communicate a rich self-awareness. Such personal relations also incorporate Maslow's notions of increased acceptance of others, deeper more profound interpersonal relations, and a more democratic character structure. These relations are characterized by mutual concern for both persons' self-actualizing. They are also characterized by good listening and authenticity, involving appropriate self-disclosure. Rogers considered congruence, genuineness, or 'realness' to be probably the most important element in the ordinary interactions of life, while empathy has the highest priority where the other person is anxious and vulnerable.

• *Ethical living.* Person-centred theory is based on a view that people, at their core, are trustworthy organisms. This shows itself in the social relations of self-actualizing people in at least two ways. First, they are capable of a wide identification with other human beings, so they are likely to seek others' self-actualizing along with their own. Consequently, they are careful not to infringe on the rights of others while pursuing their own ends. Second, they appear to be able to distinguish sharply between ends and means and between good and evil. Maslow (1970) described such people, atheists included, as religious people or people who walk in the path of God. Qualities which are likely to contribute to such people's ethical living are: trust in internal rather than in external authority; an indifference to material things, such as money and status symbols; an attitude of closeness to and reverence for nature; and a yearning and seeking for spiritual values that are greater than the individual.

Other attributes of effective people, such as desire for privacy and more frequent mystic or peak experiences, are mentioned in the person-centred literature, but will not be described further here. The central attributes of fully functioning or self-actualizing people are the six already identified: openness to experience, rationality, personal responsibility, self-regard, capacity for good personal relations, and ethical living. All these attributes are both the ends and the means of the actualizing tendency and all involve effective self-conceptions. Self-actualizing people possess actualizing self-concepts!

The counsellor in the process

Person-centered counselling does not rely on techniques or on doing things to clients. Rogers believed that in counselling 'it is the *quality* of the interpersonal encounter with the client which is the most significant element in determining effectiveness' (Rogers, 1962, p. 416). Person-centered counselling is a process that can intensely involve the thoughts and feelings of both clients and their counsellors. There is no formal assessment since all clients are viewed as being out of touch with their actualizing tendencies on account of their conditions of worth. If counsellors were, from their own external frames of reference, to assess clients they would risk replicating the circumstances that had led clients to acquire and maintain their conditions of worth. There is a coherence between how person-centred counsellors see the origins of clients' self-alienation and inner schisms and how they can assist them to grow and become healed. Person-centred counsellors try to provide the attitudinal conditions that are the antidote to the emotional deprivations that their clients have experienced.

What are the conditions for client growth and reintegration? In 1957 Rogers presented his six necessary and sufficient conditions for therapeutic personality change. He stated that the following conditions had to exist and continue over a period of time for constructive personality change to occur. Also, that 'No other conditions are necessary' (Rogers, 1957, p. 96). First, two people need to be in psychological contact. Second, the client is in a state of incongruence and is vulnerable or anxious. Third, the counsellor 'is congruent or integrated in the relationship'. Fourth and fifth, the counsellor experiences 'unconditional positive regard for the client', and 'an empathic understanding of the client's internal frame of reference and endeavours to communicate this to the client' (p. 96). Sixth, the counsellor is at least successful in communicating empathic understanding and unconditional positive regard to the client. Rogers regarded congruence, unconditional positive regard and empathy as 'the attitudinal conditions that foster therapeutic growth . . .' (Rogers & Sanford, 1985, p. 1379). He stressed that they were not all or none conditions, but exist on continua.

Congruence. Other words for congruence are genuineness, realness, openness, transparency and presence. Congruence is the most basic of the attitudinal conditions. Counsellors need to be in touch with the feelings that they experience, have them available to awareness, and 'to live these feelings, be them in the relationship, and . . . communicate them if appropriate' (Rogers, 1962, p. 417). Counsellors should encounter their clients in direct person-to-person contact. They should avoid an intellectual approach in which clients get treated as objects. Congruent counsellors are not playing roles, being polite and putting on professional facades.

Rogers acknowledged that no one fully achieves congruence all the time. Imperfect human beings can be of assistance to clients. It is enough for counsellors, in particular moments in immediate relationships with specific persons, to be completely and fully themselves with their experiences accurately symbolized into their self-concepts.

Congruence does not mean that counsellors 'blurt out impulsively every passing feeling . . .' (Rogers, 1962, p. 418). Nor does it mean that they allow their sessions to become counsellor-centred rather than client-centred. However, it can mean that they take the risk of sharing a feeling or giving feedback that might improve the relationship because it is expressed genuinely. An example is that of counsellors sharing their experience of fatigue rather than trying to cover it up. Such openness may restore the counsellor's energy level and allow the client to see that they are dealing with a real person. Another example is that Rogers thought that, if he felt persistently bored with a client, he owed it to the client and their relationship to share the feeling. He would own the bored feeling as located in himself rather than make it into an accusatory statement. Also, he would share his discomfort at sharing the feeling and communicate that he would like to be more in touch with the client. Rogers strove to overcome the barrier between them by being real, imperfect and sharing his genuine feeling. He would hope that the client could use this as a stepping stone to speak more genuinely.

Another insight into congruence may be obtained from what Rogers says about the concept of presence. In counselling, both counsellors and clients can attain altered states of consciousness in which they feel they are in touch with and grasp the meaning of the underlying evolutionary flow (Heppner, Rogers & Lee, 1984; Rogers, 1980). There can be a mystical and spiritual dimension in counselling. Rogers considered he was at his best as a counsellor when he was closest to his inner intuitive self and 'when perhaps I am in a slightly altered state of consciousness. Then simply my *presence* is releasing and helpful to the other' (Rogers, 1980, p. 129). In such a state, behaviours which may be strange, impulsive, and hard to justify rationally turn out to be right. Rogers writes: 'it seems that my inner spirit has reached out and touched the inner spirit of the other. Our relationship transcends itself and becomes a part of something larger. Profound growth and healing and energy are present' (Rogers, 1980, p. 129).

Unconditional positive regard. Other terms used to describe this condition include non-possessive warmth, caring, prizing, acceptance and respect. Unconditional positive regard relates to Rogers' deep trust in his clients' capacity for constructive change if provided with the right nurturing conditions. Rogers stressed the importance of the counsellor's attitude towards the worth and significance of each person. The counsellor's own struggles for personal integration are relevant to unconditional positive regard since they can only be respectful of clients' capacities to achieve constructive self-direction to the extent that respect is an integral part of their own personality make-ups.

Unconditional positive regard involves the counsellor's willingness for clients 'to *be* whatever immediate feeling is going on – confusion, resentment, fear, anger, courage, love, or pride . . .' (Rogers, 1986, p. 198). This respect is equivalent to the love expressed by the Christian concept of 'agape', without any romantic or possessive connotations. Rogers makes the analogy between the kind of love parents can feel for their children, prizing them as people regardless of their particular behaviours at any moment. Counsellors do not show positive regard for their clients – *if.* If they are smarter, less defensive, less vulnerable and so on. Person-centred theory explains the need for clients to seek counselling because in their pasts they were shown positive regard – *if.*

There are boundaries to show unconditional positive regard, for instance if a client were physically to threaten a counsellor. Also, unconditional positive regard does not mean that counsellors need, from their frames of reference, to approve of all their clients' behaviours. Rather, unconditional positive regard is an attitude and philosophical orientation, reflected in counsellor behaviour, that clients are more likely to move forward if they feel prized for their humanity and they experience an emotional climate of safety and freedom in which, without losing their counsellor's acceptance, they can show feelings and relate events.

Empathy. Other terms for empathy include accurate empathy, empathic understanding, an empathic way of being, an empathic stance, and an empathic attitude. Rogers (1957) wrote: 'To sense the client's private world as if it were your own, but without ever losing the "as if" quality – this is empathy . . .' (p. 99). There are various facets to an empathic way of being with clients. Counsellors need to 'get into the shoes of' and 'get under the skin' of their clients to understand their private subjective worlds. They need to be sensitive to the moment by moment flow of experiencing that goes on both in clients and in themselves. They need the capacity to pick up nuances and sense meanings of which clients are scarcely aware. With tact, sensitivity and awareness of what clients can handle, they need to communicate their understandings of their sensings of clients' worlds and personal meanings. Also, counsellors should communicate their commitment to understanding their clients' worlds by frequently checking the accuracy of their understandings and showing their willingness to be corrected. An empathic attitude creates an emotional climate in which clients can assist their counsellors to understand them more accurately. Rogers was aware that often clients receive empathic messages from unintended counsellor 'throw-ins', such as casual remarks and involuntary facial expressions.

Following are two examples of empathy. The first is an excerpt from an interview conducted by Rogers in 1983 with a woman who says she is having a lot of problems letting go of her 20-year-old daughter who is in college (Raskin & Rogers, 1989, p. 174).

> **Rogers** . . . you feel her sort of slipping away, and you . . . and it hurts. . . .and –
> **Client** Yeah. I'm just sort of sitting here alone. I guess like, you know, I can feel her gone and I'm just left here.
> **Rogers** Umm-hmm. You're experiencing it right now: that she's leaving home and here you are all alone.
> **Client** Yeah. Yeah. Yeah. I feel really lonely. (Cries).

Though the second example of empathy comes from an encounter group (Rogers, 1975, p. 3), the empathic process it demonstrates holds true for working with individual clients. A man has been making vaguely negative statements about his father. First, the facilitator enquires whether he might be angry with his father, When the man says he doesn't think so, the facilitator says 'Possibly dissatisfied with him?', to which the man rather doubtfully responds, 'Well, yes, perhaps.' Then the facilitator enquires whether the man is disappointed in his father, to which he quickly responds 'That's it! I *am* disappointed that he's not a strong person. I think I've always been disappointed in him ever since I was a boy.'

In the above example, the facilitator is not interpreting the client, nor would Rogers. Rather the facilitator progressively checks out his understanding to grasp exactly what the man wishes to say. Gendlin (1988) mentions how Rogers would take in each correction until the client indicated 'Yes, That's how it is. That's what I feel' (p. 127). Characteristically this statement would be followed by a silence in which the client fully received the empathic understanding. Very often during these silences, clients would get in touch with something deeper.

A word now about what empathy is *not*. True empathy does not have any judgemental or diagnostic quality about it. Also, empathy is most definitely not a 'wooden technique of pseudo-understanding in which the counselor "reflects back what the client has just said"' (Rogers, 1962, p. 420). In his 1975 article on empathy, Rogers observed how at first he found it helpful to think that the best response was to 'reflect' feelings back to clients, but that later on in his career the word 'reflect' made him cringe. To Rogers, empathy is an attitude, a very special form of companionship, a gentle and sensitive way of being with clients. However well intended, mechanical reflections form no part of offering empathy.

The client in the process

Already goals for person-centred counselling have been discussed. Here, I draw parallels between how presence of the three counsellor attitudinal conditions of congruence, unconditional positive regard and empathy can influence client congruence, unconditional positive regard and empathy.

Congruence. Given the right facilitative climate, clients will feel less need to be defensive and to look for external regard. Though painful at times, they may progressively take more risks in disclosing themselves to their counsellors. Counsellors who accept clients and prize their rights to be their true selves allow them to share parts of themselves that they may find embarrassing, abnormal or frightening. Also, they give clients the opportunity to share parts of themselves that they like, without being negatively judged for such disclosures. As the counselling relationship develops, a mutuality of congruence can develop between counsellor and client with each making it easier for the other to be real in the relationship. For some clients, the relationship can transcend itself into becoming a profound spiritual experience in which they, like their counsellors, attain an altered state of consciousness. Also, an outcome of successful person-centred counselling is that clients become more congruent in their outside relationships.

Unconditional positive regard. Here I refer to clients' regard for themselves rather than for their counsellors. Most often clients lack self-esteem. Rogers (1975) suggested a number of ways in which an empathic attitude may raise clients' level of regard. First, having the hidden and unacceptable parts of themselves understood and accepted dissolves clients' alienation and helps connect them to the human race. Second, being cared for and valued for their true selves allows clients to think 'this other individual trusts me, thinks I'm worthwhile. Perhaps I *am* worth something. Perhaps *I* could value *myself*. Perhaps I could care for myself' (p. 7). Third, not being judged by their counsellors may lead clients to judge themselves less harshly, thus gradually increasing the possibility of self-acceptance. Also, as clients gain in self-esteem, they are likely to shift their focus-of-evaluation from other people's standards and beliefs to their own. Thus, they become less vulnerable to the damaging effects of conditions of worth.

Empathy. The three counsellor attitudinal conditions make it easier for clients to be empathic to themselves both inside and outside of counselling. At varying rates, clients' self-concepts can allow more of their experiencing into awareness. Having their feelings sensitively listened to provides clients with the opportunity to experience and explore these feelings and so understand themselves better. Furthermore, clients learn the importance of listening on their own to their feelings as a guide to their actions and future directions. Also, the more empathic clients are able to be to themselves, the more likely they are to experience and show empathy to their counsellors and other people, thus improving the quality of their relationships with them.

In short, the counsellor attitudinal conditions of congruence, unconditional positive regard and empathy allow clients to become more effective counsellors and growth enhancers for themselves. Counsellors who insufficiently possess these attitudinal conditions may increase their clients' incongruence, negative self-regard and lack of empathy to themselves and others. However, in the right hands, person-centred counselling can be a powerful approach for assisting clients to become persons.

Further applications

Person-centred counselling has been presented here in relation to individual work. However, Rogers' interests and influence were much more extensive. Rogers championed the use of person-centred principles in encounter groups, classroom teaching, management, and peace and conflict resolution.

I end this chapter with a beautiful saying of Lao-Tse that resonated very deeply with Rogers and summarizes the crux of his counselling approach.

> It is as though he/she listened
> and such listening as his/her's enfolds us in a silence
> in which at last we begin to hear
> what we are meant to be.

CHAPTER REVIEW AND SELF-REFERENT QUESTIONS

Chapter review questions

1. Why did Rogers call his counselling approach person-centred?

2. What does Rogers mean by the actualizing tendency?

3. Critically review Rogers' concept of the actualizing tendency. What evidence might support or negate Rogers' views about the concept?

4. What does Rogers mean by organismic valuing process?

5. What does Rogers mean by experience and experiencing?

6. What does Rogers mean by awareness?

7. What are conditions of worth and how do they develop?

8. What are Rogers' four possible outcomes for how people can react to their experiences?

9. Specify how low-functioning people process their experiences differently from high-functioning people.

10. With reference to a person's self-concept and experience, what does Rogers mean by the term incongruence? Provide an example.

11. What does Rogers mean by subception and what is its function?

12. What is the role of assessment in person-centred counselling?

13. Why does Rogers present how to counsel in terms of attitudinal conditions rather than techniques?

14. What does Rogers mean by congruence?

15. What does Rogers mean by unconditional positive regard?

16. What does Rogers mean by empathy?

17. What are your views on Rogers' six necessary and sufficient conditions for therapeutic personality change?

18. As an outcome of person-centred counselling, what does it mean for clients to become more congruent?

19. As an outcome of person-centred counselling, what does it mean for clients to possess more unconditional positive regard?

20. As an outcome of person-centred counselling, what does it mean for clients to become more empathic?

21. What do you consider the strengths and weaknesses of Rogers' model of the person?

22. What do you consider the strengths and weaknesses of Rogers' model of counselling practice?

Self-referent questions

1. Are you aware of any of your conditions of worth? If so, what are they and how did you acquire each of them?

2. Examine a past or current relationship which you think has helped or is helping you to attain a more adequate self-concept. What characteristics of the other person were or are helpful?

3. Examine a past or current relationship which you think has hindered you from attaining a more adequate self-concept. What characteristics of the other person were or are harmful?

4. Assess yourself on each of the following attributes of fully functioning or self-actualizing people: openness to experience, rationality, personal responsibility, self-regard, capacity for good personal relations and ethical living.

5. If you counsel, how congruent are you and how do you know?

6. If you counsel, how well do you offer unconditional positive regard and how do you know?

7. If you counsel, how empathic are you and how do you know?

8. What relevance, if any, has the theory and practice of person-centred counselling for how you counsel?

9. What relevance, if any, has the theory and practice of person-centred counselling for how you live?

Annotated bibliography

Rogers, C.R. (1949). A theory of therapy, personality, and interpersonal relationships, as developed in the client-centered framework. In S. Koch (Ed.), *Psychology: A Study of Science* (Study 1, Vol. 3, pp.184–256). New York: McGraw-Hill.
Rogers regarded this chapter as one of his most significant publications. He worked for three or four years on it and was proud of its thoroughness and rigour. He endeavoured to make every major statement in it something that could be tested by research. This chapter is the major reference for readers wishing to understand Rogerian theory.

Rogers, C.R. (1951). *Client-centered Therapy*. Boston: Houghton Mifflin.
This book describes the attitudinal orientation of the counsellor, the therapeutic relationship experienced by the client, the process of counselling and various issues and applications of the client-centred approach. The book concludes with an important 19-proposition statement of Rogers' theory of personality and behaviour.

Rogers, C.R. (1957). The necessary and sufficient conditions of therapeutic personality change. *Journal of Consulting Psychology, 21,* 95–103.
Also regarded by Rogers as one of his most significant publications, this article presents and discusses six conditions for effective counselling practice. The paper elaborates the counsellor conditions of congruence, unconditional positive regard and empathic understanding.

Rogers, C.R. (1961). *On Becoming a Person*. Boston: Houghton Mifflin.
Another publication regarded by Rogers as one of his most significant. Rogers acknowledged the book as certainly his most popular and thought it had spoken to people all over the world. The book comprises seven parts: speaking personally; how can I be of help?; the process of becoming a person; a philosophy of persons; the place of research in psychotherapy; what are the implications for living?; and the behavioural sciences and the person.

Rogers, C.R. (1975). Empathic: An unappreciated way of being. *The Counseling Psychologist, 5,* 2–10.
This paper, reprinted in *A Way of Being*, is Rogers' reevaluation of the attitudinal condition of empathy. It is his major statement on the subject.

Rogers, C.R. (1980). *A Way of Being*. Boston: Houghton Mifflin.
A collection of 15 papers written between 1960 and 1980, this book is divided into four parts: personal experiences and perspectives; aspects of a person-centred approach; the process of education – and its future; and looking ahead – a person-centred scenario. As the book jacket says, '*A Way of Being* is a cohesive presentation of a person-centered approach to life.' This book is written in the same reader-friendly style as *On Becoming a Person*.

Further references

Rogers

Heppner, P.P., Rogers, M.E. & Lee, L.A. (1984). Carl Rogers: Reflections on his life. *Journal of Counseling and Development, 63,* 14–20. (An interview with Rogers).

Meador, B.D. & Rogers, C.R. (1979). Person-centered therapy. In R.J. Corsini (Ed.). *Current Psychotherapies* (2nd ed., pp.131–84). Itasca, IL: Peacock.

Raskin, N.J. & Rogers, C.R. (1989). Person-centered therapy. In R.J. Corsini & D. Wedding (Eds.).*Current psychotherapies.* (4th ed., pp.15–194). Itasca, IL: Peacock.

Rogers, C.R. (1939). *The Clinical Treatment of the Problem Child.* Boston: Houghton Mifflin.

Rogers, C.R. (1942). *Counseling and Psychotherapy.* Boston: Houghton Mifflin.

Rogers, C.R. (1962). The interpersonal relationship: the core of guidance. *Harvard Educational Review, 32,* 416–29.

Rogers, C.R. (1964). Toward a modern approach to values: The valuing process in the mature person. *Journal of Abnormal and Social Psychology, 68,* 160–7.

Rogers, C.R. (1969). *Freedom to Learn.* Columbus, OH: Charles E. Merrill.

Rogers, C.R. (1970). *Encounter Groups.* London: Penguin.

Rogers, C.R. (1973). *Becoming Partners: Marriage and its Alternatives.* London: Constable.

Rogers, C.R. (1974). In retrospect: forty-six years. *American Psychologist, 29,* 115–23.

Rogers, C.R. (1977). *Carl Rogers on Personal Power.* London: Constable.

Rogers, C.R. (1983). *Freedom to Learn for the 80's.* Columbus, OH: Charles E. Merrill.

Rogers, C.R. (1986). Client-centered therapy. In I. Kutash & A. Wolf (Eds.). *Psychotherapist's Casebook: Theory and Technique in the Practice of Modern Therapies* (pp.197–208). San Francisco: Jossey Bass.

Rogers, C.R. (1989). The case of Mrs. Oak. In D. Wedding & R.J. Corsini (Eds.), *Case Studies in Psychotherapy* (pp. 63–85). Itasca, IL: Peacock.

Rogers, C.R., Gendlin, E.T., Kiesler, D.J. & Traux, C. (1967). *The Therapeutic Relationship and its Impact: A Study of Psychotherapy with Schizophrenics.* Madison, WI: University of Wisconsin Press.

Rogers, C.R. & Sanford, R.A. (1985). Client-centered psychotherapy. In H.I. Kaplan, B.J. Sadock & A.M. Friedman (Eds.). *Comprehensive Textbook of Psychiatry* (4th ed., pp. 1374–88). Baltimore, MA: William & Wilkins.

Rogers, C.R. & Skinner, B.F. (1956). Some issues concerning the control of human behavior: A symposium. *Science, 124,* 1057–66.

Rogers, C.R. & Stevens, B. (1967). *Person to Person: The Problem of Being Human.* London: Souvenir Press.

Walker, A.M., Rablen, R.A. & Rogers, C.R. (1960). Development of a scale to measure process changes in psychotherapy. *Journal of Clinical Psychology, 16,* 79–85.

Others

Combs, A.W. & Snygg, D. (1959). *Individual Behavior* (Rev. ed.). New York: Harper & Row.

Gendlin, E.T. (1962). *Experiencing and the Creation of Meaning.* New York: The Free Press of Glencoe.

Gendlin, E.T. (1981). *Focusing* (2nd ed.). New York: Bantam Books.

Gendlin, E.T. (1988). Carl Rogers (1902–1987). *American Psychologist, 43,* 127–8.

Goodyear, R.K. (1987). Editorial. In memory of Carl Ransom Rogers (January 8, 1902–February 4, 1987). *Journal of Counseling and Development, 65,* 523–4.

Gordon, T. (1970). *Parent Effectiveness Training: The Tested New Way to Raise Responsible Children*. New York: Wyden.

Maslow, A.H. (1962). *Toward a Psychology of Being*. Princeton, NJ: Van Nostrand.

Maslow, A.H. (1970). *Motivation and Personality* (2nd ed.). New York: Harper & Row.

McCleary, R.A. & Lazarus, R.S. (1949). Autonomic discrimination without awareness. *Journal of Personality*, *18*, 171–9.

Mearns, D. & Thorne, B. (1988). *Person-centred Counselling in Action*. London: Sage.

Nelson-Jones, R. (1977). A factor analysis of the Counsellor Attitude Scale. *British Journal of Guidance and Counselling*, *5*, 185–8.

Nelson-Jones, R. & Patterson, C.H. (1975). Measuring client-centred attitudes. *British Journal of Guidance and Counselling*, *3*, 228–36.

Thorne, B. (1992). *Carl Rogers*. London: Sage.

Rogers on film

Rogers, C.R. (1965). Client-centred therapy. In E. Shostrom (Ed.). *Three Approaches to Psychotherapy*. Santa Ana, CA: Psychological Films.

THREE
Gestalt Counselling

PREVIEW

- *Fritz Perls, its originator, regarded gestalt counselling as an existential approach. Gestalt means form, shape, pattern or configuration. The human organism is a unified whole which can only exist in an environmental field. Consequently mind-body and person-environment splits are erroneous.*
- *Life is characterized by a continuous process of balance and imbalance in the organism, with homeostasis being the process whereby the organism satisfies its needs by restoring balance. No sooner is one gestalt completed than another comes into being. The contact boundary is the boundary between organism and environment and it is here that psychological events take place.*
- *Healthy functioning involves identifying with one's forming organismic self and keeping in touch with one's senses. An aggressive attitude towards experience is necessary if it is to be de-structured and then assimilated as one's own.*
- *People need frustrations in order to learn to mobilize their own resources to manipulate the environment. However, often children experience interruptions from significant others which interfere with their capacity for self-support and cause them to suppress their emotions.*
- *Between the self zone and the outer zone is an intermediate zone consisting of maya or fantasy activity. Anxiety or stage fright is the result of this fantasy activity. In neurosis there is a continuous fight between reality and maya.*
- *The four main neurotic mechanisms or contact boundary disturbances are introjection, projection, retroflection and confluence. The structure of neurosis consists of five layers: the cliché layer; the Eric Berne or Sigmund Freud layer of manipulative roles and games; the impasse; the death or implosive layer; and the explosion.*
- *Goals for counselling include self-support rather than environmental support, being in touch with one's senses and existential centre, self-actualizing rather than self-image*

actualizing, responsibility or freedom of choice, and the ability to form and close strong gestalts.
- *Change involves focusing on the how of clients' contact boundary disturbances in the now. Gestalt approaches to counselling practice include the awareness technique, sympathy and frustration, eliciting fantasies, drama techniques, dreamwork, and various rules and games.*
- *Gestalt counselling developments include less emphasis on frustrating clients, more counsellor self-disclosure, and use of psychoanalytic formulations to describe character structure.*

INTRODUCTION

Gestalt counselling or therapy, according to Perls, its main architect, is an existential approach 'not just occupied with dealing with symptoms or character structure, but with the total existence of a person' (Perls, 1969a, p. 71). Towards the end of his life Perls (1969a) wrote that he considered gestalt counselling one of the three then-existing types of existential counselling, the two others being Frankl's logotherapy and Binswanger's daseins counselling. Clients who come for gestalt counselling are in states of existential crisis and need to learn to take responsibility for their existences. Perls considered all other existential philosophies borrowed concepts from other sources; for example, Binswanger from psychoanalysis, Tillich from Protestantism, and Sartre from Communism. Gestalt counselling is the only existential approach which has support in its own formation since gestalt formation, the emergence of needs, is a primary biological phenomenon. He observed: 'Gestalt therapy is a philosophy that tries to be in harmony, in alignment with everything else, with medicine, with science, with the universe, with what *is*' (Perls, 1969a, p. 17).

Fritz Perls

Friederich (Frederick or Fritz) Soloman Perls (1893–1970), the originator of gestalt counselling, was born in Berlin, the son of a Jewish travelling salesman of Palestinian wines. He grew up with his two sisters in a disturbed family in which his parents had many bitter fights, both verbal and physical. Perls' mother used carpet-beating rods on him but he claims she did not break his spirit; instead he broke the carpet-beaters. He saw his father as a hypocrite who preached one thing and lived another and who progressively isolated himself from his family. Perls wrote: 'Basically I hated him and his pompous righteousness, but he could also be loving and warm. How much my attitude was influenced by my mother's hatred of him, how much she poisoned us children with it, I could not say' (Perls, 1969a, pp. 250–1). During his puberty years, a period during which he was initiated into both sex and acting, Perls was the black sheep of his family. Throughout his life Perls was a rebel rather than a complier, a man with a very quick eye for others' phoniness and pseudo-authenticity, and somewhat of an exhibitionist himself. His early experiences of rejection and insecurity may have deeply influenced his later life.

Perls was a student at the universities of Freiburg and Berlin, and received his MD from the latter institution in 1920. His psychological training included, in 1926, a post as assistant to Kurt Goldstein at the Frankfurt Neurological Institute and, in the early 1930s, attendance first at the Vienna Institute of Psychoanalysis and then at the Berlin Institute of Psychoanalysis. In 1933, with the rise of Hitler, Perls fled from Germany to Holland. At the time of his departure his analyst was Wilhelm Reich and his supervisors were Otto Fenichel and Karen Horney. He wrote: 'From Fenichel I got confusion; from Reich, brazenness; from Horney, human involvement without terminology' (Perls, 1969b, p. 39). In 1934, on the recommendation of Ernest Jones, Freud's friend and biographer, Perls moved to Johannesburg as a training analyst. The following year he established the South African Institute for Psychoanalysis. In 1942 his first book, *Ego, Hunger and Aggression*, was published in South Africa, with the British edition published in 1947. Several chapters in this book were written by Perls' wife Laura, whom some consider the co-founder of gestalt counselling (Yontef & Simkin, 1989).

In 1946 Perls emigrated to the United States and established a private practice in New York City. In 1951 he published *Gestalt Therapy*, a book co-authored by Ralph Hefferline and Paul Goodman. In 1952 he established the New York Institute of Gestalt Therapy and, in 1954, the Cleveland Institute for Gestalt Psychotherapy. In 1960 Perls moved to the West Coast of the United States and, in 1964, joined the staff of the Esalen Institute at Big Sur, California, as resident associate psychiatrist. In 1969, he moved to Cowichan on Vancouver Island in British Columbia where he established a gestalt community. Also in 1969, Perls published *Gestalt Therapy Verbatim* and the autobiographical pot-pourri of prose, poetry and psychology entitled *In and Out of the Garbage Pail*. On 14 March 1970, after a brief illness, Perls died at the age of 76. At the time of his death Perls was working on two books, *The Gestalt Approach* and *Eye Witness to Therapy*, and these were published posthumously in 1973 as a single book entitled *The Gestalt Approach and Eye Witness to Therapy*.

Perls' ideas were largely formed in the Austro-Germanic world. Freudian psychoanalysis was a big influence, though ultimately Perls was to go his own way. He was also influenced by Reich's idea of character armour, whereby resistances become total organismic functions. A major influence was the work of the gestalt psychologists with whom Perls considered he had a peculiar relationship, admiring much of their work but unable to go along with them when they became logical positivists. He did not read any of their textbooks, although he read some papers by Lewin, Wertheimer and Kohler. He observed: 'Most important for me was the idea of the unfinished situation, the incomplete gestalt' (Perls, 1969b, p. 62). The academic gestaltists never accepted Perls and he did not regard himself as a pure gestaltist. Moreno, with his ideas on therapy by means of psychodrama, was a further influence on Perls.

Perls had extensive experience of personal relations including many 'affairs'. Other influences on Perls included American humanistic psychology, Eastern religions, meditation, psychedelics and body work. In his autobiographical book *In and Out of the Garbage Pail*, Perls admits to many compulsions including smoking and 'leching'. He also wrote poems and painted. While Perls may have not always possessed the amount of responsibility (response-ability or freedom of choice) for which his counselling approach strives, he appears to have been a tremendously vital and charismatic person. The gestalt prayer of this restless gypsy was:

I do my thing, and you do your thing
I am not in this world to live up to your expectations
And you are not in this world to live up to mine.
You are you, and I am I,
And if by chance, we find each other, it's beautiful.
If not, it can't be helped.

(Perls, 1969a, inside front cover page)

ASSUMPTIONS

Perls (1973) wrote in his introduction to *The Gestalt Approach* that gestalt theory was grounded in experience and observation, had changed with years of practice and application and was still growing. The following presentation is almost exclusively based on Perls' own writings. Though others have developed the approach after Perls' death, no other really major figure has emerged.

Gestalt

The German noun *gestalt* means form or shape and among the meanings of the verb *gestalten* are to shape, to form, to fashion, to organize and to structure. Other terms for gestalt are pattern, configuration or organized whole. Perls observed: 'The basic premise of Gestalt psychology is that human nature is organized into patterns or wholes, that it is experienced by the individual in these terms, and that it can only be understood as a function of the patterns of wholes of which it is made' (Perls, 1973, p. 5). The major thrust of the experimental work of the gestalt psychologists was to show that humans do not perceive things in isolation but organize them through their perceptual processes into meaningful wholes (for example, a row of dots may be perceived as a straight line).

People's visual fields are structured in terms of 'figure' and 'background' or 'ground'. Whereas 'figure' is the focus of interest (an object or pattern etc.), 'ground' is the setting or context. Perls and his colleagues (Perls, Hefferline & Goodman, 1951) noted that the interplay between figure and ground was dynamic. For instance, the same ground may, with differing interests and shifts of attention, give rise to different figures. Also, a given figure may itself become ground in the event that some detail of its own becomes figure.

The holistic doctrine

The human organism is a unified whole. In particular Perls objected to the old mind-body split. The emergence of psychosomatic medicine made the close relationship of mental and physical activity increasingly apparent. In fact mental activity seemed to be an activity of the whole person carried out at a lower energy level than those activities called physical. Human beings are wholes engaging in fantasizing, play-acting and doing. For instance, people's actions provide clues as to their thoughts and their thoughts provide clues about what they would like to do. In short, people do not have organisms but *are* organisms engaged in activities of the same order which are often wrongly dichotomized into mental and physical activities.

Another erroneous dichotomy is that between self and external world. Individuals are not self-sufficient but can only exist in an environmental field. Environments do not create individuals nor do individuals create environments. Rather, each is what it is because of its relationship to the other and the whole. For instance, in the example of a person seeing a tree, there is no sight without something to be seen nor is anything seen if there is no eye to see it.

There are numerous other false dichotomies such as those between emotional (subjective) and real (objective); infantile and mature; biological and cultural; love and aggression; and conscious and unconscious. For instance, regarding the split between infantile and mature, it is often lack of certain childhood traits which devitalizes adults while other traits called infantile may be the introjections of adult neuroses. A consistent theme of the gestalt approach is to search for the overall pattern rather than for false dichotomies.

Homeostasis and balance

The basic tendency of every organism is to strive for balance. The organism is continuously faced with imbalance that is disturbing through either external (demands from the environment) or internal (needs) factors. Life is characterized by a continuous interplay of balance and imbalance in the organism. Homeostasis or organismic self-regulation is the process by which the organism satisfies its needs by restoring balance when faced with a demand or need which upsets its equilibrium. Health constitutes the appropriate operation of the homeostatic process, whereas sickness means that for too long a time the organism has remained in a state of disequilibrium, unable to satisfy its needs. Death constitutes a total breakdown of the homeostatic process.

Though psychological and physiological are interrelated, the organism may be perceived as having psychological as well as physiological contact needs. A simple example of a physiological need is that, for the organism to be in good health, the water content of the blood must be kept at a certain level, neither too low nor excessive. If, for instance, the water content of the blood falls too low the individual feels thirst, with its symptoms of dry mouth and restlessness and the wish to restore the imbalance by drinking. A possible example of a more psychological need is that of mothers to keep their children happy and contented. Consequently, even when sleeping, they may be very sensitive to the cries and whimpers of the offspring.

The homeostatic process also operates where several needs are experienced simultaneously. However, here a selective process takes place based on the organism's need for survival and for self-actualization. Perls observed that 'Every individual, every plant, every animal has only one inborn goal – to actualize itself as it is' (Perls, 1969a, p. 33). Thus, with the simultaneous experiencing of many needs, the individual attends to the dominant survival and self-actualization need before attending to the others. Put another way, the dominant need or the need which presses most sharply for satisfaction becomes the foreground figure while the other needs recede, at least momentarily, into the background. Perls (1969a) wrote about doing away with the whole of instinct theory and simply considering the organism as a system that needs balance if it is to function properly. Though, practically, people have hundreds of unfinished situations in them, the most urgent situation always emerges. Individuals, to be able to satisfy their needs (to complete or to close incomplete *gestalten*), must be able both to sense what they need and to manipulate themselves and their environments to obtain what is necessary.

Life is basically an infinite number of unfinished situations or incomplete gestalts: no sooner is one gestalt completed than another comes up. The homeostatic process is the means by which the organism maintains itself 'and the only law which is constant is the forming of gestalts – wholes, completeness. A gestalt is an organic function. A gestalt is an ultimate experiential unit' (Perls, 1969a, p. 16). With the introduction of the concept of the homeostatic process, it was possible to see gestalt formation as a primary biological drive, with the gestalt being the basic experiential unit, having such properties as figure and ground and completeness or incompleteness.

Contact boundary and contact

Earlier I mentioned that Perls disdained the split between self and the external world, considering that the organism and the environment stood in a relationship of mutuality to one another. The contact boundary is the boundary between organism and environment and it is at this boundary that psychological events take place. Perls and his colleagues (1951) considered that 'psychology studies the operation of the contact-boundary in the organism/environment field' (p. 229). Such 'contact' or 'being in touch with' involves both sensory awareness and motor behaviour. The organism's sensory system provides it with a means of orientation, with the motor system providing a means of manipulation. Both orientation and manipulation take place at the contact boundary. In healthy functioning, once the system of orientation has performed its function, the organism manipulates itself and the environment in such a way that organismic balance is restored and the gestalt is closed.

All thoughts, feelings and actions take place at the contact boundary. In healthy functioning, people have an effective contact withdrawal rhythm or means of meeting psychological events at the contact boundary. Contacting the environment represents forming a gestalt, whereas withdrawal is either closing a gestalt completely or mobilizing resources to make closure possible. More simply, contact and withdrawal may respectively be viewed as acceptance and rejection of the environment. The components of contact and withdrawal are almost invariably present, but the neurotic person has a reduced capacity to discriminate between the appropriateness of these dialectical elements and consequently behaves with reduced effectiveness.

The self and self-actualization

The self is the system of contacts at the contact boundary at any moment. The self exists where there are boundaries of contact and its activity is that of forming figures and grounds. The self always integrates the senses, motor coordination and organic needs. It is the integrator or artist of life and though it 'is only a small factor in the total organism/environment interaction . . . it plays the crucial role of finding and making the meanings that we grow by' (Perls *et al.*, 1951, p. 235).

The self consists of the identifications and alienations at the contact boundary. For instance, individuals may identify with their families, but feel alien to people from different countries. Inside the boundary tends to be perceived as good and outside as bad. Self-actualization may be viewed as the expression of appropriate identifications and alienations. Healthy functioning involves identifying with one's forming organismic self, not inhibiting one's creative excitement, yet alienating what is not organismically one's own. Sickness involves restricting one's areas of contact through alienating parts of one's forming organismic self by means of false identifications.

Perhaps a more accessible way of stating this is to make a distinction between self-actualizing based on the existential principle that 'a rose is a rose is a rose' and self-image actualizing in which people live for their image of how they should be rather than how they are. Perls (1969a) believed 'Every external control, even *internalized* external control – "you should" – interferes with the healthy working of the organism. There is only one thing that should control: the *situation*' (p. 20). If people understand the situations which they are in, and let these situations control their actions, then they learn how to cope with life. An even more simple view of Perls' ideas on self-actualization may be gained from his dictum: 'So lose your mind and come to your senses' (Perls, 1970a, p. 38).

Excitement

Humans secure their energy from the food and air they take in. Perls used the word excitement to describe the energy we create, because it coincides with the physiological function of excitation. Excitement varies according to the task on the basis of hormonal differentiation: for instance it gets tinged with some other substance, for example adrenalin for anger, or sexual hormones for erotic contact. Much of our excitement goes into energizing the motor system because the muscles link people with the environment. Even for most emotional events, emotion is transferred into movement. However, some excitement goes into energizing the senses. Healthy people allow their excitement to get to their senses and muscles, but unfortunately many people allow much of their excitement to be drained off into their fantasy life, into their computer (unproductive thinking), and into self-image actualization. Perls (1969a) believed modern humans live in a state of low grade vitality in which the average person lives only 5 to 15 per cent of his potential and the person who has even 25 per cent of his potential available is considered a genius.

Emotion

Emotion, which is the organism's direct evaluative experience of the organism/environment field, is immediate rather than regulated by thoughts and verbal judgements. Emotion is a continuous process since all instances in people's lives carry some feeling tone of pleasantness or unpleasantness. Excitement is modified into specific emotions according to the situation that has to be met and the emotions mobilize the sensory and motor system so that needs may be satisfied. Gestalt counselling attaches great importance to the emotions, which are not only essential as energy or excitement regulators but are also 'unique deliveries of experience which have no substitute – they are the way we become aware of our concerns, and, therefore, of what we are and what the world is' (Perls *et al.*, 1951, p. 96).

ACQUISITION

Aggression, assimilation and introjection

An aggressive attitude towards experience is necessary if it is really to be assimilated or made the organism's own. An analogy may be made between the aggression required for eating and that required for assimilating experience. Food needs to be destroyed or de-structured before what is valuable to the organism can be retained and undesirable substances can be eliminated. Any undesirable substance which is not eliminated may be poisonous and detrimental to the organism. Every organism in an environmental field grows by incorporating, digesting or destructuring, and then assimilating or absorbing selectively new matter, whether it be food, lectures or parental influence. Loving parents are likely to provide their children with experiences which they will assimilate since they are relevant to their own needs as they grow from environmental support to self-support.

Not all experience, however, goes through the destructuring and assimilation process required for healthy functioning. Introjections are experiences which are swallowed as a whole rather than being properly digested. The outcome of introjection is that undesirable as well as desirable substances have been retained, thus weakening the organism. Hateful parents are likely to provide their children with experiences which have to be introjected or taken in whole even though they are contrary to the needs of the organism.

Frustration and manipulation

The young baby is virtually totally dependent on its mother, but as time goes by the child learns to communicate, to crawl and walk, to bite and chew, and to accept and reject. In short, the child learns to realize some part of its potential for existence. Growth comes about through learning to overcome frustrations by mobilizing one's innate resources to manipulate the environment to satisfy needs. The term manipulation refers to a person's ways of mobilizing and using the environment to satisfy needs. Both healthy and unhealthy organisms manipulate the environment, with healthy organisms manipulating it on an underlying basis of self-support, whereas unhealthy organisms seek environmental rather than self-support.

Perls wrote: 'Without frustration there is no need, no reason to mobilize your resources, to discover that you might be able to do something on your own, and in order not to be frustrated, which is a pretty painful experience, the child learns to manipulate the environment' (Perls, 1969a, p. 35). Perhaps it would be more accurate to say that with the right kind of frustrations the child learns to manipulate the environment in such a way as to meet its needs and restore effective organismic balance. However, with lack of frustration (producing the spoiled child) or with frustrations which block or are beyond the child's coping capacity, the outcome is likely to be that the child starts to mobilize the environment by playing phoney roles and games: for instance, playing stupid, playing helpless, playing weak and flattering. These false manipulations cause individuals to alienate parts of themselves, be it their eyes, ears or genitals.

Interruptions of contact

Humans are forced to learn much more through education than by using their biologically based instincts. Consequently, much of the animal's intuition as to what is the 'right' procedure is either missing or blocked in people. Instead, there is a whole range of composite fantasies, handed down and modified through the generations, as to what constitutes the 'right' procedures. These procedures perform mostly support functions for social contacts (viz. manners and ethics) and have the disadvantage of not necessarily being biologically based. Consequently there frequently are interruptions in the contact provided by on-going organismic processes which, if left alone, would be conducive to self-support. Examples of such interruptions are 'Don't touch that' or 'Don't do this'. Even withdrawals may be interrupted, as in 'You stay here now, keep your mind on your homework and don't dream'. People often incorporate their parents' interruptions as introjections in their own lives, for example 'Grown men don't cry'. Unhealthy organisms or neurotics are self-interrupters who need to become aware both of the fact that they are interrupting themselves and also of what they are interrupting.

Suppression of emotion

Suppression of emotion is a major way in which adults interrupt the contact of their children. Such adults, who frequently have been brought up in environments in which 'the authorities' were afraid of emotion, tend to squelch the emotions of their children and thus prevent their emotions from undergoing natural development and differentiation. This is mainly achieved through an overemphasis of the 'external world' and the demands of 'reality' and a belittling of organismic needs and emotions. The outcome of this is that children 'adjust' to such unremitting pressure by dulling their body-sense and losing some of their vitality. However, because emotions are inherent to the organism, this suppression of emotions does not eliminate 'undesirable' emotions. Instead, it disturbs 'the intricate organism/environment field by setting up a great number of situations which, *unless avoided, are immensely emotion-arousing!*' (Perls *et al.*, 1951, p. 97).

MAINTENANCE

Though Perls often used the terms neurosis and neurotic, he considered that problems of poor gestalt formation and closure were extremely widespread. He wrote: 'Modern man lives in a state of low grade vitality. Though generally he does not suffer deeply, he also knows little of true creative living. Instead of it he has become an anxious automation' (Perls, 1973, p. ix). In this section I examine the gestalt view of how people maintain their contact deficiencies. Needless to say, an individual's difficulties are compounded by living in a culture or environment where self-image actualizing rather than self-actualizing is common.

Zones of awareness

There are three zones or layers of awareness. The *outer* zone (OZ) consists of awareness of the world, of those things, facts and processes that are available to everyone. The *self* zone (SZ) is the place within the skin. Though the SZ refers to our authentic organismic selves, within it there is an *intermediate* zone (DMZ), often called 'mind' or consciousness, which prevents people from good contact or being 'in touch' with themselves or the world. The DMZ is a zone of fantasy activity which consumes excitement and leaves little energy over for being in touch with reality. Perls sometimes used the Indian word *maya* to describe the DMZ. *Maya* means illusion or fantasy and is a kind of dream or trance. More colloquial and crude is Perl's use of the term 'mind-f**king' to describe the activity of the DMZ which hinders people from coming to their senses.

Anxiety and stage fright

Gestalt theory has both a physiological and psychological definition of anxiety. The physiological definition is: 'Anxiety is the experience of breathing difficulty during any blocked excitement' (Perls *et al.*, 1951, p. 128). The idea underlying this definition is that heightened energy mobilization, with the need for more air (an increase in the rate and amplitude of breathing), occurs whenever there is strong concern and contact. As such it is a healthy way of being in erotic, aggressive, creative and other sorts of exciting or energy mobilizing situations. A less healthy response is to control, interfere with and interrupt the excitement by trying to continue breathing at the rate that was adequate prior to it. This leads to a narrowing of the chest to force exhalation in order to create a vacuum into which fresh air can rush. Anxiety, derived from the Latin word *angustia* meaning narrowness, is the product of an emergency measure caused by the conflict between excitement and control.

The psychological definition of anxiety is that it is 'the gap between the now and the later' or 'stage fright' (Perls, 1969a, pp. 32–3). As such it is the result of the fantasy activity of the DMZ. This fantasy activity is rehearsing for a future that people do not really want to be because they are afraid of it. Perls wrote: 'We fill in the gap where there should be a future with insurance policies, status quo, sameness, *anything* so as not to experience the possibility of openness towards the future' (Perls, 1969a, pp. 48–9). People who are in the now and have access to their senses are unlikely to be anxious because their excitement can flow immediately into the kind of spontaneous, creative and inventive activity which achieves solutions to unfinished situations. They are not blocked from good contact with themselves and the environment by *maya* or fantasies, prejudices, apprehensions and so on. They are prepared to take reasonable risks in living. Perls distinguished between catastrophic fantasies, which entail too much precaution, and anastrophic fantasies which entail too little. He thought some people managed a balance between catastrophic and anastrophic fantasies, thus having both perspective and rational daring.

Neurosis

Neurotic individuals allow society to impinge too heavily on them. They cannot clearly distinguish their own needs and see society as larger than life and themselves as smaller. Society can consist of any one of a number of groups, for example, the family, the state, the social circle and co-workers. When the neurotic and one or more of these groups simultaneously experience different needs, the neurotic is incapable of distinguishing which need is dominant and thus can make neither a good contact nor a good withdrawal. Consequently one or more of the contact boundary disturbances of neurosis seem the most effective way to maintain balance and a sense of a self-regulation in situations where the odds appear to be overwhelmingly adverse.

Perls distinguished between health, psychosis and neurosis. In health, people are in touch with the realities both of themselves and of the world. In psychosis, people are out of touch with reality and in touch with *maya*, especially fantasies about megalomania and worthlessness. In neurosis a continual fight is taking place between *maya* and reality.

Contact boundary disturbances

The neuroses, which entail significant contact boundary disturbances, operate primarily through four mechanisms, albeit interrelated. These neurotic boundary disturbances are 'nagging, chronic, daily interferences with the processes of growth and self-recognition' (Perls, 1973, p. 32). However, not all disturbances in the organism/environment search for balance are evidence of or produce neurosis. Introjection, projection, confluence and retroflection are the four mechanisms of contact boundary disturbance.

I have already mentioned *introjection* as the process by which material from outside is swallowed whole rather than digested properly with the valuable elements being assimilated and the undesirable or toxic elements discarded. Introjects, or undigested thoughts, feelings and behaviour, are the results of the process of introjection. Introjection may be viewed as the tendency to 'own' as part of the self what actually is part of the environment. Two outcomes of introjection are: first, that the introjects prevent individuals from getting in touch with their own reality because all the time they are having to contend with these foreign bodies; and, second, that the introjects may be incompatible with one another and thus contribute to personality disintegration.

Projection is the reverse of introjection in that it is the tendency to 'own' as part of the environment what actually is part of the self. Projection can take place on two levels: in relation to the outer environment and in relation to the self. Perhaps most commonly, projection involves shifting those parts of ourselves that we dislike and devalue on to others rather than recognizing and dealing with the tendencies in ourselves. Projections are associated with introjects because people usually devalue themselves in relation to introjected self-standards, whose unacceptable derivatives in terms of self-evaluations are then projected on to the environment. Projection in relation to the self takes place when people disown as part of themselves areas in which or certain impulses that arise.

For instance, people may say of their anger 'It took control of me' whereby the anger is given an objective existence outside of themselves so that they can make it responsible for their troubles and avoid full recognition of the fact that *it* is part of *themselves.*

With *confluence,* the individual lacks any distinction or experiences no boundary at all between self and environment. People who are unaware of the contact boundaries between themselves and others are neither able to make good contact with them nor, where appropriate, to withdraw. A feature of confluence is demanding likeness and refusal to tolerate differences. Two examples of confluence are marital partners and parents who, respectively, refuse to see their spouses and children as different from themselves.

In *retroflection,* individuals fail to discriminate between self and others accurately by treating themselves the way they originally wanted to treat other people or objects. For instance, the harassed mother at the end of a long day in which everything has gone wrong may turn her destructive impulses against herself. Retroflection means literally 'to turn sharply back against'. When people retroflect they redirect their activity inward and substitute themselves instead of the environment as the targets of their behaviour. Retroflection is not necessarily neurotic. In certain situations it may be to the individual's advantage to suppress particular responses. However, retroflection is pathological when it is chronic, habitual and out of control.

Perls was sensitive to the use of language both in representing and helping to sustain contact boundary disturbances. For example, in introjection the personal pronoun 'I' is used when the real meaning is 'they'; in projection the pronouns 'they' or 'it' are used when the real meaning is 'I'; in confluence the pronoun 'we' is used when there may really be differentness; and retroflection uses the reflexive 'myself' as in the statement 'I am ashamed of myself'.

The following is Perls' (1973) succinct summary of the lack of discrimination, interferences and interruptions entailed in the four main contact boundary disturbances: 'The introjector does as others would like him to do, the projector does unto others what he accuses them of doing to him, the man in pathological confluence doesn't know who is doing what to whom, and the retroflector does to himself what he would like to do to others' (p. 40).

Layers of neurosis

Perls (1969a, 1970) came to see the structure of neurosis as consisting of five layers. First, the cliché layer, for example the meaningless tokens of meeting such as a handshake or 'Good morning'. Second, the Eric Berne or Sigmund Freud layer, the layer where people engage in the counter-productive manipulations of phoney roles and games (e.g. the bully, the very important person, the cry baby, the nice little girl, the good boy). When this role-playing layer is worked through, then the counsellor and client come to the third layer called the impasse or sometimes the sick-point. This layer is characterized by a phobic attitude manifested in avoidance and flight from authentic living. In particular suffering is avoided, especially the suffering of frustration. A major feature in the maintenance of neuroses is that people are not willing to undergo their pain of the impasse, the feeling of being stuck and lost. Behind the impasse is the death or implosive layer, which appears either as fear of death or a feeling of not being alive. Here people implode by contracting and compressing themselves.

The explosion is the final neurotic layer. There are four basic kinds of explosions from the death layer: into grief, if a person works through a loss which has not been assimilated; into orgasm for sexually blocked people; into anger; and into joy. The explosions, which may be mild, depending on the amount of energy invested in the implosive layer, connect with the authentic, organismic person. An example involving the later layers of neurosis is that of a young woman who has recently lost her child and who needs to be able to face her nothingness and her grief to be able to come back to life and make real contact with the world.

PRACTICE
Goals

Clients come to gestalt counselling because they are in existential crises. Perls had a rather cynical view of their motivation, stating: 'Anybody who goes to a therapist has something up his sleeve. I would say roughly 90% don't go to a therapist to be cured, but to be more adequate in their neuroses' (Perls, 1969a, p. 79). Gestalt goals for counselling revolve around the client's movement from environmental support to self-support. Beginning clients are mainly concerned with solving problems. Gestalt counsellors assist clients to support themselves not only in solving current problems but in living more authentically. In order to be self-supporting clients need to be in touch with their organismic existential centres (I am what I am). People who are in touch with their organismic selves or with their senses are self-actualizing or self-supporting.

Yontef and Simkin (1989) observe that the only goal of gestalt counselling is awareness. Clients require awareness both in particular areas and also of the processes or automatic habits by which they block awareness. The process of self-actualizing involves an effective balance of contact and withdrawal at the contact boundary and the ability to use energy or excitement to meet real rather than phoney needs. Furthermore, self-actualizing involves being able to withstand frustration until a solution emerges. Self-supporting people take responsibility for their existences and possess *response-ability* or freedom of choice. They are able appropriately to use aggression to assimilate their experiences and they are largely free from the neurotic contact boundary disturbances of introjection, projection, retroflection and confluence. Also, they possess relatively little self-destructive unfinished business since they are good at forming and closing strong gestalts.

Perls favoured conducting gestalt counselling in workshops which included, as an adjunct at Esalen, communal baths. He required six elements for his performance: '1) My skill 2) Kleenex 3) The hot seat 4) The empty chair 5) Cigarettes 6) An ashtray' (Perls, 1969b, p. 227). Perls viewed all counselling interviews as experimental. Counsellors need to try things out to help clients become aware of how they are now functioning as persons and organisms. Sometimes he would do mass experiments or exercises, but mostly he worked with a series of single people, or sometimes couples, in front of the group. Some of his methods, the use of which 'hinges on questions of *when, with whom,* and *in what situation'* (Shepherd, 1970, p. 324), are now reviewed.

Awareness technique

Gestalt counselling is an experiential rather than a verbal or interpretive approach. Assessment data about how clients interrupt their contact with life are collected as counsellors and clients work together. Gestalt counselling demands that clients experience themselves as fully as possible in the here and now, both to understand their present manipulations and contact boundary disturbances and also to re-experience the unfinished business of past problems and traumas. Perls (1973) regarded the simple phrase 'Now I am aware' as the foundation of his approach. The 'now' because it keeps counsellors and clients in the present and reinforces the fact that experience can only take place in the present, the 'aware' because it gives both counsellors and clients the best picture of clients' present resources. Awareness always takes place in the present and opens up possibilities for action.

Clients are asked to become aware of their body language, their breathing, their voice quality and their emotions as much as of any pressing thoughts. Below are some examples of Perls directing his client Gloria's attention to her non-verbal behaviour, taken from the *Three Approaches to Psychotherapy* film series (Dolliver, 1991, p. 299; Perls, 1965).

> 'What are you doing with your feet now?'
> 'Are you aware of your smile?'
> 'You didn't squirm for the last minute.'
> 'Are you aware that your eyes are moist?'
> 'Are you aware of your facial expression?'

Since clients are self-interrupters they often find it difficult to remain in the here and now. The awareness technique is really a concentration technique, sometimes called focal awareness, by which clients learn to experience each now and each need and also how their feelings and behaviour in one area are related to feelings and behaviour in other areas. Thus they come to an awareness not only of the fact that they are interrupting their contact with themselves and the world, but also of what they are interrupting and how they are doing it through the neurotic mechanisms of introjection, projection etc. Clients are also asked to do some homework which consists of reviewing the session in terms of systematic application of the awareness technique.

Sympathy and frustration

Empathizing with the client is insufficient since the counsellor is withholding himself and, at worst, allowing confluence. Sympathy alone spoils the client. What is needed is a combination of sympathy and of frustration. Clients must be frustrated in their efforts to control the counsellor by neurotic manipulations and instead learn to use their powers of manipulation to meet their real needs. The counsellor focuses on getting clients to become more aware and not to become phobic when they start feeling uncomfortable.

Perls provided situations in which his clients experienced being stuck in frustration and then frustrated their avoidances still further until they were willing to mobilize their *own* resources. He repeatedly frustrated clients until they were face to face with their blocks, inhibitions, and ways of avoiding having eyes, ears, muscles, authority, and security in themselves. Frustration often leads to the discovery that the phobic impasse does not exist in reality but in fantasy, in that clients have been preventing themselves from using their own available resources through catastrophic expectations. Furthermore, frustration helps clients to express their needs and requests directly rather than to cover them over with neurotic manipulations. The imperative is the primary form of communication and clients who can actually state what they need and mean what they state have made the most important step in their counselling.

Eliciting fantasies

The limitation of the awareness technique, as stated earlier, is its slowness. In order to speed up therapy Perls made considerable use of fantasizing, be it verbal, written or acted out. Below is an example taken from the *Three Approaches to Psychotherapy* film series in which Perls encourages Gloria to describe a fantasy (Dolliver, 1991, p. 300; Perls, 1965).

'Can you describe the corner you'd like to go to?'
'Imagine you are in this corner and you are perfectly safe. Now what would you do in that corner?'
'What should I do when you are in that corner?'

During the interview, Perls also asked Gloria to describe her fantasies about him (Dolliver, 1991, p. 301).

'Now what can I do to you?'
'How old must I be?' (for Gloria to scold him)
'How should I be? Give me a fantasy. How could I show my concern for you?'
'What would I do? How would I conceal my feelings?'

Dolliver observes that whenever Gloria offered Perls feedback about her experience of him, Perls always regarded it as a transference fantasy representing her projected attributes.

Drama techniques

'Monotherapy', perhaps better termed monodrama, is a form of psychodrama with a difference. In monotherapy, instead of having other people as well as the client involved in the drama, the client creates his own stage and plays all the roles under his own direction and expression.

In the *shuttle* technique clients are asked to shuttle their attention from one area to another. For instance, it is possible for a client to shuttle between the visualization of a memory and the organismic reliving of it in the here and now. Another example involves getting clients to shuttle between their feelings in and about an incident and their projections in the incident. For example, a client who feels angry with a colleague for 'apple-polishing' his boss may shuttle to experiencing his own needs and desires for approval from the boss. A further example is that of getting clients to shuttle between talking and listening to themselves. After each sentence, clients are asked: 'Are you aware of this sentence?'. The purpose here is to help clients stop compulsive talking which interrupts their experiencing of themselves and listening to others.

Drama and fantasy work can involve both the *hot seat* and the *empty chair*. The hot seat is occupied by the individual with whom at any given time the counsellor is working in front of the group. The empty chair is a second chair which is a 'projection-identification gimmick . . . waiting to be filled with fantasised people and things' (Perls, 1969b, p. 224). Essentially, it is a method of highlighting the shuttling process by getting clients to change chairs as they shuttle between parts of themselves or between different people in a drama.

Topdog–underdog dialogues are one of the main examples of the use of the shuttle technique involving both fantasy work and the empty chair. Perls believed that in their fantasies many people played self-torture games in which they were fragmented into an inner conflict between controller (topdog) and controlled (underdog). The topdog (or super ego) is righteous, authoritarian, full of 'shoulds' and 'should nots', perfectionistic and manipulates with threats of catastrophe if his demands are not carried out. The underdog (or intra ego) is cunning and manipulates by wheedling, being defensive, apologetic, playing the cry-baby and so on. Typical underdog statements are 'Mañana', 'I try my best' and 'I have such good intentions'. Through shuttling between these polarities, clients are helped to understand the structure of their behaviour and also to bring about a reconciliation between these two fighting clowns by becoming more in touch with their organismic selves.

Dreamwork

Perls (1970b) regarded dreams as the royal road to integration. Dreams are existential messages, not just unfinished situations, current problems or symptoms. Especially if the dreams are repetitive, a very important existential issue for the client is likely to be involved. There are four stages to dreamwork. First, the client relates the dream. Second, the client retells the dream or a section of it as a drama by changing the past tense into the present tense, for example 'I was climbing a mountain' becomes 'I am climbing a mountain'. Perls would ask clients to say their dreams, or part of their dreams, again 'in the *present tense:* as if you were dreaming it *now*' (Perls, 1970b, p. 205).

Third, the client becomes the stage director, sets the scene and talks to the different actors. For example, when working with Mary Anne's dream, Perls introduced the action element with the statement: 'Now let's start acting it out. Tell this to the man. Talk to the man – express your resentment' (Perls, 1970b, p. 206). Fourth, the client is encouraged to become the different actors, the props and all that is there. Clients do not have to work with a whole dream. Even if they re-identify with just one or a few elements in the dream the exercise is valuable.

The fourth stage of dreamwork may be facilitated by the empty chair technique to allow for dialogue between the different people, objects or parts of the self that are encountering each other. These dreamwork encounters provide opportunity for two things; the integration of conflicts and re-identification with those parts of the self that are alienated, especially the assimilation of projections. Dreamwork is an excellent way of finding the holes in a client's personality. These tend to be manifested as voids and blank spaces which are accompanied by nervousness and confusion.

Rules and games

Rules

There are some basic rules for gestalt groups which are usually described at the outset (Levitsky & Perls, 1970; Perls, 1970a). Most of these rules also transfer to individual work and include the following.

• *The principle of the now.* This involves encouraging communications in the present tense, for example by the question 'What is your now?'

• *I and thou.* Using the personal pronoun 'I' rather than 'It' and sending messages directly to the other.

• *Using responsibility language.* For example, rephrasing 'I can't do that' to 'I *won't* do that'.

• *Using the awareness continuum.* Focusing on the now, what and how of behaviour rather than on the why.

• *No gossiping.* This is another way of stating that communications should be addressed directly to the other rather than talking about other people when they are present.

• *Changing questions into statements.* Group members are encouraged not to ask the kind of questions which manipulate the environment for support, but rather to change those passive questions into more active and self-supporting statements.

Games

There are numerous gestalt games and experiments which are proposed whenever the counsellor deems it appropriate. Some illustrative games are listed below with the first two being particularly recommended for warming up a group at the beginning of a session. Many of the games and experiments are relevant to working with individual clients.

• *'I have a secret.'* Each person thinks of a well-guarded secret involving feelings of guilt and shame and, without sharing it, imagines (projects) how others might react to it.

• *'I take responsibility.'* With each statement, clients are asked to use the phrase '. . . and I take responsibility for it'. For instance, 'I am aware that I am moving my leg, and I take responsibility for it'.

• *Games of dialogue.* Games of dialogue can be used for any significant split in the personality, for example: topdog–underdog, nice guy–scoundrel, masculine–feminine, etc.

• *Making the rounds.* The client elaborates a theme or a feeling (for example, 'I can't stand anyone in this room') by making a specific statement to each person.

• *Unfinished business.* When clients identify unfinished business (for instance with parents, siblings and friends), they are asked to complete it. Resentments are the most common forms of unfinished business.

• *Playing the projection.* For example, the individual who says 'I can't trust you' may be asked to play an untrustworthy person to identify and assimilate his own untrustworthiness.

• *Reversal.* This game is based on the principle that overt behaviour often represents the reversal of underlying or latent impulses. For example, the good young lady is asked to play a spiteful bitch.

• *Rehearsal.* Since much thinking is internal rehearsal for playing social roles, group members are encouraged to share their rehearsals.

• *Exaggeration.* The exaggeration technique may focus on either movement and gesture or on verbal statements. In each instance, clients are asked progressively and repeatedly to exaggerate the behaviour. Examples of exaggeration requests from Perls' interview with Gloria are as follows (Dolliver, 1991, p. 300; Perls, 1965).

> 'Can you develop this movement?'
> 'Develop it as if you were dancing.'
> 'Now exaggerate this.'
> 'What you just said, talk to me like this.'
> 'Do this more.'

• *Marriage counselling games.* These include partners facing each other and taking it in turns to say 'I resent you for . . . ' followed by 'What I appreciate in you is . . .'. Also, the discovery game whereby partners alternately describe each other in sentences starting with 'I see . . .'. The idea here is to get partners relating to the reality of rather than their fantasy of the other person.

Gestalt counselling developments

Since Perls' death, the practice of gestalt counselling has altered in many ways (Yontef & Simkin, 1989). First, there is less emphasis on frustration and abrasively confronting clients perceived as manipulative. Gestalt counsellors are likely to take a softer approach and be more concerned with their clients' perceptions. Second, gestalt counsellors are more likely to reveal themselves, including their fears, defensiveness and confusions. Gestalt counsellors are encouraged to make 'I' statements to enhance their contact with clients and clients' focusing. In describing how she works, Laura Perls (1970c) provides examples of disclosing her awareness and feelings, sharing personal problems and life experiences, and using physical contact. Her guiding principle is to use such disclosures only if they might help clients take their next steps.

Third, gestalt counsellors may openly use psychoanalytic formulations to describe character structure. Fourth, gestalt counselling is conducted on both an individual and group basis, and often in combination. Some gestalt counsellors use Perls' working with individuals in front of the group style. Other gestalt counsellors make greater use of the interactions between and contributions from group members than Perls did. Fifth, there 'is also an increased attention to theoretical instruction, theoretical exposition, and work with cognition in general' (Yontef & Simkin, 1989, p. 331).

A further development is that gestalt therapy techniques have been integrated into other approaches. For example, gestalt techniques and experiments are commonly used in conjunction with transactional analysis (Dusay & Dusay, 1989; James & Jongeward, 1971).

CHAPTER REVIEW AND SELF-REFERENT QUESTIONS

Chapter review questions

1. What did Perls mean by gestalt?

2. In gestalt theory what is the relevance of the homeostatic process?

3. What did Perls mean by the contact boundary?

4. How did Perls view self-actualizing?

5. What did Perls mean by excitement?

6. What did Perls mean by emotion?

7. Why did Perls consider it important for people to take an aggressive attitude to experience?

8. In growing up what is the role of frustration?

9. Discuss the role in human development of interruptions of contact and suppression of emotion.

10. Describe each of Perls' three layers of awareness.

11. What was Perls' view on the role of anxiety in maintaining neurosis?

12. Describe each of the following mechanisms of contact boundary disturbance: introjection; projection; retroflection; and confluence.

13. Describe each of Perls' five layers of neurosis.

14. What are the goals of gestalt counselling?

15. How do gestalt counsellors use awareness techniques?

16. How and why do gestalt counsellors use sympathy and frustration?

17. How and why might a gestalt counsellor elicit a client's fantasies?

18. What is the shuttle technique?

19. What do the terms hot seat and empty chair mean?

20. What did Perls mean by topdog–underdog dialogues?

21. What is the purpose of dreamwork and what are its four stages?

22. What are some rules of gestalt counselling and why are they important?

23. What are some games of gestalt counselling and how might gestalt counsellors use them?

24. What are some of the ways the practice of gestalt counselling has developed since Perls' death?

Self-referent questions

1. What specific events in your life may have influenced you to come to your mind and lose your senses?

2. Assess how you relate to your environment in terms of each of Perls' mechanisms of contact boundary disturbance:
(a) introjection
(b) projection
(c) confluence
(d) retroflection.

3. What are the phoney roles and games that you use to obtain environmental support rather than rely on self-support?

4. Sit in a comfortable chair and, for the next three minutes, say to yourself 'Now I am aware . . .' each time you become aware of your body language, your breathing, your emotions, and any pressing thoughts. For example, 'Now I am aware I'm uncrossing my legs.'

5. Spend the next three minutes focusing on your response-ability for your life by staying in the now and saying to yourself about all your current behaviour '. . . and I take responsibility for it.'

6. Use the shuttle technique and change chairs as you shuttle between different parts of yourself or between yourself and another person.

7. What is your fantasy of how it would be like for you to be in the hot seat being counselled by a gestalt counsellor?

8. What relevance, if any, has the theory and practice of gestalt counselling for how you counsel?

9. What relevance, if any, has the theory and practice of gestalt counselling for how you live?

Annotated bibliography

Perls, F.S., Hefferline, R.F. & Goodman, P. (1951). *Gestalt Therapy*. London: Souvenir Press. This book contains an introduction and two volumes. Volume 1 is a series of eighteen experiments: experiments 1 to 11 focus on contacting the environment, techniques of awareness, and directed awareness; experiments 12 to 18 focus on retroflection, introjection and projections. Volume 2 is a major statement of gestalt theory consisting of three parts: introduction; reality, human nature, and society; and theory of the self. This detailed book is for serious students and counsellors.

Perls, F.S. (1969a). *Gestalt Therapy Verbatim.* New York: Bantam Books.
This book consists of three parts: talk, dreamwork seminar, and intensive workshop. The talk and dreamwork seminar parts are selected and edited material from audiotapes made at weekend dreamwork seminars conducted by Perls at the Esalen Institute, Big Sur, California between 1966 and 1968. The talk part of the book provides an easily readable introduction to gestalt theory.

Perls, F.S. (1969b). *In and Out of the Garbage Pail.* New York: Bantam Books.
As the book's cover says, 'Joy. Sorrow. Chaos. Wisdom. The free-floating autobiography of the man who developed Gestalt Therapy.' A pot-pourri of self-disclosure by means of prose and poetry. This book is a good way to meet Perls, the man.

Perls, F.S. (1973). *The Gestalt Approach and Eyewitness to Therapy.* New York: Bantam Books.
This book is a combination of two projects that Perls was working on at the time of his death. *The Gestalt Approach* is Perls' final statement of his theory and was written because he regarded his two previous theoretical works, *Ego, Hunger and Aggression* and *Gestalt Therapy,* as too outdated and difficult to read. *Eyewitness to Therapy* provides descriptions of gestalt counselling in action.

Yontef, G.M. & Simkin, J.S. (1989). Gestalt therapy. In R.J. Corsini and D. Wedding (Eds.), *Current Psychotherapies* (4th ed., pp. 323–61). Itasca, IL: Peacock.
This chapter both presents Perls' ideas on gestalt theory and practice and also discusses developments in gestalt counselling since his death.

Further references

Perls

Levitsky, A. & Perls, F.S. (1970). The rules and games of gestalt therapy. In J. Fagan and I.L. Shepherd (Eds.), *Gestalt Therapy Now: Theory, Techniques, Applications* (pp. 140–9). Palo Alto, CA: Science & Behavior Books.

Perls, F.S. (1947). *Ego, Hunger and Aggression.* London: Allen & Unwin.

Perls, F.S. (1970a). Four lectures. In J. Fagan and I.L. Shepherd (Eds.), *Gestalt Therapy Now: Theory, Techniques, Applications* (pp. 14–38). Palo Alto, CA: Science & Behavior Books.

Perls, F.S. (1970b). Dream seminars. In J. Fagan and I.L. Shepherd (Eds.), *Gestalt Therapy Now: Theory, Techniques, Applications* (pp. 204–33). Palo Alto, CA: Science & Behavior Books.

Perls, L. (1970c). One gestalt therapist's approach. In J. Fagan and I.L. Shepherd (Eds.), *Gestalt Therapy Now: Theory, Techniques, Applications* (pp. 125–9). Palo Alto, CA: Science & Behavior Books.

Others

Clarkson, P. & Mackewn, J. (1993). *Fritz Perls.* London: Sage.

Dolliver, R.H. (1991). Perls with Gloria re-viewed: Gestalt techniques and Perls' practices. *Journal of Counseling and Development, 69,* 299–304.

Dusay, J.M. & Dusay, K.M. (1989). Transactional analysis. In R.J. Corsini & D. Wedding (Eds.), *Current Psychotherapies* (4th ed., pp. 405–53). Itasca, IL: Peacock.

Fagan, J. & Shepherd, I.L. (Eds.) (1970). *Gestalt Therapy Now: Theory, Techniques, Applications.* Palo Alto, CA: Science & Behavior Books.

Greenberg, L.S. & Clark, K.M. (1979). Differential effects of the two chair experiment and empathic reflections at a conflict marker. *Journal of Counseling Psychology, 26,* 1–8.

Greenberg, L.S. & Dompierre, L.M. (1981). Specific effects of gestalt two-chair dialogue on intrapsychic conflict in counselling. *Journal of Counseling Psychology, 28,* 288–94.

Greenberg, L.S. & Higgins, H.M. (1980). Effects of two-chair dialogue and focusing on conflict resolution. *Journal of Counseling Psychology, 27,* 221–4.

Houston, J. (1982). *The Relative-sized Redbook of Gestalt.* London: The Rochester Foundation.

James, M. & Jongeward, D. (1971). *Born to Win: Transactional Analysis with Gestalt Experiments.* Reading: MA: Addison-Wesley.

Mackewn, J. (1994). Modern Gestalt – an integrative and ethical approach to counselling and psychotherapy. *Counselling, 5,* 105–8.

Polster, E.A. & Polster, M. (1973). *Gestalt Therapy Integrated.* New York: Brunner/Mazel.

Schiffman, M. (1971). *Gestalt Self-therapy: And Further Techniques for Personal Growth.* Berkeley, CA: Wingbow Press.

Shepherd, I.L. (1970). Limitations and cautions in the Gestalt approach. In J. Fagan & I.L. Shepherd (Eds.), *Gestalt Therapy Now* (pp. 234–8). Palo Alto, CA: Science & Behavior Books.

Zinker, J.C. (1977). *Creative Process in Gestalt Therapy.* New York: Brunner/Mazel.

Perls on film

Perls, F. (1965). Gestalt therapy. In E. Shostrom (Ed.) *Three Approaches to Psychotherapy.* Santa Ana, CA: Psychological Films.

Journal

The Gestalt Journal, published twice a year, is devoted primarily to articles on gestalt counselling. Subscription information: P.O. Box 990, Highland, NY, USA.

FOUR
Transactional Analysis

PREVIEW

- *Transactional analysis was originated by Eric Berne and comprises a theory of personality, a theory of social interaction, and an analytic tool for counselling. Humans start from a fundamentally OK life position, which early experiences often cause them to lose.*

- *Ego states are patterns of feeling, thinking and behaviour. Each person has three ego states: Parent, Adult and Child, representing influences copied from parent figures, age-appropriate reality appraisal, and relics of the individual's childhood, respectively. Further analyses of ego states tend to focus on elaborating the Parent and Child. At any time the ego state which is most cathectic with psychic energy will have executive power.*

- *People are motivated principally by stimulus, recognition, and structure hungers. Six ways of structuring social time are: withdrawal, rituals, activities, pastimes, games and intimacy.*

- *Transactions involve the exchange of strokes, or units of recognition, between the ego states of those involved in a social interaction. Transactions between ego states can be complementary, crossed or ulterior.*

- *Scripts are preconscious life plans by which people structure their time and have their destinies determined. They are based on early decisions when the young person moves into one of the Not-OK life positions and relinquishes some autonomy in order to acquiesce to parental injunctions.*

- *The script matrix is a way of conceptualizing directives given from the ego states of parents to those of any particular child. Parents hamper the ego-state development of their children through injunctions, attributions and discounts.*

- *Games, which involve ulterior transactions and a payoff, are developed on the basis of a script decision and justify a life position. Ways in which maladaptive behaviour is maintained include: script payoffs, game payoffs, the illusion of autonomy involving ego-state contamination, ego-state exclusion, and inadequate information.*

- *The goals of transactional analysis include autonomy through the development of an integrated Adult. Awareness, spontaneity and intimacy are three features of autonomous people.*

- *Counsellors and clients negotiate contracts specifying treatment goals. Structural analysis of ego states, transactional analysis, game analysis and script analysis are approaches to the transactional analysis practice.*

- *The use of egograms, reparenting, and the incorporation of gestalt techniques and exercises represent more recent developments in transactional analysis.*

INTRODUCTION

Eric Berne, the originator of transactional analysis, stated that the criterion distinguishing his approach from other approaches was that it was based on the personality theory of Child, Parent and Adult ego states. The dividing line between what was and what was not transactional analysis rested on whether or not human behaviour was explained in terms of such ego states. (Throughout this chapter Parent, Adult and Child start with a capital letter when describing ego states.)

Although Berne was strongly influenced by Freud, the theory and practice of transactional analysis are very different from those of psychoanalysis. Berne sees an element of his approach, called script analysis, as being 'para-Freudian' rather than anti-Freudian (Berne, 1970, p. 400), and conceivably the same might be said for the whole of transactional analysis. He also differed from other humanistic theorists and from Freud in his greater emphasis on social psychology, or the analysis of social, as well as intrapsychic, transactions.

Eric Berne

Eric Berne (1910–70) was born Eric Lennard Bernstein in Montreal, Canada, and grew up in a poor Jewish section of the city. His father appears to have been a dedicated general practitioner who often took Berne on his rounds. His mother was a professional writer and editor who, after her husband died in 1921, supported Berne and his sister by her writing. James (1977) considers that the little Child in Berne was traumatised by his father's death. Certainly his father appears to have had a strong influence on Berne, whose goal was always to cure patients. This influence is reflected in the Latin dedication in Berne's seminal book *Transactional Analysis in Psychotherapy*, which translates as 'In Memory of My Father David, Doctor of Medicine, Master of Surgery, and Doctor to the Poor' (Berne, 1961). Berne' journalist mother appears to have been a strong stimulus for his writing about curing patients.

Berne studied English, psychology and pre-medicine at McGill University in Montreal and received his BA in 1931. In 1935 he obtained his MD and Master of

Surgery degree from the same institution. Berne then went to the United States, where he became an American citizen. After an internship at Englewood Hospital in New Jersey, he became a psychiatric resident at Yale University School of Medicine. Reacting to the anti-Semitism of this period, he changed his name to Berne and began a private psychiatric practice in Norwalk, Connecticut. He also contracted the first of three marriages, each of which ended in divorce. Berne became Clinical Assistant at Mt Zion Hospital in New York and, in 1941, began training at the New York Psychoanalytic Institute, where he was analysed by Paul Federn, a former colleague of Freud.

In 1943 Berne entered the Army Medical Corps as a psychiatrist and it was during the war period that he started working with groups. On his discharge in 1946 he moved to Carmel, California, and finished *The Mind in Action,* since revised and now published as *A Layman's Guide to Psychiatry and Psychoanalysis.* He also resumed his psychoanalytic education at the San Francisco Psychoanalytic Institute and underwent a training analysis with Erik Erikson. In 1950 he took a position at Mt Zion Hospital, San Francisco, and restarted private practice. For the remainder of his life he worked both in San Francisco and in Carmel, 125 miles away.

From his days in the army, Berne developed a research interest in intuition and developed the concept of ego image, which is a therapist's intuitive image of a person which in some ways describes his ego. Ego images are largely based on observation and listening to what patients say about themselves. During the period 1954 to 1958 Berne developed his ideas on the diagnosis of ego states or structural analysis; the analysis of individual transactions; the analysis of a series of transactions with covert as well as overt content, otherwise known as game analysis; and the longitudinal view of a patient's whole life, from which it was possible to extrapolate and predict his future, now called script analysis. Berne's first transactional analysis group started in September 1954 and his ideas were developed further in a series of regular seminars in Carmel which, in 1958, were succeeded by the San Francisco Social Psychiatry Seminars, later called the Eric Berne Seminars.

Berne was moving away from orthodox psychoanalysis and, in 1956, his application for membership of the San Francisco Psychoanalytic Institute was rejected for the third time. Of this event he comments: '. . . after fifteen years the psychoanalytic movement and the writer officially parted company (on the most friendly terms) . . .' (Berne, 1961, p. 13). When, some years later, the Psychoanalytic Institute offered him membership, he declined with thanks. Berne had increasingly felt that the effective counsellor had to be more active than was allowed in orthodox psychoanalysis and had to practise transactionally rather than from the head of a couch. At the November 1957 Western Regional Meeting of the American Group Psychotherapy Association in Los Angeles he presented a paper entitled 'Transactional analysis: a new and effective method of group therapy', which was published in 1958. During three successive summers he broadened his experience by going to the South Pacific to study socialization and mental illness in various island cultures. By 1961 he had visited mental hospitals in about 30 different countries in Europe, Asia, Africa and the islands of the Atlantic and Pacific to test his ideas in various racial and cultural settings.

Berne's most systematic book, *Transactional Analysis in Psychotherapy,* was published in 1961. In 1963 he published a discussion of the application of transactional analysis to groups in *The Structure and Dynamics of Organizations and Groups*. In 1964 his ideas on analysing psychological games were publicly presented in *Games People Play*, though these ideas had appeared three years earlier in a private edition of the book. The principles of transactional analysis for counsellors are explained in his 1966 book *Principles of Group Treatment*, and his ideas on script analysis are developed in *What Do You Say After You Say Hello?*, published posthumously in 1972. Berne also wrote *The Happy Valley* for children and *Sex in Human Loving* for both non-professionals and professionals. The *Transactional Analysis Bulletin* started in 1962 with Berne as editor. In 1964 the International Transactional Analysis Association (ITAA) was formed as a training and accreditation body for transactional analysis. Now the European Association for Transactional Analysis also performs training and accreditation functions.

During the 1960s, along with his writing and private practice, Berne held a number of appointments. These included Consultant in Psychiatry to the Surgeon General, US Army; Attending Psychiatrist to the Veterans Administration Mental Hygiene Clinic; Lecturer in Group Therapy, Langley-Porter Neuropsychiatric Clinic; Visiting Lecturer in Group Therapy, Sanford Psychiatric Clinic; and Adjunct Psychiatrist, Mt Zion Hospital, San Francisco. Early in 1970 Berne and his third wife were divorced. He died of a heart attack on 15 July the same year. Berne's work was continued by a number of his colleagues who attended the San Francisco seminars, including Claude Steiner, who developed script analysis.

It is interesting to speculate on Berne's own life script. The son of a doctor and a writer, he spent his life curing and writing about curing people. Some idea of his professional ideals may be gleaned from the introduction to his *Principles of Group Treatment*, which is written for those who wish to become 'real doctors' as contrasted with the 'non-real' or 'unreal' variety. A 'real doctor': (a) has the overriding consideration through his practice of curing his patients; (b) plans his treatment so that at each phase he knows what he is doing and why he is doing it; (c) clearly distinguishes research and experimentation from good medical or surgical care, the former always being subsidiary to the latter; and (d) takes complete responsibility for the welfare of his patients (Berne, 1966, p. xvii). The development of transactional analysis represents Berne's own commitment to being a 'real doctor'.

ASSUMPTIONS

Berne saw transactional analysis both as a theory of personality and social interaction and as a method of counselling. Some of his assumptions and basic concepts are presented below.

The fundamental OK position

Berne had a positive view of human nature, which is stated in the transactional-analytic position of 'I am OK; you are OK'. Another way he expressed this is by his statement 'Every human being is born a prince or a princess; early experiences convince some that they are frogs, and the rest of the pathological development follows from this' (Berne, 1966, pp. 289–90).

Related to the basic assumption of human OKness are two further assumptions. First, Berne regarded practically every human being as possessing the complete neurological apparatus for adequate reality-oriented or Adult functioning. The only exceptions were those with the most severe type of organic brain injuries. Thus the counselling task is that of how to strengthen this already existing apparatus so that it may take its normal place in the client's psychic organization. Second, Berne believed that people have a built-in drive to both mental and physical health. The transactional analyst's job is to help nature by removing obstructions to patients' emotional and mental development, thus letting them grow in their own directions.

Ego states

Central to transactional analysis is the notion of ego states. Berne (1961) wrote: 'An ego state may be described phenomenologically as a coherent system of feelings related to a given subject, and operationally as a set of coherent behaviour patterns; or pragmatically as a system of feelings which motivates a related set of behaviour patterns' (p. 17). Though not always emphasized by Berne, ego states involve thinking as well as feeling and behaviour.

Each human being exhibits three kinds of ego states, and at any given moment any individual in a social grouping will predominantly exhibit one or another of these states. The three ego states, depicted in Figure 4.1, are described as follows.

1. A *Parent* or exteropsychic *ego state* is a set of feelings, thoughts, attitudes, and behaviours which resemble those of parental figures. It is both an accumulation of data and a way of relating to people. The Parent ego state may be seen in one of two

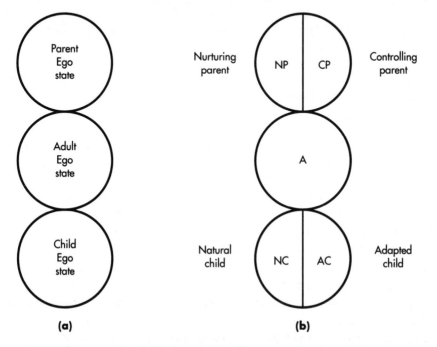

Figure 4.1 (a)Structural and (b) descriptive diagrams of personality.

forms. The *controlling* or prejudicial Parent is manifested as a set of seemingly arbitrary and rigid rules, usually prohibitive, which may either agree or disagree with the rules of a person's culture. The *nurturing* Parent is manifested as sympathy and care for another individual or for oneself. Thus the Parent can be over-controlling and inhibiting or supportive and growth-enhancing. The Parent ego state may also influence a person's Adult or Child ego states. The function of the Parent is to conserve energy and to diminish anxiety by making certain decisions automatic.

2. The Person in an *Adult* or neopsychic *ego state* autonomously and objectively appraises reality and makes judgements. Berne likened the neopsyche to a partially self-programming probability computer and stressed that the criterion of its adequacy with the use made of data available to a given individual. Characteristics by which an Adult ego state may be recognized include organization, adaptability and intelligence.

3. A *Child* or archaeopsychic *ego state* is a set of feelings, thoughts, attitudes and behaviour patterns which are archaic relics of an individual's childhood. Berne considered that we all carry within ourselves a little boy or girl who feels, thinks, acts and responds just as we did when we were children of a certain age. The Child ego state is exhibited in two major forms. The *adapted* Child is manifested by feelings and behaviour which inferentially are under parental influence, such as sulking, compliance, rebelliousness, withdrawal and inhibition. The *natural* Child is manifested by spontaneous expression such as self-indulgence or creativity. Berne considered the natural Child to be the most valuable part of the personality. The proper function of a 'healthy' Child is to motivate the Adult so as to obtain the greatest amount of gratification for itself. This it does by letting the Adult know what it wants and by consulting the Parent about its appropriateness.

Structural analysis of ego states

Structural analysis consists of diagnosing and separating one feeling-thinking-and-behaviour pattern or ego state from another. Further analysis of ego states does not provide new ones but subdivisions of existing ones. Such analysis tends to be called second-order structural analysis and can get very detailed. In particular, it focuses on further analysis of the Parent and Child.

In Figure 4.2 the Parent is divided into two components, one derived from the father and one derived from the mother. Children incorporate some characteristics of each parent into their Parent ego state, including the ways in which their parents exhibited thinking and feeling when expressing values. Consequently, second-order structural analysis includes the Parent, Adult and Child ego states of both parents.

Within the Child ego state, Parent, Adult and Child ego states, which were already there when the child made its basic decision concerning its life script, can be observed. Berne (1972) sometimes called the parent in the Child the 'electrode', and Steiner (1974) described it as the 'Pig Parent'. Berne called the parent in the Child the electrode because when it 'pushes the button', the person automatically does something negative. Examples of such negative behaviour, the origins of whose injunctions are unclear, include excessive alcohol consumption, reckless gambling, and getting sexually turned off if feeling strongly aroused.

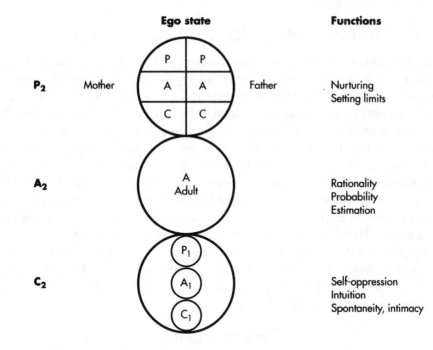

Figure 4.2 Second-order structural diagram of personality.

Berne saw the adult in the Child (A_1) as a keen and perceptive student of human nature, which he called the Professor (Berne, 1961). Steiner calls A_1 the Little Professor and observes that it is the ego state which Berne himself used in his studies on intuition, when he would guess the occupations of people using his own intuition (Steiner, 1974). The adult in the Child is the source both of intuitive and creative thinking and of delusion, since it may not always be right. The child in the Child ego state (C_1) is the source of innate wants and feelings. Spontaneity is a central characteristic of the child in the Child, but sometimes this spontaneity can be self-destructive.

Psychic energy and cathexis

Transactional analysis is a dynamic theory of personality in that it uses the concepts of psychic energy and of cathexis or distribution of energy. At a given moment the ego state which is most strongly cathectic will have executive power. Berne wrote of the flow of cathexis which gives rise to shifts in ego states. He believed that the most convenient way of acknowledging the differentiation of ego states was to view each state as having a boundary which separates it from other ego states. Under most conditions ego-state boundaries are semi-permeable. Shifts in ego state depend on three factors: (a) the forces acting on each state; (b) the permeability of the boundaries between ego states; and (c) the cathectic capacity of each ego state. Berne (1961) observed that it is the quantitative balance between these three factors which determines the clinical condition of the client and thus indicates the counselling procedures.

Stimulus, recognition and structure hunger

The psychobiological basis of social psychiatry is that the ability of human beings to maintain coherent ego states depends on a changing flow of sensory stimuli. Berne cited Spitz's work (Spitz, 1945), which demonstrated that sensory deprivation in infants resulted not only in psychological changes but also in organic deterioration. Berne posited that there were three principal forms of drive, hunger or motivation. First, stimulus hunger, with the most favoured forms of stimuli being those offered by physical intimacy. He acknowledged the dangers of over-stimulation as well as those of under-stimulation. Second, there is recognition hunger, which may be viewed as a partial transformation of infantile stimulus hunger. Berne used the term 'stroking' to denote any act implying recognition of another's presence. There are numerous rituals, such as saying 'Hello!', which imply recognition and give gratification. Biologically, even negative recognition has an advantage over no recognition at all. Put colloquially, 'Folks need strokes!' Third, there is structure hunger, or the everyday problem of how to structure one's waking hours. Such time structuring is concerned only with social time or the time people spend with others.

Time structuring

Berne observed that if two or more people were in a room together they had six possible kinds of social behaviour or time structuring from which to choose. These are discussed below.

• *Withdrawal*. Here two people do not overtly communicate with one another, for example if they are on a bus or are withdrawn schizophrenics. In withdrawal, people remain wrapped up in their own thoughts.

• *Rituals*. Rituals are stylized signs of mutual recognition dictated by tradition and social custom. At the simplest level, two people saying 'Good morning' engage in a ritual.

• *Activities*. Activities, more commonly called work, are not just concerned with dealing with the material means of survival. They also have a social significance in that they offer a framework for various kinds of recognition and satisfactions. Berne considered that work transactions were typically Adult-to-Adult, oriented mainly towards external reality.

• *Pastimes*. Pastimes are semi-ritualistic, topical conversations which last longer than rituals but are still mainly socially programmed. Pastimes might include 'Ain't it Awful?' and 'Motor Cars'. The focus of pastimes tends to be external to the participants rather than directly self-referent.

• *Games*. Games, in contrast to pastimes, are sequences of transactions which are based more on individual than on social programming. A psychological game is a set of covert or ulterior as well as overt transactions which lead to a predictable outcome or payoff. Frequently these payoffs involve negative feelings or 'rackets' such as anger and depression. Collecting racket feelings is known as collecting 'trading stamps', which may some day be cashed in for behaviours such as a good cry or going out and buying some new clothes. More drastically, 'trading stamps' may be cashed in for divorce or attempted suicide. Each game has a motto by which it can be recognized, for example 'Why don't you – Yes but' and 'If it weren't for you'.

• *Intimacy.* Berne defined bilateral intimacy as 'a candid, game-free relationship, with mutual free giving and receiving and without exploitation' (Berne, 1972, p. 25). Intimacy represents individual and instinctual programming in which social programming and ulterior motivations are largely, if not totally, suspended. Intimacy is the most satisfying solution to stimulus, recognition, and structure hunger, and unfortunately it is not very common for people to live as 'princes' and 'princesses'. Berne's ideas of intimacy included, but was not restricted to, sexual intimacy.

Types of transactions

In transactional analysis a stroke or unit of recognition is viewed as the fundamental unit of social interaction. An exchange of strokes constitutes a transaction. Thus rituals, activities, pastimes, games and intimacy may all be viewed as involving transactions. During transactions, at any given time each person is likely to have one of their three ego states predominantly energized or 'cathected'. Thus transactions take place between ego states and, at its simplest level, transactional analysis involves diagnosing the ego states involved in a stimulus and response exchange. In other words, the transactional stimulus may come from the Parent, Adult or Child of one person and the transactional response from the Parent, Adult or Child of the other person.

There are three main types of transactions: complementary, crossed and ulterior.

Complementary transactions

Complementary transactions are ones in which the directions of the stimulus-response transactions are consistent, such as discussing the ills of the world (Parent-Parent), talking about work (Adult-Adult), or having fun together (Child-Child). Another way of stating this is that complementary transactions are ones in which people receive a response from the ego state that they have addressed. An example of a complementary transaction is given in Figure 4.3. There are nine possible types of complementary transaction (PP, PA, PC, AP, AA, AC, CP, CA, CC). Berne's first rule of communication was that communication will proceed smoothly as long as transactions are complementary. In the example in Figure 4.3 Mike responds (a) from the ego state addressed by Bill and (b) to the ego state from which Bill addressed him.

Crossed transactions

In a crossed transaction the transactional response (a) comes from an ego state different from the one addressed, and/or (b) may go to an ego state which did not send the original stimulus. Berne's second or converse rule of communications was that communication is broken off when a crossed transaction occurs. In fact, the break may be only slight and momentary. However, at the other extreme, communication may be broken off completely. Figure 4.4 is an example of a crossed transaction. There are 72 possible types of crossed transactions, but only a few occur frequently.

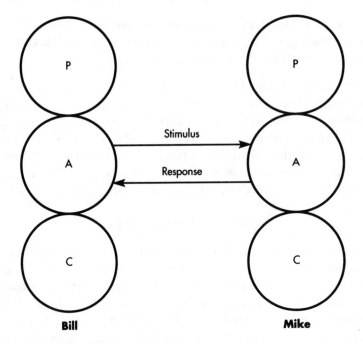

Figure 4.3 A complementary transaction.
Stimulus: 'Pass me the salt.'
Response: 'Here it is.'

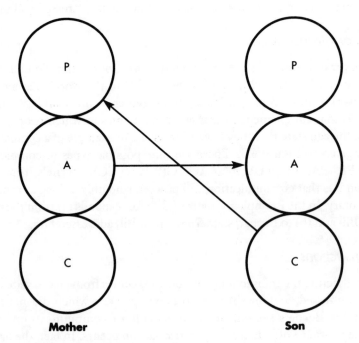

Figure 4.4 A crossed transaction.
Stimulus: 'Would you please help with the washing-up?'
Response: 'Why do you always keep asking me?'

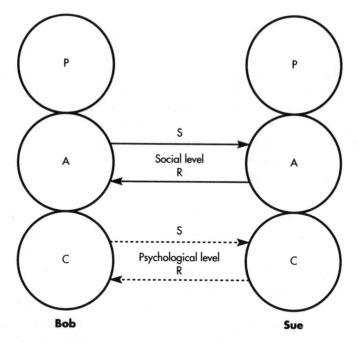

Figure 4.5 An ulterior transaction.
Social level – Bob: 'That was a great film. How about coming back to my place for a drink?'
Sue: 'Yes, I'd like that.'
Psychological level – Bob: 'Let's have some fun together.'
Sue: 'I'm available.'

Ulterior transactions

An ulterior communication is where, under the guise of an overt and socially more acceptable communication, an individual engages in an underlying and socially more risky communication. Another way of viewing this is that in much human interaction there is an underlying psychological as well as an overt social agenda. Psychological games, by definition, involve ulterior transactions.

Ulterior transactions may occur in everyday situations such as when a salesman says to a customer, 'Perhaps you shouldn't buy that beautiful and expensive fur coat', when his psychological message is 'Come on, I want you to buy it'. Potential sexual situations are other everyday situations in which ulterior transactions may occur. Figure 4.5 illustrates such an ulterior transaction.

ACQUISITION
The script

Berne regarded a script as a preconscious life plan by which people structured their time. Scripts determine their destinies, including their approach to relationships and to tasks.

He considered that scripts are usually based on childlike illusions which may persist throughout a whole lifetime. People's scripts are the produce of parental programming plus the decisions they made in response to parental programming. Scripts lead people to have an illusion of personal autonomy when in fact they are carrying out, often unthinkingly, the directives of their scripts. At times, however, some people may question their scripts and this may cause identity crises which may or may not be resolved satisfactorily by removal of some of the blockages to genuine autonomy and a well-functioning Adult. Berne's view of human life, as contrasted with human nature, was pessimistic, as he tended to see humans as driven by script directives which led to ways of time structuring seriously detrimental to attaining autonomy and creative activity.

The script matrix

The script matrix is a diagram used to help understand the development of people's scripts. It is helpful to an understanding of the transmission of scripts if the matrix depicts a second-order structural breakdown of the Child. Figure 4.6 depicts such a script matrix for a hypothetical person, Mary. The diagram aims to show how script directives are transmitted to her. Although during her upbringing it is desirable for Mary to experience much of the nurturing Parent ego state of her parents, plus their reasoning Adult and spontaneous Child, she may also be experiencing negative directives from the parent in the Child ego state of one or both of her parents. As depicted in Figure 4.6, the directives to Mary may be contradictory.

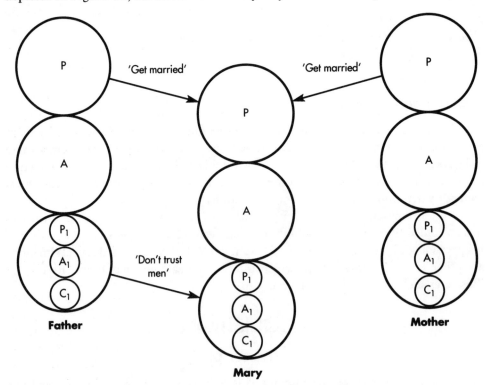

Figure 4.6 Script matrix showing transmission of script directives.

Although a chapter in Berne's 1961 book *Transactional Analysis in Psychotherapy* is devoted to analysis of scripts, he acknowledged the valuable work of Steiner in devising the script matrix and in helping to develop script theory. Berne proposed that it was the parent of the opposite sex who usually tells the child what to do and the parent of the same sex who usually demonstrates how to do it. Steiner (1974) added that it was the Child in the parent who gives the restrictive directives or injunctions and the Adult in the parent who gives the child the pattern or programme of behaviour.

Injunctions, attributions and discounts

Although directives from parents can be nurturing and conducive to the child's emotional development, they can also be restrictive, reflecting the fears and insecurities of the Child in the parent.

Injunctions are expressed as messages beginning with 'Don't'. They can be relatively mild or highly restrictive. Steiner (1974) suggests the following as injunctions by which people learn to block intimacy: (a) do not give strokes if you have them to give; (b) do not ask for strokes when you need them; (c) do not accept strokes if you want them; (d) do not reject strokes when you do not want them; and (e) do not give yourself strokes. He believes that these injunctions are the basis of depression. Other injunctions may stop people from thinking, especially perhaps if they are female, or they may interfere with the capacity to experience feelings, especially perhaps for males.

Steiner states that children are also strongly influenced by *attributions*, or being told what they are and what they must do, and how they are feeling. Family reinforcement schedules tend to reward children who follow attributions and punish children who disobey injunctions.

Children are also liable to receive *discounts* from their parents. Steiner regards a discount as a crossed transaction in which a person says something from an Adult ego state to another person's Adult and the other person responds from his or her Parent or Child. For instance, children's inquisitiveness may be discounted by parental rebuffs. More generally, a discount in TA is the minimization of some aspect of oneself, another person, or a situation.

Decisions

On the basis of early transactions related to feeding, toilet training, weaning and family relationships, the young person starts developing a view of the world. Where children are given unconditional protection they are less likely to develop restrictive scripts. However, when parents make their nurturing conditional on their child's submission to their injunctions and attributions, the child may make a conscious decision to adhere to parental wishes even though this means the sacrifice of autonomy. These decisions tend to be made in the pre-school years and are as realistic as the capacity of the adult in the Child or Little Professor at the time of the decision. As a result of this decision, however, the child tends to take a different and more negative position and also develops a script. Berne acknowledged that some scripts could be winners' scripts.

Life positions

The fundamental assumption of transactional analysis is that of human OKness as expressed in the statement or life position of 'I'm OK – You're OK'. By making a decision children move out of this position. Instead, they adopt one of three other life positions, namely: 'I'm not-OK – You're OK'; 'I'm OK – You're not-OK'; and 'I'm not-OK – You're not-OK'. Each of these three 'not-OK' positions reflects and sustains impaired ego state development. Also, 'not-OK' positions militate against the development of intimacy and are the bases on which individuals play out their games. Just as stimulus, recognition and structure hunger can be viewed as motivators, it is also possible to view the need to justify a basic life position as a motivator. Perhaps, though, it is more accurate to consider position hunger as a refinement of the other motivators, indicating how their fulfilment is to be attained.

Berne (1966) gave an example of a decision leading to a life position in the case of Rita. Rita, when little, used to run to greet her father when he came home from work. As time went on her father's behaviour became erratic because of his drinking and he would push Rita away. One day her father had a particularly bad row with her mother. Rita, who was 6 years, 2 months and 23 days, was bewildered and frightened and at 5 p.m. that afternoon she made a decision that she would never again love a man. In order to maintain her decision, Rita took a position regarding her father that, even when amiable and sober, he was fundamentally bad. Over time she generalized her position to most other men, the not-OKness of whom she epitomized in the slogan 'All men are beasts'. Her position also became the basis of a game in which her seductive behaviour provoked 'decent' men to make advances, which she then rejected. Berne observed that Rita's seductive manoeuvres were an attempt to establish an intimate relationship which she was unable to carry through.

Development of games

During children's upbringing they are taught the rituals, activities and pastimes appropriate to their situations in life. They also learn games through significant experiences in their family life from the earliest months. Berne (1964) gave as an example of how a game might be learned the case of three-year-old Mike who, when his seven-year-old brother was allowed to leave the dinner table and lie down because of a stomach-ache, said 'I have a stomach-ache too', as though he wanted the same consideration. Mike's parents, however, did not co-operate and thus may have saved him from the game of pleading illness (social transaction) in order to gain some privilege for himself (ulterior or psychological transaction). Berne thought that games are imitative in nature, and also that they are deliberately initiated by the neopsychic adult or Little Professor in the Child, frequently between the ages of two and eight. As illustrated by Rita, games are often formulated to help justify a life position.

The counterscript

In the development of a script, the person is given not only script injunctions and attributions from their parents' parent in the Child, but also counterscript messages from their parents' Parent. Berne (1972) used the word 'prescription' for counterscript messages and observed that prescriptions were usually transmitted from grandparents. Examples of prescriptions are 'Be a good boy (or girl)!' and 'Work hard'. Script injunctions and counterscript prescriptions are often contradictory, and life may involve an alternation between compliance first to one and then to the other. The counterscript may lead to a period of time in which an unhappy life plan gives way to a happier period. However, in the end the script injunctions always prevail, though again the possibility of winners' scripts should be acknowledged. Steiner (1974) indicates that an alcoholic's Parent may give the counterscript 'Be sober' while the parent in the Child is giving the injunction 'Don't think! Drink'. In Figure 4.6 Mary's parents' Parent counterscript prescription was 'Get married' while her father's parent in the Child injunction was 'Don't trust men'. Frequently injunctions are transmitted non-verbally by approval or disapproval of certain kinds of behaviour, and this may make them harder to bring into awareness than when they are transmitted more openly.

MAINTENANCE

In the preceding section the ways in which people acquire scripts and games were described. The question to be answered in this section is why people persist in acting out scripts and playing games rather than enjoying autonomy and intimacy, or, in other words, why people stay frogs when it might seem more rewarding to revert to being princes or princesses. Part of the answer is that both scripts and games have their rewards or payoffs.

Script payoffs

Berne (1972) defined the script payoff as the ultimate destiny or final display that marks the end of a life plan. He considered that there were four main payoffs in clinical practice: be a loner, be a bum, go crazy or drop dead. While these ultimate destinies are one way of viewing the concept of script payoff, another way is to look at it in terms of current as contrasted with ultimate rewards. Steiner (1974) observes that when people enter their counterscript phase, despite a superficial sense of well-being, they experience a deep visceral discomfort. However, people experience visceral comfort when reverting to script behaviour. This is because adherence to script injunctions represents acquiescence to parental wishes, albeit the parental parent in the Child, and thus is associated with the well-being and comfort of parental protection. Steiner notes that an alcoholic, even in the pain of a hangover, is receiving approval for acquiescing to the parental Child's injunction 'Don't think! Drink'. Steiner is perhaps more pessimistic about scripts than many other TA counsellors.

Game payoffs

Games too have their payoffs, which are related to the life positions adopted in their players' scripts. For instance, the payoff in Rita's script was manipulating men to boorish behaviour which confirmed her position that men are not-OK. Berne (1964) observed that, beyond their social function of time structuring, games are urgently needed by some for the maintenance of their health. Their life positions are so tenaciously maintained that to interfere with or deprive them of the payoffs from their games may cause disturbance, or even psychosis. Thus game analysis must be approached cautiously.

An example of a game with a payoff is 'If it weren't for you'. A person can complain endlessly that if it were not for a husband, wife, child, boss or some other person, they could engage in an activity from which at present they feel restricted. Sometimes, however, these other people are being used to defend the person against the realization that, if it were not for them, he or she might be unable to perform a difficult or anxiety-evoking task. Also, if the task were performed, it would no longer be possible to cause the other person discomfort by saying 'If it weren't for you'. This game validates the life-position that others are not-OK.

The illusion of autonomy

Berne (1972) believed that only the strongest can live without illusions and that one of the illusions which is hardest to relinquish is that of autonomy or self-determination. An autonomous person knows what is practical and Adult, what he accepts that comes from others, and what he does that is determined by early impulses. The illusion of autonomy is where a person does not acknowledge feelings and behaviours which come from his Child and Parent ego states, but instead believes that they come from the Adult ego state.

Berne distinguished between delusions and illusions, both of which are contaminations of the Adult ego state and, as such, prevent it from effectively dealing with here-and-now situations. Delusions are the prejudices and directives from parents which a person treats as though they were his own ideas. Illusions are those wishful ideas, impulses and early tastes coming from the Child which are accepted as Adult and rational. The significance of the illusion of autonomy is that an individual, being unaware of the delusions and illusions which are causing 'frog-like' behaviour, lacks the necessary insight and motivation for change. Thus destructive ways of time structuring are sustained rather than ameliorated. What is needed is a re-alignment and strengthening of the Adult ego-boundary to allow accurate processing of all relevant information.

Contamination and exclusion

With a truly autonomous person the ego-boundaries are strong, yet appropriately permeable to allow psychic energy to move between Parent, Adult and Child ego states. The illusion of autonomy indicates a structure where ego-boundaries are insufficiently well defined and the Adult ego state is being contaminated by the Parent and/or Child ego states. Exclusion, on the other hand, occurs in situations where psychic energy becomes exclusively cathectic in a constant Parent, a constant Adult, or a constant Child (Berne, 1961). Thus one ego-state is strongly cathectic while the other two are decommissioned. Berne believed that the excluding Parent is to be found in 'compensated' schizophrenics, where exclusion is the principal defence against confused Child or archaeopsychic activity. He gave as an example of an excluding Adult,

Dr Quint, who had a sincere commitment to data processing as a way of life yet possessed no healthy Child or Parent characteristics. Narcissistic impulsive personalities exhibit the excluding Child, where both rational and nurturing and limit-setting ego states are avoided. The excluding Parent, Adult or Child may defend itself, for instance by the use of intellectualization in the case of the excluding Adult.

Inadequate information

The last point to be made regarding the maintenance of maladaptive behaviour is that the effectiveness of the Adult is dependent on the adequacy of the information available to it. Furthermore, the Adult may need to develop some skills of effective Adult functioning, including the ability to collect and adequately assess relevant information. James and Jongeward (1971) state that the computer phrase 'Garbage in, garbage out' applies to the Adult or, for that matter, to any other ego state.

PRACTICE
Goals

Transactional analysis seeks to help clients obtain an 'I'm OK – you're OK' life position. For clients who have been turned by their life's experiences from princes and princesses into frogs, there are two kinds of counselling goals. The first goal is getting better or 'progress', which Berne regarded as making clients more comfortable frogs. Transactional analysis aims for the second kind of goal, which Berne described as 'getting well, or "cure", which means to cast off the frog skin and take up once more the interrupted development of the prince or princess' (Berne, 1966, p. 290). Achieving autonomy or the integrated Adult are two ways of stating this second goal of transactional analysis.

Autonomy

Autonomy refers to the capacity for 'non-script' behaviour which is reversible, 'with no particular time schedule, developed later in life, and not under parental influence' (Berne, 1972, p. 418). Autonomous behaviour is the opposite of script behaviour. It involves the overthrow of and then persistent struggle against sinking back into: (a) the weight of a whole tribal or family historical tradition; (b) the influence of the individual's parental, social and cultural backgrounds; and (c) seeking ulterior payoffs from games. Furthermore, autonomy consists of the active development of personal and social control so that significant behaviour becomes a matter of free choice. Berne summarized the process of the attainment of autonomy as 'obtaining a friendly divorce from one's parents (and from other Parental influences) so that they may be agreeably visited on occasion, but are no longer dominant' (Berne, 1964, p. 183).

The attainment of autonomy involves the person's regaining three basic capacities of the fundamental OK position: awareness, spontaneity and intimacy.

• *Awareness.* Awareness means the capacity to see and hear directly and not in the way in which one was brought up. It means living in the here-and-now, open to the sensations coming from the environment in the way a painter, poet or musician might be.

• *Spontaneity.* Spontaneity means the capacity to feel directly and to express feelings directly and not in the way in which one was brought up. The spontaneous person can choose feelings, be they Parent, Adult or Child feelings.

• *Intimacy.* Intimacy means the capacity to relate to another person or persons in an aware, spontaneous, loving and game-free way. Berne regarded intimacy as essentially a function of the natural uncorrupted Child.

The integrated adult

With the integrated Adult, certain child-like and parent-like qualities get integrated into the Adult ego state in a manner different from contamination. The integrated Adult can have both child-like qualities, such as charm and openness of nature, and ethical qualities, such as courage, sincerity, loyalty and reliability, which Berne (1961) observed as meeting a world-wide ethos. Thus the integrated Adult or neopsychic ego state ideally should exhibit three kinds of elements or tendencies: first, archaeopsychic elements like personal attractiveness and responsiveness; second, neopsychic elements like objective data-processing; and third, exteropsychic elements like personal responsibility.

Contractual goals

Transactional analysis takes a contractual approach to counselling. A key question in such an approach is 'How will both you and I know when you get what you came for?' (Dusay & Dusay, 1989, p. 427). Counsellor and client negotiate a contract that defines both treatment goals and mutual responsibilities in achieving the goals. Contract goals can include: physiological changes, for instance lowering of diastolic blood pressure; relief of psychological symptoms, such as impotence or a specific phobia; specific behaviour changes, for instance not hitting children, refraining from alcohol or drugs, holding a job for a specified time period, or passing examinations; and attaining quantifiable goals, such as increased earnings (Berne, 1966).

Contracts are open to amendment as counselling proceeds. Updates and changes of goals are frequent. Furthermore, the counsellor's or client's ultimate goal may differ from the set of operational criteria for improvement stated as initial goals. During counselling, transactional analysts always observe determinants underlying symptoms and responses. Berne (1966) gave the example of the counsellor who wished to investigate a client's archaic attitudes towards parental figures. He stated goals in terms of alleviation of symptoms first, and later proposed an amendment to the contract that focused on the goal of altering attitudes towards parent figures.

Transactional analysis approaches

In this section I discuss Berne's approach to transactional analysis. In a subsequent section I review some developments in transactional analysis after his death. For Berne transactional analysis was an umbrella term for four different, but interrelated, approaches to treatment. These approaches are structural analysis, transactional analysis, game analysis and script analysis. Berne (1961) saw a progression from structural analysis, through transactional and game analysis, to script analysis, though he realized that the script analysis state was not always attained.

Berne originally designed transactional analysis as a group counselling adjunct to psychoanalysis (Dusay & Dusay, 1989). One advantage to conducting transactional analysis in groups is that members can observe each other's ego states and thus learn about their own. Another advantage is the scope groups offer for observing transactions and games. Still another benefit is that script analysis performed with individual clients can resonate and have relevance for other group members.

Structural analysis

As mentioned earlier, structural analysis consists of diagnosing and separating one feeling-thinking-and-behaviour pattern or ego state from another. Structural analysis helps clients to identify and become aware of both the existence and the contents of their ego states. Its aim is to free people to have appropriate access to all their ego states without debilitating exclusions and contaminations. A related aim is to help the Adult to remain in control of the personality in stressful situations.

Transactional analysis

Berne (1961) saw one aim of transactional analysis as social control or the ability of the Adult to decide when to release the Parent or Child and when to resume the executive. If a person does not have social control, others can consciously or unconsciously activate that person's Parent or Child ego states in ways which may not be helpful. Transactional analysis proper, as Berne (1972) called it, is the analysis of single transactions by means of transactional diagrams. Clients are helped to understand the ego state transactions involved in situations and relationships in which they are experiencing difficulty as a means towards greater competence in handling them.

Game analysis

Game analysis is another way of attaining social control. Just as an understanding of structural analysis is a prerequisite of transactional analysis, so an understanding of analysis of single transactions is a prerequisite of understanding the more complex series of transactions called games. In games analysis the client is encouraged to learn more satisfying way of structuring time and acquiring strokes. The methods of game analysis include helping a client to see what game he or she is playing, what the moves are, what the racket or bad feeling payoffs are, and how the games justify a life position. It is also important to help the client to express constructively the natural Child need or feeling which he or she has been discounting.

Script analysis

The script analyst must take care not to behave in ways which promote a client's script. The purpose of script analysis is to get clients out of their script and thus to behave autonomously. The counsellor needs to listen carefully to and observe the client's verbal and non-verbal behaviour for script signs or signals. Additionally, script analysis may involve the use of a script checklist to help both analyst and client to know the client's script (Berne, 1972). Script analysis aims to help clients abandon their early decisions, *previously* made in different circumstances and with an incomplete neopsychic or Adult apparatus, by *now* making and enacting redecisions for change.

A script antithesis is a counselling intervention which directly contradicts a parental injunction and thus brings temporary or permanent release from a script. Berne (1972) believed that the final common pathway of a patient's behaviour is the preconscious dialogue between Parent, Adult and Child, or voices in the head, which can easily be brought into consciousness. Redecision can be helped by getting into the client's head another voice, that of the counsellor. This process involves the three 'Ps' of script antithesis: potency, permission and protection. Potency is defined by whether the counsellor's voice in the client's head has been powerful enough to prevail over the voices or injunctions of the client's parents in the Child. Permissions can be positive or negative. Positive permissions or licences involve the counsellor saying 'Let him/her do it!', whereas with negative permissions or releases the therapist is saying 'Stop pushing him/her into it!'. When clients follow a script antithesis and go against a parental injunction, their Child may get very anxious. Protection means that during the period of change the client can call upon their counsellors to exercise their potency again in time of need.

Transactional analysis developments

Dusay and Dusay state that, to date, there have been four transactional analysis phases: the ego state phase (1955–62); the transactions and games phase (1962–6); the script analysis phase (1966–70); and a fourth post-Berne phase 'stimulated by the action techniques of the human-potential movement, Gestalt, psychodrama, encounter, and many of the other explosive, energy-liberating systems' (Dusay & Dusay, 1989, p. 448). While using the same language and concepts, transactional analytic counsellors work in different ways. Below are some developments in the fourth TA phase.

Use of egograms

Ego states may be viewed not only in terms of their content, but also in terms of the degree to which they are 'cathected' both before and after treatment. Dusay (1972; Dusay & Dusay, 1989) devised a diagram called the egogram which graphs the extent to which each of a person's ego states undergo cathexis. An egogram shows in bar-graph form how much of a person's energy exists in the five functional ego states: Critical Parent (CP); Nurturing Parent (NP); Adult (A); Free Child (FC); and Adapted Child (AC). A bar graph profile identifies what may be the client's probable types of problems and where their strengths and weaknesses lie. Figure 4.7 is an example of an egogram.

Dusay (1972) suggested a constancy hypothesis: namely, that the amount of psychic energy within a person is constant and that if energy is taken away from one ego state more will be available for other ego states. Thus, as treatment progresses, the AC ego state may be less strongly cathectic, while the A and FC ego states may attain stronger cathexes. In terms of the Figure 4.7 egogram, the height of AC would become lower, with the amount taken away distributed between raising the heights of A and FC.

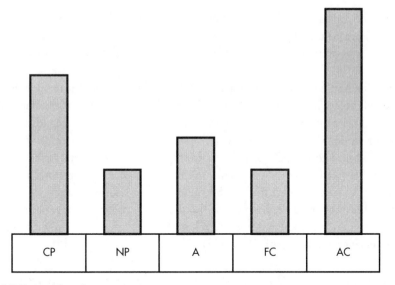

| CP | NP | A | FC | AC |

Figure 4.7 Example of an egogram.

Dusay and Dusay (1989) observe that each person has different ego-state imbalances. They use a variety of techniques and exercises for people needing to raise or lower the energy cathected in specific ego states: for example, assertiveness techniques for those low in Critical Parent; empathy techniques for those low in Nurturing Parent; thinking exercises for those low in Adult; creative and intuitive activities for those low in Free Child; and compromise and getting along with others exercises for those low in Adapted Child.

Reparenting

Stewart and Joines (1987) identified a cathexis school of transactional analysis based on Schiff's reparenting work with schizophrenics (Schiff, 1969, 1970, 1975). In residential treatment centres, severely disturbed clients with a tendency to regress and relive early childhood experiences were 'reparented' by positive parents. This level of intense and continuing counselling involvement is not appropriate for non-psychotic clients. Nevertheless, counsellors may act as 'replacement parents' for less disturbed clients, giving them positive messages and permissions to replace restrictive injunctions received from their natural parents.

Incorporating gestalt methods

Gestalt and psychodrama methods may be used in conjunction with transactional analysis. The Gouldings (Goulding, 1974; Goulding & Goulding, 1976; 1979) have developed an approach called *redecision therapy* that combines TA and gestalt theory and practice. They believe that early decisions are made from a feeling rather than a thinking position. Therefore, to get out of script decisions people must get in touch with their original feelings at the time of the decisions, deal with unfinished emotional business, and make more appropriate *redecisions* (Stewart and Joines, 1987). The

Gouldings see impasses as developing between ego states. They use the gestalt empty-chair technique to enable clients to have dialogues between ego states. During this process, clients may connect with and reveal strong feelings suppressed since childhood.

Another example of the incorporation into TA of gestalt techniques are the exercises and experiments in James and Jongeward's (1971) book *Born to Win*. For instance, as part of an exercise on the Adapted Child, readers are asked 'Can you admit to any top-dog and/or under-dog positions with yourself?' and 'Can you relate these to your Parent and Child ego states?' (p. 155). Contemporary transactional analysis appears to be widely influenced by Perls' emphasis on the importance of emotional awareness and expression. The Dusays end their 1989 review of transactional analysis by observing that the techniques used 'have and will be distinctly shifted from major reliance on insight and understanding (which is still thought to be important) to an approach that is more experiential and emotive' (p. 448).

CHAPTER REVIEW AND SELF-REFERENT QUESTIONS

Chapter review questions

1. What is an ego state?

2. Describe each of the following ego states: Parent, Adult, and Child.

3. Why is transactional analysis a dynamic theory of personality?

4. What are stimulus, recognition and structure hungers?

5. What did Berne mean by time structuring and what are the ways in which people can structure time?

6. Provide an example of and draw a diagram for each of the following types of transactions: complementary, crossed, and ulterior.

7. What did Berne mean by a script?

8. What are games and how do people develop them?

9. What are script payoffs and game payoffs?

10. What is the significance of the illusion of autonomy?

11. What are ego state contaminations and exclusions?

12. Why does transactional analysis take a contractual approach to counselling?

13. Why and how are gestalt techniques sometimes incorporated into transactional analysis?

Self-referent questions

1. Do a first-order PAC structural analysis on yourself (Figure 4.1a), indicating thoughts, feelings and behaviours belonging to your:
   (a) Parent ego state;
   (b) Adult ego state;
   (c) Child ego state.

2. Provide an example from your own life of each of the following types of transactions:
  (a) complementary
  (b) crossed
  (c) ulterior.

3. Draw a script matrix for yourself as in Figure 4.6 and indicate some of the main script injunctions and counterscript prescriptions you received from your parents.

4. Into which of the four life positions would you place yourself: 'I'm OK – You're OK'; 'I'm not-OK – You're OK'; 'I'm OK – You're not-OK'; and 'I'm not-OK – You're not-OK'? Give reasons for your choice.

5. Assess yourself on each of the following goals of transactional analysis:
  (a) awareness;
  (b) spontaneity;
  (c) intimacy;
  (d) the integrated Adult ego state.

6. Take a relationship with a significant other in your life (parent, spouse, child, colleague, etc.) and analyse one or more of the transactions in it in terms of the Parent, Adult and Child ego state, or states, cathectic in each person.

7. Identify some of the games you play, including the moves involved and their negative feeling payoff or your racket. Suggest an easily remembered name for each of your games.

8. Identify any early decisions you made which are no longer appropriate. Formulate appropriate statements of redecision which will allow you to change the ways in which you are currently scripted to feel and behave.

9. Assume that you have 100 units of energy to divide among your Critical Parent, Nurturing Parent, Adult, Free Child, and Adapted Child ego states. In terms of the way you usually feel and behave, draw an egogram distributing the 100 units of energy among the five ego states.

10. What relevance, if any, has the theory and practice of transactional analysis for how you counsel?

11. What relevance, if any, has the theory and practice of transactional analysis for how you live?

Annotated bibliography

Berne, E. (1961). *Transactional Analysis in Psychotherapy*. New York: Grove Press.
This book is Berne's major statement of structural analysis and transactional analysis. It consists of four parts: psychiatry of the individual and structural analysis; social psychiatry and transactional analysis; psychotherapy; and frontiers of transactional analysis. A case study is provided as an appendix.

Berne, E. (1964). *Games People Play*. New York: Grove Press.
This book is Berne's international best-seller. It consists of three parts: analysis of games; a thesaurus of games; and beyond games. The chapters in the thesaurus of games cover: life, marital, party, sexual, underworld, consulting room, and good games. Berne gave each game a catchy title.

Berne, E. (1966). *Principles of Group Treatment.* New York: Oxford University Press.
This book is a systematic treatise on the use of transactional analysis in groups. The book's first part describes the basic principles of group treatment. The focus of the book's second part is transactional analysis, its general principles and basic techniques, and the handling of the more common games that occur in the course of group treatment.

Berne, E. (1972). *What Do You Say After You Say Hello?* London: Corgi Books.
Published posthumously, this book elaborates Berne's ideas on scripts. The book is divided into five parts: general considerations; parental programming; the script in action; the script in clinical practice; and scientific approaches to script theory.

Dusay, J.M. & Dusay, K.M. (1989). Transactional analysis. In R.J. Corsini & D. Wedding (Eds.), *Current Psychotherapies* (4th ed., pp. 405–53). Itasca, IL: Peacock.
This chapter overviews the development of transactional analysis both during and after Berne's life. Basic concepts are explained and practical applications outlined. The authors emphasize the use of egograms.

Further references

Berne

Berne, E. (1958). Transactional analysis: A new and effective method of group therapy. *American Journal of Psychotherapy, 12,* 735–43.

Berne, E. (1963). *The Structure and Dynamics of Organizations and Groups.* Philadelphia: J.B. Lippincott.

Berne, E. (1968). *A Layman's Guide to Psychiatry and Psychoanalysis.* Harmondsworth: Penguin. First published in 1947 as *The Mind in Action.*

Berne, E. (1968). *The Happy Valley.* New York: Grove Press.

Berne, E. (1970). *Sex in Human Loving.* Harmondsworth: Penguin.

Berne, E., Steiner, C.M. & Dusay, J.M. (1973). Transactional analysis. In R.R.M. Jurjevich (Ed.), *Direct Psychotherapy* (Vol. 1, pp. 370–93). Coral Gables FL: University of Miami Press.

Others

Dusay, J.M. (1971). Eric Berne's studies of intuition 1949–62. *Transactional Analysis Journal, 1,* 34–44.

Dusay, J.M. (1972). Egograms and the 'constancy hypothesis'. *Transactional Analysis Journal, 2,* 27–41.

English, F. (1973). TA's Disney world. *Psychology Today,* April, pp. 45–9 and 98.

Goulding, M. & Goulding, R. (1979). *Changing Lives through Redecision Therapy.* New York: Brunner Mazel.

Goulding, R. (1974). Thinking and feeling in psychotherapy (three impasses). *Voices, 10,* 11–13.

Goulding, R. & Goulding, M. (1976). Injunctions, decisions and redecisions. *Transactional Analysis Journal, 6,* 41–8.

Gregg, G. (1973). Eric Berne: A drive to simplify and make it. *Psychology Today,* April, pp. 50–1.

Holland, G.A. (1973). Transactional analysis. In R.J. Corsini (Ed.), *Current Psychotherapies,* (pp. 353–99). Itasca, IL: Peacock.

James, M. & Jongeward, D. (1971). *Born to Win,* Reading, MA: Addison Wesley.

James, M. *et al.* (1977). *Techniques in Transactional Analysis for Psychotherapists and Counselors.* Reading, MA: Addison Wesley.

Schiff, J. (1969). Reparenting schizophrenics. *Transactional Analysis Bulletin, 8,* 158–64.

Schiff, J. (1970). *All My Children,* New York: Evans.

Schiff, J. (1975). *The Cathexis Reader.* New York: Harper & Row.

Spitz, R. (1945). Hospitalism, genesis of psychiatric conditions in early childhood. *Psychoanalytic Study of the Child, 1,* 53–74.

Steiner, C.M. (1971). *Games Alcoholics Play.* New York: Grove Press.

Steiner, C.M. (1974). *Scripts People Live.* New York: Bantam Books.

Stewart, I. (1989). *Transactional Analysis Counselling in Action.* London: Sage.

Stewart, I. (1992). *Eric Berne.* London: Sage.

Stewart, I. & Joines, V. (1987). *TA Today: A New Introduction to Transactional Analysis.* Nottingham: Lifespace.

Woollams, S. & Brown, M. (1979). *The Total Handbook of Transactional Analysis.* Englewood Cliffs, NJ: Prentice-Hall.

Woollams, S. & Brown, M. & Huige, K. (1976). *Transactional Analysis in Brief* (3rd edn.). Ann Arbor, MI: Huron Valley Institute.

Journal

The *Transactional Analysis Journal,* published quarterly, presents theoretical, applied and research articles about TA. For information, contact: International Transactional Analysis Association, 1772 Vallejo Street, San Francisco, CA 94123, USA. Telephone: (415) 885-5992.

FIVE
Reality Counselling

PREVIEW

- *Reality counselling is based on control theory. Control theory's fundamental assumption is that people's behaviour is always their best attempt to control the world to satisfy their needs. People's needs comprise the physical need for survival and the psychological needs for belonging, power, freedom and fun.*

- *People develop personal picture albums consisting of pictures in their heads of how to satisfy their needs. Total behaviour is the sum of the four components of acting, thinking, feeling and physiology. People as control systems behave to get the pictures they want.*

- *Children develop pictures in their heads through experiences of getting their needs satisfied. They learn total behaviours by creatively choosing different ways to control the world and by imitation.*

- *Reasons that people choose to maintain their misery are: to keep angering under control, to attract help, to excuse not taking more effective action, and to control others.*

- *Reasons that most people remain unaware that they choose misery are: mistaking short-term pure feelings for long-term feeling behaviours, most of their painful choices becoming automatic, and not wanting to lose self-esteem. People can also choose to stay controlled by others' misery.*

- *Reality counsellors always require a clear control theory reason for anything they do. The main goal of reality counselling is to help clients take effective control of their lives.*

- *The counselling relationship is characterized by involvement, compassion, caring, honesty and not giving up on clients. Reality counsellors teach control theory through their initial structuring, using control theory concepts, and by direct teaching.*

- *Early on, reality counsellors attempt to identify clients' wants and needs. Clients are asked to evaluate their behaviour by questions like 'How are you behaving now?' and 'Is your behaviour getting you what you want?' If clients are not getting what they want, reality counsellors ask them questions like 'What do you think might be better?' and work with them to develop plans for satisfying their needs and the pictures in their heads.*

- *Counsellors seek commitment to plans and, where appropriate, train clients in behaviours they need to succeed. No excuses and no punishment are two principles when evaluating clients' progress in implementing plans.*

- *Applications of reality counselling and control theory include marriage counselling, group counselling and working with school administrators and teachers to assist students.*

INTRODUCTION

Reality counselling, otherwise known as reality therapy, is a counselling approach developed in the 1950s and 1960s by William Glasser, a California-based psychologist. Glasser (1984a) admits that originally the approach had no systematic theory but rested on the assumption that people are responsible for what they do. In the early 1980s, Glasser (1981, 1984b) added control theory as a theoretical base for the practice of reality counselling. Glasser (1989) writes: 'Control theory contends that *our behavior is always our best attempt to control the world and ourselves as part of that world so that we can best satisfy our needs'* (p. 5). The object of reality counselling is 'teaching people to control their lives effectively' (Glasser, 1984a, p. 342).

William Glasser

William Glasser (1925–) grew up in Cleveland, Ohio, where he studied chemical engineering at Case Institute of Technology. At 19 Glasser was extremely shy, though this did not prevent him from marrying during his college years. For three years he studied for a PhD in clinical psychology at Western Reserve University, but he did not complete the degree. In 1953, Glasser obtained his MD from Western Reserve. He then commenced psychiatric training at the Veterans Administration Brentwood Hospital and, in 1957, completed his final year at the University of California at Los Angeles. Reality counselling stems from Glasser's dissatisfaction with psychoanalytic psychiatry as taught during his training. He thought that there was too much emphasis on clients' feelings and past history and insufficient emphasis on what clients were doing and on 'What are you doing about what you are doing?' (Evans, 1982, p. 460). Also he noticed that many of his teachers did not practise what they taught and that what seemed to work was not what they said worked.

In 1956, after an attempt at private practice which was hampered by a shortage of referrals, Glasser accepted a position with the California Youth Authority as head psychiatrist at the Ventura School for Girls. Glasser (1984a) observes that reality counselling evolved in its initial phase from his work with delinquent teenage girls (1956–67), with private outpatients with a variety of problems (1956–82), and with physically injured clients in a rehabilitation centre (1957–66). A further influence was the work of his former residency consultant and mentor G.L. Harrington with severely psychotic patients at a Veterans Administration Hospital (1955–62). In 1961, Glasser's first book, *Mental Health or Mental Illness?*, was published, followed in 1965 by *Reality Therapy*.

Also in 1965, Glasser began consulting in the California school system, spending much time in elementary schools in the deprived Watts area of Los Angeles. This work led to his focus on applying his ideas to education and institutional change and not just to individuals. In 1968, Glasser opened the Institute for Reality Therapy in Brentwood, a suburb of Los Angeles. Also, that year he created the Educator Training Center to research and develop programmes for the prevention of school failure. In 1969, Glasser's *Schools without Failure* was published. In this book he supported the idea that education was causing students to fail because of noninvolvement, nonrelevance, and limited emphasis on thinking and that schools needed to move towards the opposite philosophy of involvement, relevance, and thinking. By 1974, Glasser was saying 'I've all but given up my private practice' (Barr, 1974, p. 67).

Glasser's interest in control theory was stimulated after his 1976 book *Positive Addiction* in which he discussed how addictions like running and meditation are extremely strengthening. While reading widely on how the brain functions during meditation, he discovered William Powers' 1973 book *Behavior: The Control of Perception*. Powers' theory of how the brain functions as a control system provided a theoretical base both for positive addiction and reality counselling. Glasser writes: 'As Powers defines it, a control system acts upon the outside world, or upon itself as a part of the outside world to fulfill some purpose intrinsic to the system' (Glasser, 1984a, p. 321). People with psychological disorders fail in their attempts to control the world to satisfy what they need right now. Glasser's 1981 book *Stations of the Mind* related control theory to the practice of reality counselling. In 1982, Glasser began teaching control theory to the general public. His 1984 book *Control Theory* both describes the theory and then shows how people can apply it to gain greater control over their lives. Glasser's recent books, *The Quality School* (1992) and *The Quality School Teacher* (1993), apply control theory ideas to school management and teaching, respectively.

Glasser has three children. His wife Naomi, who died in December 1992, was very supportive of his work and edited two books of case studies, *What Are You Doing?* (1980) and *Control Theory in the Practice of Reality Therapy* (1989). Glasser continues training and certifying reality therapists through the Institute for Reality Therapy and remains positively addicted to promoting, both in the United States and overseas, his control theory, reality counselling, educator training and institutional change ideas.

ASSUMPTIONS

Reality counselling is based on control theory. Some of the basic concepts of control theory include the following.

Active language

Behaviour is made up of thinking, doing and feeling components. While doing and thinking are always expressed as verbs, such as running and meditating, feelings are usually expressed as adjectives, for instance depressed, or nouns, for instance depression. However, people not only choose how they think and act, they choose how they feel. A feeling like depression does not happen to people, they choose to depress. Consequently, Glasser uses verbs rather than nouns and adjectives to refer to feelings. Examples of the use of verbs to denote feelings are depressing for depression, anxietying for anxiety, headaching for headache, angering for anger, and phobicking for phobia. Active language attempts to describe the behaviour that people choose in their attempts to control the world to satisfy their needs.

Basic needs

Control theory sees humans as driven by basic needs that are genetic in origin. All human behaviour represents an attempt to control the world to best satisfy these needs. People have no rest from their needs. Once aware of a need they have no choice but to attempt to satisfy the need and, when any particular need is satisfied, other needs emerge. Human life is a constant struggle to satisfy these different needs and to solve the ever-present conflicts between them. The five basic needs are for *survival, belonging, power, freedom* and *fun*.

• *The need to survive and reproduce.* This physical need is located in the old brain, which is located in a small group of structures clustered at the top of the spinal cord. People's genes instruct their old brain to carry out all the survival activities that promote health and reproduction.

Glasser distinguishes between the old brain and the cerebral cortex or 'new brain' that evolved much later. There is much communication between the small unconscious old brain and the huge conscious new brain, which is the source of awareness and of voluntary behaviour. For most people, the old brain with the assistance of the new brain satisfies the survival need reasonably well. However, much of life is concerned with satisfying the more complex and often conflicting needs that arise in the conscious new brain. Glasser (1984b) calls these 'psychological needs' because people have to satisfy their genetic instructions psychologically rather than physically. He stresses that their source is still biologic and their genetic instructions no less urgent than the genetic instructions for the physical need to survive and reproduce. Following are the four psychological needs.

• *The need to belong – to love, share and co-operate.* This need may be satisfied by family, friends, groups, classes and even pets, plants and favourite inanimate objects, such as a boat or computer.

• *The need for power.* This need may be satisfied by status, recognition and getting others to obey us. The need for power is often in competition with the need to belong. The need to belong propels people into relationships that can then turn into power struggles.

• *The need for freedom.* People need freedom to choose how they live their lives or at least some aspects of their lives. They need to move around as they like, express themselves freely and associate with whom they choose. The need for freedom can conflict with other needs, for instance the need to belong as either a spouse or parent. Also, it is fundamental that chosen need satisfying behaviours should not prevent others from engaging in need satisfying behaviours.

• *The need for fun.* The need for fun is as fundamental a need as the other needs. Fun is a basic genetic instruction for all higher animals because that is how they learn. Fun removes the drudgery from learning and enhances motivation. Even in old age, learning without play is difficult.

Pictures in heads

Throughout their lives, people develop personal picture albums consisting of detailed pictures of what they want to satisfy their needs. Glasser (1984b) gives the example of the baby who was screaming and then given a chocolate-chip cookie which was much liked. Immediately the baby took a picture of the cookie and stored it away as something to look for when hungry again. Human senses combine into a sensory camera that, among others, can take visual, auditory, gustatory and tactile pictures. Glasser prefers the word pictures to perceptions both because it is easier to understand and because about 80 per cent of perceptions stored in personal albums are visual.

Personal picture albums are a small and selective part of total memory. The personal picture album is a special world that Glasser now calls the quality world. It is more than an ideal world of 'What I would like to be' since it contains very specific pictures of what will satisfy my needs for love, worth, success, fun and freedom right now. People must have at least one picture for every need. It is virtually impossible to have a need without quickly finding a picture to satisfy it. However, people commonly have pictures in their albums that cannot be satisfied in the real world. Furthermore, the pictures in their heads may be neither rational nor compatible with each other.

People can add pictures in their heads or remove them if they do not satisfy needs. When people change important pictures, they change their lives. The only way pictures can be taken out of albums is to replace them with something that fits the same basic need reasonably well. For example, the picture of a loved one is usually replaceable with someone else. Sometimes people choose a lifetime of misery because they cannot replace pictures: for example battered wives who stay with husbands because they remain the only 'possible' pictures of loving persons. Changing our own pictures is difficult. Changing other people's pictures is even more difficult and can only be achieved through negotiation and compromise. It is the pictures in each person's head, and nobody else's, that cause them to do what they do.

The pictures in people's heads are central to understanding the control theory view of motivation. Behaviour always starts with the pictures in people's heads. Behaviour is generated by the difference between the pictures in people's heads, what they want, and what is going on in the real world, what they have. When a difference exists, people behave to reduce this difference. It is a biological fact that people must choose to do something to reduce the difference. However, what they do is almost invariably their choice.

Total behaviour

In control theory, behaviour is how people attempt to control the world to satisfy needs rather than a response to stimulation. Behaviour is more than conduct or action. Glasser uses the term total behaviour to describe his expanded concept of behaviour. Total behaviour, the whole, is always the sum of the following four components:

• *Acting.* The acting component consists of active behaviours like walking or running, which involve voluntarily moving some part of the body. However, some involuntary actions accompany routine activities: for instance swallowing when eating.

• *Thinking.* The thinking component consists of voluntarily generating thoughts as well as involuntarily generating them, for instance in dreams.

• *Feeling.* The feeling component consists of a wide variety of pleasurable and painful feelings that people can choose to generate.

• *Physiology.* The physiological component, for instance sweating, involves the voluntary and involuntary body mechanisms involved in the doing, thinking and feeling components of total behaviour.

Glasser (1989) provides the example of a client who admits to being depressed. From the viewpoint of control theory, this client is depressing or choosing to depress. The four components of this depressing total behaviour are as follows. The acting component may be sitting round lethargically. The feeling component is pain and misery. The thinking component may be thoughts like 'What's the use? There is nothing I can do.' The physiology component may be stomach ache and trouble sleeping. The more this depressed client can both realize that the feeling component is just one of the four components of a total behaviour and use a verb like depressing to describe the behaviour, the more the client will be in control of his or her life. The client who admits to depressing or choosing to depress then is forced to acknowledge that he or she has a choice and possibly could do something different and better.

Glasser (1989) uses the analogy of total behaviour as a four-wheel drive car, with each component as one wheel of the car. The front wheels are the acting and thinking components and the rear wheels are the feeling and physiology components. The needs are the engine and the driver steers in the direction closest to the picture most wanted from his or her special world album. As in a car, the person has total voluntary control of where to steer the front wheels of his or her 'car'. Whatever clients' problems are, they can choose to steer their life 'cars' in better directions than they do now. However, clients have nowhere near the degree of voluntary control over the rear wheels of feeling and physiology that they have over the front wheels of acting and thinking. Consequently, reality counselling focuses on helping clients change their actions and thoughts (the front wheels) much more than their feelings and physiology (the rear wheels).

People as control systems

As control systems people, like all living organisms, are always attempting to control the world for the purpose of fulfilling basic needs genetically built into their systems. People as control systems act upon the world and themselves as part of the world to attempt to get the picture that they want. All living organisms have two fundamental ways to control the world. First, they need to perceive what in the world can possibly get them the picture they see as satisfying their need. This is the input dimension of controlling the world. Second, they need to act upon or control what they see as satisfying their need, the output dimension. For instance, thirsty people first have to perceive what thirst is and how it can be satisfied by water. Second, to satisfy their thirst they must act upon or control the world by looking for water and, if this is unobtainable, for some other fluid.

People as control systems choose all their behaviour to satisfy one or more basic needs. Neurotic, psychotic, psychosomatic and addictive behaviours are ineffective attempts that people make to control the world to satisfy their needs. Most ineffective behaviours, for instance angering, are consciously chosen. Other behaviours, for instance psychosomatic behaviour like arthritis or heart disease, may be less conscious and blocked from awareness because people find it too painful to realize that they choose their misery. Regarding stress, Glasser (1984a) considers that there are few, if any, genuinely stressful situations in the outside world. People use the term stress to describe situations that they cannot control satisfactorily with the behaviours that they choose.

Though control systems like to be in control, no control system likes to be controlled. If others attempt to control people or if people attempt to control themselves in ways that frustrate their needs, they will always choose to rebel. Sometimes the rebellion is direct. Most often the rebellion is in indirect ways like choosing to depress, migraine or be ill. No one can control another person unless that person is persuaded that it satisfies some picture in their heads.

ACQUISITION
Learning about needs

At birth, people do not know what their needs are or how to satisfy them. However, babies do know how they feel. They also know that when their needs are not satisfied they do not feel good. This knowledge enables them to gain some idea of what their needs are. For instance, babies do not have concepts of food, eating or survival. However, they know when they hurt and, when fed, they usually feel better. As this occurs, babies first begin to know about food and then later about eating and about their survival need. People can also learn about their psychological needs for power, belonging, fun and freedom in that they know that, when these needs are satisfied, they feel better. Even if never clear what their needs are, through their efforts to feel good people will still try to satisfy these needs.

Acquisition of pictures in heads

Already, the example has been given of the baby who was given a chocolate-chip cookie when screaming, took a psychological picture of it, and stored it in a personal picture album as something to look for when hungry. As people go through life, they store in their personal picture albums anything that they believe will satisfy one or more of their basic needs. Glasser (1984b) considers it likely that people have hundreds and even thousands of pictures that will satisfy each need. People may acquire pictures in their heads that put them at risk. For example, anorexic people have pictures in their heads about the desirability of being excessively thin. Alcoholics have pictures about satisfying their needs through alcohol.

Acquisition of total behaviours

Babies know that to survive they must do all that they can to control the world around them to meet their needs. For the sake of their survival, babies are born with the total behaviour of angering. Angering is the baby's way of signalling to the world that he or she has unmet needs. In order to encourage independence, shortly after birth most mothers stop allowing their babies totally to control them with angering. When babies scream and nothing happens they quickly learn to look for different behaviours, for instance smiling, with which to control their worlds. Humans are creative and, aided by imitating, quickly learn other total behaviours. Children's most effective teachers are people they care for and respect. Other ways of learning new behaviours to control the world include going to school, reading books and watching television.

Glasser (1989) considers that, usually early in life, everyone learns to add misery, craziness, sickness, and dysfunctional angering behaviours like fighting to their existing repertoires of total behaviours. It is common for children to pout and depress to control adults or to fight to control other children. Thus children add miserabling or angering as ways to control themselves and others to meet their needs. In these examples, children learn to choose behaviours that may have short-term payoffs. However, as time goes by, the same choices are likely to lessen people's control over their lives because they are more likely to produce negative than positive consequences for self and others.

Raising children

Glasser (1984b) advises: *Try as hard as possible to teach, show and help your children to gain effective control over their lives'* (p. 198). Children are going to live according to their own and not their parents' pictures. Too often parents try to mould their children to their pictures and, by doing so, create power struggles. It is important that parents keep their children's pictures of them as loving people. However, if parents allow this, children can take advantage of their parents' love to control them.

Children are born without knowing how to fulfil their needs. Glasser (1984b) distinguishes between doing things *for, to* and *with* children and leaving them alone. Many parents do too much *for* their children in ways that assist them to have less control over their lives later. Also, parents do far too much *to* their children, for instance yelling at them and punishing them when they don't do as parents want. Most parents do too little *with* their children, for example playing with them or discussing mutual interests. Also, at all ages, parents do not leave children alone enough, for instance letting them cry out temper tantrums or make their own entertainment on rainy days. Allowing children space to achieve goals on their own can lead to feelings of success that satisfy their power needs. In short, children learn most about how to be in control of their lives from adults who do things with them and encourage them to do things for themselves.

Inevitably, children will break rules and challenge parents. Since both parents and children have strong needs for power, negotiation and compromise are the only ways that they can get along with each other. Control theory distinguishes between discipline and punishment. Discipline always starts with trying to teach children to follow reasonable rules through negotiation. Parents attempt to assist children to see that there are better pictures and behaviours that would be within the rules. Punishment starts and finishes with trying to force children to follow rules, whether reasonable or not, by trying to inflict pain if they refuse. Parents make no attempt to give them the opportunity to negotiate and review other pictures and behaviours within the rules. Punished children feel deep losses of power and control.

When negotiating plans with children, parents should try to do as much with and as little to or for them as possible. Where children do not want to change or negotiate, parents can impose sanctions appropriate to the child's age until the problem is worked through: for instance, going to one's room for ten minutes might be a maximum sanction for a five-year-old and an evening without television appropriate for a ten-year-old. Sanctions should not be so great that children lose their willingness to try to correct the situation. Also, it is preferable that parents not impose sanctions unless they have previously discussed with the child the consequences of not complying. Parents always should explain to children their element of personal choice regarding the sanction, that they either comply or choose to accept the consequences of not complying.

MAINTENANCE

Glasser (1989) sees all clients at the start of counselling as choosing some form of self-destructive behaviour that represents their misguided attempts to regain control over their poorly controlled and frustrating lives. People who are depressing, guilting, angering, and headaching insufficiently realize both their needs and that they can make better choices about satisfying them than their current choices.

Reasons for choosing misery

There are four distinct reasons why people choose the suffering, pain and misery in their lives.

1. *To keep angering under control.* By about the age of two, most children realize that angering will not get them what they want and look for alternatives. Children unable to go for walks when everyone else is busy may choose to keep angering under control. Instead, they may choose depressing from their behavioural repertoire. Depressing, despite its pain, may be a safer and more effective way for children to take control over others. By the time people become adults, they have created and learned from others a wide variety of painful feeling behaviours that they substitute for displaying anger, for instance depressing, anxietying, guilting or headaching.

2. *To attract help.* Depressing is a very powerful way of getting help. Many people are vulnerable to being controlled by being the targets of depressing behaviour.

3. *To excuse not taking more effective action.* Pain, misery and depressing are commonly used as excuses for either doing nothing, being frightened of doing something, or a mixture of the two. The choice to stay miserable, despite the pain, protects people from becoming aware of the need to work on problems. Also, depressing can hide their fears of failure which might make their lives even harder to control than they are now.

4. *To control others.* Depressing is a way of gaining powerful control over others. Glasser (1984b) gives the example of physically healthy Carol who chooses to depress for the purposes of controlling her middle-aged daughter Phyllis to give her attention. Carol knows that she can get Phyllis to choose to guilt. When Phyllis chooses to guilt, this is a way of controlling her own anger.

Reasons for remaining unaware of choosing misery

A major reason that people maintain their choosing to stay miserable behaviour is that they remain unaware that they are doing so. They do not want to take the responsibility of doing something about it if they were to accept that their misery is a choice. Following are three important reasons blocking people from becoming aware that negative feelings involve choices.

1. *Mistaking short-term pure feelings for long-term feeling behaviours.* What people feel is divided into two stages. First, there is the immediate experiencing of a feeling, which Glasser (1984b) calls 'pure feeling'. These pure feelings are derived from the early evolutionary need to be aware of threats to survival and tell people whether or not they are in control. Such feelings are not chosen and begin to diminish as soon as they occur. Second, people choose a long-term feeling behaviour, for instance depressing or loving, to prolong either the pain or the pleasure initiated by the pure unchosen feeling.

Glasser (1984b) gives the example of Tom, who had the pure feeling of a sharp pang of disappointment when he opened his pay packet and saw a dismissal slip. This pain alerted him that he had lost control of an important part of his life. Then Tom chose the long-term pain of depressing that quickly superceded the pure pain of the initial disappointment. However, since it is difficult to tell when the switch occurs, people tend to confuse the pure, brief, unchosen pain with the chronic chosen pain.

2. *Making painful choices automatically.* Frustrated children often consciously choose whether to sulk or to anger. However, for adults who have been making such choices over a period of years, the choice process has become automatic and below awareness. Distinctly painful behaviours, such as headaching, are limited to about twenty, and most people use only four or five that 'work well' for them. People are more likely to acknowledge their responsibility for choosing pleasurable total behaviours than for choosing painful ones.

3. *Not wanting to lose self-esteem.* People's need for power and self-esteem is so strong that, if they were to acknowledge that they choose painful feelings, this knowledge might cause them to experience some loss of control. Consequently, to maintain control of themselves as well as of others, people repress from awareness that they are

choosing much of the misery they feel. However, to regain control people need to acknowledge that they choose their misery and can choose other behaviours and, if necessary, change the pictures in their heads to satisfy their needs.

Staying controlled by others' misery

Glasser states that one of the most important axioms of control theory is *'Never let anyone control you with the pain and misery he or she chooses'* (Glasser, 1984b, p. 202). People can give up control to others who have their own control agendas. For instance, in the above example of Phyllis and her mother Carol, Phyllis is colluding in creating her own misery and guilting by allowing her mother to control with her misery. Carol is not going to change on her own accord since choosing misery is her way of keeping control of her life. Phyllis needs to realize that Carol is choosing all the misery about which she complains. Then she needs to regain control by separating herself from her mother's control: for instance, by setting regular times to visit and not going over for 'emergencies'. Also, she needs to stop colluding in letting her mother take control by asking 'How do you feel, Mum?'

PRACTICE
Goals

In reality counselling, there are no rigid rules. However, counsellors should always have a clear control theory reason for anything they do. Glasser (1984a) regards all counselling as teaching. The overall goal of reality counselling is to teach clients how to take effective control of their lives.

More specifically, reality counselling has the following goals. First, reality counsellors try to impart to clients the control theory framework for understanding their behaviour. Second, the approach aims to raise clients' awareness of their choosing behaviours and how they try to control their worlds through them. Third, reality counselling increases clients' sense of their responsibility for making choices that work for them. Clients are taught that they need no longer be victims of self-defeating past and current choices. Fourth, clients are assisted to identify and understand their basic needs for survival, belonging, power, freedom and fun. Fifth, reality counselling assists clients to have realistic pictures in their heads to satisfy their basic needs. Sixth, reality counselling teaches clients to evaluate the effectiveness of their total behaviour in light of what they want and choose different behaviours as needed. Seventh, reality counsellors assist clients to develop and implement specific behaviours that will help them meet their needs in the present and future. Eighth, reality counselling teaches clients how to avoid allowing themselves to be controlled by others' negative controlling behaviour.

Glasser (1989) writes that 'what we really do is help clients to help themselves' (p. 14). Clients are better prepared not only to deal with current problems, but to prevent or solve future problems.

The counselling relationship

The counsellor-client relationship is very important. A first step in counselling is to 'make friends' with clients. Most clients who come for counselling are lonely. Counsellors should be caring and involved human beings to whom clients can relate and by whom they can feel supported. However, being involved also means being honest about the limits of involvement, such as length of sessions and rules about between session contact. Compassion, acceptance and patience are further desirable counsellor attributes. In addition, without trivializing their work together, both counsellors and clients are encouraged to use humour.

In reality counselling a tension exists between showing compassion and communicating to clients that their needs must be met and their problems solved in the present. Reality counsellors try to avoid allowing clients to control them with the same inadequate behaviours that they use to control others, such as angering, depressing and anxietying. Usually reality counsellors, while showing sympathy for what clients have experienced, do not allow them to dwell on past hurts and sufferings. However, on occasion, clients may be allowed to dwell on their pasts and talk about their feelings to strengthen the relationship for subsequent work on the role of their present choices in sustaining problems.

Reality counsellors are strongly committed to their clients. (Glasser (1984a) advises them 'Never give up' (p. 337). Counsellors persevere with clients to the point where clients realize that counsellors will neither allow themselves to be controlled nor give up. Good friends do not give up easily.

Teaching control theory

Glasser (1989) observes that reality counsellors 'make an active effort to teach control theory to any client they believe may be receptive to these ideas' (p. 1). Counsellors approach this task in a number of ways.

• *Initial structuring.* Reality counsellors try to instil hope in clients early on by letting them know that, during counselling, they will learn to make better choices and, in doing so, gain better control over their lives. Clients are also informed that they will have to work hard to achieve and maintain this control.

• *Using control theory concepts.* Counsellors teach control theory concepts by getting clients to rework their problems within these concepts. For instance, clients learn to use concepts like basic needs, pictures in head and total behaviour. In addition they learn the basic assumption of control theory that their behaviour is always their best attempt at controlling the world and themselves so that they can best satisfy their basic needs for survival, belonging, power, freedom and fun. Furthermore, counsellors work with clients on the assumption that the only behaviour they can control is their own.

• *Direct teaching.* Assuming clients are receptive and capable of understanding the ideas, reality counsellors can ask them to read Glasser's book *Control Theory* and together they can discuss its contents. Then counsellors and clients can analyse the clients' problems according to control theory. Though not necessary to counselling, much time may be saved by clients reading and using the book.

Assisting identification of wants and needs

Counsellors attempt to discover what clients want or are 'controlling for' by their current behaviour. When counsellors ask clients 'What do you want?', they are asking 'What do you really want right now?' Counsellors try to find out how much clients are in touch with what they really want. The less in touch they are, the more difficult it can be to work with them. Clients may answer that they want to obtain another job, have a better relationship with someone, or find someone to love. Then counsellors try to get them to describe in some detail the pictures in their head of what they want right now. Where clients focus on wanting to change someone else, they are refocused on how they can change themselves, since their behavioural systems cannot control others. In short, counsellors help clients focus on what it is possible for them to achieve.

Reality counsellors introduce clients to the control theory concept of basic needs. Then they can assist clients to explore which of their basic needs they are wanting to satisfy. Brierly (1989) mentions the 'needs tray' technique whereby clients are asked 'If I had a tray and you could have one or more of these needs today before you leave, which would you choose: love, personal power, fun or freedom?' (p. 174). Clients' answers can illuminate where counselling might focus. Clients are in a better position to generate and evaluate pictures in the head for satisfying needs when clear about the needs they wish to satisfy.

Evaluating total behaviour

Evaluating total behaviour consists of two main parts: clarifying current behaviour and assessing its adequacy.

How are you behaving now?

When clients identify what they want and need, the next step is to ask clients 'What are you doing now?' or 'What behaviours are you choosing now?' Frequently clients talk as though they are passive victims of circumstances or of other people. Clients who sit at home depressed and yet say they want love choose the action behaviour of sitting at home, the feeling behaviour of depressing, the thinking behaviour of 'I'm too depressed to do anything', and any accompanying physiological symptoms or behaviours, for instance disturbed sleep.

Often reality counsellors ask significant others that clients are trying to control or feel controlled by to join the client in a session. The purpose of this is to help both clients and counsellors understand the client's behaviour better. Sometimes these ancillary people also benefit from the session.

In particular, reality counsellors focus on the action and thinking components of total behaviour because they are the components most amenable to change. Also counsellors look for effective behaviours that clients have in their repertoires and may enquire about times in the past when clients functioned effectively. Counsellors look for strengths both to help clients understand their assets and also because often it is easier to develop behaviours that are already in clients' repertoires than others which are not.

Is your behaviour getting you what you want?

Reality counsellors assist clients to judge their behaviour in light of their wants and needs. As well as 'Is your behaviour getting you what you want?', other questions that reality counsellors use to get clients to evaluate their behaviour include: 'Is what you're doing getting you what you want?', 'How is your behaviour helping you?', and 'Is this what is best for you?' The purpose of such questions is to encourage clients to realize that the behaviours they are choosing are not getting them what they claim they need. For instance, the client who wants love and sits at home and depresses is forced to face the fact that by this behaviour he is choosing not to obtain love. The middle-aged client Phyllis, who wants more independence yet keeps responding whenever her mother Carol complains, is forced to realize that her behaviour is not getting her what she wants. Evaluating behaviour questions encourages clients to acknowledge that their current choices are not giving them effective control over their lives.

Planning and changing total behaviour

Planning and changing behaviour involves the following components: searching for alternative behaviours, negotiating plans, getting commitment to plans, developing relevant behaviours, and evaluating progress in implementing plans.

If your current behaviour is not getting you what you want, then what do you think might be better?

Once clients realize that their current behaviour is not giving them effective control over their lives, they are ready to look at alternative ways of regaining control. Reality counsellors realize that clients are sensitive to being told what to do, so they ask questions that encourage clients to come up with their own better behaviour. Such questions include: 'If your current behaviour is not getting you what you want, then what do you think might be better?', 'What are better choices than the ones you are currently making?', and 'What can you do to regain more control over your life?'.

Tell me your plan?

Plans are ways that clients can satisfy important pictures in their heads outside of counselling. Reality counsellors lead clients to develop their own plans rather than do it for them. This involves counsellors working closely with clients, yet encouraging their self-reliance. Plans focus particularly on the doing and thinking components of total behaviour since, to use the earlier analogy, these are the front wheels of the car. Plans can include finding new pictures that are satisfying. Plans should be feasible in terms of clients' abilities and motivation. They should not attempt too much too soon since clients seeking to regain control may need small successes to build up confidence for more difficult tasks.

When planning, reality counsellors often ask questions that pin clients down to clarifying the specific details of their plans. For instance, when a teenage girl who has never looked for a job says she is going to do so, the counsellor might ask what time and day she is going to start, what she plans to wear, and how she is going to look up what jobs to apply for. In addition, the counsellor might pin down the client regarding what she would do if her first three or four attempts at going for a job interview were unsuccessful. In general, the more reality counsellors pin down clients with respect to the details of their behaviour change plans, the more chance clients have of successfully implementing them.

Glasser (1984b) presents the case of Randy, a business school graduate student who was phobicking about going to class because, if he finished business school, he might not obtain the high-level job that he pictured in his head. Together Glasser and Randy developed a plan which focused on the action component of total behaviour and had implications for the thinking component. Randy was to disclose his phobia to his instructors and ask them if he could sit at the back of the class near the open door, leave quietly if it became too difficult to stay, pull himself together in the empty hall, and then return to class. By this means he was able to regain some control in a previously out-of-control situation. Partly because his instructors did not reject him when he disclosed his phobia, Randy also altered the self-defeating perfectionist pictures in his head. He obtained more realistic pictures both of job requirements and of his resources as a potential employee. Randy implemented his plan with the feelings behaviour outcome that he stopped phobicking almost entirely.

Do you commit yourself to making an effort to follow your plan through?

It is one thing to make a plan and another to have the commitment to implementing it. Reality counsellors seek commitments from clients to implementing plans. If counsellors have established themselves as need-fulfilling people in clients' internal worlds, clients will take their commitments to them seriously. In addition, clients are making commitments to themselves. Strong commitments enhance the likelihood of strong follow through. Also, a key to feelings of control is the ability to make and follow through on plans.

Developing relevant behaviours

Where necessary, reality counsellors work with clients to develop specific behaviours required to implement plans. For instance, in the above case of the teenage girl who has never looked for a job, a reality counsellor might develop her skills by role-playing an employer interviewing her. Brierly (1989) gives the example of 'practising' conversational skills in her office with Susan, a shy, quiet-spoken young woman of 20, to build her skill level to where she could succeed when trying out her new behaviours.

Evaluating progress: No excuses and no punishment

Clients are asked to implement plans as homework. Reality counsellors check clients' progress. They assume that commitments to reasonable plans can always be fulfilled. In accepting no excuses counsellors might say 'I'm not interested in why you can't do it. I'm interested in when you can do it and how you can do it' (Glasser, 1984a, p. 336). Reality counsellors assist clients to keep focusing on what they can do now rather than lose control by looking for reasons to be miserable and ineffective. Frequently reality counsellors use confrontations: for instance, 'You said you will do it, when will you do it?' Less frequently, they use even stronger confrontations like telling clients that they are full of bull or firmly saying 'Wake up, you can't control me with your usual behaviour.' However, in instances where plans genuinely turn out to be unreasonable, counsellors and clients work together to remake better ones.

Counsellors praise clients who succeed in carrying out plans. Any kind of negative statement by counsellors is viewed as punishment. Punishment weakens clients' involvement with their counsellors and reinforces their failure identities. The negative consequences stemming from not carrying out plans are viewed as quite different from punishment.

Further applications

Reality counselling based on control theory is used in marital work. Early on it is important to clarify whether the partners want to evaluate the advantages and disadvantages of continuing the marriage or whether they have made a definite decision to try to preserve the marriage. Marital counselling focuses on how couples can live together without controlling each other in ways that they do not want to be controlled.

Reality counsellors also work in groups, often as joint leaders. Group members can help each other to evaluate the adequacy of current behaviours in satisfying needs and pictures in the head, planning alternative behaviours and making commitments. For example, a member's plan can be written down and a public commitment made by having each member of the group read and sign it.

Reality counselling and control theory principles are widely used in educational settings. Much of Glasser's recent writings (Glasser, 1990, 1992, 1993) have been focused on improving the skills of administrators and teachers in creating environments in which students can learn to take effective control of their lives.

CHAPTER REVIEW AND SELF-REFERENT QUESTIONS

Chapter review questions

1. Why does Glasser favour using active language?

2. What are the basic needs and what is their role in control theory?

3. What are pictures in the head and what is their role in control theory?

4. What is total behaviour? Provide an example.

5. What is meant by viewing people as control systems?

6. How do people acquire ineffective behaviours?

7. Critically discuss Glasser's views on raising children.

8. Why do people choose their misery? Do you agree with Glasser that misery is often chosen?

9. How do people remain unaware that they are choosing their misery?

10. What are the goals of reality counselling?

11. In reality counselling, what is the nature of the counsellor–client relationship?

12. How might reality counsellors teach control theory to clients?

13. How do reality counsellors assist in identifying clients' wants and needs?

14. Why do reality counsellors ask questions like 'How are you behaving now?'

15. Why do reality counsellors ask questions like 'Is your behaviour getting you what you want?'

16. Why do reality counsellors ask questions like 'If your current behaviour is not getting you what you want, then what do you think might be better?'

17. What are plans and how do reality counsellors assist clients to make plans?

18. Why do reality counsellors seek commitment to plans?

19. Why does Glasser advocate no excuses and no punishment when counsellors assess clients' progress in implementing plans?

Self-referent questions

1. Do you think Glasser's view of basic needs is accurate in reflecting your basic needs?

2. Critically assess the extent to which you are a control system.

3. In an area where your current total behaviour is not getting you what you want, think through what might be better ways of behaving and make a plan to behave more responsibly.

4. What relevance, if any, has the theory and practice of reality counselling for how you counsel?

5. What relevance, if any, has the theory and practice of reality counselling for how you live?

Annotated Bibliography

Glasser, W. (1984a). Reality therapy. In R.J. Corsini (Ed.). *Current Psychotherapies* (3rd ed., pp. 320–53). Itasca, IL: Peacock.
This chapter summarizes the theory and practice of reality counselling, integrating control theory into the approach. The chapter includes an annotated bibliography of Glasser's books to that date.

Glasser, W. (1984b). *Control theory: A New Explanation of How We Control Our Lives*. New York: Harper & Row.
This book starts with presenting the major concepts of control theory such as the basic needs, pictures in our heads, total behaviour and people as control systems. The middle part of the book includes chapters on psychosomatic illness and addictive drugs. The contents of the final part of the book have a self-help emphasis on taking control of your life and health, controlling others or ourselves with pain and misery, and how to start using control theory. The book does not focus on the use of control theory in counselling.

Glasser, W. (1965). *Reality Therapy: A New Approach to Psychiatry*. New York: Harper & Row.
This book represents an evolutionary stage in the development of reality therapy. Part one, entitled 'Theory', covers basic concepts of reality therapy and the differences between reality

therapy and conventional therapy. Part two, entitled 'Practice', contains chapters on the use of reality therapy with seriously delinquent adolescent girls, hospitalized psychotic patients and clients in private practice. The final chapter discusses the application of reality therapy to the public schools.

Glasser, W. (1989). Control theory. In N. Glasser, (Ed.) *Control Theory in the Practice of Reality Therapy: Case Studies* (pp. 1–15). New York: Harper & Row.

This chapter summarizes some of the main concepts in control theory and discusses their application to counselling.

Glasser, N. (Ed.) (1989). *Control Theory in the Practice of Reality Therapy: Case Studies*. New York: Harper & Row.

In the 1980s, Glasser added control theory to reality counselling. The book consists of 13 case studies, each written by a different counsellor certified by the Institute for Reality Therapy. Many of the case studies focus on assisting young people to assume more responsibility for their lives, often despite the behaviour of elders. Some case studies focus on the problems of families and parents and one case study focuses on working with a prisoner in a maximum security segregation unit. Each chapter ends with William Glasser's comments, highlighting points about reality counselling illustrated in the case study.

Further references

Glasser

Glasser, W. (1961). *Mental Health or Mental Illness?* New York: Harper & Row.

Glasser, W. (1969). *Schools without Failure.* New York: Harper & Row.

Glasser, W. (1972). *The Identity Society.* New York: Harper & Row.

Glasser, W. (1976). *Positive Addiction.* New York: Harper & Row.

Glasser, W. (1981). *Stations of the Mind.* New York: Harper & Row.

Glasser, W. (1990). *The Quality School: Managing Students without Coercion.* New York: Harper & Row.

Glasser, W. (1992). *The Quality School: Managing Students without Coercion* (2nd ed.). New York: Harper & Row.

Glasser, W. (1993). *The Quality School Teacher.* New York: Harper & Row.

Glasser, W. & Karrass, C. (1980). *Both-win Management.* New York: Lippincott.

Others

Barr, N.I. (1974). The responsible world of reality therapy. *Psychology Today, 7* (9), 64–8.

Brierly, S.A. (1989). Breaking away from the family mold and developing a strong comfortable identity. In N. Glasser (Ed). *Control Theory in the Practice of Reality Therapy: Case Studies* (pp. 163–80). New York: Harper & Row.

Evans, D.B. (1982). What are you doing? An interview with William Glasser. *Personnel and Guidance Journal, 60,* 460–5.

Glasser, N. (Ed.) (1980). *What Are You Doing? How People Are Helped through Reality Therapy.* New York: Harper & Row.

Powers, W.T. (1973). *Behavior: The Control of Perception.* Chicago: Aldine.

Wubbolding, R.E. (1988). *Using Reality Therapy.* New York: Harper & Row.

Wubbolding, R.E. (1994). Reality Therapy: What is it? *Counselling, 5,* 117–19.

Journal

The *Journal of Reality Therapy* publishes articles on theory, practice and research into reality counselling. Information about the journal is available from:

Dr Lawrence Litwack, Editor, Journal of Reality Therapy, 203 Lake Hall, Boston Bouve College, Northeastern University, 360 Huntington Avenue, Boston, MA 02115, USA.

PART THREE

Existential

SIX

Existential Counselling

PREVIEW

- *Yalom and May's existential counselling is a dynamic approach which focuses on clients' confrontations with universal existential concerns. Existence is an active process involving becoming something. Unwelt, Mitwelt and Eigenwelt are three forms of being-in-the-world.*

- *Anxiety can be normal or neurotic. Existential counsellors focus on helping clients cope with anxieties that are inherent in human existence. Guilt can be normal, neurotic or existential, the latter being guilt over transgressing one's potential.*

- *Human life involves confronting four existential ultimate concerns: death, freedom, isolation and meaninglessness.*

- *Young and old alike use denial as a means of coping with death anxiety. The rapid disintegration of traditional structures and pace of technological change are increasingly forcing humans to confront issues of responsibility, meaning and isolation.*

- *Existential counselling offers a psychodynamic model in which the core inner conflicts centre around awareness of existential concerns leading to anxiety which in turn may be handled by defence mechanisms. Defences against the anxiety generated by death, freedom, isolation and meaninglessness are reviewed.*

- *Existential counselling's main goal is that clients experience their existences as real. Within the context of authentic relationships, existential counsellors help clients confront and come to terms with their inner conflicts in relation to death, freedom, isolation and meaninglessness. The major focus is on clients' current situations and enveloping fears.*

- *Counselling approaches to death anxiety include giving clients permission to talk about it, identifying defence mechanisms, and working with dreams and reminders of finiteness.*

- *Counselling approaches to freedom and responsibility include identifying defences and avoidance strategies, freeing up wishing, and facilitating willing and deciding.*

- *Counselling approaches to isolation anxiety include helping clients to confront isolation, identifying defence mechanisms and interpersonal pathology, and offering healing counsellor-client relationships.*

- *Counselling approaches to meaninglessness anxiety include redefining the problem, identifying defences, and assisting engagement in the stream of life.*

- *Though primarily an individual approach, existential counselling can be conducted beneficially in groups.*

INTRODUCTION

The word existence is derived from the Latin word *existere*, literally meaning 'to stand out, to emerge'. Existence is not a static process, but entails the process of coming into being or becoming (May, *et al.*, 1958). Existential approaches to counselling are concerned with the science and processes of being. The science of being is known as *ontology*, from *ontos*, the Greek word for being. Existential counsellors assist clients to stand out or to affirm their existences, despite and within the constraints involved in existence.

The existential approaches to counselling are rooted in existential philosophy. Prominent existential philosophers include Kierkegaard, Nietzsche, Heidegger and Sartre. Kierkegaard's existentialism was located within a Christian framework and he described the dread, anxiety and despair – 'the sickness unto death' – of humans estranged from their essential nature (Kierkegaard, 1954). Nietzsche was an atheist existentialist who presented a nihilistic picture of the world in which 'God is dead' as the background for human self-affirmation (Tillich, 1952). Heidegger's (1962) *Being and Time* focused on the quest for being and analysed the concept the *dasien*, being there or existence. Sartre, a Marxist, echoed Nietzsche's thoughts about a godless world. He emphasized humans' inescapable need, in their struggle against despair and non-being, to make the choices that create the essence of their existences (Sartre, 1956). So long as they are alive, humans have no exit from the need to define themselves.

Existential approaches to counselling have also been influenced by religious philosophers such as Buber, the Jewish theologian, and Tillich the Protestant Christian theologian. Buber (1965, 1970) thought that humans were not separate entities but existed as creatures of the 'in-between'. The two special types of in-between relationships were 'I–It' relationships, involving functional relationships in which others were objects, and 'I–Thou' relationships, involving mutual influence and a full experiencing of another. Tillich's (1952) book *The Courage to Be* examines human existence within a religious framework. For Tillich the courage to be is 'the ethical act in which man affirms his own being in spite of those elements which conflict with his essential self-affirmation' (p. 3).

Existential approaches to counselling go beyond dealing with surface problems to assist clients to confront the basic issues of their existence: anxiety, despair, death, loneliness, alienation, and meaninglessness. All the preceding issues have the potential to generate 'existence pain' (Yalom, 1989, p. 4). Existential counselling approaches are also concerned with questions of freedom, responsibility, love and creativity.

Yalom (1980) observes that counselling approaches 'reflect, and are shaped by, the pathology that they must treat' (p. 223). He distinguishes between the counselling needs of restrictive and sexually repressed Viennese people at the end of the nineteenth century and the counselling needs of the compulsively permissive American culture at the end of the twentieth century. In former times, much of people's existences were defined for them, whereas now people face far more of a challenge to create and define their own existences.

There are many existential approaches to counselling. Yalom and May's existential counselling and Frankl's logotherapy are two such approaches that widely influence contemporary counselling. This chapter describes the theory and practice of Yalom and May's existential counselling and the next chapter reviews Frankl's logotherapy.

Irvin Yalom and Rollo May

Irvin Yalom

Irvin Yalom was born in Washington, DC in 1931, the son of Russian immigrant parents who, in the 1920s, had arrived penniless in the United States. Yalom 'spent too many hours in my childhood silently hating my mother's vicious tongue' (Yalom, 1989, p. 147), though he admired his father. Yalom grew up facing two additional existential predicaments because 'In the streets, the black attacked me for my whiteness, and in school, the white attacked me for my Jewishness' (Yalom, 1989, p. 88). In 1952 Yalom received his BA degree from George Washington University, and in 1956 he obtained his MD from Boston University. During the next six years he was an intern at New York's Mt Sinai Hospital, a psychiatric resident at Baltimore's Johns Hopkins Hospital, a consultant at the Patuxent Institution in Maryland, and a US Army Captain in Honolulu. In 1962 Yalom was appointed an instructor in psychiatry at Stanford University School of Medicine, followed by appointments as assistant professor, associate professor and professor in 1963, 1968, and 1973, respectively. Yalom married his wife Marilyn in 1963 and they have four children. Although in 1993 Yalom retired from Stanford, he remains very active as an author and psychotherapist.

Yalom has published numerous scientific papers. In addition, he is the author of *The Theory and Practice of Group Psychotherapy, Existential Psychotherapy, Inpatient Group Psychotherapy, Love's Executioner and Other Tales of Psychotherapy*, and co-author of *Encounter Groups: First facts, Everyday Gets a Little Closer*, and *Concise Guide to Group Psychotherapy*. Also, Yalom has collaborated with his former therapist, Rollo May, to write a chapter about existential counselling for *Current Psychotherapies* (May & Yalom, 1989). In 1993 Yalom's *When Nietzsche Wept* won the Commonwealth Club's Gold Medal for Fiction for the Best Novel of 1992. Among his other accomplishments, Yalom has a deep commitment to articulate and polished writing.

Rollo May

Rollo May 1909–94 was born in Ohio. One of seven children, his father was a YMCA secretary who moved his family quite often. May's parents' relationship was discordant and his family life unhappy, a stimulus for his later interest in counselling. May describes his mother as a 'bitch-kitty on wheels' (Rabinowitz, Good & Cozad, 1989, p. 437). His only sister, who was older than him, was psychotic and spent some time in a mental hospital. May obtained relief from family misery by sitting and playing on the shores of the St Clair river. A rebel during high school, May studied liberal arts at Oberlin College, obtaining his BA in 1930. May then went to Greece for three years where he taught boys aged 12–18 and studied ancient Greek civilization. In addition, one summer vacation he went to Vienna where he studied individual psychology with Alfred Adler. In 1938 May received his BD from Union Theological Seminary, where he met and developed an ongoing friendship with Paul Tillich, who had recently been expelled from Nazi German. Tillich was a major influence on his thinking. In 1949 May obtained his PhD in clinical psychology from Teachers College of Columbia University. While pursuing his doctoral degree, May came down with tuberculosis. His recovery involved spending nearly two years bed-ridden in an upstate New York sanitarium where he spent much time reading and thinking about the nature of anxiety. Ultimately, this work led to his writing *The Meaning of Anxiety*. During his New York City years, May conducted a private practice, authored books and articles, was an adjunct professor at the New School of Social Research and New York University, and served as a training analyst and supervisor at the William Alanson White Institute. May then lived in San Francisco where he wrote, taught and saw clients. May was divorced twice and, in 1989, confided 'I've always had good friends and lovers, but I'm scared to death of marriage' (Rabinowitz, Good & Cozad, 1989, p. 437). He died on 22 October 1994 at the age of 84.

Reflecting his early interest in English literature, May has been a prolific author of books and articles. Over a long period he has been at the forefront of applying existential and humanistic ideas to counselling. May's books include *The Art of Counseling, The Meaning of Anxiety*, his edited book *Existence: A New Dimension in Psychiatry and Psychology* (which includes two important chapters by him), *Psychology and the Human Dilemma, Love and Will, Power and Innocence: A Search for Sources of Violence, The Courage to Create, Freedom and Destiny* and *My Quest for Beauty*. Though he enjoyed his twilight years, May observed: 'I wouldn't want to go through this life again. I mean, one time is enough. I don't know that I'd do anything differently, but it would be too boring' (Rabinowitz, Good & Cozad, 1989, p. 439).

ASSUMPTIONS
Being and non-being

May (May, Angel & Ellenberger, 1958) observes that being is a participle of a verb and implies that someone is in the process of becoming something. He states that, when used as a noun, being means *potentia*, the source of potential. An analogy is that the acorn has the potential to become an oak. However, this analogy is only partially accurate for humans because they have the capacity for self-consciousness. Humans can choose their own being. The choices that they make about being are not just concerned with whether or not to commit suicide but are relevant to every instant of their lives.

Because of widespread collectivist and conformist trends in society, modern humans have repressed their sense of being. People's sense of being refers to their whole experience of existence, both conscious and unconscious. They need to experience themselves as beings in the world and have a basic 'I-am' experience, expressed by one of May's clients as 'Since I Am, I have the right to be' (May *et al.*, 1958, p. 43). The 'I-am' experience is not the solution, but rather the precondition for the solution to clients' problems.

The opposite of being is non-being or nothingness. Existence implies the possibility of not existing. Death is the most obvious form of non-being. However, there are numerous other threats to being in the form of loss of potentiality through anxiety and conformity and through lack of clear self-awareness. In addition, destructive hostility and physical sickness can pose threats to being. However, people who are able to confront non-being can emerge with a heightened sense of being including a greater awareness not only of themselves but of others and the world around them.

The three forms of being-in-the-world

Existential counselling distinguishes three modes of the world that characterize people's existence as being-in the world. First, there is the *Umwelt*, the 'world around'. The *Umwelt* represents the natural world, the laws of nature and the environment. For animals and human beings alike, the *Umwelt* includes biological needs, drives, instincts. Also, it includes each organism's daily and life cycles. The natural world is accepted as real.

Second, there is the *Mitwelt*, the 'with-world'. This is the social world of relating to fellow humans singly and in groups. Both in personal and group relationships people influence each other and the structure of meaning that develops. May writes: *'The essence of relationship is that in the encounter both persons are changed'* (May *et al.*, 1958, p. 63). How people relate in intimate relationships, for instance their degree of commitment, influences the meaning of the relationships for them. Similarly, how much of themselves people put into groups influences the meaning of the groups for them.

Third, there is the *Eigenwelt*, or 'own world'. The *Eigenwelt* is uniquely present in humans and entails self-consciousness and self-awareness. Also, the *Eigenwelt* entails grasping the personal meaning of a thing or person. Individuals need to own their relationships to things and people: for instance, 'This flower is beautiful' means 'For me, this flower is beautiful'.

The three modes of being are interrelated. For instance, love entails more than the biological drives of the *Umwelt*. Furthermore, it entails more than the social or interpersonal relationship of the *Mitwelt*. In addition, love requires the *Eigenwelt*, in that, when relating to another, people need to be sufficient to themselves.

Normal and neurotic anxiety

To be human is to be anxious. Anxiety is an unavoidable part of human life. May (1950) distinguishes between normal and neurotic anxiety. He defines anxiety as 'the threat to our existence or to values we identify with our existence' (May, 1977, p. 205). In the course of normal development everyone experiences various threats to their existence. One source of normal anxiety is human's existential vulnerability to nature, sickness and death. Another source is the need to progressively become independent from parents with the tensions and crises that this process can create. However, people can use such threats constructively as learning experiences and continue to develop.

The reaction of normal anxiety has three characteristics. First, it is proportionate to the objective threat in the situation being confronted. Second, it does not involve repression. Third, it can be used creatively to identify and confront the conditions bringing it about. Existential counsellors view their main function as helping clients come to terms with the normal anxieties that are part of human existence.

Neurotic anxiety possesses the opposite characteristics to normal anxiety. Neurotic anxiety is a disproportionate reaction to an objective threat, involves repression, and is destructive rather than constructive. Another way of viewing neurotic anxiety is that people subjectively react to objective threats in terms of their inner psychological patterns and conflicts. The repression and blocking of awareness involved in neurotic anxiety leaves people more vulnerable to threats since they lose access to important information with which to distinguish and deal with the threats.

Normal, neurotic and existential guilt

Like anxiety, guilt is part of human existence. A distinction may be drawn between normal and neurotic guilt. Neurotic guilt derives from *imagined* transgressions against others, parental injunctions and societal conventions. Normal guilt is a call to conscience and sensitizes people to the ethical aspects of their behaviour.

Existential or ontological guilt represents another form of guilt. May distinguishes between three forms of existential guilt. The first form, which corresponds to *Eigenwelt*, is failure to live up to potential. As such, people can be guilty of transgressions against themselves. The second form, which corresponds to *Mitwelt*, relates to distorting the reality of one's fellow humans. The third form of existential guilt, which involves *Umwelt* as well as the other two modes-of-being, is 'separation guilt' in relation to nature as a whole.

Existential guilt is universal. It is rooted in self-awareness. Existential guilt does not arise from violation of parental injunctions, 'but arises from the fact that I can see myself as the one who can choose or fail to choose' (May, *et al.*, 1958, p. 55). Thus existential guilt is inexorably linked with the notion of personal responsibility. Existential guilt is not in itself a form of neurotic guilt, though it possesses the potential to turn into neurotic guilt. However, if correctly addressed, existential guilt can have constructive outcomes both in terms of greater humility and sensitivity to others and in increased creativity.

Transcendence

Humans' unique capacity to think and talk in symbols allows them the possibility of transcending time and space. Humans can project themselves into the past and into the future. In addition, humans can transcend themselves in their social relations and see themselves as other see them and give appropriate weight to others' perceptions. The capacity to transcend immediate, concrete situations provides humans with the basis of both their freedom and the responsibility.

Transcendence is derived from the Latin word *transcendere*, meaning to 'climb over and beyond'. The ability to transcend immediate situations is part of the ontological nature of human beings. Existing involves humans in a continuous process of emerging in which they transcend their pasts and presents to create their futures. Unless seriously ill or blocked by anxiety or despair, all humans engage in this process.

Existential ultimate concerns

Yalom (1980) has identified four existential ultimate concerns – death, freedom, isolation, and meaninglessness – with considerable relevance for counselling.

• *Death*. Life and death, being and non-being, are interdependent rather than concurrent. Death is the fundamental source of anxiety, whether it be neurotic, normal or existential. Perhaps the term 'death terror' denotes the force of death concern better than 'death anxiety'. Death anxiety, the fear of ceasing to be, can be both conscious and unconscious. From early in their lives children are extremely preoccupied with death. Strong death anxiety is likely to be repressed. To cope with the terror of potential non-being, people erect denial-based defences against death anxiety. To a large extent psychopathology has its origins in failed attempts to transcend death. The first existential conflict is that between awareness of the inevitability of death and the wish to continue to live: the conflict between fear of non-being and wishing to be.

• *Freedom*. Humans are 'condemned to freedom' (Sartre, 1956, p. 631). Humans do not live in a well-ordered and structured universe. There is no secure ground undergirding existence. Rather, there is lack of structure and groundlessness which generates both anxiety and dread. Because of their freedom, humans are also condemned to responsibility. They are not only responsible for imbuing the world with significance, but they are entirely responsible for their lives, for their actions and their failures to act. The second existential conflict is that between people's confrontation with groundlessness and freedom and their wish for ground and structure.

• *Isolation*. There are three forms of isolation. *Interpersonal isolation*, often experienced as loneliness, means that people are in varying degrees cut off from others. This may be through deficient social skills, psychopathology or by choice and of necessity. *Intrapersonal isolation* means that people are blocked from awareness of or dissociated from parts of themselves. Whereas interpersonal isolation may not contain pathology, intrapersonal isolation does so by definition. *Existential isolation* is rooted in the human condition in that each person enters, lives in, and leaves the world alone. Ultimately there is an unbridgeable gap between self and others. Yalom (1980) observes that existential isolation refers to an even more fundamental form of isolation, namely 'separation from the world' (p. 355). The third existential conflict is that between people's awareness of their fundamental isolation and their wish for contact, protection and to be a part of a larger whole.

• *Meaninglessness.* What is the meaning of life? Humans require coherence, purpose and significance. They organize random stimuli into figure and ground. They are neuropsychologically organized to seek patterns and meaning. However, the human paradox is that of existence in an indifferent universe with no predetermined meaning. A distinction may be made between cosmic meaning, whether human life fits into some overall cosmic pattern, and terrestrial meaning, the meaning of *my* life. With the decline in religious beliefs, modern humans are faced with the need to discover secular personal meaning in the absence of cosmic meaning. This leads to the fourth inner existential conflict: how do humans confront their need for meaning in an indifferent world that has no meaning?

Existential psychodynamics

Yalom (1980) offers the following definition of existential counselling and psychotherapy: 'Existential psychotherapy is a dynamic approach to therapy which focuses on concerns that are rooted in the individual's existence' (p. 5). In personality theory, the term dynamics relates to the concept of energy or force. The notion of psychodynamic conflict relates to the clash between opposing forces. The Freudian model of dynamic conflict was that of the clash between ego and instinctual sexual and aggressive drives. To Freud, the deeper conflicts were associated with the earliest psychosexual conflicts. Existential psychodynamics differ in two important ways from Freudian psychodynamics. First, existential conflicts and existential anxiety flow from people's inescapable confrontations with the givens of existence: death, freedom, isolation and meaninglessness. Second, existential dynamics do not assume a developmental or archaeological model where first is synonymous with deep. When existential counsellors and clients explore deeply, they do so not by focusing on everyday concerns but thinking deeply about existential ultimate concerns.

ACQUISITION

Despite existential anxieties and conflicts being inescapable parts of life, the question still remains of how people develop different modes of dealing with the ultimate concerns of existence.

Death

Young children, even though not intellectually equipped to understand what death means, grasp its essence. Yalom (1980) believes that children then deny their first knowledge of death. Mechanisms of denial include such beliefs as death is temporary, children do not die, I will not die because I am special, and there is an ultimate rescuer. Coming to terms with the concept of death is a major developmental task which some children handle better than others. Exposure to death can be for good or ill. Factors likely to be helpful include the presence of already existing ego resources, good genes and supportive adults able to deal with their own death anxieties. However, exposure to death can be traumatic when these factors are insufficiently present. Deaths of siblings and of parents can be especially frightening and can exceed children's coping resources.

Research indicates that both neurotic and psychotic psychiatric patients have lost a parent more frequently than the general population. The degree of cultural acceptance of death also influences how much anxiety death will generate in both adults and children.

The quality of death education that parents offer to their children affects their awareness and acceptance of death. Children are often shielded from death by misinformation, denial, fairy tales, euphemisms and assurances that children do not die. As with sex, children do not ignore the issue but turn to other sources of information of varying degrees of reliability. Western cultures offer no real guidelines as to how parents should educate their children about death, and this not helped by many adults seeking comfort in childlike beliefs.

Freedom

The modern day emphasis on freedom and responsibility as existential concerns derives from the breaking down of traditional belief systems, religions, rituals and rules. In the twentieth century, there has been a rapid disintegration of structures and values. Permissive parenting has left many young people with the need to choose but without clear guidelines as to how or what to choose. Numerous people are unprepared for the freedom they now have. Frequently, when confronted with the existential fact of their responsibility for their lives, they experience difficulty in handling this realization. Now people are less often faced with what they *must* do; instead, the emphasis is on what they *want* to do. In what may be a transitional period between old and new ways of being in the world, many people have failed to learn adequately how to wish, how to will and how to decide and stay committed to their decisions.

Isolation

Cultural and technological change plays a large part in the creation of *interpersonal* isolation. In the United States and other Western cultures there has been a decline in community links – churches, local shops, neighbours who know each other and have local roots, family doctors and so on. *Intrapersonal* isolation stems from obstructions and frustrations that occur early in life and threaten some vital aspect of the individual's nascent sense of self. *Existential* isolation is closely interwoven with interpersonal isolation. Many people fail to develop the inner strength, confidence and sense of identity that enable them to face existential isolation. Never having received genuine growth-inducing love, they do not know how to offer it to others. If committed and authentic counsellor-client relationships can help clients confront and come to terms with their existential isolation, it can safely be inferred that clients have insufficiently experienced such relationships in their pasts.

Meaninglessness

Many factors in contemporary culture contribute to people having a diminished sense of life's meaning compared to their forebears in the pre-industrial agricultural world. First, instead of meaning being supplied by religion, now most people neither believe in religion nor go to church. Second, the spread of urbanization and industrialization has contributed to people losing a sense of meaning through their contact with nature. No longer are most people closely connected with the cycles of the land and of farm animals. Third, most contemporary humans no longer belong to and have roles in rural communities but instead often live in relatively impersonal urban communities. Fourth, many contemporary humans are alienated from their work and feel that they engage in mechanical and routine tasks of little intrinsic interest. Fifth, contemporary humans are less beset with basic survival needs, such as food, shelter, and water. With their greater security and leisure they are confronted increasingly by the abyss of meaninglessness. Time on their hands means time to be haunted by issues of meaning. In addition, in economic recessions, many people are confronted by unemployment and a subsequent loss of meaning. Sixth, contemporary humans face the possibility of nuclear annihilation and global environmental destruction. If the world is not going to last, why bother?

MAINTENANCE

Existential model of defence mechanisms

How do people maintain insufficient awareness and psychopathological behaviour within the existential framework? They evolve both conscious and unconscious psychological operations to deal with the anxiety generated by existential ultimate concerns. These psychological operations or *defence mechanisms* are of two types. First, there are conventional defence mechanisms, such as projection, which defend people against anxiety regardless of its source. Second, there are specific defences of each of the four ultimate concerns which defend people against these fundamental fears. These defence mechanisms may not only be relevant to individual clients but may also be reinforced by whole cultures colluding in them.

Figure 6.1 depicts the existential model of defence mechanisms in reaction to awareness at some level of an inner conflict raised by an ultimate concern. Such defence mechanisms provide a modicum of psychological safety at the expense of restricting people's potential for growth and of generating existential guilt.

Death anxiety defences

Though the specific defences for each ultimate concern are mentioned separately, they may overlap. Furthermore, they require recombining or merging into an overall existential model of psychopathology. Children's modes of coping with death awareness and death terror involve denial. For children and adults alike, Yalom (1980) has identified two major death anxiety defence mechanisms. First, there is the defence of

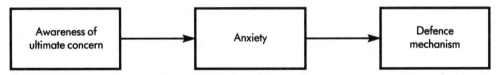

Figure 6.1 Existential model of defence mechanisms.

specialness. While at the conscious level most people accept their lives as finite, deep down they can develop irrational beliefs about their own immortality and inviolability. Where this defence is weak or absent, then people may develop one of a number of clinical syndromes, including: compulsive heroism, being a 'workaholic' and turning a deaf ear to time's message, narcissism, and the drive for power and control. Frequently, such people seek counselling when they can no longer ward off their death anxiety through these pretences.

Belief in an ultimate rescuer is the second major defence mechanism against death anxiety. This represents the belief that, however bad things may get, the individual is not alone in an indifferent universe and some omnipresent servant will come to the rescue. People using the defense of the ultimate rescuer may restrict their lives by locating and serving a 'dominant other'. Most people do not acknowledge their belief system until it fails to serve its purpose: for instance, if they acquire a fatal illness or their 'dominant other' dies or psychologically withdraws.

Freedom anxiety defences

Freedom anxiety defences protect individuals from awareness of their responsibility for the authorship of their lives. Awareness of responsibility entails being 'aware of creating one's own self, destiny, life predicament, feelings and, if such be the case, one's own suffering' (Yalom, 1980, p. 218). Compulsivity is one defence against responsibility awareness. Yalom gives the example of Bernard, a 25-year-old salesman who was compulsively driven in the areas of sex, work, and leisure. His compulsivity obliterated choice, yet Bernard was responsible for creating as well as maintaining his compulsivity. Other defences against freedom anxiety include: displacing responsibility on to others, including counsellors; denying responsibility by posing as the innocent victim or losing control; avoidance of autonomous behaviour; and pathology in wishing, willing and deciding.

Isolation anxiety defences

In isolation anxiety defences people do not relate to others in their own right but use them for defensive functions. One defence against ultimate aloneness is to seek affirmation in others' eyes. Such people exist so far as they are part of others' consciousness and receive approval from them. Frequently, under the guise of loving, they can hide their inability to love. However, ultimately, others are likely to get fed up with meeting their needs for affirmation. Fusion with an individual or group is another isolation anxiety defence. Rather than confront and come to terms with their fundamental isolation, people feel and think they are not alone because they are part of others. In addition, compulsive sexuality is a defence against isolation anxiety. Sexually compulsive people treat their partners as objects rather than persons. They do not take the time to know and be known. Instead, their serial relationships are caricatures of the real thing.

Meaninglessness anxiety defences

People handle meaninglessness anxiety in different ways. Compulsive activity is one way of avoiding a confrontation with meaninglessness. Individuals compulsively engage in any of a range of activities as a reaction to an underlying deep sense of purposelessness. Sooner or later many individuals who have compulsively sought money, pleasure, power, recognition and status start questioning their values. Crusadism is a form of compulsive activity where people seek out issues that they can make into time and energy consuming crusades. Nihilism is another defence against meaninglessness anxiety. Here people avoid confronting meaninglessness by disparaging all sources of meaning that others find in their lives, for instance love or service.

PRACTICE
Goals

Existential counselling is more a mode of viewing human beings than a rigorous system. In the final analysis, existential counsellors view clienthood as ubiquitous. However, generally clients are more troubled than their counsellors.

The overriding goal of existential counselling is that clients experience their existence as real. The underlying assumption is that the fundamental neurotic process is repression of the ontological sense involving the loss of a sense of being and the truncation of awareness and potential. Since counselling is primarily concerned with helping clients experience their existence, any symptomatic 'cure' is a by-product or secondary goal. Existential counsellors attempt to avoid a technical, mechanical approach to clients that can lead to clients obtaining a symptomatic 'cure' at the expense of constricting their existence. Great stress is placed in viewing clients in human rather than behavioural terms and on authentic counsellor–client relationships.

Existential counsellors seek to assist clients to understand their inner conflicts in relation to the ultimate existential concerns of death, freedom, isolation and meaninglessness. They attempt to identify clients' maladaptive defence mechanisms and help raise awareness of their negative consequences. As well as assisting clients to develop other ways of coping with primary or existential anxiety, existential counsellors work to lessen secondary anxiety by correcting restrictive ways of relating to self and others. Counsellors may use a variety of interventions employed by other approaches so long as they are consistent with a basic existential framework.

An obvious case of the appropriate use of an existential approach to counselling is when clients face boundary situations associated with ultimate concerns. Such existential crises include death, personal and work transitions, irreversible decisions and becoming unexpectedly isolated, among others. The decision to work on existential conflicts should be a joint counsellor–client decision. Long-term counselling is most appropriate for thoroughly addressing existential issues. However, aspects of an existential approach, for instance an emphasis on responsibility and authenticity, can also be incorporated into briefer counselling.

The counsellor–client relationship

The quality of the counsellor–client relationship is central to existential counselling. The counselling relationship is not viewed in terms of transference and little time is spent trying to dig up clients' pasts. Since existential counsellors emphasize the depth of confrontations with ultimate concerns at the given moment, they try to understand their clients' *current* situations and enveloping fears.

Presence, authenticity and commitment are words that describe the quality of relationship that existential counsellors strive to offer. Existential counselling conducted on an individual basis takes place between two real people. The existential counsellor is not a shadowy reflector but a live human who tries to understand and experience the client's being. May believes that any counsellor is existential who, despite technical knowledge, can still relate to clients 'as "one existence communicating with another", to use Binswanger's phrase' (May *et al.*, 1958, p. 81).

Counsellors who are present to clients do not impose their own thoughts and feelings on them. Nor do they transfer to clients thoughts and feelings coming from previous relationships, which is sometimes called *countertransference*. Yalom (1989) recalls that he had always been repelled by fat women and had to work through these feelings to be fully present to a grossly overweight client who entered his office. Furthermore, existential counsellors are conscious that clients have many ways of inviting involvement with counsellors in order to avoid their own problems.

Yalom (1980) talks about surreptitious 'throw-ins' making all the difference in counselling. He cites a number of critical incidents in counselling in which counsellors showed their commitment and engaged their clients in human rather than stereotyped encounters. An example is that of a counsellor seeing an acutely ill client for a long emergency session on a Saturday afternoon. In Yalom's case study *Every Day Gets a Little Closer* (Yalom & Elkins, 1974), written from both the counsellor's and the client's perspectives, he was struck by the importance his client attached to small personal touches such as warm looks and compliments about the way she looked. In addition to presence, characteristics of good counsellor–client relationships include: caring, extending oneself, touching clients at a profound level and wisdom (Yalom, 1980). Counsellors help clients 'by being lovingly present with that person; by being trustworthy, interested; and by believing that their joint activity will ultimately be redemptive and healing' (Yalom, 1989, p. 227).

Self-disclosure

Counsellor self-disclosure is an important issue in existential counselling. The overriding goal is that of an authentic relationship in the client's best interests. Existential counsellors can use two kinds of self-disclosure. First, they can disclose information about their own struggles to come to terms with existential ultimate concerns and be human. Yalom (1989) regards himself as having erred on the side of too little self-disclosure and writes that 'whenever I have shared a great deal of myself, patients have invariably profited . . .' (p. 164). Second, existential counsellors can have a process as contrasted with a content focus. They can use their thoughts and feelings about what is going on in the here-and-now to try to improve the counselling relationship. For instance, Yalom (1989) felt bored with his overweight client, Betty. First he tried to sort out how much of his boredom was countertransference. Then, he pinpointed two reasons for his boredom: Betty was always revealing something that occurred elsewhere, and she hid behind a mask of false gaiety. He tactfully confronted

Betty by saying that he thought she masked her pain by staying jolly and asking her permission to interrupt and point out when she was entertaining him the moment it occurred. This self-disclosure acted as a springboard for deepening their relationship.

Counselling and death

Gains from increased death awareness

Increased awareness of death can lead to heightened appreciation of life. Terminally ill cancer patients react to the diagnosis in varying ways. Many patients do not fully hear what their doctors say. Some are flooded with existential terror. Others acknowledge the news briefly, regroup their defences, engage in internal processing, and then are ready for more information. Many cancer patients are able to use their illness as an opportunity for personal growth. They reassess priorities; choose not to do the trivial; gain an enhanced sense of living in the present; become more in touch with nature; communicate more deeply with loved ones; and have fewer interpersonal fears about rejection and taking risks. Mechanisms for change in cancer patients include the belief that existence cannot be postponed and the wisdom of counting your blessings. Increased death awareness can also bring about a radical shift in perspective in clients who are not terminally ill.

Approaches to increasing death awareness

Yalom cites as a good working rule for clinicians: 'death anxiety is inversely proportional to life satisfaction' (Yalom, 1980, p. 207). Approaches to increasing death awareness may increase clients' anxiety in the short term. The objective is not to anaesthetize the anxiety but to help clients come to terms with it and use it constructively. The following are some ways used by existential counsellors to increase clients' death awareness.

• *Giving permission.* Existential counsellors can cue clients that discussion of issues concerning death is valued in counselling. Some of this cuing may be by encouraging and showing interest in clients' disclosures in the area. Another part of giving permission is that of avoiding colluding in clients' denial of death. Counsellors can play active roles in keeping counselling superficial. They require the ability to tolerate their own death anxiety to follow adequately clients' leads. Some counsellors may require further personal counselling until they work through personally and professionally debilitating death anxiety blockages.

• *Identifying defence mechanisms.* Two of the main defence mechanisms against death anxiety are the belief in specialness and the belief in the existence of an ultimate rescuer. Existential counsellors collaborate with clients to identify such maladaptive defence mechanisms and their negative consequences. Clients are assisted to acknowledge the reality of their finiteness rather than deny it. Existential counsellors require tact, persistence and good timing to help clients to identify and relinquish childlike ways of viewing death.

• *Working with dreams.* Existential counsellors encourage clients to share their dreams. In dreams and nightmares unconscious themes can appear without being repressed or heavily edited. Death themes are common in dreams and nightmares. Discussion and analysis of dreams relates to clients' current existential conflicts. However, clients are not always ready to deal with the material revealed in the dreams. Marvin was a 64-year-old client of Yalom's (Yalom, 1989). The following is a nightmare of his, Yalom's private reflections about it, and what happened afterwards.

Marvin's nightmare (p. 242):

> The two men are tall, pale and very gaunt. In a dark meadow they glide along in silence. They are dressed entirely in black. With tall black stovepipe hats, long-tailed coats, black spats and shoes, they resemble Victorian undertakers or temperance workers. Suddenly they come upon a carriage, ebony black, cradling a baby girl swaddled in black gauze. Wordlessly, one of the men begins to push the carriage. After a short distance he stops, walks around to the front, and, with his black cane, which now has a glowing white tip, he leans over, parts the gauze, and methodically inserts the white tip into the baby's vagina.

Yalom's private reflections about the meaning of Marvin's nightmare (p. 245):

> I am old, I am at the end of my life's work. I have no children, and I approach death full of dread. I am choking on darkness. I am choking on the silence of death. I think I know a way. I try to pierce the blackness with my sexual talisman. But it is not enough.

Afterwards, when Yalom asked Marvin to associate to his dream he said nothing. When Marvin was then asked what he made of all the death imagery, he preferred to discuss the dream from the perspective of sex rather than of death.

• *Working with reminders of finiteness.* Counsellors can assist clients to identify and constructively deal with their death anxiety by being 'tuned-into' the signs of mortality that are parts of normal life. The death of loved ones can be a powerful reminder of personal mortality. The death of parents means that ours is the next generation to die. The death of children can invoke a sense of powerlessness in relation to cosmic indifference. Also, where it is an only child who dies, parents realize that they will not be immortal through passing on their seed. In addition, severe illness can confront clients with their finiteness and vulnerability.

Transitions remind clients of their mortality. Such transitions include the passage from adolescence to adulthood, commitment to a permanent relationship, children leaving home, and marital separation and divorce. In middle age many clients become more aware of death, realizing that they are no longer growing up but instead growing old. In addition, retirement or unexpected career threats can powerfully increase death awareness.

In daily life reminders of the passage of time are ever present. Physical signs of ageing – for instance greying, wrinkling, skin plaques, stiffening of the joints, loss of stamina, poorer eyesight – shatter the illusion of permanent youthfulness. Going to reunions shows that everyone else is ageing. Frequently, since they are milestones of the ageing process, birthdays and anniversaries can generate existence pain as well as or instead of joy.

• *Aids to increasing death awareness.* While many existential counsellors would not use artificial aids to increase clients' death awareness, some counsellors use them. Clients can be asked to write their obituaries or fill out death anxiety questionnaires. In addition they can be taken on guided fantasies regarding their deaths, imagining 'where', 'when', 'how', and the funeral. Yalom (1980) describes two different ways of getting clients to interact with the dying: observing a group of terminally ill people and introducing a person with terminal cancer into an everyday counselling group.

• *Desensitizing clients to death.* Counsellors can assist clients to deal with death terror by exposing them over and over to the fear in lessened doses. Yalom (1980) cites that in working with groups of cancer patients, he often has seen their dread gradually diminish through sheer familiarity.

• *Understanding anxieties associated with death.* Counsellors may break down and identify the anxieties associated with death. A distinction needs be made between the true helplessness arising from the fundamental existential fact of death and the ancillary feelings of helplessness. Clients can be encouraged to regain more of a sense of control over aspects of their lives they can influence. Also, clients can be helped to identify and rationally confront their ancillary fears, such as having a painful death, loneliness and concern over loved ones. In the adult's unconscious dwell childlike irrational terrors about death. Such terrors can be brought into the open and assessed realistically.

Counselling and freedom

Counselling in relation to the ultimate concern of freedom focuses on increasing clients' awareness of their responsibility for their lives and on assisting them to assume this responsibility. Yalom (1980) reports that all the research data suggest that successful counselling clients become more aware of their personal responsibility for their lives. Counsellors can use a wide variety of techniques to assist in the awareness and assumption of responsibility.

• *Identifying defences and methods of responsibility avoidance.* Counsellors can help clients to understand the functions of certain of their behaviours, for instance compulsiveness, in avoiding responsibility for choices. In addition, counsellors can explore with and, if necessary, confront clients with their responsibility for their own distress. For instance, when lonely clients keep belittling others, the counsellor can say 'And you are lonely'.

A general guideline is that when clients complain about their situations, counsellors enquire about how they created them. In addition, counsellors can focus on how clients use responsibility avoidance language: for instance, saying 'I can't' instead of 'I won't'.

• *Identifying responsibility avoidance in the here-and-now.* Clients' responsibility avoidances can manifest themselves in the counsellor–client relationship. Counsellors need awareness of their own feelings about clients to identify how they might elicit similar reactions from others. For instance, a woman with a history of relating to abusive men may distort her perception of her male counsellor and behave towards him in ways that, in another context, might elicit the abuse she dreads. Counsellors can also confront clients with their here-and-now attempts to transfer responsibility for what happens either inside or outside of counselling on to them. If so, counsellors may need to work through clients' resistances such as 'If I knew what to do, I wouldn't need to be here.'

• *Confronting realistic limitations.* All human beings have realistic adverse circumstances with which to deal. Counselling can help clients to change their attitude to or reconstrue external circumstances that they cannot alter. In addition, counsellors can assist clients in identifying areas in their lives that they can influence. For instance, counsellors dealing with cancer patients can assist them to assume more responsibility for their relationships to their doctors, such as assertively requesting information about their illness.

• *Confronting existential guilt.* Existential counsellors view one of the functions of anxiety as a call to conscience. One source of anxiety is guilt about failure to actualize potential. For instance, a client who engaged in compulsive sexual behaviour also had difficulty being assertive in his business life. Identifying how he transgressed his potential as a human being through limiting his life through compulsive sex was the springboard for his gaining the confidence to become more assertive. No longer was the client inwardly terrified about exposure of all the shameful episodes in his life. As his compulsiveness declined, his sense of being a chooser increased. A distinction exists between guilt for bad choices made in the past and refusal to make new choices. So long as clients continue to behave in the present as they did in the past, then they cannot forgive themselves for their past choices.

• *Freeing up wishing.* Wishing precedes willing (May, 1969). However, for clients to wish they need to be in touch with how they feel. Working with affect-blocked clients can be a slow and repetitive process. Dramatic breakthrough methods are avoided since their effects tend not to be sustained. Instead, within the context of authentic relationships, existential counsellors explore the source and nature of clients' blocks and the underlying feelings they try to express. In addition, counsellors repeatedly ask affect-blocked clients questions like 'What do you feel?' and 'What do you want?'

• *Facilitating deciding.* Existential counsellors encourage clients to see that every action is preceded by decision. Decisions are difficult because alternatives exclude. As such, decisions are boundary situations in which people create themselves, despite their fundamental groundlessness. Many clients paralyse their decision-making capacity through 'what-ifs': for instance, 'What if I lose my job and can't find another?'

Counsellors can assist clients to explore the ramifications of each 'what-if' and analyse the feelings they generate. While ensuring that responsibility for decisions remains with clients, counsellors can assist them to generate and evaluate decision options. Counsellors can encourage clients to make decisions actively in ways that reinforce acceptance of their power and resources.

Where necessary, existential counsellors try to disencumber their clients' wills. Counsellor acceptance is crucial for clients learning to trust their wills and gain the belief that they have a right to act. Following are 'insights' that existential counsellors commonly offer to will-stifled clients: 'Only I can change the world I have created'. 'There is no danger in change', 'To get what I really want, I must change', and 'I have the power to change'. Decisions to change may take place over a considerable period of time.

Counselling and isolation

Following are ways in which existential counsellors assist clients in confronting and dealing better with the ultimate concern of isolation.

• *Confronting isolation.* Counsellors can help clients realize that, ultimately, everyone is alone. Clients can learn both what they can and what they cannot obtain from relationships. Counsellors can ask clients to experiment with periods of self-enforced isolation in appropriate doses. Benefits of this experiment can include increased awareness both of the terror of loneliness and of hidden resources and courage.

• *Identifying defence mechanisms.* Clients can be helped to identify defences that they use to cope with the conflict between the need to belong and the fact of existential isolation. Becoming aware that existing in the eyes of others, fusion with others and compulsive sexuality are defence mechanisms against existential anxiety can act as a springboard for doing something about them.

• *Identifying interpersonal pathology.* Using the ideal of a need-free or 'I-thou' relationship as a yardstick, clients' ways of avoiding real relationships with others can be identified. To what extent do they relate to others as objects to satisfy their wants and needs? How well can they love others? How good are they at listening and revealing themselves? What are their specific distancing operations? Counsellors can instruct clients in 'the ABCs of the language of intimacy . . .' (Yalom, 1989, p. 43). Such ABCs include how to own and express feelings.

• *Using the counsellor–client relationship to illuminate pathology.* Existential counsellors have reservations about seeing clients as transferring feelings and attitudes from important past relationships on to them. Instead they prefer to use the counsellor–client relationship to illuminate pathology that may interfere with current and future relationships. Frequently clients distort aspects of their relationship with their counsellors. Counsellors can raise clients' awareness of such distortions, including their consequences for other relationships.

• *The healing relationship.* As mentioned earlier, existential counsellors strive to develop real relationships with clients. Even though counsellor–client relationships are temporary, the experience of intimacy can be permanent. The relationship can be powerfully affirming for clients because someone whom they respect and who *really* knows them fully accepts them. Counsellors who have deep relationships with clients can help them face their existential isolation. Also, they help clients realize that they alone are responsible for their lives.

Counselling and meaninglessness

Following are some ways in which existential counsellors work with clients complaining of lack of meaning in their lives.

• *Redefining the problem.* When clients complain that 'life has no meaning', they appear to assume that life has a meaning that they cannot find. The existential position is that people are meaning-giving rather than meaning-getting. Existential counsellors raise clients' awareness that there is no inherent meaning in life, but that they are responsible for creating their own meaning. Frequently, what is subsumed under meaninglessness is best pursued under the other ultimate concerns of death, freedom and isolation.

• *Identifying meaninglessness anxiety defences.* Existential counsellors can assist clients to become more aware of their meaninglessness anxiety defences. To what extent does their search for money, pleasure, power, recognition and status stem from their failure to confront the existential issue of meaninglessness? Clients can be helped to recognize the consequences and costs of their defences. Their defences against meaninglessness may contribute to their leading superficial lives that create the very problems that consciously or unconsciously they seek to avoid.

• *Assisting engagement in life.* Counsellors should approach the problem of meaninglessness by assisting their clients to become more engaged in the stream of life. They should assume that the desire to engage in life is always present in clients. Counsellors can offer clients authentic relationships that demonstrate their own engagement in the counselling process. They can explore clients' long range hopes and goals, belief systems, capacity to love and attempts to express themselves creatively. In addition they can identify and try to remove blocks in their clients' progress towards engagement. Clients may find insufficient meaning in their relationships, work, leisure, creative pursuits and religious strivings. Each area can be analysed for obstacles that clients can then work to remove.

Group counselling

Often existential counselling is conducted in counselling groups of eight to ten members. Counselling groups provide here-and-now information on members' ways of avoiding or assuming responsibility. Also, the interactional format of groups gives counsellors and members opportunities to observe and work on interpersonal distortions and maladaptive behaviours. Existential group counsellors attempt to take group members through the following sequence: learning how their behaviour (1) is viewed by others, (2) makes others feel, (3) creates the opinions others have of them, and (4) influences their opinions of themselves. In addition, groups can work on issues surrounding the ultimate concerns of death and meaninglessness. For instance, in groups of cancer patients the issue of confronting death is likely to be a major area for work.

CHAPTER REVIEW AND SELF-REFERENT QUESTIONS

Chapter review questions

1. What does the word existential mean?

2. What are the characteristics of the three forms of being-in-the-world?

3. How is normal anxiety distinguished from neurotic anxiety?

4. What is meant by existential guilt?

5. What are the characteristics of each of the four existential ultimate concerns?

6. What are the inner conflicts associated with each of the four existential ultimate concerns?

7. When growing up, how do people learn about how to cope with death?

8. What factors in contemporary society contribute to existential anxiety about freedom, isolation, and meaninglessness?

9. What are existential psychodynamics and what is the existential model of defence mechanisms?

10. What are some death anxiety defences?

11. What are some freedom anxiety defences?

12. What are some existential isolation anxiety defences?

13. What are some meaninglessness anxiety defences?

14. What are the goals of existential counselling?

15. What are desirable characteristics of existential counsellor–client relationships?

16. Describe some potentially beneficial outcomes for clients of increased death awareness.

17. Describe approaches existential counsellors can take for working with clients' death anxiety.

18. Describe approaches existential counsellors can take to enhance clients' responsibility awareness and assumption.

19. Describe approaches existential counsellors can take for working with clients' problems of existential isolation.

20. Describe approaches existential counsellors can take for working with clients' problems of meaninglessness.

21. What are some uses of existential group counselling?

Self-referent questions

1. To what extent do you experience your existence as real? Answer as specifically as possible.

2. To what extent and in what ways do you experience existential anxiety? What are some of your main defences against existential anxiety?

3. Assess the degree to which you currently take personal responsibility for making or creating your existence. In what ways might you engage in less responsibility avoidance and in greater responsibility assumption?

4. Do you consider that meaninglessness is a major problem for people in Western society? If so, how does this affect you personally?

5. What relevance, if any, has the theory and practice of Yalom and May's existential counselling for how you counsel?

6. What relevance, if any, has the theory and practice of Yalom and May's existential counselling for how you live?

Annotated bibliography

Yalom, I.D. (1980). *Existential Psychotherapy*. New York: Basic Books.
This book is a major contribution to the counselling literature. It develops a psychodynamic theory of existential anxiety centred on humans' confrontations with the ultimate concerns of death, freedom, isolation and meaninglessness. The book suggests ways in which existential counsellors assist clients to confront and come to terms with each of these sources of existential anxiety. Both theory and practice are illuminated by numerous vignettes and case examples.

Yalom, I.D. (1989). *Love's Executioner and Other Tales of Psychotherapy*. London: Bloomsbury.
The human face of existential counselling. A series of beautifully written case studies in which Yalom works with his clients. Both counsellor and clients come alive as real people struggling with the concerns of existence. The book provides Yalom's insights into 'grey areas' regarding their own behaviour that existential counsellors are likely to face.

May, R. & Yalom, I.D. (1989). Existential psychotherapy. In R.J. Corsini & D. Wedding (Eds.), *Current Psychotherapies* (4th ed., pp. 363–402). Itasca, IL: Peacock.
This chapter provides an overview of the theory and practice of May and Yalom's approach to existential counselling.

May, R., Angel, E. & Ellenberger, H.F. (Eds.) (1958). *Existence: A New Dimension in Psychiatry and Psychology*. New York: Basic Books.
May authored the first two of the ten chapters in this book. Chapter 1 is on 'The origins and significance of the existential movement in psychology'. Chapter 2 is on 'Contributions to existential psychotherapy'. Both are important contributions for the serious student of the theory and practice of existential counselling.

May, R. (1950). *The Meaning of Anxiety*. (rev. ed. 1977). New York: Ronald Press.
This book was an early presentation of the importance of anxiety as a normal as well as a neurotic condition. The first part, entitled 'modern interpretations of anxiety', looks at its roots in philosophy, biology, psychology and contemporary culture. The book's second part, entitled 'clinical analysis of anxiety', presents a series of case studies and May's conclusions about anxiety drawn from them.

Further references

Yalom

Lieberman, M.A., Yalom, I.D. & Miles, M.B. (1973). *Encounter Groups: First Facts.* New York: Basic Books.

Yalom, I.D. (1983). *Inpatient Group Psychotherapy.* New York: Basic Books.

Yalom, I.D. (1985). *The Theory and Practice of Group Psychotherapy.* (3rd ed.). New York: Basic Books.

Yalom, I.D. (1991). *When Nietzsche Wept.* New York: Basic Books.

Yalom, I.D. & Elkins, G. (1974). *Every Day Gets a Little Closer.* New York: Basic Books.

Yalom, I.D. & Vinogradov, S. (1989). *Concise Guide to Group Psychotherapy.* Washington, DC: American Psychiatric Press.

May

May, R. (1939). *The Art of Counseling.* Nashville: Cokesbury.

May, R. (1953). *Man's Search for Himself.* New York: Norton.

May, R. (1967). *Psychology and the Human Dilemma.* Princeton, NJ: Van Nostrand.

May, R. (1969). *Love and Will.* New York: Norton.

May, R. (1972). *Power and Innocence: A Search for the Sources of Violence.* New York: Norton.

May, R. (1975). *The Courage to Create.* New York: Norton.

May, R. (1977). *The Meaning of Anxiety.* (rev. ed.). New York: Norton.

May, R. (1981). *Freedom and Destiny.* New York: Norton.

May, R. (1985). *My Quest for Beauty.* New York: Norton.

Rabinowitz, F.E., Good, G. & Cozad, L. (1989). Rollo May: A man of myth and meaning. *Journal of Counseling and Development, 67,* 436–41. (Interview with Rollo May).

Others

Buber, M. (1965). *Between Man and Man.* New York: Macmillan.

Buber, M. (1970). *I and Thou.* New York: Charles Scribner.

Bugental, J. (1956). *The Search for Existential Identity.* New York: Holt, Rinehart & Winston.

Bugental, J. (1976). *The Search for Authenticity.* New York: Holt, Rinehart & Winston.

Bugental, J.F.T. (1987). *The Art of the Psychotherapist.* New York: Norton.

Deurzen-Smith, E. (1988). *Existential Counselling in Practice.* London: Sage.

Heidegger, M. (1962). *Being and Time.* London: SCM Press.

Kierkegaard, S. (1954). *Fear and Trembling and the Sickness unto Death.* Garden City, NY: Doubleday.

Sartre, J.P. (1956). *Being and Nothingness.* New York: Philosophical Library.

Tillich, P. (1952). *The Courage to Be.* New Haven, CT: Yale University Press.

SEVEN

Logotherapy

PREVIEW

- *Logotherapy's purpose is to assist clients in their search for meaning. The will to meaning is the primary motivational force in humans. The search for meaning involves both conscious activity and getting in touch with the spiritual unconscious.*

- *Conscience, the origins of which are located in the spiritual unconscious, can intuitively reveal an individual's unique meanings in specific situations. The religious unconscious exists within the spiritual unconscious.*

- *Human freedom is 'freedom to' accept responsibility for fulfilling meaning within the confines of death and destiny. Self-transcendence, in which people reach out for meaning beyond themselves, is an essential characteristic of human existence. Sources of meaning include: work, love, suffering, the past, and the supra-meaning.*

- *The existential vacuum occurs when people suffer from an inner void and lack meaning in life. Existential frustration results when the will to meaning is frustrated. The existential vacuum is not in itself neurotic but can lead to noogenic neurosis. Humanity is becoming more neurotic and the mass neurotic triad consists of depression, addiction and aggression.*

- *Causes of the existential vacuum include the weak instinctual basis of human behaviour compared to other animals, the erosion of values and traditions, and tendencies to reductionism where humans are viewed as determined rather than determining.*

- *Ways in which people maintain the existential vacuum include repression, avoiding responsibility and insufficiently emphasizing self-transcendence.*

- *The goal of logotherapy for the existential vacuum and noogenic neuroses is to help clients find meaning in their lives. Logotherapists are responsibility educators. In addition, goals for the psychogenic neuroses and somatogenic psychoses are described.*

- *Within the context of humane relationships, logotherapy for existential concerns focuses on increasing existential awareness and on assisting clients to finding meaning. Methods for focusing on meaning include: teaching clients the importance of assuming responsibility for meaning, helping clients listen to their consciences, asking clients about meanings, broadening horizons about sources of meaning, eliciting meaning through Socratic questioning, using logodrama, offering meanings, and analysing dreams.*

- *Paradoxical intention and dereflection are logotherapeutic techniques for working with psychogenic neuroses.*

- *Medical ministry, in which logotherapists assist clients to find meaning in the suffering, is advocated for somatogenic psychoses.*

INTRODUCTION

The last chapter focused on Yalom and May's existential approach to counselling. This chapter focuses on another leading approach, Viktor Frankl's logotherapy. Logotherapy is sometimes called the third Viennese school of psychotherapy, the other two being Freud's psychoanalysis and Adler's individual psychology. Another way of viewing logotherapy is that it is a supplement rather than a replacement for psychotherapy (Frankl, 1975a). Logos is a Greek word that connotes both 'meaning' and 'spirit', the latter without any primary religious connotation. Humans are meaning seeking beings and the search for meaning in itself is not pathological. Existence confronts people with the need to find meaning in their lives. The main purpose of logotherapy is to assist clients in their search for meaning.

Viktor Frankl

Viktor E. Frankl was born on 26 March 1905 in Vienna, Austria, the son of Jewish parents. As a schoolboy he corresponded with Freud and, in 1924, his first article was published at Freud's invitation in the *International Journal of Psychoanalysis*. Frankl was both influenced by and reacted against some of the ideas of Freud and Adler. In addition, he was influenced by the existential philosophers, such as Heidegger, Jaspers and Scheler. The origins of logotherapy go back to Frankl's early struggles to find meaning in his own existence. Frankl readily confesses that when a young man '. . . I had to go through the hell of despair over the apparent meaninglessness of life, through total and ultimate nihilism, until I could develop an immunity against nihilism. I developed logotherapy.' (Frankl, 1988, p. 166).

He coined the term logotherapy in the 1920s and in the 1930s used the word *Existenzanalyse,* existential analysis, as an alternative word for logotherapy. To avoid confusion he mostly refrains from using the term existential analysis in his English-language publications. In 1928 Frankl founded the Youth Advisement Centres in Vienna, heading them until 1938. In 1930 he received his MD from the University of Vienna. From 1930–8 he was on the staff of the Neuropsychiatric University Clinic. From 1938–42 he was Specialist in Neurology and Psychiatry, and then Head of the Neurological Department, at the Jewish Hospital in Vienna. During this time he wrote the draft of his first book. Shortly before America entered the Second World War, Frankl was given the opportunity to immigrate to the United States. He let this opportunity pass because he chose to abide by the commandment 'Honor father and mother and you will dwell in the land' (Frankl, 1988, p. 59). He thought that, by retaining his hospital position, he might protect his parents from being sent to a concentration camp.

From 1942 to 1945 Frankl had the harrowing experience of being imprisoned in Nazi concentration camps, including Auschwitz and Dachau (Frankl, 1963). On arrival at Auschwitz, Frank was shaved of all his body hair. He was number 119,194. The manuscript of his first book was confiscated. During the next three years he survived selections of who should live or die, forced labour, brutal Capos (guards), beatings, malnutrition, disease, the vagaries of fate and the existential challenge to find meaning in his suffering. Most of the time his work consisted of digging and laying tracks for railway lines. Only in the last few weeks of his internment did he work as a doctor.

During this period Frankl had the opportunity to observe human nature under extreme circumstances. Most prisoners made the choice to vegetate. However, other prisoners deepened spiritually and took the camps' difficulties as tests of their inner strength. They rose to the challenge of finding meaning in their lives. Frankl quotes Nietzsche: 'He who has a *why* to live for can bear almost any *how*' (Frankl, 1963, p. 121). Despite adversity, these prisoners retained their freedom to choose both in their inner life and in how they behaved towards others. They turned their tragedies into triumphs. Though Frankl managed to survive, his parents, brother and wife died in concentration camps. His sister was the only other surviving family member.

In 1946 Frankl became Head of the Department of Neurology at the Poliklinik Hospital in Vienna. In 1947 he was appointed Assistant Professor of Psychiatry and Neurology at the University of Vienna and, in 1955, full Professor. Frankl has been president of the Austrian Medical Society of Psychotherapy. In addition, he has been Distinguished Professor of Logotherapy at the US International University in California and also Visiting Professor at Stanford, Harvard, and Duquesne universities, among others. Frankl has lectured widely in Europe, Australia, South America, Asia and Africa.

Frankl has been a prolific author writing over 30 books, some of which have been translated into many languages, and numerous articles. His books include *The Doctor and the Soul: From Psychotherapy to Logotherapy, Man's Search for Meaning: An Introduction to Logotherapy* (which by 1992 had sold over five million copies), *Psychotherapy and Existentialism: Selected Papers on Logotherapy, The Will to Meaning: Foundations and Applications of Logotherapy, The Unconscious God: Psychotherapy and Theology,* and *The Unheard Cry of Meaning: Psychotherapy and Humanism.* Frankl has epitomized his life in the following words: 'I have seen the meaning of my life in helping others to see in their lives a meaning' (Frankl, 1988, p. 160).

ASSUMPTIONS
Freedom of will

Frankl uses the term existential in three ways. First, the term existential refers to *existence* itself, which is a specifically human mode of being. Second, existential refers to the *meaning* of existence. Third, existential refers to the striving to find meaning in personal existence or, put another way, the will to meaning. Life is transitory. However, this transitoriness does not make life meaningless. Instead, the transitory aspects of life are potentialities. Humans need to realize the transitory possibilities. They are constantly choosing which of the mass of transitory potentialities will be actualized and which condemned to nonbeing.

Humans possess freedom of will. Alone among animals they possess the capacity for self-detachment. Humans are capable of reflecting upon and judging their choices. What matters is not the particular features of people's character or their drives and instincts but the stand they take towards them. People are free to shape their own characters and responsible for what they make out of themselves. When people rise above the somatic and psychic dimensions of their existence, they enter a new dimension which is termed the noological dimension. In this noological dimension are located distinctly human functions, for instance reflection, the capacity to make self into an object, and conscientiousness.

Will to meaning

The will to meaning is the fundamental motivational force in humans. People are confronted with the need to detect meaning literally until their last breaths. Frankl writes 'Man's search for meaning is a primary force in his life . . . This meaning is unique and specific and can be fulfilled by him alone; only then does it achieve a significance that will satisfy his own will to meaning' (Frankl, 1963, p. 154). As Frankl observed in his concentration camp experiences, people need something to live for. Humans are beings who encounter other people and reach out for meanings to fulfil. However, meaning does not coincide with being, rather it sets the pace for being. Human existence is at risk unless people live in terms of transcendence towards something beyond themselves.

Logotherapy focuses on the will to meaning whereas psychoanalysis focuses on the will to pleasure and individual psychology focuses on the will to power. Frankl acknowledges that Freud and Adler did not use those precise terms. Both pleasure and power are by-products or derivatives of the will to meaning. The will to meaning is not a rationalization of instinctual drives nor concerned with reducing tension and returning to a state of homeostasis. What people need is not a tensionless state but the tension of striving for some meaning that is worthy of them.

The will to meaning also differs as a motivating force from self-actualizing. Frankl views self-actualization as only a side-effect of the will to meaning. People can only actualize themselves to the extent that they fulfil meaning.

Consciousness and the unconscious

What is the source or referent point against which people can detect meaning in their lives? The search for meaning can involve both conscious activity and getting in touch with unconscious layers of the self.

Consciousness

Humans are spiritual beings and logotherapy focuses on their spiritual existence. In this context, the word spirit has no religious connotations. Spiritual phenomena in humans can be either conscious or unconscious. Consciousness implies awareness. Logotherapy aims to increase clients' consciousness of their spiritual selves. Humans need to be conscious of their responsibility for detecting and acting in terms of the unique meaning of their lives in specific situations in which they are involved.

The spiritual unconscious

Each human has an existential, personal spiritual core. Centred around their spiritual core, people are not only individualized but integrated in their somatic, psychic and spiritual aspects. Though the border between the conscious and the unconscious is 'fluid', Frankl regards the spiritual basis of human existence as ultimately unconscious. The deep centre of each human is unconscious.

A sharp distinction exists between the instinctual unconscious and the spiritual unconscious. Freud saw the unconscious as a reservoir of repressed sexual and aggressive instincts. Depth psychology, instead of focusing on repressed instincts, seeks to follow humans into the depths of their spirits. However, the self does not yield to total self-reflection and, in a sense, this makes human existence basically unreflectable. Frankl writes: 'Existence exists in action rather than reflection' (Frankl, 1975a, p. 30).

Conscience

The origins of conscience are located in the spiritual unconscious. Logos is deeper than logic. Existentially authentic decisions take place completely unreflectedly and unconsciously. Frankl writes: 'It is the task of conscience to disclose to man the *unum necesse*, the one thing that is required' (Frankl, 1975a, p. 35). Conscience can intuitively reveal the unique possibilities for meaning to be actualized in specific situations. Conscience or the 'ethical instinct' is highly individual in contrast to the other instincts which work for the greatest number of the species. In addition to moral conscience, Frankl believes love and art are rooted in the emotional, intuitive, nonrational depths of the spiritual unconscious.

Freedom can be considered in terms of 'from what' and 'to what'. The 'to what' is responsibleness to conscience. Conscience has a transcendent quality. People can only be the servants of their conscience when instead of a monologue they can have a dialogue with it as something other than themselves. Through conscience a trans-human agent 'is sounding through' (Frankl, 1975a, p. 53). Conscience has a key position in disclosing the essential transcendence of the spiritual unconscious. Conscience is the voice of transcendence and is itself transcendent.

The religious unconscious

The existential analysis of dreams makes obvious the fact of repressed and unconscious religiousness. Not only is *libido* repressed but also *religio*. Conscience is not the last 'to what' of responsibleness. Though humans are responsible for themselves, they are not responsible before themselves. This 'to what' of responsibleness is prior to responsibleness itself. Unconscious religiousness, or the religious unconscious, exists within the spiritual unconscious. Humans have always stood in an intentional relation to transcendence, even if only on an unconscious level. This 'unconscious God' is hidden in two ways. First, the human relationship to God is hidden. Second, God is hidden. Even in highly irreligious people, religiousness is latent.

The religious unconscious is an existential agent rather than an instinctual factor. Frankl calls it 'a deciding being unconscious rather than a being driven by the unconscious' (Frankl, 1975a, p. 65). In relation to Jung, he stresses that unconscious religiousness stems from the personal centre of each individual rather than from an impersonal pool of images shared by mankind.

Repression of religiousness, as with repression of other aspects of the unconscious, leads to neurosis: ' . . . once the angel in us is repressed, he turns into a demon' (Frankl, 1975a, p. 70). The existentiality of religiousness needs to be spontaneous. Genuine religiousness must unfold at its own pace. Humans commit themselves to it by choosing to be religious.

Meaning of life and death

Meaning of life

Frankl writes that 'being human means being responsible for fulfilling the meaning potential inherent in a given life situation' (Frankl, 1975a, p. 125). Being human means being at the same time different, conscious and responsible. The concept of responsibility is the foundation of human existence. Human freedom is not a 'freedom from', but rather a 'freedom to', namely the freedom to accept responsibility. Freedom is what people 'are': it is not something that they 'have' and can therefore lose. People have many potentialities within them. They are not fully conditioned or determined. Rather, moment by moment they are free to decide what they will become in the next moment. Their decisions determine which of their potentialities gets actualized. During no stage of their lives can people 'escape the mandate to choose among possibilities' (Frankl, 1955, p. 85).

All the time people are questioned by life. The way to respond is by being responsible for their lives. Working with the matter that fate has supplied them, people are like sculptors who chisel out and hammer unshaped stone so that it takes more and more form. Though always surrounded by biological, sociological and psychological restrictions, humans can either conquer and shape them or deliberately choose to submit to them.

Meaning of death

Death does not rob life of its meaning. If people were immortal they might put off doing things indefinitely. Death belongs to life and gives it meaning. People's responsibility springs from their finiteness. Consequently, they need to realize the full gravity of the responsibility that they bear throughout every moment of their lives. Destiny, like death, is essential to the meaning of life. Destiny refers to those factors that are beyond people' power. Freedom can be viewed not only in the contexts of life and death but also in the context of destiny. The opportunities and tribulations that come people's way are unique. Nevertheless, people still can exercise their inner freedom to take a stand against their destiny.

Self-transcendence

Self-transcendence is an essential characteristic of human existence. Humans are essentially beings who reach out beyond themselves. They become most human when they transcend the boundaries of their selves by either fulfilling a meaning or encountering another person lovingly. Frankl sees the basic human need as a search for meaning rather than a search for the self. Identity is only achievable through being responsible for the fulfilment of meaning. People can become overly focused on themselves. The self-transcendent quality of human life is most apparent when people forget themselves. Frankl regarded the main lesson he learned from Auschwitz and Dachau was that unless life pointed to something beyond itself, survival was pointless, meaningless and impossible.

Suffering from neurotic problems that reflect difficulties in self-transcendence is the converse of people finding meaning by transcending themselves. Hyperreflection and hyperintention are two of the main ways in which people choose not to transcend themselves. Hyperreflection is a tendency to overbearing self-reflection. Hyperintention is a tendency to pay excessive attention to achieving that which one desires.

Sources of meaning

Frankl suggests that self-transcendence is achievable by discovering or detecting meaning in three different ways: by doing a deed, by experiencing a value, and by suffering (Frankl, 1963). Elsewhere Frankl (1967, 1988) talks of three principal ways in which people can find meaning in life: (1) by what they give to life (creative values); (2) by what they take from life (experiential values); and (3) through the stand they take towards a fate they can no longer change, for instance an inoperable cancer (attitudinal values). In addition, past experiences and religion are two further areas in which people can discover meaning.

Meaning in work

Work is a major area in which people can reach out beyond themselves. The meaning of work goes beyond a particular occupation to include the manner in which people bring their unique human qualities to their work. For instance, a nurse may go beyond her regimented duties to say a kind word to a critically ill patient. Frankl views all work as allowing such opportunities, though he acknowledges that some jobs are very routine. In such instances, much creative meaning may need to be found in leisure pursuits.

Unemployment is an example of how people can be affected by lack of creative meaning. Frankl views unemployment neurosis, characterized by apathy and depression, as an existential position. Some people respond to the existential challenge of unemployment by remaining active and involved and so stay free of unemployment neurosis. Employment can also be for good or ill. Some people run away from the emptiness of their existence by taking refuge in their work or profession. Achieving creative meaning in life is not synonymous with work satisfaction alone.

Meaning in love

Unlike in psychoanalysis, in logotherapy love is not regarded as a secondary phenomenon to sex. While sex can be an expression of mature love, it is not a form of love in itself. Love as a form of self-transcendence has various characteristics. It entails relating to another person as a spiritual being. As such, love involves understanding or grasping the inner core of the personality of another person. People are moved to the depths of their spiritual beings by their partner's spiritual core. Infatuation seldom lasts long. When gratified, the sex drive vanishes promptly. Love, however, has a quality of permanence in that the spiritual core of the other person is unique and irreplaceable. Furthermore, love can outlast death in that the essence of the unique being of the beloved is timeless and imperishable.

Another characteristic of love is that, since it is directed at what the other 'is' rather than at the other as a possession, it leads to a monogamous attitude. A further characteristic is that it involves seeing the potential in the beloved and helping him or her achieve this potential. In addition, in a real love relationship there is no room for jealousy since the other person is not treated as a possession.

Frankl (1967) is at pains to point out that love is not the only and not even the best way to fill life with meaning. However, he distinguishes between neurotic failure and failure to attain love imposed by destiny.

Meaning in suffering

Human destiny has a twofold meaning: to be shaped where possible and to be endured where necessary. Attitudinal values are inherent in the stand that people take to circumstances that they cannot change, for instance an incurable illness or concentration camp internment. Through attitudinal values even the tragic aspects of human existence – the 'tragic triad' of pain, guilt and death – can be turned into something positive and creative. However, people need be careful not to accept fate too readily. The time to enlist attitudinal values is only when they can be certain that they cannot alter their fates.

Inescapable negative situations give people the opportunity 'to actualize the highest value, to fulfill the deepest meaning, the meaning of suffering' (Frankl, 1963, p. 178). People have choices in how they respond to suffering. For instance, life can retain meaning up to the last moment for people with terminal illnesses who accept the challenge to suffer bravely. Frankl quotes Goethe: 'There is no predicament that we cannot ennoble either by doing or enduring' (Frankl, 1955, p. 115). Some people can rise to the challenge of suffering and grow richer and stronger because of it. Though people may be helpless victims of fate, they can still exercise the inner freedom to turn their predicaments into accomplishments at the human level.

Meaning from the past

Though the search for meaning is primarily oriented towards people's futures, the past can still be a source of meaning. Often people discount their past experiences as a source of meaning. In Auschwitz concentration camp, Frankl went through considerable soul searching about the meaning of suffering when the manuscript of his first book was confiscated. However, he came to realize that nothing in his past was lost but was in fact irrevocably stored. The meaning of his life did not depend on whether a manuscript of his was printed. His experiences in the past constituted a full granary. Often in times of suffering, but not always so, the search for meaning can entail acknowledging and identifying sources of meaning in the past relevant to creating meaning in the present. Even short lives can still have pasts full of meaning. However, for those who have led sterile lives, their unconditional faith in an unconditional meaning may turn their failure into a triumph (Frankl, 1988).

The supra-meaning

People are incapable of understanding the ultimate meaning of human suffering. However, that does not mean that suffering does not have an ultimate meaning. Frankl (1963, 1988) uses the term supra-meaning to denote the ultimate meaning of suffering and life. People cannot break through the dimensional differences between the human world and the divine world. The supra-meaning can only be grasped by faith and not by intellectual means. Unlike in secular existential philosophy, the human task is not to endure life's meaninglessness. Instead people need to bear their inability to grasp in rational terms life's ultimate meaningfulness. Trust in God precedes people's ability to have faith in life's ultimate meaning. As always, the infinite God is silent rather than dead.

The trend in modern life is not away from religion but away from an emphasis on differences between individual denominations. Frankl (1988) does not advocate a form of universal religion. Instead he sees a trend towards a profoundly personalized religion in which people address themselves to the ultimate being in their own individual language and words.

The existential vacuum

The existential vacuum describes a state in which people complain of an inner void. They suffer from a sense of meaninglessness, emptiness and futility. The existential vacuum is an 'abyss experience' in contrast to the peak experience described by Maslow.

Frankl suggests three causes of the existential vacuum. First, unlike other animals, humans are no longer programmed by drives and instincts telling them what to do. Second, humans are no longer told by traditions, conventions and values what they should do. Sometimes they do not know what they wish to do and retreat into conformism, doing what others do, or into totalitarianism, doing what others wish them to do. Third, especially in America, students are exposed to 'reductionism'. Humans are viewed as drives, instincts, creatures of conditioning, reaction formations and defence mechanisms rather than as deciding agents. Frankl cites as an example of reductionism the case of a couple who were told, during the induction into the

American Peace Corps, that they were helping the less privileged because of their unconscious need to prove themselves superior (Frankl, 1975a, p. 94).

Existential frustration

Existential frustration results when the will to meaning is frustrated. Apathy and boredom are the main characteristics of existential frustration. Existential frustration is not in itself pathological nor pathogenic. People's concern, even their despair, over the meaning of their lives is a spiritual distress rather than a disease. Frankl regards the existential vacuum, with its attendant frustration, as 'something sociogenic and not at all a neurosis' (Frankl, 1975a, p. 139). Despair over the meaninglessness of life can be a sign of intellectual sincerity and honesty. In his more recent writings, Frankl (1977, 1988) states that there is no doubt that the existential vacuum is spreading.

Noogenic neurosis

The existential vacuum can lead to neuroticism. The term noogenic neurosis refers to those cases where the existential vacuum leads to clinical symptomatology. Frankl defines the noogenic neurosis as 'a neurosis which is caused by a spiritual problem, a moral or ethical conflict, as for example, a conflict between the mere superego and the true conscience . . .' (Frankl, 1988, p. 89). Existential frustration plays a large part in noogenic neuroses. Such neuroses arise from spiritual conflicts to do with people's aspirations for a meaningful existence and the frustration of their will to meaning. Doctors and counsellors need to distinguish sharply between the spiritual dimension of problems as against the instinctual.

The mass neurotic triad

Frankl speaks of the neuroticization of humanity because of the existential vacuum. The worldwide effects of the existential vacuum go beyond feelings of meaninglessness and noogenic neuroses. Frankl uses the term 'mass neurotic triad' (Frankl, 1975a, p. 96) for the three main effects: depression, addiction and aggression. Regarding depression, there is ample evidence that suicide rates are increasing, especially among the young. Frankl sees the cause as the spreading existential frustration. Regarding addiction, people with low purpose in life are more likely to try to find feelings of meaningfulness in drugs than those with high purpose in life. A frequently cited reason for taking drugs is the desire to find meaning in life. Also, many alcoholics suffer from a sense of meaninglessness in their lives. Regarding aggression, not only does sexual libido thrive in an existential vacuum but 'aggressive destrudo'. Frankl believes that statistical evidence favours his hypothesis that people are most likely to become aggressive when they are caught in feelings of emptiness and meaninglessness.

ACQUISITION

A sense of meaninglessness is not necessarily acquired through learning. It can be part of the human response to life and, if worked through satisfactorily as in Frankl's own case, a growth experience. However, Frankl believes that the existential vacuum and existential frustration are becoming more widespread. Furthermore, there is an increasing neuroticization of humanity. If this is the case, individuals are more likely to acquire a sense of meaninglessness because they grow up in cultures and societies in which it is harder to find meaning than in the past. First, the erosion of traditional values and the tendencies to reductionism make it more difficult for many people to find meaning in their lives. Second, because there are fewer people in society who have satisfactorily found meaning, it is more difficult for young people to grow up learning from models who are successful at realizing the spiritual aspects of themselves. Put another way, young people may suffer from a lack of access to meaning educators and exemplars. Despite Frankl's belief in people's potential humanness, '*humane* humans are, and probably will always remain a minority' (Frankl, 1975a, p. 84).

MAINTENANCE
Maintaining the existential vacuum

How do people maintain their sense of meaninglessness? Some suggestions may be inferred from Frankl's writings.

• *Repression.* Logotherapy concerns itself with the frustration and consequent repression of the will to meaning. Frankl observes 'Not eros but logos is the victim of repression' (Frankl, 1975a, p. 131). People repress their spirituality and religiousness. Thus they remain out of touch with their spiritual centres which are the deepest sources for a sense of meaning. Their repression of the will to meaning blocks their perception of the existence of meaning.

• *Avoiding responsibility.* Among mechanisms mentioned by Frankl for avoiding responsibility for the search for meaning are conformism, totalitarianism, and taking refuge in the neurotic triad of depression, addiction and aggression.

• *Erosion of traditions and values.* The erosion of traditions has a continuing influence on creating and maintaining the existential vacuum.

• *Reductionism.* Reductionist models of psychology and education lead people to believe, and then maintain their beliefs, that they are determined rather than determining.

• *Insufficient emphasis on self-transcendence.* Much of modern psychology focuses on self-actualization and on self-expression. People continue to be insufficiently helped to realize that happiness and fulfilment are by-products of self-transcendence, forgetting oneself rather than excessively focusing on oneself.

• *Neuroticization of humanity.* The fact that problems and symptoms of meaninglessness are widespread makes it harder for individuals to obtain assistance in their personal search for meaning, thus contributing to maintaining their inner void.

PRACTICE
Goals

Frankl divides what he terms mental illness into three categories: noogenic (neurosis), psychogenic (neurosis), and somatogenic (psychosis). The existential vacuum is not a neurosis. However, the goals of logotherapeutic counselling are similar whether the existential vacuum is on its own or is a part of a noogenic neurosis.

Logotherapy is the treatment of choice for dealing with the existential vacuum. The meaning of logotherapy is in helping clients find meaning in their lives. Logotherapeutic counsellors seek to confront and reorient clients towards their life's tasks. Logotherapy is an education for responsibility that seeks to unblock clients' will to meaning. With their will to meaning unblocked, clients are more likely to find ways of self-transcendence through creative, experiential and attitudinal values. Clients need to become aware of their existential responsibleness for finding their life's meaning through their conscience. However, making the spiritual unconscious conscious is only a transitory phase in the counselling process. What counselling seeks to achieve is first to convert an unconscious potential into a conscious act and then to allow it to recede back into an unconscious habit. Frankl (1975a) is at pains to stress that, while a religious counsellor may bring religion into counselling, logotherapeutic counsellors have to refrain from setting preconceived religious goals.

The overcoming of symptoms of existential frustration, such as apathy and boredom, is a by-product of searching for and discovering meaning. Furthermore, when clients find more meaning in their lives, any symptoms they possess from the mass neurotic triad of depression, addiction and aggression are likely to get better if not disappear altogether.

The psychogenic neuroses include obsessive-compulsions and phobias where the counselling goal is to overcome clients' tendencies to hyperintention or trying too hard. Also the psychogenic neuroses include sexual and sleep problems where the goal is to overcome clients' tendencies to hyperreflection or excessive self-consciousness.

With the psychoses, such as endogenous depression and schizophrenia, logotherapy may be used in conjunction with medication that addresses the somatic aspect that has become diseased. Logotherapy itself deals with the healthy part of the personality and frequently its goal is to help clients find meaning in their suffering.

A broader goal of Frankl's logotherapy is the rehumanization of psychiatry. Psychiatrists and counsellors should not view the mind as a mechanism and the treatment of mental illness merely in terms of technique. Within the limits of their environment and endowment, humans are ultimately self-determining. In the concentration camps, some chose to behave like swine and others like saints.

Logotherapy for the existential vacuum

How does the logotherapist deal with clients in states of existential vacuum? Though Frankl has not systematically listed his methods, below are some suggestions drawn from his writings.

A humane relationship

Frankl (1988) observes that counselling usually consists of both strategies and I–Thou relationships. He also stresses that logotherapy cannot become too individualized. Thus, though the logotherapist is a responsibility educator, it is in the context of a committed and caring relationship which respects the uniqueness of each client. Frankl appreciates humane humans and is concerned for the rehumanization of psychiatry. His work shows much compassion and wisdom. By offering humane relationships, logotherapists provide contexts for assisting clients to find their own meanings.

Diagnosing the existential vacuum

Logotherapists are alert to overt signs, for instance saying 'My life lacks meaning' and covert signs, for instance apathy and boredom, that indicate clients feel an inner void. Issues of meaning are considered legitimate areas in which clients can work, though noogenic neuroses account for 'only about 20 percent of the case material accruing to our clinics and offices' (Frankl, 1988, p. 68). Often Frankl reassures 'non-patients' that their existential despair is an achievement rather than neurosis. It is a sign of intellectual depth rather than of superficiality.

Increasing existential awareness

Following are methods by which Frankl increases existential awareness of the finiteness of life and the importance of responsibility.

• *Explaining.* Explaining that finiteness gives meaning to human existence rather than robs life of meaning.

• *Offering maxims.* One of Frankl's leading maxims is 'Live as if you were living for the second time and had acted as wrongly the first time as you are about to act now' (Frankl, 1955, p. 75).

• *Using similes.* Clients can be instructed to imagine their lives as moving pictures that are being 'shot'. However, the irreversibility of life is brought home to them by being told that they cannot 'cut' anything and that nothing can be retrospectively changed. Another simile is that of clients as sculptors who have a limited time span for completing their works of art, but are not informed of when the deadline will be.

Focusing on finding meaning

Frankl stresses that meaning is an individual matter. Logotherapists must both individualize how they work and improvise. Logotherapy is neither teaching, preaching or moral exhortation. Frankl (1963) uses the analogy of the ophthalmologist who enables people to see the world as it really is. Similarly, the logotherapeutic counsellor's role is that of widening and broadening clients' visual fields so that the whole spectrum of meaning and values becomes visible to them.

Following are some methods by which Frankl focuses on issues of meaning.

• *Teaching the importance of assuming responsibility for meaning.* Frankl views his task as helping clients achieve the highest possible activation of their lives. He shares his views that human life never, under any circumstances, ceases to have a meaning. Clients need to learn that they are always responsible for detecting the meaning of specific situations in their unique lives. Logotherapy teaches clients to view their lives as an assignment. For religious logotherapists working with religious clients, this can go one stage further in that they assist clients to see that they are not only responsible *for* fulfilling their life's tasks but they are also responsible *to* the taskmaster.

• *Assisting clients to listen to their consciences.* Frankl often says that meaning must be found and cannot be given. Clients are guided in their search for meaning by their consciences. A client requires an alert conscience if he is 'to listen to and obey the ten thousand demands and commandments hidden in the ten thousand situations with which life is confronting him' (Frankl, 1975a, p. 120). Though counsellors cannot give meanings to clients, they can provide existential examples of their commitment to the search for meaning.

• *Asking clients about meanings.* Counsellors can ask clients about creative accomplishments they might bring about and support them as they search for answers. Clients can also be helped to explore and identify meanings in their relationships and in their suffering.

• *Broadening horizons about sources of meaning.* Logotherapeutic counsellors can assist clients to obtain broader views of sources for meaning. Frankl (1955) cites a client who declared her life was meaningless and that she would only get better if she found a job that fulfilled her, such as working as a doctor or nurse. Frankl assisted her to see that it was not only the job that she did but her attitude towards how she performed her job that might allow her a unique opportunity for fulfilment. Furthermore, in her private life outside her occupation she could find meaning as a wife and mother.

• *Eliciting meaning through Socratic questioning.* Frankl (1988) gives the example of the female client who expressed concern with life's transitoriness. Frankl asked her to identify a man whose accomplishments she respected and she named her family doctor. Then by means of a series of questions he led her to acknowledge that, even though the doctor died and even though through lack of gratitude some patients might not remember what they owed him, the meaningfulness of his life remained.

• *Eliciting meaning through logodrama.* Frankl (1963) gives an example of eliciting meaning through a 'logodrama' in a counselling group. A woman, admitted to his clinic after a suicide attempt, had lost a son who died aged 11 and was left alone with an older son who had infantile paralysis. Frankl first asked another woman in the group to imagine she was 80 and to look back on a life that was childless but full of financial success and prestige. This woman ended by saying her life had no purpose. Frankl then asked the mother of the handicapped son similarly to look back over her life. During her reply she realized her life was full of meaning because she had made a better and fuller life possible for her crippled son.

• *Offering meanings.* Frankl provides the example of an elderly and severely depressed doctor who could not get over his grief for his beloved wife who had died two years earlier. First, Frankl asked him what would have happened if he had died first. The doctor replied that she would have suffered terribly. Whereupon Frankl replied: 'You see, Doctor, such a suffering has been spared her, and it is you who have spared her this suffering; but now, you have to pay for it by surviving and mourning her' (Frankl, 1963, pp. 178–9).

• *Analysing dreams*. Logotherapists can work with clients' dreams to lift spiritual phenomena into consciousness. Frankl (1975) gives the example of the woman who dreamed that, along with her dirty wash, she took a dirty cat along to the laundry. On going to pick up her wash, she found the cat dead. Her free associations indicated that 'cat' was the symbol for 'child' and 'dirty' was the 'dirty linen' of gossip surrounding her daughter's love life, about which the mother had been very critical. Frankl saw the dream as expressing a warning to the mother not to keep tormenting her daughter or else she might lose her. Religious logotherapists may also analyse dreams to bring the religious unconscious into consciousness. Frankl believes that many people conceal and repress their religiousness because of 'the intimate quality inherent in genuine religiousness' (Frankl, 1975a, p. 48).

Logotherapeutic techniques for psychogenic neurosis

Paradoxical intention and dereflection are the two main logotherapeutic techniques for the psychogenic neuroses (Frankl, 1955, 1975b). Both techniques rest on the essential human qualities of self-transcendence and self-detachment.

Paradoxical intention

Paradoxical intention's use is recommended for the short-term treatment of obsessive-compulsive and phobic clients. With phobias, paradoxical intention targets anticipatory anxiety whereby clients react to events with fearful expectations of their recurrence. These fearful expectations cause excessive attention, or hyperintention, which prevents clients from accomplishing what they want. In short, anticipatory anxiety brings about the very things that clients fear.

In paradoxical intention, clients are invited to intend precisely that which they fear. Their fear is replaced by a paradoxical wish through which 'the wind is taken out of the sails of the phobia' (Frankl, 1955, p. 208). In addition, paradoxical intention enlists clients' sense of humour as a means of increasing their sense of detachment towards their neuroses by laughing at them.

Frankl provides many examples of paradoxical intention, for instance a young physician who was afraid of perspiring on meeting people. Whenever he met someone who triggered his anticipatory anxiety he said to himself: 'I only sweated out a litre before, but now I am going to pour out at least ten litres!' (Frankl, 1955, p. 139). After one session of paradoxical intention he freed himself of a phobia that had lasted four years. Another example is that of the medical student whose fear of trembling led her to begin trembling when the anatomy instructor entered the dissecting room. She overcame her problem by using the paradoxical intention technique. Whenever the instructor came she said to herself: 'Oh, here is the instructor! Now I'll show him what a good trembler I am – I'll really show him how to tremble!' (Frankl, 1955, p. 140). However, whenever she tried, she was unable to tremble.

While obsessive compulsive neurotics also display fear, their fear is more fear of themselves than 'fear of fear'. They fear the potential effects of their strange thoughts. However, the more these clients fight their thoughts, the stronger their symptoms become. If counsellors succeed in assisting clients through paradoxical intention to stop fighting their obsessions and compulsions, their symptoms soon diminish and may finally disappear.

An example of paradoxical intention with an obsessive compulsive is that of a married woman who had been suffering for 14 years from a counting compulsion and a compulsion to check whether or not her dresser drawers were in order and securely locked (Frankl, 1955, p. 143). Her doctor demonstrated how to practise paradoxical intention. She was shown how to throw things carelessly into her dresser and to say to herself 'These drawers should be as messy as possible!' After two days her counting compulsion disappeared and after the fourth day she felt no need to recheck her dresser. She continued her improvement and, whenever occasionally any obsessive–compulsive ideas returned, she was able to ignore them or make them into a joke.

Dereflection

Just as paradoxical intention tries to counteract hyperintention, excessive intention, dereflection aims to counteract hyperreflection, or excessive attention. Frankl (1988) considers the compulsive tendency to self-observation particularly a problem in the United States. Paradoxical intention tries to assist clients to ridicule their symptoms, while dereflection assists clients to ignore them.

Sexual neuroses, such as frigidity and impotence, are one area for dereflection. Clients must be dereflected from their disturbance to the task at hand. Frankl (1963) provides the example of the young woman who complained of being frigid. In her childhood she had been sexually abused by her father. However, this event in itself did not cause her frigidity. Then, because she read popular psychoanalytic literature, she feared all the time that her traumatic sexual abuse experiences would create sexual difficulties. As a result of excessive intention to confirm her femininity and excessive attention to herself, the orgasm was no longer an unintended effect of her commitment to her partner. When her attention was dereflected from herself and refocused towards her partner, she experienced spontaneous orgasms.

Another example of dereflection is that of a woman who became very thin because she compulsively observed her swallowing and feared her food would go down the wrong way. The client was dereflected by the formula: 'I don't need to watch my swallowing, because I don't really need to swallow, for actually I don't swallow, but rather *it* does' (Frankl, 1955, p. 235). She learned to trust the automatically regulated functioning of her organism.

Medical ministry for somatogenic psychoses

Frankl (1988) uses the term medical ministry for how the logotherapeutic counsellor works with somatogenic cases where the somatic cause cannot be removed. Frankl regards it as a responsibility of the medical profession to comfort and console the sick. The medical ministry is not to be confused with the pastoral ministry. Where possible, the logotherapeutic treatment of clients with endogenous depressions and psychoses is aimed at working with the non-diseased part of clients to assist them in finding meaning in the attitude that they take towards their suffering. A residue of freedom is left even to people with psychoses and their innermost core is not touched by their psychosis. It is extremely demoralizing for sick people to believe that their suffering is meaningless.

An example of medical ministry with a somatogenic case is that of a 17-year-old schizophrenic Jewish youth who had been institutionalized in Israel for 2½ years because of the severity of his symptoms. The youth started doubting his Jewish faith and blamed God for having made him different from other people. Frankl suggested to him that perhaps God wanted to confront him for a specific period in his life with the task of his confinement. The young man said that is why he still believed in God and that possibly God wanted him to recover. Frankl responded that what God wanted was not only his recovery but that his spiritual level should be higher than before his illness. Afterwards the youth improved dramatically and Frankl believes that he enabled him to find meaning 'not only despite but because of psychosis' (Frankl 1988, p. 131).

CHAPTER REVIEW AND SELF-REFERENT QUESTIONS

Chapter review questions

1. What is the will to meaning?

2. How does Frankl distinguish between consciousness and the unconscious? What are some important characteristics of the unconscious?

3. What is the role of conscience?

4. What are Frankl's ideas on freedom and responsibility?

5. What does Frankl mean by self-transcendence?

6. Describe each of the following sources of meaning:
   meaning in work;
   meaning in love;
   meaning in suffering;
   meaning from the past;
   the supra-meaning.

7. What is the existential vacuum?

8. What is existential frustration?

9. What are the characteristics of the mass neurotic triad?

10. What are some ways in which the existential vacuum is acquired?

11. What are some ways by which the existential vacuum is maintained?

12. What do the following terms mean:
    noogenic neuroses;
    psychogenic neuroses;
    somatogenic psychoses?

13. What are the goals of logotherapy? Please specify according to category of human distress.

14. What is the role of the counselling relationship in logotherapy?

15. What are some methods by which Frankl increases clients' existential awareness of their finitude?

16. Describe how a logotherapeutic counsellor might use each of the following methods to focus clients on finding meaning in their lives:

teaching the importance of assuming responsibility for meaning;
assisting clients to listen to their consciences;
asking clients about meanings;
broadening horizons about sources of meaning;
eliciting meaning through Socratic questioning;
eliciting meaning through logodrama;
offering meanings;
analysing dreams.

17. Describe the technique of paradoxical intention and give an example of its use.

18. Describe the technique of dereflection and indicate its uses.

19. What does Frankl mean by medical ministry?

Self-referent questions

1. To what extent do you experience the existential vacuum and suffer from existential frustration?

2. Assess the extent to which you find meaning in each of the following sources: work, love, suffering, the past, and the supra-meaning.

3. If currently you have insufficient meaning in your life, how might you help yourself to find more meaning?

4. If possible, apply the technique of paradoxical intention to coping with a problem in your life.

5. If possible, apply the technique of dereflection to coping with a problem in your life.

6. What relevance, if any, has the theory and practice of logotherapy for how you counsel?

7. What relevance, if any, has the theory and practice of logotherapy for how you live?

Annotated bibliography

Frankl, V.E. (1963). *Man's Search for Meaning: an Introduction to Logotherapy*. New York: Washington Square Press.
Part one of this small volume, entitled 'Experiences in a concentration camp', provides a highly readable and moving account of Frankl's experiences as a concentration camp inmate. Frankl recounts instances of human brutality, weakness and nobility. He incisively describes qualities making for psychological survival and growth. The second part of the book, entitled 'Basic

concepts of logotherapy', was written some years later. It provides a clearly written and concise introduction to logotherapy theory and practice. This book provides an excellent introduction to Frankl, the man and the counsellor.

Frankl, V.E. (1955). *The Doctor and the Soul: From Psychotherapy to Logotherapy.* Harmondsworth: Penguin.
This book traces the development of logotherapy. Frankl then discusses the meanings of life, suffering, work and love. Then he gives his views of the psychology of anxiety neurosis, obsessional neurosis, melancholia and schizophrenia. Next come descriptions of the logotherapeutic techniques of paradoxical intention and dereflection. Frankl ends the book by presenting logotherapy as a form of medical ministry.

Frankl, V.E. (1988).*The Will to Meaning: Foundations and Applications of Logotherapy.* New York: Meridian.
This book arose from a series of lectures Frankl gave in 1966. Part one of the book, entitled 'Foundations of logotherapy', covers metaclinical implications of psychotherapy, self-transcendence as a human phenomenon, and what is meant by meaning. Part two, entitled 'Applications of logotherapy', discusses the existential vacuum, logotherapeutic techniques and medical ministry. The book concludes with a chapter on dimensions of meaning and then has an afterword on the de-gurufication of logotherapy.

Frankl, V.C. (1975a). *The Unconscious God: Psychotherapy and Theology.* New York: Simon & Schuster.
The first part of this book, entitled 'The unconscious God', was originally published in 1948 in Austria. Frankl asserts that there is not only an instinctual unconscious but a spiritual unconscious as well. Within the spiritual unconscious there exists unconscious religiousness. Frankl discusses unconscious religiousness as well as the relationship between psychotherapy and theology. The second part of the book, entitled 'Postscript 1975: New research in logotherapy', presents Frankl's ideas interspersed with references to research.

Frankl, V.E. (1967). *Psychotherapy and Existentialism: Selected Papers on Logotherapy.* Harmondsworth: Penguin.
This book is a compilation of many of Frankl's most important articles regarding the theory and practice of logotherapy.

Further references

Frankl

Frankl, V.E. (1953). Logos and existence in psychotherapy. *American Journal of Psychotherapy, 7,* 8–15.
Frankl, V.E. (1954). Group psychotherapeutic experiences in a concentration camp. *Group Psychotherapy, 7,* 81–90.
Frankl, V.E. (1955). The concept of man in psychotherapy. *Pastorol Psychology, 6,* 16–26.
Frankl, V.E. (1958). On logotherapy and existential analysis. *American Journal of Psychoanalysis, 18,* 28–37.
Frankl, V.E. (1959). The spiritual dimension in existential analysis and logotherapy. *Journal of Individual Psychology, 25,* 157–65.
Frankl, V.E. (1960). Paradoxical intention: A logotherapeutic technique. *American Journal of Psychotherapy, 14,* 520–35.
Frankl, V.E. (1962a). Basic concepts of logotherapy. *Journal of Existential Psychiatry, 3,* 111–18.

Frankl, V.E. (1962b). Psychiatry and man's quest for meaning. *Journal of Religion and Health,* *1,* 93–103.

Frankl, V.E. (1963). Existential dynamics and neurotic escapism. *Journal of Existential Psychiatry, 4,* 27–42.

Frankl, V.E. (1966a). Logotherapy and existential analysis: A review. *American Journal of Psychotherapy, 20,* 252–60.

Frankl, V.E. (1966b). Self-transcendence as a human phenomenon. *Journal of Humanistic Psychology, 6,* 97–106.

Frankl, V.E. (1967). Logotherapy and existentialism. *Psychotherapy: Theory, Research and Practice, 4,* 138–43.

Frankl, V.E. (1972). The feeling of meaninglessness: A challenge to psychotherapy. *American Journal of Psychoanalysis, 32,* 85–9.

Frankl, V.E. (1975b). Paradoxical intention and dereflection. *Psychotherapy: Theory, Research and Practice, 12,* 226–37.

Frankl, V.E. (1985). *The Unheard Cry for Meaning: Psychotherapy and Humanism.* New York: Simon & Schuster.

Frankl on audio and video cassette

A full listing of Frankl audio-visual materials is in Section 4 of the Bibliography of *The Will to Meaning,* pp. 182–5.

PART FOUR

Psychoanalytic

EIGHT

Psychoanalysis

PREVIEW

- *Psychoanalytic theory groups human instincts into two broad categories, the erotic or life instincts and the death or destructive instincts. The energy of the life instincts is termed 'libido'. To a large extent people are motivated by the pleasure principle. Mental life takes place on conscious, preconscious and unconscious levels.*

- *The mental apparatus consists of three agencies: the id, which is constantly striving for instinctual satisfaction; the super-ego, which represents parental and moral influence; and the ego, which aims to meet the instinctual demands of the id on the basis of the reality principle. The ego has three task-masters – the external world, the id and the super-ego – and each may cause it anxiety. Psychical energy is distributed among the three mental agencies, which may be in harmony or in conflict with each other.*

- *People are sexual from infancy, though they tend to be subject to amnesia about this. Humans are constitutionally bisexual and infantile sexuality contains great tendencies to perversion.*

- *Sexual development takes place in two phases: a pre-genital phase up to the end of the fifth year and a genital phase starting at menarche and puberty. The period in between is the latency period. There are some differences in sexual development between the sexes, including development during the Oedipus situation.*

- *While the child's ego is relatively weak, it develops defensive mechanisms to ward off the strong sexual impulses emanating from the id. Thus much of its early sexual life becomes repressed or is not allowed access to consciousness. Excessive repression may lead to the development of neurosis. Since the ego is weakened by having to maintain the repression, it does not have access to the repressed material, and the repressed impulses become transformed into neurotic symptoms.*

- *The aim of psychoanalysis is to strengthen the client's ego by lifting childhood repressions, filling in gaps in memory and allowing acts of judgement to be made through the ego's present strength rather than its previous weakness. Concepts of psychoanalytic practice such as free association, transference and interpretation are reviewed.*

INTRODUCTION

Around the end of the nineteenth century Freud started writing about psychoanalysis. His work is considered worthy of inclusion in this book for a number of reasons. First, psychoanalytic theory provides a tremendously fruitful source of concepts concerning personality. For instance, Freud's instinct theory throws light on the biological basis of human functioning, while his ideas on defensive mechanisms provide a valuable insight into the way in which people sustain self-defeating behaviour. Second, psychoanalytic theory possesses a unique historical interest not only in terms of its being an early major psychological theory, but also because of its influence on other theorists. In varying degrees Freud has influenced humanistic and existential psychologists and psychiatrists. For example, points of contact with transactional analysis include the tripartite structure of personality and the importance of early experience. Also, Rogers' concept of levels of awareness resembles Freud's idea of levels of consciousness. Others influenced by Freud include Jung, Adler, Horney, Sullivan and Fromm, the last four of whom are often termed the 'neo-Freudians'. In addition, under the leadership of Melanie Klein an English school of psychoanalysis emerged, emphasizing the importance of primitive fantasies of loss (the depressive position) and persecution (the paranoid position) in the pathogenesis of mental illness (Arlow, 1989). Winnicott and Bowlby were other prominent English analysts whose work was influenced by Freud.

A third reason for including this chapter is that psychoanalytic concepts regarding practice, such as free association, interpretation, transference and resistance, merit the attention of all counsellors. Fourth, some counsellors and many psychiatrists are of an analytic orientation. Some analysts use 'pure' Freudian theory; others accept some of his ideas while modifying others. Communication with such people is likely to be facilitated by an understanding of their theoretical framework.

Sigmund Freud

Sigmund Freud (1856–1939) was born at Freiberg, a small town in what is now Czechoslovakia. He was the eldest son of his father's second wife, who subsequently bore five daughters and two other sons. Jones (1963) writes of Freud's mother's pride in and love for her first-born and also mentions that when he was two Freud's libido had been aroused towards his mother on seeing her naked. Freud writes: 'My parents were Jews, and I have remained a Jew myself' (Freud, 1935, p. 12). His father, Jakob, was a wood merchant who, when Freud was four, moved his family to Vienna. Freud's early years in Vienna were hard, and throughout his upbringing his family appears to have been short of money.

When he was nine Freud went to high school (Sperl Gymnasium), where he was at the top of his class for seven years, enjoyed special privileges, and was required to pass few examinations. Freud was a hard worker who enjoyed reading and studying. On leaving school with distinction at 17 he faced the choice of a career, which for a Viennese Jew had to be in industry, business, law or medicine. He recalls not feeling any particular predilection for medicine, since his interests were directed more towards human concerns than natural objects. Freud writes '. . . and it was hearing Goethe's beautiful essay on Nature read aloud by Professor Carl Bruhl just before I left school that decided me to become a medical student' (Freud, 1935, p. 14).

In 1873 Freud enrolled at the University of Vienna to study medicine, though when he was there his academic interests were more wide-ranging. In 1876 he began the first of his researches, a study of the gonadic structure of eels. Soon afterwards he entered Ernst Brucke's physiological laboratory, where he worked, with short interruptions, from 1876 to 1882. During this period Freud focused chiefly on work connected with the histology of nerve cells. He found 'rest and satisfaction' in Brucke's laboratory as well as scientists 'whom I could respect and take as my models' (Freud, 1935, p. 15). He thought especially highly of Brucke himself. Freud recalls being decidedly negligent in pursuing his medical studies. Nevertheless, in 1881 he passed his final examinations to become a Doctor of Medicine with the grade of 'excellent'.

In 1882 Freud left Brucke's laboratory, where the year before he had been appointed a demonstrator. For financial reasons, probably influenced by falling in love, Freud decided to earn his living as a physician. He entered the General Hospital of Vienna, where he gained experience in various departments and became an active researcher in the Institute of Cerebral Anatomy. During this period 'with an eye to material considerations, I began to study nervous diseases' (Freud, 1935, p. 18). Because of inadequate opportunities for learning this subject, Freud was forced to be his own teacher. He published a number of clinical observations on organic diseases of the nervous systems and, in 1885, was appointed lecturer in neuropathology. Around this period Freud both took and conducted research into the use of cocaine. Jones (1963) observes: 'For many years he suffered from periodic depressions and fatigue or apathy, neurotic symptoms which later took the form of anxiety attacks before being dispelled by his own analysis' (pp. 54–5). Cocaine apparently calmed the agitation and eased the depression. Jones also mentions that all his life Freud was subject to severe bouts of migraine which were refractory to any treatment.

On the award of a travelling fellowship Freud went to Paris where, from October 1885 to February 1886, he studied at the Sâlpetrière (hospital for nervous diseases) under Charcot. He was very impressed with Charcot's investigations into hysteria, confirming the genuineness of hysterical phenomena, including hysterical paralyses and contractures by hypnotic suggestion. In 1886 he returned to Vienna to marry Martha Bernays and to set up a private practice as a specialist in nervous diseases. His 'therapeutic arsenal contained only two weapons, electrotherapy and hypnotism . . .' (Freud, 1935, p. 26). He soon dropped electrotherapy and increasingly realized the limitations of hypnotic suggestion. During the period 1886 to 1891 he did little scientific work, though in 1891 he jointly published the first of his studies on the cerebral paralyses of children.

In the early 1880s Freud had developed a close friendship with Joseph Breuer, a prominent Viennese physician, who told him how, between 1880 and 1882, he had successfully treated a young girl with hysterical symptoms. His method was to hypnotize her deeply and then encourage her to express in words her reminiscences of earlier emotional situations which were oppressing her. In the late 1880s Freud began repeating Breuer's technique with his own patients, aware 'of the possibility that there could be powerful mental processes which nevertheless remained hidden from the consciousness of man' (Freud, 1935, p. 29). In 1893 Freud and Breuer wrote a preliminary paper on the cathartic method and, in 1895, published their book *Studies of Hysteria*.

During the 1890s the transition from catharsis to psychoanalysis proper took place. Jones (1963) writes: 'there is ample evidence that for ten years or so – roughly comprising the nineties – he suffered from a very considerable psychoneurosis . . . yet it was just in the years when the neurosis was at its height, 1897–1900, that Freud did his most original work' (p. 194). Although he showed no conversion symptoms, he had extreme alterations of mood between elation and self-confidence, and depression and inhibition. In the latter moods Freud could neither write nor concentrate, apart from his professional work. Additionally, he had occasional attacks of dread of dying and also became very anxious about travelling by rail.

During the period 1887 to 1900 Freud had an intense friendship with Wilhelm Fleiss, a nose and throat specialist two years younger than himself. Fleiss saw sexual problems as central to his own work, encouraged Freud and gave him permission to develop his theories. Jones notes Freud's dependency on Fleiss's good opinion and calls him Freud's 'sole public' during this period. Jones rated Fleiss as intellectually much inferior to Freud.

Against this background, Freud started developing his ideas on the sexual bases of neuroses, abandoned hypnotism yet retained his practice of requiring the patient to lie on a sofa while he sat behind. During 1897 to 1899 he wrote his major work, *The Interpretation of Dreams*. In the summer of 1897 Freud undertook a psychoanalysis of his own unconscious, and this self-analysis generated material for the book. Freud discovered his childhood passion for his mother and jealousy for his father, which he considered a pervasive human characteristic; he termed it the Oedipus complex. It took eight years to sell the first edition of 600 copies of *The Interpretation of Dreams*. Jones (1963) observes of Freud's self-analysis: 'The end of all that labour and suffering was the last and final phase in the evolution of Freud's personality. There emerged the serene and benign Freud, henceforth free to pursue his work in imperturbable composure' (p. 205). Fromm's (1959) biography is less kind, suggesting that Freud continued to exhibit some insecurity and egotism in areas of both his professional and his personal life. In 1905 Freud published what is perhaps his other major work, *Three Contributions to the Theory of Sex*, which traces the development of sexuality from its earliest childhood beginnings.

In his autobiographical study Freud observed that, after the preliminary cathartic period, the history of psychoanalysis falls into two phases. From 1895–6 until 1906 he worked in isolation, but thereafter the contributions of his pupils and collaborators increasingly grew in importance. The historical development of Freud's ideas will be left at this stage. Suffice it to say that for the remainder of his life he published numerous books and articles, not only on psychoanalysis as a method of treating the disturbed but also on the relevance of his theories to everyday life. In 1910, at a congress held at Nuremberg, the analysts formed themselves into an International Psychoanalytical

Association divided into a number of local societies but under a common president. By 1935 the number of the Association's supporters had increased considerably. The growth of psychoanalysis, however, was not smooth, and it aroused considerable antipathy.

Freud was in the habit of smoking an average of 20 cigars a day and, in 1923, learned that he had cancer of the jaw. He lived the last 16 years of his life in pain which was often extreme, and a total of 33 operations were performed on his jaw. In 1938 Nazism caused Freud to leave Austria with his family and settle in England, which he had first visited when he was 19 and which he much admired. He died in London a year later. The following is Freud's summary of his life's work:

> Looking back, then, over the patchwork of my life's labours, I can say that I have made many beginnings and thrown out many suggestions. Something will come of them in future, though I cannot myself tell whether it will be much or little. I can, however, express a hope that I have opened up a pathway for an important advance in our knowledge.
>
> (Freud, 1935, pp. 135–6)

Elsewhere, Freud had observed that he was by temperament a conquistador or adventurer, with the accompanying traits of curiosity, boldness and tenacity. A modern term for Freud might be an 'ideas person'.

ASSUMPTIONS

Although many of Freud's basic concepts are to be found in *The Interpretation of Dreams*, he was developing and refining his ideas continuously. Thus the same concept may appear in different sources, only some of which will be mentioned here. In general, this chapter represents Freud's later presentation of his work.

The pleasure principle

Originally presented as the unpleasure principle, the pleasure principle follows from the constancy hypothesis that 'the mental apparatus endeavours to keep the quantity of excitation in it as low as possible or at least to keep it constant' (Freud, 1961, p. 3). Thus everything which increases the quantity of excitation will be felt as unpleasurable and anything which diminishes it will be experienced as pleasurable. Freud qualified the idea of the dominance of the pleasure principle by observing that, although in the mind there exists a strong tendency towards the pleasure principle, there are also other forces opposing it, with the final outcome not always fulfilling the tendency towards pleasure.

The instincts

Instincts represent somatic or biological demands upon the mind. While acknowledging the possibility of distinguishing many instincts, Freud assumed that these could be grouped into two basic instincts, *Eros* and the *destructive instinct*. The erotic instincts 'seek to combine more and more living substance into even greater unities', while the death instincts 'oppose this effort and lead what is living back to an inorganic state' (Freud, 1973, p. 140). Eros includes the instincts of self-preservation, the preservation of the species, ego–love and object–love, and its energy is called *libido*. Throughout life the basic instincts may either work together (for instance the sexual act is also an acts of aggression) or oppose each other.

Freud saw instincts as historically acquired and conservative and stated: 'It seems, then, that an instinct is an urge inherent in life to restore an earlier state of things' (Freud, 1961, p. 30). Given the fact that living things appeared later than inanimate ones and arose out of them, the death instinct may be viewed as a compulsion to repeat this earlier inorganic state. Consequently, the aim of all life is death. Eros, however, does not follow the same formula. Freud believed that sexual instincts were the single exception among the instincts in not seeking to restore an earlier state of things.

Freud viewed the inclination to aggression as an original instinctual disposition in humans. He quoted Plautus: 'Homo homini lupus', a translation of which is 'Man is a wolf to man'. The aggressive instinct is the derivative and main representative of the death instinct. The evolution of civilization represents the struggle between the life and death instincts in the human species. The fateful question that Freud posed at the end of *Civilization and its Discontents* was whether Eros would assert itself, 'But who can foresee with what success and what results?' (Freud, 1962c, p. 92).

The unconscious and consciousness

Heavily influenced by his study of dreams, Freud made a distinction between the unconscious and consciousness. He observed: 'The interpretation of dreams is the royal road to a knowledge of the unconscious activities of the mind' (Freud, 1976, p. 769). From the very beginning, he stated that there were two kinds of unconscious. First, there is the *unconscious* (Ucs), or unconscious proper, which is material that is inadmissible to consciousness because of repression. In other words, with the unconscious the censorship on material coming into awareness is very strong indeed. The object of psychoanalysis is to help make some of this material accessible to awareness, though during the process strong resistances may be aroused, not least because of the forbidden sexual connotations of much of what is being repressed.

The second kind of unconscious is the *preconscious* (Pcs), which consists of everything that can easily move from the unconscious state to the conscious one. Thus the preconscious is latent and capable of becoming conscious, while the unconscious is repressed and is unlikely to become conscious without great difficulty. Material may remain in the preconscious, though usually it finds its way into consciousness without any need for psychoanalytic intervention. The preconscious may be viewed as a screen between the unconscious and the conscious, with, as in the case of dreams, modifications being made in unconscious material through censorship.

Consciousness (Cs or Pcpt Cs) has the function of a sense organ for the perception of psychical qualities. Unlike the two kinds of unconscious, consciousness has no memory and a state of consciousness is usually very transitory. Materials becomes conscious, or flows into the consciousness sense-organ, from two directions: the external world and inner excitations. Furthermore, the function of speech enables internal events such as sequences of ideas and intellectual processes to become conscious.

Structure of the mental apparatus

Freud structured the mental apparatus into three systems or agencies: the id, the ego and the super-ego. Psychological well-being depends on whether these three systems are interrelating effectively. Figure 8.1 is Freud's own sketch of the structural relations of the mental apparatus, though he acknowledges that the space occupied by the unconscious id ought to have been much greater (Freud, 1973, p. 111).

The id

The *id* or 'it' is the oldest of these systems and contains everything that is inherited and fixed in the constitution. The instincts, which originate in the somatic organization, find their mental expression in the id. The id, filled with energy from the instincts, strives to bring about the satisfaction of instinctual needs on the basis of the pleasure principle, Thus the activity of the id is directed towards securing the free discharge of quantities of excitation. The psychical processes of the id are known as primary processes because they are present in the mental apparatus from the first. Furthermore, no alteration in the id's mental processes is produced by the passage of time. Freud viewed the id as 'a chaos, a cauldron full of seething emotions', which 'knows no judgements of values: no good and evil, no morality' (Freud, 1973, pp. 106–7). The id consists of wishful impulses. It is not governed by logic, and this applies especially to the law of contradiction, since it contains contrary impulses side by side. In short, the id is the individual's primary subjective reality at the unconscious level.

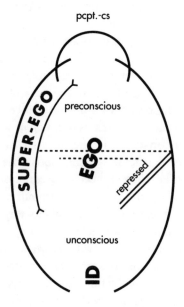

Figure 8.1 Structural relations of the mental apparatus.

The ego

The *ego* or 'I' is first and foremost a bodily ego ultimately derived from bodily sensations, in particular those coming from its surface. The ego is a portion of the id which has undergone a special development or modification through the influence of the external world. The ego acts as an intermediary between the id and the external world and ideally represents reason and common sense, whereas the id contains instinctual passions and would destroy itself without the intervention of the ego. The ego strives to bring the reality principle to bear upon the id in substitution for the pleasure principle. The processes of the ego, which include perception, problem solving and repression, are later developments or secondary processes, in contrast to the original or primary processes of the id. Nevertheless, the ego seeks pleasure and the avoidance of unpleasure, differing from the id only in the means of attaining common ends. A foreseen increase in unpleasure is met by a signal of anxiety. As Figure 8.1 shows, the perceptual-conscious system is the outer later of the ego, which also includes much preconscious and unconscious material.

The ego is in control of voluntary movement but interposes thought between experiencing a need and acting on it. The ego deals with external events through perception, memory, avoiding excessive stimuli, adapting to moderate stimuli and engaging in activities designed to modify the external world to its advantage. Regarding internal events in relation to the id, the ego attempts to control instinctual demands by deciding the timing and manner of their gratification or by suppressing their excitations. Freud makes the analogy of the id being the horse, while the ego is the rider. He observes that often, however, the ego is weak in relation to the id and so is in the habit of transforming the id's will into action as if it were its own.

The super-ego

The third agency is the *super-ego*, which is a residue formed within the ego in which parental influence is prolonged. Parental influence may be defined broadly as including cultural, racial and family influences. As the person grows up, the nature of the 'parental' influence may vary, partly because parents may behave differently. Also, teachers, admired figures in public life and many others may contribute to the development of an individual's super-ego, which normally departs more and more from original parental influences.

The function of the super-ego, which engages in self-observation, is to contain the demands of the id through moral influence on the ego. Originally the child engages in instinctual renunciation through fear of loss of love or through fear of aggression from an *external* or parental authority. Subsequently a secondary situation develops in which the external restraint is internalized and thus instinctual renunciation comes about through fear of an *internal* authority, or super-ego.

A characteristic of the super-ego is the ego-ideal, based on the admiration which the child felt for the perfection it saw in its parents and which it strives to emulate. In fact the terms 'super-ego' and 'ego-ideal' are virtually synonymous. The ego-ideal consists both of precepts – 'You ought to be like this' – and prohibitions – 'You ought not to be like that'. These precepts and prohibitions are based in part on the identifications and repressions resulting from the resolution of the Oedipus complex. They represent the individual's conscience, transgressions of which are likely to result in a sense of inferiority and guilt and also possibly in a need for punishment. Freud observed: 'The super-ego is the representative for us of every moral restriction, the advocate of a striving towards perfection – it is, in short, as much as we have been able to grasp psychologically of what is described as the higher side of human life' (Freud, 1973, p. 98).

In addition to the demands of the instincts and of the external world, the ego has to take into account the demands of the super-ego. Individuals vary in the severity of their super-egos, which may be benign or punitively harsh and restricting. Conflicts can arise between ego and super-ego, with large portions of both agencies remaining unconscious.

Anxiety

Freud defined anxiety as a specific state of unpleasure accompanied by motor discharge along definite pathways. He saw anxiety as the universal reaction to the situation of danger and the ego as the sole seat of anxiety. In later life, a source of anxiety which is involuntary occurs whenever a dangerous situation arises. Another source is anxiety generated by the ego when danger is merely threatened and the ego feels weak in relation to it. Hence there are three kinds of anxiety, one for each of the ego's three 'taskmasters': (a) *realistic* anxiety regarding the dangers of the external world; (b) *moral* anxiety regarding conflict with the super-ego; and (c) *neurotic* anxiety regarding conflict with the strength of the id's instinctual impulses. Thus anxiety is either a reaction to actual danger or a signal involving the perception of impending danger.

Psychical energy, cathexis and anti-cathexis

Psychoanalysis is often referred to as having a dynamic view of psychology. What this means is that the concept of psychical or mental energy and its distribution among the id, ego and super-ego is central to psychoanalysis. The id is the source of this somatically based psychical energy, being filled with energy reaching it from the instincts. Sexual excitation is an example of instinctual psychical energy. As the ego and the super-ego are formed they also become charged with energy.

The words 'cathexis' and 'cathectic' describe the idea of psychical energy being drawn to mental agencies and processes, somewhat analogous to an electric charge. Cathexes are the charges of instinctual energy seeking discharge, whereas anticathexes are charges of energy which block and inhibit such discharge. The id has only primary-process instinctual cathexes seeking discharge. However, the ego and the super-ego have both urging cathexes and restraining anti-cathexes. Throughout life the ego is the avenue by which libidinal cathexes are transferred to objects and into which they may also be withdrawn again. Two characteristics of libidinal cathexes are mobility, the ease with which they pass from one object to another, and, in contrast, fixation, or being bound to particular objects.

Bisexuality

Freud observed that it was a long-known anatomical fact that in every normally formed male or female there are traces of the apparatus of the other sex, though in atrophied form. Anatomically there may have been an original predisposition to bisexuality, which in the course of the development of the human species has largely been altered to monosexuality.

Psychologically Freud believed that the sexual impulse is probably entirely independent of its object and therefore not originated by chemical attraction. Another way of stating this is that there is only one libido and it cannot be assigned a sex. Therefore the direction of both heterosexual and homosexual object selection requires further explanation. By studying covert sexual excitations, psychoanalytic research discovered that all men were capable of homosexual object selection and actually accomplish this in the unconscious. Furthermore, homosexual libidinous feelings 'play no small role as factors in normal psychic life' and an even greater role as 'causative factors of disease' (Freud, 1962a, p. 10). Freud believed that the same free attachment to male and female objects as observed in childhood and primitive and prehistoric states forms the basis on which both heterosexual and homosexual or inverted sexual development takes place. A degree of homosexuality is congenital in everyone, with the final determination of sexual behaviour being the result of the intensity of constitutional predisposition as well as of life experiences and restrictions in one or other direction. Both the woman and the man develop out of a child with a bisexual disposition.

ACQUISITION
Infantile sexuality and amnesia

Freud distinguished between the sexual impulse, the sexual object, and the sexual aim. The sexual impulse is the sexual aspect of libido, the sexual object is the person in whom sexual attraction is lodged, and the sexual aim refers to the action, such as touch or intercourse, towards which the sexual impulse strives. Freud further made a sharp distinction between 'sexual' and 'genital', considering that sexual life consists of gaining pleasure from erotogenic zones of the body and that this is not necessarily in the service of reproduction. Additionally, sexual life includes affectionate and friendly impulses often called 'love'. In a sense, all adult sexual behaviour whose goal is not reproduction, a heterosexual object and intercourse may be considered perverse. Adult sexual behaviour does not suddenly emerge at puberty but has developed out of prior sexual dispositions and experiences.

Sexual life starts soon after birth. Infantile sexuality, in the absence of genital maturation and of ego and super-ego development, lacks a central co-ordinating focus. Instead the component sexual instincts seek their own pleasure. Infantile sexuality is fundamentally auto-erotic in that the infant finds its pleasure in the object of its own body. Freud believed that the infantile sexual disposition contained great tendencies to perversion and that normal sexual behaviour develops partly in response to organic changes and partly as a result of psychic inhibitions and repressions.

The years of childhood are when the individual is most impressionable. Nevertheless, people are largely unaware of the beginnings of their sexual life and tend to view their childhood as if it were a prehistoric time. However, infantile and childhood sexual experiences leave deep traces in the individual's psychical life, acting as significant determinants for future development. Freud used the term 'infantile amnesia' to refer to the phenomenon by which a veil is drawn over early sexual experiences.

Sexual development

The onset of sexual life is diphasic. The first or pre-genital phase of sexual development is a steady process which reaches a climax towards the end of a child's fifth year. After this there is a lull or period of latency. The second or genital phase starts with the re-emergence of the sexual impulse at menarche or puberty. The pre-genital and genital phases of sexual organization are distinguished by whether or not the genital zones have assumed a dominating role.

The pre-genital phase

The pre-genital phase itself consists of three separate phases of sexual organization through which individuals normally pass smoothly, though fixations or arrested development may occur at each phase. Both sexes seem to pass through the early stages of sexual development in the same manner. The first organ to be an erotogenic zone is the mouth, and hence sexual development starts with the *oral* phase. The infant's act of sucking goes beyond that needed for the taking of nourishment to what may be viewed as the seeking of sexual organ-pleasure independent of nourishment. The oral phase can be further subdivided. The first sub-stage is where there is a focus only on oral incorporation, whereas the second sub-stage is 'oral-sadistic', with the emergence of biting activity. These two sub-stages of the oral phase are the first manifestation of the phenomenon of ambivalence.

The second organ to become an erotogenic zone is the anus, and normal sexual development proceeds from the oral to the *sadistic-anal* phase. The active aspect of this phase is the impulse for mastery (sadism), with the strengthening of the musculature of the body and control of sphincter functions. The erotogenic mucous membrane of the anus also manifests itself as an organ with a passive sexual aim. Character traits associated with this phase are orderliness, parsimony and obstinacy, which together define the so-called 'anal character'.

The third organ to become an erotogenic zone is the genital apparatus. The period of sexual development in which the male sexual organ (the phallus) and the female clitoris become important is known as the *phallic* phase, which starts in about the child's third year. Here pleasure is obtained from masturbation. During the phallic phase the sexuality of early childhood reaches its greatest intensity and it is during this phase that male and female sexual development become differentiated.

The *Oedipus* phase is part of the phallic phase for both sexes. Put simply, at an early age the little boy develops an object-cathexis for his mother and identifies with his father. During the phallic phase the body's libidinal object-cathexis of his mother intensifies and he wishes to get rid of his father and to take his father's place with his mother. The threat of castration causes the boy to abandon and repress his incestuous wishes. The resolution of the boy's Oedipus complex involves renouncing his object-cathexis of his mother, which may lead to an identification with his mother or, more normally, to an intensification of his identification with his father, consolidating the masculinity in his character. The Oedipus situation is often more complex because of the child's bisexual disposition. Thus, instead of affection for his mother and ambivalence towards his father, he may have a mixture of affection for and ambivalence towards each parent. Freud observes that 'in both sexes the relative strength of the masculine and feminine sexual dispositions is what determines whether the outcome of the Oedipus situation shall be an identification with the father or with the mother' (Freud, 1962b, p. 23). Perhaps it is more accurate to consider the outcome as a predominant rather than an exclusive identification with one or the other parent. Freud further asserts that, especially with neurotics, a bisexual Oedipus complex should be assumed.

As with the body, the girl's mother is the first object of her love. During the phallic phase the clitoris is her predominant erotogenic zone. Freud believed that during the girl's development to femininity she should change both her predominant erotogenic zone (to the vagina) and also the sex of her love object. The powerful attachment of the girl to her mother is ended when the girl, discovering the inferiority of her clitoris and the fact that she does not have a penis, holds her mother responsible. According to Freud penis envy or the wish for a penis is a very important feminine trait. The wish for a penis-baby from the father replaces the wish for a penis, and it is at this stage that the girl has entered her Oedipus situation, desiring her father and wishing to be rid of her mother. Again the situation may be complicated by her bisexual disposition. Girls remain in their Oedipus situation for an indeterminate length of time and resolve it late and often incompletely. Where the boy is encouraged to surmount the Oedipus complex through fear of castration, the girl has no such motivation. As time goes by the female Oedipus complex weakens, partly as a result of inevitable disappointments from her father.

The latency period

The period from around the beginning of the child's sixth year, probably later for girls, to menarche and puberty constitutes the sexual latency period. Latency may be total or partial and, during this period, sexual inhibitions develop. One of the mechanisms by which sexual energy is diverted is called sublimation or the displacement of libido to new aims and cultural pursuits. Furthermore, as the individual develops libidinous impulses may call forth contrary anti-cathexes or reactions (reaction formations) such as disgust, shame and morality.

The genital phase

The *genital* phase, which starts at menarche or puberty, involves the subordination of all sources of sexual feeling to the primacy of the genital zones. Earlier libidinal cathexes may be retained, included in sexual activity or preliminary or auxiliary acts, or in some way repressed or diverted. Puberty brings a greater increase of libido in boys, but in girls there is an increase in repression, especially regarding clitoral sexuality. Also at menarche and puberty, along with the overcoming of incestuous object-choices, comes the breaking away from parental authority. Given a reasonably adequate prior sexual development, the individual is now ready to engage in a heterosexual genital relationship.

Identification

Identification is an important concept for understanding ego and super-ego development. Identification may be viewed in three ways: first, as the original form of emotional tie with an object; second, as a regressive substitute for a libidinal object-tie by means of introjection of the object with the ego, so that the ego assumes the characteristics of the object (e.g. a female patient imitating her father's cough); and third, as a feeling generated by the perception of a common quality with another person who is not libidinally cathectic. The development of the super-ego may be seen in terms of identification with the parental agency, by which young people, wishing to be like their parents, mould their egos after the fashion of those taken as their models. Identification is part of the normal process of development. However, the ego may be restricted, as well as enhanced, depending on the nature of the identification.

Defensive mechanisms

During the child's early years its ego is relatively feeble, yet it has to deal with strong instinctual sexual impulses. At this stage anxiety may be generated by loss of an object or loss of love, which may persist into later life. Later sources of anxiety include fear of castration during the phallic phase and fear of the super-ego during and after the latency period.

In order to cope with the sources of anxiety the ego utilizes defensive mechanisms. Freud doubted that the ego could do without them during normal development. In many instances, however, the ego pays a high price for the use of the mechanisms, since they restrict its functioning, also using in their anti-cathexes psychical energy which might better be expended elsewhere. Defensive mechanisms are infantilisms which operate unconsciously and may impede realistic behaviour long after they have outlived their usefulness. Individuals do not make use of all the possible mechanisms of defence but select some, which become fixated in their egos. The establishment of defensive mechanisms is largely a feature of the child's struggle against its sexuality during the first five years of life.

When the ego observes that an emerging instinctual demand may place it in danger, the defensive ways in which it strives to contain the instinctual cathexis include the following.

• *Repression.* The process of repression is of two kinds. First, material which is in the preconscious and hence admissible to consciousness is pushed back into the unconscious. Second, unconscious material may be forbidden by censorship to enter the preconscious and hence has to remain unconscious. For example, either kind of repression might apply to an individual's latent sexually perverted impulses. Repression is the central underlying defensive mechanism of the ego, the basis of all other defences.

• *Sublimation*. Sublimation involves displacing instinctual sexual impulses into socially more acceptable channels. For instance, painters may express their sexuality in displaced form in their art. Sublimation is not necessarily pathological.

• *Reaction-formation*. In reaction-formation the ego acknowledges impulses contrary to the ones by which it is threatened. For instance, sexual impulses may be warded off by excessive shame, disgust and loathing of sexuality.

• *Denial*. With denial, the ego wards off some claim from the external world, which it experiences as painful, by denying the perceptions that would involve acknowledging the reality of the situation. For example, people may deny feedback from others about their aggression.

• *Fixation*. When people get highly anxious about moving on to the next phase of their sexual development, they may lag behind or become fixated in varying degrees to an earlier stage in terms of satisfaction of their instincts. For instance, children may cling dependently to their mothers' love rather than make new object-cathexes.

• *Regression*. Another danger in sexual development is that, under threat, an individual will return to an earlier phase at which she may previously have been fixated. In fact, regressions may be of two kinds: a return to the incestuous objects first 'cathected' by the libido and a return of the sexual organization as a whole to an earlier phase.

• *Projection*. With projection the ego deals with the threat of an unacceptable instinctual impulse by externalizing it. Thus, instead of acknowledging the extent of their own libidinal and aggressive impulses, individuals may become very aware of such characteristics in others and actually attribute them incorrectly.

Normal development

To summarize, the Freudian view of the normal development of personality may be seen in terms of three interrelated strands. One strand involves the individual's libidinal development, which starts with a mixture of constitutional and infantile predispositions which mature into genital sexuality in successive but overlapping phases, interrupted by the latency period. The second strand involves the development of both the ego, as it gains in ability to mediate between instinctual demands and the reality of the external world, and the super-ego, based on identifications with parental influences. The third strand is the establishment of favoured defensive mechanisms on the part of the ego to ward off the anxiety caused by the strength and persistence of the id's libidinal impulses. Thus normal development may be viewed as passing through successive stages of sexual maturation without major fixations and regressions, developing an ego which copes reasonably effectively with the external world, developing a super-ego based on identifications which are constructive and not punitively moralistic, and evolving defensive mechanisms which drain off some of the energy of the id without serious restriction of ego functioning. Normal development is a dynamic process entailing a continuing distribution and redistribution of psychical energy among id, ego and super-ego, the three systems of the mental apparatus.

Development of neurosis

Freud saw biological, phylogenetic and psychological factors as each contributing to neurosis. The biological factor is that the human animal is born relatively unfinished and thus has to undergo a protracted period of helplessness and dependence. This helplessness creates the initial situation of danger regarding fear of object loss, which in turn creates the human's need to be loved, which it never renounces.

The phylogenetic factor is inferred from the interruption in human sexual development of the latency period, whereas the sexual maturation of related animals proceeds uninterrupted. Freud believed that something momentous must have taken place in the history of the human species to bring about this situation and that its pathogenic importance is that most of the instinctual demands of infantile sexuality are treated as dangers to be guarded against by the ego. Furthermore, there is the danger that the sexual impulses of puberty will follow their infantile prototypes into repression.

The psychological factor involves three elements which together make for a pathogenic neurotic conflict. The first element is that of frustration of libidinal impulses or the damming up of the sexual instinct by the ego. Repressions are especially likely to take place in infancy and early childhood, when the ego is underdeveloped and feeble in relation to the strength of the sexual impulses. Freud observed: 'We recognize the essential precondition of neuroses in this lagging of ego development behind libidinal development' (Freud, 1949, p. 113). The process of repression takes place under the influence of anxiety, in that the ego anticipates that satisfaction of the emerging sexual cathexis will lead to danger. In fact the ego allows an initial reproduction of the feared unpleasure. This feeling of anxiety brings the unpleasure-pleasure mechanism into operation and so causes the ego to repress the dangerous instinctual impulse. By the act of repression, however, the ego has renounced a portion of its organization and the repressed instinctual impulse remains inaccessible to its influence.

The second psychological element is that the frustrated sexual impulses may not disappear, instead getting transformed into neurotic symptoms. Freud saw symptoms such as hysterical or conversion symptoms as the substitute satisfactions for the frustrated sexual instincts. Repression, however, does not always result in symptom formation. For instance, in a successful dissolution of the Oedipus complex the repressed sexual impulses may be destroyed, with their libido being put permanently to other uses.

The third psychological element is that, while the repressions may be effective during early childhood and the latency period, they may turn out to be inadequate with the re-awakening and intensification of the sexual instincts at menarche and puberty. When this occurs the individual may experience an intense neurotic conflict with all its suffering. Without assistance in undoing its repressions, the ego will have little or no influence over the transformed instincts of the repressed id. Furthermore, the conflict is often heightened through an alliance of the id and super-ego against the ego.

Freud (1973) gives as an example of normal and neurotic development the story of the caretaker's and the landlord's little daughters. When young, the two girls played games which took on a sexual character, including exciting each other's genitals. These experiences awakened sexual impulses which afterwards found expression in masturbation. The caretaker's daughter, unscarred by her early sexual activity, which she regarded as natural and harmless, took a lover and became a mother. While still a child the landlord's daughter, as a result of education, got the idea that she had done something wrong. She turned into an intelligent and high-minded girl who renounced her sexuality and whose subsequent neurosis precluded her from marrying. While consciously unaware of her sexual impulses, unconsciously these impulses were still attached to her experiences with the caretaker's daughter. Freud observes that, owing to the higher moral and intellectual development of her ego, she came into conflict with the demands of her sexuality.

MAINTENANCE

Freud believed that neuroses are acquired only during early childhood, up to the age of six, even though the symptoms of the neurotic conflict may not appear until much later. He acknowledged the truth of the common assertion that the child is psychologically father of the man. Neurotic people, despite their suffering, are unable to heal their disordered egos and thus their misery is maintained. The reason for this is that, by definition, the significant repressions made by their weak childhood egos are unconscious. Thus their egos pay the price of their defensive operations by not having conscious access to the material through which the neurotic conflict might be resolved. Neurotic people's egos are weakened by their repressions and their personality functioning is impaired by psychical energy being utilized in harmful defensive anti-cathexes. Also, as long as the repressions continue, so do the conditions for the formation of neurotic symptoms through the rechannelling of frustrated libidinous impulses.

In a broader sense, maintenance of neurosis results from the unsatisfactory way in which society tries to regulate sexual matters. Freud believed that what is described as morality, or the group super-ego, requires a bigger sacrifice of libidinal impulses than is necessary or desirable. He found it impossible to side with conventional sexual morality and considered that anyone with real self-knowledge would be protected against the dangers of morality, while possibly adopting a life-style different from the conventions of society.

PRACTICE
Goals

A definition of a neurotic is someone who is incapable of enjoyment and efficiency. To be capable of enjoyment neurotics require the ability to deploy their libido on to real objects instead of transforming it into symptoms. To live efficiently the ego needs to have the energy of the libido at its disposal rather than wasting energy in warding off libidinous impulses through repression. Furthermore, people's super-egos need to be such as to allow them libidinal expression and the efficient use of their egos. Thus the objectives of psychoanalysis are threefold: (a) the freeing of impulse; (b) the strengthening of reality-based ego functioning, including widening its perceptions so that it appropriates more of the id; and (c) the alteration of the contents of the super-ego so that it represents human rather than punitive moral standards.

Psychoanalysis is a process of re-educating the ego. Repressions were instituted when clients' egos were weak. However, now not only have clients' egos grown stronger but they possess allies in analysts. Methods by which analysts help weakened egos to lift their repressions, gain insight and make realistic decisions are discussed below. The pathogenic conflicts of neurotics are different from normal mental conflicts because of the ego's weakness relative to the other mental agencies.

Freud considered psychoanalytic treatment effective for a number of nervous diseases, such as hysteria, anxiety states and obsessional neurosis. Since the alliance between the analyst and the client's ego is a mutual one, the client's ego needs to have retained a minimum degrees of coherence or reality orientation. This is not to be expected with psychotics, with whom, therefore, psychoanalysis is contra-indicated.

Free Association

A basic pact lies at the heart of analytic relationships. Freud (1949) stated: 'The patient's sick ego promises us the most complete candour . . . we, on the other hand, assure him of the strictest discretion and put at his service our experience in interpreting material that has been influenced by the unconscious' (p. 63). The fundamental rule for clients is that of free association. Clients must tell their analysts everything that occurs to them, even if it is disagreeable and even if it seems meaningless. As far as possible, clients are encouraged to put their self-criticism out of action and share all their thoughts, feelings, ideas, memories and associations. The object of free association is to help lift repressions by making unconscious material conscious.

Transference

From early in his career Freud attached great importance to his relationships with clients. He discovered that clients perceive their analysts as reincarnations of important figures from their childhoods and transfer on to them moderate to intense feelings and emotions appropriate to these earlier models. Freud speaks of transference-love and observes that this love is ambivalent, being a mixture of affection with a reverse side of hostility, exclusiveness and jealousy. The transference represents a development of the original neurosis into a transference neurosis in relationship to the analyst.

The transference has at leat three advantages. First, it may start by being positive, which helps analysts, since their clients work to please them. The weak ego can become stronger and the client achieve gains out of love for the analyst. Second, when clients put analysts in the places of their fathers or mothers, they give them access to the power their super-egos have over their egos. Analysts as new super-egos can use their power for 'a sort of *after-education* of the neurotic' (Freud, 1949, p. 67). They can remedy earlier errors in parental education. However, analysts need always respect their clients' need for independence. Third, in the transference clients reproduce, rather than just remember, important parts of their life history. They act out in front of their analysts mental attitudes and defensive reactions connected with their neuroses.

Almost invariably the transference becomes negative and hostile, thus turning into a resistance. The onset of the negative transference is connected with analysts frustrating their clients by being unwilling to satisfy their erotic demands towards them. The revival of pathogenic conflicts gives analysts access to much repressed material, insight into which helps to strengthen their clients' egos.

Handling the transference is a critical skill of analysts, who must again and again show clients the prototype of their feelings in their childhoods. Analysts need take care that transferences do not get out of hand. They can forewarn clients of this possibility and be alert to early signs of this happening. Also, they can encourage clients not to act out their transferences outside of the analytic setting.

Resistance

Free association is not really free, in that clients associate within the context of the analytic situation. Thus everything that occurs to them has some reference to that situation and they are likely to resist reproducing the repressed material. At its simplest level, resistance involves intentionally not adhering to the fundamental rule. Even if this level of resistance is overcome, resistance will find less obvious means of expression. The client's ego is fearful of potential unpleasure caused by exploring material that is has repressed in the unconscious. The ego protects itself from the repressed id by means of anti-cathexes. The more threatening the repressed material is, the more tenaciously the ego clings to its anti-cathexes and the more remote are clients' associations from the unconscious material that their analysts seek.

Freud described all the forces that oppose the work of recovery as clients' resistances. One resistance is the repression-resistance described above. A second resistance is the transference resistance, which was mentioned earlier. A third is the resistance to forgoing the gain from illness. A fourth resistance is that of the id, which may resist a change in the direction of its satisfaction and need to 'work through' to a new mode of satisfaction. The fifth kind of resistance, emanating from the super-ego, is the unconscious sense of guilt or need for punishment which resists any success through analysis. Clients must remain ill for they deserve no better. This is the most powerful kind of resistance and the one analysts most dread.

The struggle to overcome resistances is the main work of psychoanalysis and this part of analytic treatment cannot easily be hurried. Forces helping analysts to overcome resistances are clients' needs for recovery, any intellectual interest they may have in the analytic process and, most important, their positive transferences with their analysts.

Interpretation

Interpretations are constructions or explanations. They can focus both on what has happened to clients and been forgotten and on what is now happening to clients without their understanding it. Interpretation is the means by which material that is repressed and unconscious is transformed into preconscious material and consciousness. Analysts employ interpretation not only to understand the impulses of the id, but also to help clients gain insight into the defensive mechanisms and resistances that their egos use both to cope with the repressed material and to thwart the analytic endeavour. Part of the work of interpretation consists of filling in memory gaps. Analysts interpret the impulses that have become subject to repression and the objects to which they have become attached with the aim of helping clients to replace these repressions by acts of judgement appropriate to their present-day rather than to their childhood situations. The analyst works with the client's ego, encouraging it to overcome resistances and to take control of hitherto repressed libidinal energy. Unconscious impulses are exposed to criticism by being traced back to their origin.

The material for interpretation is obtained from a number of sources. These include the clients' free associations, parapraxes or slips of the tongue, dreams, and their transference relationships with their analysts. Analysts need to distinguish clearly between their own and their clients' knowledge. Appropriate timing of interpretations is very important; if attempted at the wrong time, they meet with resistance. Therefore clients need to be very near to the moment of insight before analysts make interpretations. Also, the closer interpretations are to the details of what has been forgotten, the easier it is for clients to accept them. The later stages of psychoanalysis involve a working through by repeated interpretations, and this is often the most difficult and frequently an incomplete part of analysis.

Interpretation of dreams

An important – sometimes the most important – part of the psychoanalytic technique is the interpretation of dreams. When Freud's clients were told to communicate to him every idea or thought that occurred in relation to a particular topic, among other things they told him their dreams. This taught Freud that 'a dream can be inserted into the psychical chain that has to be traced backwards in the memory from a pathological idea' (Freud, 1976, p. 175). During sleep the ego reduces its repression and thus unconscious material becomes conscious in the shape of dreams. Freud saw dreams as wish-fulfilments, the disguised fulfilment of repressed wishes. However, even in sleep the ego still retains some censorship over repressed material and the latent dream thoughts are distorted so as to make the manifest dream content less threatening. Dreams, in fact, are compromises between repressed id impulses and the defensive operation of the ego.

The interpretation of a dream involves understanding the latent dream thoughts which are disguised by the process of dream work. Elements of dream work involve condensing the latent dream thoughts into a much smaller dream content, displacing the psychical intensity between elements and using symbolism. Frequently, symbols in dreams represent sexual material. For instance, all elongated objects, such as sticks, tree trunks, knives, daggers and umbrellas, may stand for the penis. The opening of an umbrella may symbolize an erection. Boxes, cases, chests, cupboards and ovens represent the uterus. A dream of going through a suite of rooms is a brothel or harem dream. Not all dream symbols are sexual: for instance, emperors or empresses may represent parents.

Freud prepared clients in two ways for working with their dreams. First, he asked them to increase the attention that they paid to their psychical perceptions. To enhance this, it was advantageous that they 'lie in a restful attitude' (Freud, 1976, p. 175). However, he soon abandoned stressing that they need shut their eyes. Second, he explicitly insisted that clients abandon all criticism of the thoughts that they perceived (a feature of free association). Clients differed in the ease with which they could adopt the required mental attitude and abandon their critical functions.

In *The Interpretation of Dreams*, Freud gives as an example the interpretation of one of his own dreams (1976, pp. 180–99). He had been giving psychoanalytic treatment to Irma, a family friend. The treatment was partially successful in that Irma was relieved of her hysterical anxiety, but without losing all somatic symptoms. One day Freud received a visit from a junior colleague called Otto, who had been staying with Irma and her family at a country resort. Otto answered Freud's enquiry about Irma with: 'She's better, but not quite well.' Freud was annoyed with Otto's words, detecting reproof in them. That evening he wrote out Irma's case history with the idea of giving it to Dr M, a mutual friend. The following night or morning he had a dream which he noted down as soon as he awoke. The dream involved Irma, Otto, Dr M, and a friend called Leopold. Without going into great detail, in that dream Otto was implicated in infecting Irma by giving her an injection with a syringe that was probably unclean. The conclusion of Freud's interpretation of this dream was that it was Otto, not he who was responsible for the persistence of Irma's present pains. Freud observed of his dream: *'Thus its content was the fulfilment of a wish and its motive was a wish'* (Freud, 1976, p. 196).

Concluding comment

Freud saw psychoanalysis as having three main parts. First, inducing clients' weakened egos to participate in the intellectual work of interpretation to fill in the gaps of their mental resources and transfer to their analysts the authority of their super-egos. Second, stimulating clients' egos to struggle against each of the id's demands and to defeat the resistances arising in connection with them. Third, restoring order to clients' egos 'by detecting material and impulses which have forced their way in from the unconscious' (Freud, 1949, p. 77). Such material is both traced back to its origin and exposed to criticism. Freud considered that ultimately, the success of psychoanalysis depended upon the quantitative relationship between the amount of energy analysts can mobilize in clients to their advantage in comparison with the amount of energy of the forces working against them.

CHAPTER REVIEW AND SELF-REFERENT QUESTIONS
Chapter review questions

1. What is the pleasure principle?
2. How did Freud view the instincts?
3. Describe each of Freud's three levels of consciousness.
4. How did Freud describe the id and its functions?

5. How did Freud describe the ego and its functions?

6. How did Freud describe the super-ego and its functions?

7. What are the three kinds of anxiety identified by Freud?

8. Why is psychoanalysis often referred to as presenting a dynamic view of psychology?

9. What were Freud's views on bisexuality?

10. Describe each phase of the pre-genital stage of sexual development.

11. What does the term latency period mean?

12. Describe the genital stage of sexual development.

13 What is the function of defensive mechanisms? Illustrate with specific examples.

14. Describe Freud's views on the development of neurosis.

15. Describe Freud's views on the maintenance of neurosis.

16. In psychoanalysis, what is meant by the term transference and why is it so important?

17. In psychoanalysis, what is meant by the term resistance and why is it so important?

18. What did Freud mean by the term interpretation and what are some sources of material for making interpretations?

19. Describe as best you can how Freud approached the interpretation of a dream.

Self-referent questions

1. List as many of your instincts as you are able. Do you consider that Freud's idea about the destructive instincts applies to you?

2. Can you think of material or events in your life which you might view as evidence for unconscious mental processes? If so, provide examples (e.g. dreams).

3. Think back over your own sexual development. Are you aware of having been sexual as an infant, having passed through pre-genital, latency, and genital stages of sexual development, and having experienced an Oedipus situation? If you are unaware of such experiences, do you think it might be because you are repressing them?

4. What are some of the significant influences which contributed to the formation of your super-ego? With what moral guidelines, if any, do you consider that your super-ego restricts you from the realistic pursuit of pleasure?

5. Assess the adequacy with which your ego deals with each of its three taskmasters: (a) your instinctual impulses; (b) the external world; and (c) your super-ego. Do you suffer from neurotic and/or realistic and/or moral anxiety?

6. Are you aware that your ego uses defensive mechanisms to ward of anxiety? If so, what are they? Do you consider that your use of defensive mechanisms is normal or neurotic?

7. What do you consider the relevance of Freud's ideas on the interpretation of dreams to interpreting your own dreams?

8. What is the relevance of Freud's work to understanding your life?

9. How has Freud influenced the way you think about and practice counselling?

Annotated bibliography

Freud, S. (1976). *The Interpretation of Dreams.* Hardmondsworth, Penguin. Original edition 1900.
This book is Freud's major work. In it he reviews the scientific literature about dreams, demonstrates his method of interpreting dreams, and discusses dreams as fulfilments of wishes. He also examines distortion in dreams, the material and sources of dreams, dream-work and the psychology of the dream process. The present translation is based on the reprint of the eighth edition (1930), the last published during Freud's life. This volume is part of The Pelican Freud Library, which is intended to contain all Freud's major writings.

Freud, S. (1962a). *Three Contributions to the Theory of Sex.* New York: E.P. Dutton. Original edition 1905.
This book is Freud's major statement on the nature and development of human sexuality. The three contributions are entitled: the sexual aberrations, infantile sexuality, and the transformations of puberty. Apart from *The Interpretation of Dreams*, this was the only other book that Freud kept more or less systematically up to date.

Freud S. (1949). *An Outline of Psychoanalysis.* New York: W.W. Norton. Originally published posthumously in 1940.
Written just before Freud's death, this book provides an excellent concise introduction to psychoanalysis. The book consists of three parts: the mind and its workings, the practical task, and the theoretical yield.

Jones, E. (1963). *The Life and Work of Sigmund Freud.* Edited and abridged in one volume by Lionel Trilling and Steven Marcus. New York: Anchor Books. Also available in a Penguin edition.
Written in three volumes by a close associate, this book is a definitive biography of Freud. It records the main facts of Freud's life and relates his personality and life experiences to the development of his ideas. In addition, the book traces the history of the psychoanalytic movement during Freud's lifetime.

Hall, C.S. (1954). *A Primer of Freudian Psychology.* New York: Mentor Books.
This concise book presents Freud's ideas on the organization, dynamics, development of, and stabilized personality. It is a highly recommended secondary source.

Further references

Freud

Freud, S. (1935). *An Autobiographical Study.* London: Hogarth Press.

Freud, S. (1936). *The Problem of Anxiety.* New York: W.W. Norton. Originally published in 1926 under the title *Inhibitions, Symptoms and Anxiety*.

Freud, S. (1950). Analysis terminable and interminable. In S. Freud, *Collected Papers* (vol. V., pp. 316–57). London: Hogarth Press. Original edition 1937.

Freud, S. (1950). *Group Psychology and the Analysis of the Ego.* London: Hogarth Press. Original edition 1921.

Freud, S. (1961). *Beyond the Pleasure Principle.* London: Hogarth Press. Original edition 1920.

Freud, S. (1962b). *The Ego and the Id.* London: Hogarth Press. Original edition 1923.

Freud, S. (1962c). *Civilization and its Discontents*. New York: W.W. Norton. Original edition 1930.

Freud, S. (1964). *The Question of Lay Analysis*. New York: Anchor Books. Original edition 1926.

Freud S. (1973). *New Introductory Lectures on Psychoanalysis*. Harmondsworth: Penguin. Original edition 1933 (1932).

Freud, S. & Breuer, J. (1956). *Studies on Hysteria*. London: Hogarth Press. Original edition 1895.

Others

Arlow, J.A. (1989). Psychoanalysis. In R.J. Corsini and D. Wedding (Eds.) *Current Psychotherapies* (4th ed., pp. 19–62). Itasca, IL: Peacock.

Bowlby, J. (1958). The nature of the child's ties to the mother. *International Journal of Psychoanalysis, 52*, 137–44.

Brenner, C. (1973). *An Elementary Textbook of Psychoanalysis*. New York: International Universities Press.

Fromm, E. (1959). *Sigmund Freud's Mission*. London: George Allen & Unwin.

Klein, M. (1932). *The Psychoanalysis of Children*. London: Hogarth Press.

Winnicott, D.W. (1953). Transitional objects and transitional phenomena: A study of the first not-me possession. *International Journal of Psychoanalysis, 34*, 89–97.

PART FIVE
Behavioural

NINE

Behavioural Counselling: Theory

PREVIEW

- *Behavioural theory may be viewed both as an overall theory and as an experimentally based attempt to describe the laws or principles by which human behaviour is learned and maintained.*

- *Pavlov conducted extensive researches into the functioning of the cerebral hemispheres of dogs. He discovered the conditioned reflex, otherwise known as classical or respondent conditioning. For example, by pairing a conditioned stimulus (metronome) with an unconditioned stimulus (food), a dog comes to acquire a salivary response in the presence of the conditioned stimulus alone.*

- *Watson viewed behaviourist psychology, termed 'behaviourism', as an objective experimental branch of natural science focused on the behaviour of human beings. He distinguished between unlearned and learned responses. Most stimuli to which humans respond are learned. Three main habit systems are formed by conditioning: (a) visceral or emotional; (b) manual; and (c) laryngeal or verbal.*

- *Some experiments on an 11-month-old boy called Albert illustrate the conditioning of an emotional fear response to a white rat, its transfer to other furry animals and its persistence. A further experiment on another child unconditioned his fear of furry animals. The cure for personality problems is unconditioning and conditioning.*

- *Skinner viewed behaviour as being shaped and maintained by its consequences. While acknowledging the importance of classical conditioning, he went beyond this to focus on the action of the environment after the response has been made.*

- *Operant conditioning emphasizes that behaviour operates on the environment to generate consequences. Reinforcers are events which strengthen the probability of a response.*

Contingencies of reinforcement, which describe the interaction between the organism and its environment, are: (a) the occasion on which a response occurs; (b) the response itself; and (c) the reinforcing consequences.

• *Other concepts reviewed here are: positive and negative reinforcement, primary and conditional reinforcers, schedules of reinforcement, maintenance and extinction of behaviour, shaping and successive approximation, stimulus discrimination and control, and stimulus generalization. Skinner's ideas on the self, self-control, psychotherapy and environmental design are also described.*

• *Wolpe offers a reciprocal inhibition explanation for some conditioned inhibitions. Reciprocal inhibition involves eliciting a competing response in order to bring about a decrease in the strength of a simultaneous response. Wolpe induced neurotic fear responses in experimental cats and then used his reciprocal inhibition principle to decondition them to the point where they could eat in an experimental cage where previously they had received electric shocks. A number of responses incompatible with anxiety may be used in conjunction with counselling. These include relaxation, assertive and sexual responses.*

• *Eysenck considers that a theory of neurosis has to explain not only the failure of extinction, but the enhancement of neurotic conditioned responses that remain unreinforced.*

• *Eysenck's incubation theory posits that certain conditioned responses (CR) have drive properties which, when the conditioned stimulus (CS) only is presented, produce a conditioned response of fear/anxiety identical to the unconditioned response (UCR). Such a CR provides positive reinforcement for the CS-only presentation, thus causing it to evoke more fear or enhance/incubate the CR. Incubation allows the CR to exceed the strength of the UCR. Conditions which favour incubation are discussed.*

INTRODUCTION

Adherents of behavioural counselling, or behaviour therapy, view their practice as firmly rooted in experimentally derived principles of learning. However, behavioural theory is an overall theory as well as an experimentally based attempt to describe the specific laws or principles of human behaviour. As an overall theory the distinctive emphasis is on the overwhelming role of environmental contingencies in influencing the acquisition and perpetuation of behaviour. In its most radical form the behavioural model sees human actions as derived solely from two sources: biological deprivations, such as hunger and sexual tension, and the individual's learning history. There is no place for concepts such as mind and free will. However, a distinction increasingly emerging in behavioural counselling is that between approaches based solely on stimulus-response connections and those which also take into account cognitive mediating variables. The latter emphasis is less deterministic than the former.

As a set of experimentally derived principles of learning, the behavioural model offers a greater degree of specificity in analysing observable, as contrasted with intrapsychic, human behaviour than that offered by the humanistic, existential or psychoanalytic models. Much of the research on which the behavioural model is based has been performed on animals such as dogs, cats and pigeons. This raises issues of the generalizability of a model derived largely from non-human animals in laboratory settings to humans in natural settings. Nevertheless, the point remains that, at the molecular level or level of observation of specific behaviours, behavioural psychologists have made a distinctive contribution to the development of a theoretical framework for counselling.

Defining learning involves indicating both what the term includes and what it excludes. Hilgard and Bower (1966, p. 2) provisionally offer the following definition:

> Learning is the process by which an activity originates or is changed through reacting to an encountered situation, provided that the characteristics of the change in activity cannot be explained on the basis of native response tendencies, maturation, or temporary states of the organism (e.g. fatigue, drugs, etc.).

Learning is a process which involves the acquisition of and, in varying degrees, the retention of behaviours. Although it may be helped or hindered by factors such as maturation and fatigue, it refers to those elements in the acquisition and retention of behaviours which are not attributable to these factors.

This chapter differs from the preceding ones. It aims to introduce the reader to some key behavioural concepts through discussing selectively the ideas and experimental work of five leading theorists: Pavlov, Watson, Skinner, Wolpe and Eysenck. Both Wolpe and Eysenck played major roles in advancing and popularizing what is now known as behavioural counselling or behaviour therapy. The theorists are presented in roughly historical order, though their working lives may overlap.

PAVLOV'S CLASSICAL CONDITIONING

Ivan Petrovich Pavlov (1849–1936) was a Russian physiologist. In the course of his investigations into the activities of the digestive glands, he started to record all the external stimuli falling on his experimental dogs at the time their reflex reactions, such as the secretion of saliva, were manifested. Pavlov did not begin his investigations into the functioning of the cerebral hemispheres of dogs until he was 50, but spent the remainder of his life on this research, eventually with a large staff. Although he is best known for the discovery of the conditioned reflex, his researches were far more extensive.

Pavlov considered that both instincts and reflexes were alike in being inevitable response of the organism to internal and external stimuli. 'Reflex' was the preferred term since it had been used from the beginning with a scientific connotation. The whole nervous activity of animals is based on inborn reflexes, which may be either excitatory or inhibitory. Such reflexes 'are regular causal connections between certain definite external stimuli acting on the organism and its necessary reflex reaction' (Pavlov, 1927, p. 16). The inborn reflexes alone are inadequate to ensure the continued existence of the organism, with the more specialized interaction between the animals and the environment provided through the medium of the cerebral hemispheres. The 'most general function of the hemispheres is that of reacting to signals presented by innumerable stimuli of interchangeable signification' (Pavlov, 1927, p. 16).

In his book *Conditional Reflexes*, subtitled 'An investigation of the physiological activity of the cerebral cortex', Pavlov describes the precautions taken to build a laboratory so as to eliminate, as far as possible, any stimuli outside his control. In order to register the intensity of the salivary reflex, all the dogs used in his experiments were subjected to a minor operation which consisted of transferring the opening of the salivary duct from the mucous membrane of the mouth to the outside skin. In the experimental laboratory a dog would be harnessed to a stand in one section of a double chamber, while the experimenter was in the other section.

In the following experiment a conditioned reflex was obtained by pairing or linking up the action of a new stimulus with an unconditioned reflex. An experimental dog was introduced to a routine in which stimulation by a metronome was linked with feeding. If the dog was then placed in the experimental condition its salivary glands remained inactive as long as no special stimulus was introduced. However, when it was allowed to hear the sounds of a beating metronome, salivary secretion began after nine seconds, and in the course of 45 seconds 11 drops were secreted. Furthermore, in this experiment the dog turned in the direction from which it had customarily received food and began to lick its lips vigorously.

In another experiment food was shown to the animal. After five seconds salivary secretion began, and in the course of 15 seconds six drops were collected. In yet another experiment food was introduced into the dog's mouth and secretion began in one to two seconds.

Food in the dog's mouth, as contrasted with the sight of food or the association of food with the beating of a metronome, produces an inborn reflex. This reflex is brought about by the physical and chemical properties of the food acting upon the mucous membrane of the mouth and tongue. However, even salivation at the sight of food is a learned reflex, as in salivation at the beating of the metronome. Both the sight of food and the beating of the metronome are signals, and the reaction to them involves signalization through the activity of the cerebral hemispheres. Thus inborn reflexes do not involve learning or signalization, while conditioned reflexes are learned and involve signalization. The definition of reflexes as causal connections between definite external stimuli and their necessary reflex reactions still holds true when signalization is involved. The difference is that the reflex reaction to signals depends on more variables than those entailed in unconditioned reflexes.

In a further experiment on the same dog, contrary to the usual routine, stimulation by the metronome was not followed by feeding. The stimulus of the metronome was repeated for periods of 30 seconds at intervals of two minutes. Pavlov gives details indicating a lengthening of the latency period prior to secretion and a diminution of drops of saliva over successive trials. He writes that the phenomenon of the weakening of a reflex to a conditioned stimulus which is repeated a number of times without reinforcement might appropriately be termed extinction of conditional reflexes. Indeed, if the above experiment had been continued, the conditional reflex would have disappeared entirely.

Stage one

Unconditioned Stimulus (UCS) ————————▶ Unconditioned Response (UCR)

(food)   (salivation)

Stage two

Conditioned Stimulus (CS)

(metronome)

reinforced by

Unconditioned Stimulus (UCS) ————————▶ Unconditioned Response (UCR)

(food)   (salivation)

Stage three

Conditioned Stimulus (CS)———————————▶ Conditioned Response (CR)

(metronome)   (salivation)

Stage four

Conditioned Stimulus (CS) ———————————▶ Extinguished Conditioned

(metronome, no longer   Response (ECR)

reinforced by feeding)   (diminution/absence of salivation)

Figure 9.1 Diagrammatic representation of Pavlov's experiments on the conditioning and extinction of a dog's salivary response to the beating of a metronome.

Figure 9.1 diagrammatically depicts the metronome experiments, with the term 'response' substituted for 'reflex'. Food in the mouth is an unconditioned stimulus (UCS), which automatically elicits the inborn response of salivation (UCR). Through repeated reinforcement consisting of stimulation by the metronome followed by feeding, the metronome becomes a conditioned stimulus (CS), thus becoming a signal for food and eliciting the conditioned response of salivation (CR). However, if the metronome (CS) is no longer reinforced by feeding, then the conditioned response (CR) undergoes extinction and diminishes, or even disappears (ECR).

Learning a conditioned response in the above manner has come to be termed classical or respondent conditioning. Pavlov and his colleagues explored many other areas, such as conditioned inhibition and the generalization of stimuli, but these researches are not described here. Suffice it for now to say that Pavlov's experimental work constitutes a lasting and fundamental influence in the behavioural approach to counselling.

WATSON'S CONDITIONED BEHAVIOURISM

John Broadus Watson (1878–1958), sometimes viewed as the founder of behaviourism, led an unusual life. He was born in Greenville, South Carolina, to an energetic and religious mother and a philandering father, who left home when Watson was 13 years old. He was educated at Furman University in Greenville and at the University of

Chicago, where his doctoral thesis was on animal education. Watson married when he was 25. At 30 he became professor of psychology at Johns Hopkins University in Baltimore, and when 36 he was elected president of the American Psychological Association. During the 1910s Watson moved his emphasis from animal to human observation and experimentation, and from 1913 he worked hard at establishing behaviourism as a method of psychology.

In his personal life Watson had a decided tendency to respond to female stimuli, a characteristic with which his first wife was prepared to live so long as the relationships were not really serious. However, in 1919 Watson, who was then 41, met an overwhelming stimulus in the person of a 19-year-old graduate student called Rosalie Raynor. In 1920 Watson was forced to resign from Johns Hopkins University on the grounds of adultery with a student and no other university would employ him. Divorced in late 1920, Watson married Rosalie in January 1921 and lived happily with her until her tragic death in 1936.

After leaving university life Watson became a highly successful advertising executive with J. Walter Thompson's and later with Esty's agencies. In the 1920s, Watson conducted some research on children with Mary Cover Jones and also did some popular psychological writing. His two children by his second marriage, Billy and Jimmy, were brought up by behavioural methods, including an absence of overt shows of parental affection so that they would not become dependent. Billy, who became a psychiatrist interested in Freudian ideas, committed suicide a few years after Watson's death in 1958, while Jimmy underwent psychoanalysis.

Watson's books include *Animal Education, Behaviour, Psychology from the Standpoint of a Behaviorist, The Psychological Care of the Infant and Child* and *Behaviorism*. A bibliography of Watson's work can be found at the end of David Cohen's biography, *J.B. Watson, the Founder of Behaviourism*.

Behaviourism

To the behaviourist 'the subject matter of human psychology is the behavior of the human being' (Watson, 1931, p. 2). Furthermore, the behaviourist views psychology as a purely objective experimental branch of natural science, with its theoretical goal being the prediction and control of behaviour. In his 1913 paper 'Psychology as the behaviourist views it', Watson observed that he had devoted nearly 12 years to experimentation on animals and that it was natural that he should drift to a theoretical position in harmony with his experimental work. What is observable constitutes the real field of psychology and what can be observed consists of what the organism does or says, i.e. its behaviour.

Watson believed that there were two points of view dominant in the American psychological thinking of his time: introspective or subjective psychology, which he termed the old psychology, and the new and objective psychology of behaviourism. Concepts such as consciousness and introspection, the subject matter of the old psychology, were magic. Psychology, being an objective and experimental branch of the natural sciences, needs such concepts as little as do the sciences of chemistry and physics. As the behaviour of animals can be investigated without referring to consciousness, so can the behaviour of man. In fact 'the behavior of man and the behavior of animals must be considered on the same plane; as being equally essential to a general understanding of behavior' (Watson, 1913, p. 176)

Stimulus, response and conditioning

Both man and animal adjust themselves to their environments by means of hereditary and habit equipments. Through the process of evolution humans have developed sense organs, such as the eye, skin and viscera, which are most sensitive to differing kinds of stimuli. A stimulus, or thing that evokes a reaction, may come from objects in the external environment. Also, humans are affected constantly by stimuli in their internal environment arising from tissue changes in their bodies. By means of conditioning there is an ever-increasing range of stimuli to which people respond.

Stimuli evoke responses which usually involve the organism moving or altering in such a way that the stimulus no longer arouses reaction. One classification of responses is that between overt and implicit. Another general classification is that between learned and unlearned responses. Unlearned responses include all the things people do from earliest infancy, such as perspiring and breathing, prior to the processes of conditioning and habit formation which produce learned responses.

The Watsonian behaviourist sees all psychological problems and their solutions as being schematized in *stimulus* (or the more complex *situation*) and *response* terms, often abbreviated to S-R terms. In the ideal behaviourist world, given the response the stimuli can be predicted and given the stimuli the response can be predicted. Figure 9.2 illustrates this view of psychological problems.

Stimuli may be unconditioned in that from birth they call forth definite responses, such as the responses of turning the eyes away from or closing the eyes to light. On the other hand, most stimuli to which humans respond are conditioned or learned, for example all the printed words to which humans respond. Similarly, responses may be unconditioned, as in the above light example, but very frequently they are conditioned, as in the case of a two-year-old child who has learned to substitute screaming for

Unsolved

S . . . . R

Given   ? (To be determined)

S . . . . R

? (To be determined)   Given

Solved

S . . . . R

Has been determined   Has been determined

Figure 9.2 Schematization of unsolved and solved psychological problems

laughter at the sight of a dog. Watson observed that the whole body of man is built around the keynote 'rapid, and when needed, complicated reactions to simple and complex stimuli' (Watson, 1931, p. 91).

Hereditary equipment

Watson viewed humans as animals born with certain types of structure, subject to individual variations, which force them to respond to stimuli in certain ways. For instance, at birth the human responds with breathing, heartbeat, sneezing, etc. These kinds of reactions are the human's unlearned behaviour. Some unlearned behaviours, such as suckling and unlearned grasping, are short lived. Others, such as blinking, menstruation and ejaculation, begin later in life and last much longer. Unlearned behaviours form a relatively simple list of human responses, each of which, including our respiration and circulation, becomes conditioned shortly after birth. The concept of instinct is redundant in psychology, since observation of children indicates that everything which people tend to call 'instinct' is largely the result of training or conditioning and, as such, is part of the human's learned behaviour.

Watson developed the idea of the activity stream, a 'ceaseless stream of activity beginning when the egg is fertilized and becoming more complex as age increases' (Watson, 1931, p. 139). Each human action system starts with an unlearned beginning and is then made more complex by conditioning. For instance, vocal responses constitute unlearned behaviour while talking represents a conditioned action system.

Determinism and habit formation

The Watsonian behaviourist is a strict determinist. Watson believed that, given total control over a dozen healthy infants from birth, he could take any one at random and train him to become any type of person he might select, be it doctor, lawyer, artist, beggar or thief. Inheritance of capacity, talent, temperament, mental constitution and characteristics does not really exist, since these things depend on training.

Habit formation probably starts in embryonic life and is very rapid after birth. Though a baby is very helpless at birth, greater development of three habit systems differentiates the human from other animals. These habit systems are (a) visceral or emotional; (b) manual; and (c) laryngeal or verbal. The development of emotional habits will be used to illustrate the importance of conditioning.

Conditioning of emotions

Watson states that there are three types of unlearned beginnings of emotional reactions, or unlearned emotional responses, to stimuli. These responses are fear, rage and love. These emotional reactions might be viewed as unconditioned reflexes or responses. For instance, a loud sound is a fundamental stimulus for eliciting the fear response.

Watson and Raynor did a series of experiments on an 11-month-old boy called Albert (Watson & Raynor, 1920). The first experiment involved the establishment of a conditioned emotional response of fear to a white rat. This was achieved by linking on some trials the loud sound of the striking of a bar with Albert's touching the white rat.

When later the white rat was presented alone, Albert exhibited fear responses of crying, falling over and crawling away. A second experiment showed that there was a transfer of the conditioned fear response, though less strong, from the white rat to other furry animals (rabbit, dog) and objects (fur coat, cotton wool) when five days later they were presented to him. The above tests were carried out on a table covered with a mattress in a small, well lit room. A further experiment indicated, after 31 days, the persistence in a less intense form of both the conditioned fear response to the rat and the transferred fear responses to the fur coat and the rabbit. Watson and Raynor concluded that it was probable that many of the phobias in psychopathology are conditioned emotional reactions of either the direct or the transferred type. Emotional disturbances can be retraced to conditioned and transferred responses set up in infancy and childhood to all three of the fundamental human emotions.

Watson and Raynor did not remove Albert's conditioned emotional responses prior to his discharge from hospital to be adopted by a family that lived outside Baltimore. However, Mary Cover Jones, an associate of Watson's, conducted an experiment in which Peter, a boy of about three, was unconditioned or reconditioned in his 'home grown' fears of a rabbit, a white rat and related stimuli (Jones, 1924). The experimenters were given permission to give Peter his lunch of crackers and a glass of milk. Just as he began to each his lunch, the rabbit was displayed in a cage of wire mesh just far enough away not to disturb his eating. Gradually the rabbit was brought closer and closer and finally Peter would eat with one hand and play with the rabbit with the other. There was a transfer of unconditioning of fear responses to other furry objects, with degrees of success varying from total to greatly improved.

Watson contended that human emotional life is the result of the wear and tear of environmental forces. Through experiments such as those described above, an initial understanding was developing of how emotional reactions could be conditioned and unconditioned. Watson was excited and cautiously optimistic about the place of his natural science approach in the treatment of the emotionally disturbed.

Thinking and memory

Watson argued that 'thinking' referred to all subvocal word behaviour. In other words, thinking is the same as talking to oneself. Furthermore, language development represents the conditioning of verbal responses on unlearned vocal sounds. Sometimes the subvocal use of words has become an automatic habit. On other occasions, for example in reacting to a new situation, human thinking is similar to the trial-and-error behaviour of a rat in a maze. When subjects are asked to think aloud it is easy to see how they worked out their problem by word behaviour. New verbal creations, such as a poem, are arrived at by manipulating words and shifting them about until a new pattern is arrived at. There is no such thing as personal meaning in the behaviourist's theory.

Memory is viewed as the retention of verbal habits. If people meet a stimulus again after a period of time they do the habitual thinking they learned to do when the stimulus was first present. For instance, a person who meets a friend after an absence will say the old words and exhibit the old visceral reactions.

Personality and diagnosis

Watson defined personality as 'the sum of activities that can be discovered by actual observation of behavior over a long enough time to give reliable information. In other words, personality is the end product of our habit systems' (Watson, 1931, p. 274). Thus personality is defined in terms of behaviours or habits which may be observed objectively and which may give rise to accurate predictions of future behaviour. The method of studying personality is to take a cross-section of the habit systems in the activity stream at a given time, say at the age of 24. Among the activities there are dominant habit systems in each of the three broad clusters of habit systems, i.e. visceral, manual and laryngeal. An example of a dominant habit system in the laryngeal field is that of a great talker, whereas shyness may be a dominant habit system in the visceral field. Watson considered most judgements of personality to be superficial, made without a real study of the individual and often causing people serious injury as a result. He suggested five ways of obtaining a more accurate estimate of personality, namely by studying the individual's (a) education chart, (b) achievement chart, (c) spare time and recreation record, (d) emotional make-up under the practical situations of daily living and (e) responses to psychological tests.

There is no need to introduce the concept of mind into the so-called mental diseases. Diagnosis should involve an analysis of behaviour as suggested above. Personality problems are behaviour disturbances and habit conflicts which need to be cured by unconditioning and conditioning.

Ethics

The behaviourist is not interested in morals or ethics except as a scientist. Watson believed that to guide human behaviour on experimentally sound lines was beyond existing knowledge, since far too little was known about the human body and its needs. However, behaviourism is the foundation of all future experimental ethics. He possessed a vision of behaviouristic freedom unshackled by those customs and conventions which needlessly and harshly restrict the individual because they are not based on a sound understanding of the principles of behaviour. Watson would have liked to develop a world of people who could talk and behave freely everywhere 'without running afoul of group standards' (Watson, 1931, p. 303).

SKINNER'S OPERANT BEHAVIOURISM

Burrhus Frederick Skinner (1904–90) was born in Susquehanna, Pennsylvania. In 1926 he graduated from Hamilton College where, majoring in English, he had planned to become a writer. In 1928 Skinner entered Harvard University as a graduate student in psychology, obtaining his doctorate in 1931. From 1931–6 he worked as a postdoctoral fellow in the laboratory of W.J. Crozier, a distinguished experimental biologist.

Skinner held early academic appointments, from 1936–45, at the University of Minnesota and, from 1945–8, at Indiana University. In 1948 he became professor of psychology at Harvard, where he taught until he retired from active teaching in 1974.

throughout the remainder of his life Skinner continued writing and lecturing. Among his numerous academic awards, in 1958 Skinner received the American Psychological Association's Award for Distinguished Scientific Contributions.

Skinner's 19 books include his seminal work *The Behavior of Organisms, Walden Two,* a novel about a behavioural utopia, *Science and Human Behavior, Verbal Behavior,* which he considered his most important book, *Schedules of Reinforcement,* co-written with C.B. Ferster, *The Analysis of Behavior,* a programmed textbook co-authored with J.G. Holland, *Contingencies of Reinforcement, Beyond Freedom and Dignity,* and *Particulars of My Life.* Skinner 'always viewed his own work – as he views science generally – as the product of environmental contingencies and not the result of a creative mind' (Holland, 1992, p. 667).

Like Watson, Skinner was dedicated to a science of behaviour which deals with facts and searches for lawful relations among the events in nature. Pavlov's and Watson's experiments involved classical or respondent conditioning in which the organism was passive while being conditioned. In 1913 the noted experimental psychologist E.L. Thorndike propounded his Law of Effect that: 'When a modifiable connection between a situation and a response is made and is accompanied or followed by a satisfying state of affairs, that connection's strength is increased: when made and accompanied by an annoying state of affairs its strength is deceased' (Thorndike, 1932, p. 176). The Law of Effect went beyond the conditioning of reflexive responses to emphasize that the satisfying or annoying after-effects of connections influence them.

Skinner's distinctive contribution to psychology has been to elaborate the importance of the after-effects or consequences of behaviour. His fundamental principle is that 'Behavior is shaped and maintained by its consequences' (Skinner, 1971, p. 23). He was assiduous in conducting experiments which map out the details of this principle. He considered that he has gone beyond stimulus and response to take into account the action of the environment upon the organism *after* the response has been made. I now review some of Skinner's basic concepts derived from experimental research with pigeons and rats, prior to discussing some implications for human behaviour.

Operant behaviour

Skinner observes that a response which has occurred cannot be predicted or controlled, but all that can be predicted is the probability of a similar response occurring in the future. The unit of a predictive science of behaviour is an operant. The term 'operant' emphasizes that fact that behaviour *operates* on the environment to generate consequences. Thus the consequences define the properties with respect to which responses are viewed as similar. Skinner used the term 'operant' both as an adjective, as in operant behaviour, and as a noun, which indicates the behaviour defined by a given consequence. He acknowledged that Pavlov called all events which strengthened behaviour in his dogs 'reinforcement' and the resulting changes in their voluntary and involuntary behaviour 'conditioning'. However, the critical difference is that in Pavlov's work the reinforcer is paired with the *stimulus,* whereas in operant behaviour it is contingent upon a *response.* Classical and operant conditioning are the only two possible kinds of conditioning.

Contingencies of reinforcement

Skinner stressed the role of the environment in shaping and maintaining behaviour. Behaviour both operates on the environment to produce consequences and also is controlled or contingent upon the consequences produced by that environment. Any adequate description of the interaction between an organism and its environment must specify three elements: (a) the occasion on which a response occurs; (b) the response itself; and (c) the reinforcing consequences. The interrelationship of these three elements constitutes the contingencies of reinforcement. For example, in an experiment with pigeons, any stimuli deriving from the experimental space, such as sound or light, and from the operanda of the experiment, such as a translucent disc on the wall which may be pecked, and from any special stimulating devices prior to the response, are the 'occasion' of the response. The response itself might be pecking the disc and the reinforcing consequence might be food provided at a time when the pigeon is hungry.

Positive and negative reinforcement

The probability of a response is increased after both positive and negative reinforcement. Positive reinforcements consist of presenting something, such as food, water or sexual contact, in a situation. Negative reinforcements consist of removing something, such as a bright light or an electric shock, from the situation. Thus the difference between positive and negative reinforcement hinges on whether it is the presence or absence of a given reinforcer which increases the probability of a response. The withdrawal of a positive reinforcer has the same effect as the presentation of a negative reinforcer.

Primary and conditioned reinforcers

Skinner believed that all reinforcers eventually derive their power from evolutionary selection and that it is part of 'human nature' to be reinforced in particular ways by particular things. For instance, both the positive reinforcer of food and the negative reinforcer of escape from a dangerous situation have obvious survival value. Only a small part of behaviour is immediately reinforced by food, water, sexual contact or other reinforcers of evident biological significance. Such reinforcers are the primary or unconditioned ones.

Most behaviour is emitted in response to reinforcers which have become associated with or conditioned to primary reinforcers. For instance, if each time food is given to a hungry pigeon a light is turned on, the light eventually becomes a conditioned reinforcer. The light may then be used to condition an operant in the same way as food. A conditioned reinforcer is generalized when it is paired with more than one primary reinforcer. The importance of this is that a generalized conditioned reinforcer, such as money, is useful because it is not attached to just one state of deprivation, such as hunger, but to many. Therefore, under this kind of reinforcement, a response is more likely to occur. Other generalized conditioned reinforcers are attention, approval and affection.

Schedules of reinforcement

Ferster and Skinner (1957) observe that many significant features of the shaping and maintenance of behaviour can be explained only by reference to the properties of schedules of reinforcement, and also that intermittent reinforcement can be a very important source of reinforcement in its own right and not just the poor relation of inevitable or continuous reinforcement.

Non-intermittent schedules of reinforcement are:
1. Continuous reinforcement, where every response emitted is reinforced.
2. Extinction, where no responses are reinforced.

Intermittent schedules of reinforcement include:
1. Fixed interval, in which the first response occurring after a given period of time (for example, five minutes) is reinforced, with another period beginning immediately after the reinforcement.
2. Fixed ratio, in which every *nth* response is reinforced. (The word 'ratio' refers to the ratio between responses and reinforcements.)
3. Variable interval, in which reinforcements are scheduled according to a random series of intervals having a given mean and lying between arbitrary values.
4. Variable ratio, in which reinforcements are scheduled according to a random series of ratios having a given mean and lying between arbitrary values.
5. Multiple, in which one schedule of reinforcement is in force in the presence of one stimulus and a different schedule in the presence of another stimulus. For instance, there is a fixed interval when the key in the pigeon's experimental box is red, and a variable interval when the key is green.
6. Differential reinforcement of rate of response, in which a response is reinforced only if it follows the preceding response after a specified interval of time (e.g. three minutes) or before the end of a given interval (e.g. half a second).

Maintenance and extinction

Skinner did not consider the term 'learning' to be equivalent to 'operant conditioning'. Learning emphasizes acquisition of behaviour, whereas operant conditioning focuses on both acquisition and maintenance of behaviour. Thus behaviour continues to have consequences, and if these consequences or reinforcements are not forthcoming then extinction occurs. For instance, when a pigeon's behaviour, such as the lifting of its head, which has been reinforced by the consequence of food, no longer continues to receive this reinforcement, the head lifting tends to occur with a reduced frequency. Similarly, when people engage in behaviour which no longer has rewarding consequences, they find themselves less inclined to behave that way. Schedules of reinforcement are relevant to extinction. For example, the resistance to extinction generated by intermittent reinforcement may be much greater than that under continuous reinforcement. The task of a science of behaviour is to account for the probability of a response in terms of its history of reinforcement and extinction. Skinner used the term 'operant strength' to indicate the probability of a given response and observes that with humans the condition of low operant strength resulting from extinction often requires treatment. For instance, psychotherapy might sometimes be viewed as a system of reinforcement designed to reinstate extinguished behaviour.

Shaping and successive approximation

Behaviour may be shaped by reinforcing successive approximations to the desired response. Skinner gives the example of teaching a pigeon to bowl by swiping, with a sharp sideward movement of its beak, a wooden ball down a miniature alley towards a set of toy pins. When he and his colleagues waited for the complete response, which was to be reinforced by food, nothing happened. Then they decided to reinforce any response which had the slightest resemblance to a swipe and, afterwards, to select responses which more closely approximated the final form. This was a highly successful procedure and within minutes the pigeon was striking the ball as if it had been a champion squash player. In another experiment, by reinforcing successive approximations, a rat was conditioned to pull a string to get a marble from a rack, pick up the marble with its forepaws, carry it across the cage to a vertical tube rising two inches above the floor, lift the marble, and drop it into the tube.

Stimulus discrimination and control

Operant behaviour is emitted through important connections with the environment. For instance, in a pigeon experiment, neck-stretching is reinforced when a signal light is on and allowed to extinguish when a signal light is off. The contingencies of reinforcement are that a stimulus (the light) is the occasion, the response is stretching the neck, and the reinforcement is food. The process through which the response is eventually more likely to occur when the light is on is called discrimination. Another way of viewing discrimination is to say that a response has come under the control of a discriminative stimulus or, more briefly, under stimulus control. Once an operant discrimination has been conditioned, the probability of the response occurring may be increased or decreased by presenting or removing the discriminative stimulus. An example of the effect of stimulus control on humans is the increased probability of purchasing behaviour through the effective display of merchandise in a shop.

Stimulus generalization

When the reinforcing effect of one stimulus spreads to other stimuli, the effect is that of generalization or induction. For instance, if a response to a round, red spot one square inch in area is reinforced, a yellow spot of the same size and shape may also be reinforcing through the common properties of size and shape. However, by reinforcing only responses to the red spot with the above dimensions, and by extinguishing the response to the yellow spot, the red spot may be given exclusive discriminative control. An example of stimulus generalization in everyday life is reacting to people in a similar way because they resemble someone we know.

The self

Skinner regarded a self as a repertoire of behaviours appropriate to a given set of reinforcement contingencies. The traditional view of the causation of behaviour regards people as autonomous agents responsible for their own lives. The scientific view is that people are members of a species shaped by evolutionary contingencies of survival whose behaviour is under the control of the environment in which they live. Although Skinner acknowledged the nomad on horseback in Outer Mongolia and the astronaut in outer space as being different people, he believed that if they had been exchanged at birth they would have taken each other's place (though this might be interfered with by genetic factors which set limits on learning). The ways in which people perceive and know are determined by environmental contingencies. Also, consciousness or awareness is a social product shaped by the environment. Furthermore, the complex activity called thinking is explicable in terms of contingencies of reinforcement. Thus the self is a repertoire of behaviours acquired through an environmental history of reinforcement and maintained or extinguished through current contingencies of reinforcement.

Self-control

A functional analysis of behaviour implies discovering the independent variables which, once they are controlled, in turn control behaviour. In self-control, people manipulate events in their environments to control their behaviour. Self-control involves two interrelated responses. First, there is the controlling response which acts on the environment to alter the probability of the second or the controlled response. For instance, an adult may engage in the controlling response of walking away so that he is able to control his response of anger. Similarly, removal of discriminative stimuli, such as food, may help to avoid over-eating. On the other hand, presence of certain discriminative stimuli may make desirable behaviours more probable. For instance, a certain desk may act as a stimulus to study behaviour and a knot in a handkerchief may reinforce acting at a later date.

Psychotherapy

Some of the emotional and motivational manifestations of what is called mental disease may be extreme consequences of variables used in controlling the normal organism. In other words, much of the behaviour involved in mental disease is learned and therefore the role of psychotherapy is to change behaviour by manipulating the client's contingencies of reinforcement. Psychotherapy may be viewed as a form of control, the aim of which frequently is to correct the undesirable effects of excessive or inconsistent control exercised by other agencies to restrict the individual's selfish, primarily reinforced behaviour. These other agencies of control include parents and educational and religious institutions. Skinner believed that the use of punishment as a measure of control was responsible for many of the avoidance or escape and emotional by-products characteristic of mental disease.

Diagnosis in psychotherapy consists of a functional analysis to discover variables which can be used to alter unwanted behaviour. If the therapist is able adequately to identify and control these intervening variables, this leads directly to the control of dependent variables. One intervening variable in psychotherapy is the therapists's ability to be a controlling agent or potent reinforcer. Despite the client's aversive condition, which should make promise of relief reinforcing, usually the therapist's initial power is slight. However, as time goes by the therapist may become an important source of reinforcement, with approval being especially effective.

The main tool of the therapist is to be a non-punishing audience or to respond in ways which are incompatible with punishment. This may have two effects. First, behaviour which has hitherto been repressed may begin to appear in the repertoire of the client. Second, some of the effects of punishment may become extinguished. For instance, a client who feels less wrong or sinful may be less likely to emit the kinds of operant behaviour which provide escape from these self-generated stimuli. Skinner wrote: 'It is clear that psychology and psychodynamics overlap, these two fields being distinguished not in terms of subject matter or the casual factors to which appeal is made, but only in technique . . .' (Skinner, 1961, p. 200).

Not all unwanted behaviours, however, are caused by excessive use of punishment. Therefore further techniques are needed, depending on the outcomes of the functional analysis. For example, in instances where ethical and parental control have been inadequate, therapy may consist of supplying additional controlling contingencies. With the total lack of control of the psychotic it is difficult to discover effective controlling contingencies.

At other times the therapist may need to construct new controlling contingencies either by strengthening responses already in the individual's repertoire or by building additional responses. Furthermore, the therapist may have to teach a client techniques of self-control, especially if the client is still likely to be subject to continued excessive or inconsistent control. Skinner acknowledged that the use of active techniques to add, strengthen and possibly to teach self-control for specific responses may be the second stage in a therapeutic process, only to be engaged in after the therapist has established himself or herself as a non-punishing audience. Furthermore, it may be important for therapists to help clients to change their behaviours in such a way that they may find a solution for themselves, since sometimes telling clients what is wrong does nothing to alter the relevant intervening variables. In such an instance the client's behaviour in respect of the problem is a relevant intervening variable.

In psychotherapy there is always the possibility that the therapist will misuse the power to control. One form of countercontrol to prevent this abuse is the ethical standards of the psychotherapeutic profession. Nevertheless, there is still mistrust of the possibility of therapeutic control and therefore some theories of psychotherapy deny that, in the final analysis, behaviour can be controlled and that psychotherapy is one of the controlling agencies.

Environmental design

Psychotherapy is a form of control designed to correct the problems caused by other controlling agencies. Usually it is based on the assumption, common in our culture, of the autonomous person who wishes both to be free from aversive features of the environment and also to receive credit for ethical behaviour. People find it difficult to accept the fact that all control is exercised by the environment. A technology of behaviour which will help humans to design better environments is available. Although such environments will exercise control over behaviour, their task is to release people for more reinforcing activities, consequently also reducing the need for corrective psychotherapy.

The basic premise for the design of a culture is that behaviour can be changed by changing the conditions of which it is a function. Humans are the products of both biological and cultural evolutions. Though humans are controlled by a culture, it is largely of their own making. The task of evolving a more effective culture may be seen as a gigantic exercise in self-control. Skinner affirmed his belief in operant behaviourism by concluding *Beyond Freedom and Dignity* with the following statement: 'A scientific view of man offers exciting possibilities. We have not yet seen what man can make of man' (Skinner, 1971, p. 210).

WOLPE'S RECIPROCAL INHIBITION

Joseph Wolpe (1915–) was born and educated in Johannesburg, South Africa. Trained as a doctor, during the Second World War Wolpe served in the South African Medical Corps, where the failure of conventional treatments to war neuroses stimulated his interest in psychology. Wolpe became a lecturer in the department of psychiatry at the University of Witwatersrand, Johannesburg. In the late 1940s, as a result of laboratory experiments with cats as subjects, he developed a method based on reciprocal inhibition for de-conditioning neurotic fear responses. Wolpe then applied his experimental findings in his clinical work, with great success. In 1958 both the experimental work and its clinical and counselling derivatives were published in *Psychotherapy by Reciprocal Inhibition*. This book created a great stir and acted as a major impetus to the burgeoning development since the early 1960s of behavioural approaches in clinical and counselling psychology.

Wolpe emigrated to the United States where he was professor of psychiatry first at the University of Virginia at Charlottesville (1960–5), then at Temple University in Pennsylvania (1964–84) and, afterwards, at the Medical College of Pennsylvania in Philadelphia. Wolpe's other books include *The Practice of Behaviour Therapy*, *Theme and Variations: A Behaviour Therapy Casebook*, and *Life without Fear: Anxiety and its Cure*, which he co-authored with his son David. Wolpe edited the *Journal of Behavior Therapy and Experimental Psychiatry*. In 1979 he received the American Psychological Society's Distinguished Scientific Award for his pioneering research that contributed to the establishment of behaviour therapy. Wolpe acknowledges his debt to other learning theorists, especially Pavlov and Hull, in developing his approach to the learning and unlearning of neurotic behaviour.

Theory

Extinction: conditioned, reactive and reciprocal inhibitions

Wolpe, in a discussion of the extinctive or unlearning processes, observed that a partial recovery of the response, known as spontaneous recovery, takes place if the stimulus is not applied for some time. The partial nature of spontaneous recovery indicates that two elements are involved in the inhibition of a response during extinction: reactive inhibition, which describes an inhibitory state dissipating with time, and negative conditioning, which leads to a permanent decrease in response probability. The Miller–Mowrer explanation of the extinctive process posits that every time an organism makes a response to a stimulus, there follows a fatigue effect which has an inhibitory effect on a closely following repeat of the same response. Stimuli present at the time are in closest contiguity with the drive reduction associated with cessation of the activity and, in some measure, become conditioned to an inhibition of a response to which previously they were positively joined. The result of this is that, at the next presentation of these stimuli, the strength of the response decreases, even after a time interval long enough to eliminate all reactive inhibition effects. However, when the response is a reinforced one, the positive effects override the development of conditioned inhibition. In other words, in this explanation of conditioned inhibition, the inhibition is built up during extinction through traces of the conditioned stimuli being simultaneous with reactive inhibition of the conditioned response.

Wolpe offered a further explanation of conditioned inhibition. He noted that old habits are often eliminated by allowing new habits to develop in the same situation. The term *reciprocal inhibition* encompasses all situations in which the elicitation of one response appears to bring about a decrement in the strength of evocation of a simultaneous response. He hypothesized that if an incompatible response were to inhibit the conditioned response and lead to much drive reduction, then a significant degree of conditioned inhibition of the original response would be developed. Eventually, his work led to his framing the following general reciprocal inhibition principle:

> If a response antagonistic to anxiety can be made to occur in the presence of anxiety-evoking stimuli so that it is accompanied by a complete or partial suppression of the anxiety responses, the bond between these stimuli and the anxiety responses will be weakened.

(Wolpe, 1958, p. 71)

In a later work, Wolpe suggests that the term mutual inhibition might be more comprehensible than reciprocal inhibition (Wolpe & Wolpe, 1988).

The learning and unlearning of neurotic fears and habits in cats

Wolpe conducted fundamental laboratory research on the learning and unlearning of neurotic fears (Wolpe, 1958). The subjects were 12 domestic cats between the ages of six months and three years. Lasting neurotic effects were induced in all the cats by the administration of several electric shocks in a small experimental cage. Six of the cats were subject to a procedure by which, after control observations, the cat was given five to ten grid shocks preceded by a 'hoot' lasting two to three seconds. The other six cats were subject to a different procedure in which they were first conditioned to perform food-approach responses to a buzzer. This response was strongly reinforced over eight to 16 experimental sessions. The next stage of the procedure involved sounding the buzzer and shocking the cat when it made its food-approach response until it ceased to do so. The mean number of shocks required was four.

The immediate responses of the cats to the shocks included combinations of the following: rushing hither and thither, clawing at the cage, getting up on hind legs, crouching, trembling, howling, pilo-erection and rapid respiration. Persistent responses displayed by all animals were: (a) resistance to being put into the experimental cage; (b) signs of anxiety when inside the cage; and (c) refusal to eat meat pellets anywhere in the cage even after one, two or three days' starvation. The above symptoms were invariably intensified by presentation of the original auditory stimuli. Furthermore, all cats showed some of these symptoms outside the experimental cage.

The learned neurotic reactions of six of the cats were associated with inhibition of feeding. This suggested to Wolpe that under different conditions feeding might inhibit the neurotic reactions. The neurotic anxiety reactions were subsequently removed, or unlearned, in all cats by getting them to eat in the presence of successively larger doses of anxiety-evoking stimuli. The cats were subject to a number of procedures. One procedure was to place the cat in the experimental cage and move pellets of meat towards its mouth on the flat end of a four-inch rod held in the experimenter's hand, in the hope that the human hand would act as a stimulus to overcome the inhibition to eating. After some persistence, four of the nine cats undergoing this procedure were induced to eat. However, only one of the three cats whose food-approach responses had been shocked was induced to eat in this way. The three cats not subject to the human-hand procedure were induced to eat by Masserman's 'forced solution' procedure. This involved repetitions of a procedure, in the experimental cage, of gradually pushing a hungry, neurotic cat by means of a movable barrier towards an open food box containing appetizing food.

The five cats which remained unaffected by the human-hand method were eventually induced to eat in the experimental cage by a procedure which involved a hierarchy of anxiety-evoking rooms ranging from the most anxiety-evoking, the experimental room or Room A, to the least anxiety-evoking, which turned out to be the passage outside Room D. The five cats initially ate at different points in the hierarchy, but by a method of gradual ascent all cats were eventually induced to eat in Room A and then in the experimental cage. By similar methods the cats' neurotic responses to the conditioned auditory stimuli were inhibited.

Wolpe explained the success of his experiments by stating that, when stimuli to incompatible responses are present simultaneously, the occurrence of the response that is dominant in the circumstances involves the reciprocal inhibition of the other. Thus, as the number of feedings increased, the anxiety responses gradually became weaker, so that to stimuli to which there was initially an anxiety response there was ultimately a feeding response with inhibition of anxiety.

The learning of neurotic or useless fears and habits in humans

Wolpe views neurotic behaviour as any persistent habit of unadaptive behaviour acquired by learning in a physiologically normal organism. A habit is defined as 'a set of responses that is consistently triggered by the same circumstances' (Wolpe & Wolpe, 1988, p. 19). People can have habits of movement, emotion and thought. Neurotic habits almost invariably involve anxiety, which is the autonomic response pattern that is characteristically a part of the organism's response to noxious stimulation. The terms 'anxiety' and 'fear' can be used interchangeably. The criterion for the severity of a neurosis is generally the level of unadaptive anxiety. Anxiety impairs the functioning of the organism in many ways, including impairments of movement, emotion and thought.

There are two main sources of neurotic fears and habits: classical conditioning and cognitive misinformation. Habits of useless fears can be autonomically conditioned on the basis of single or multiple intense fear events. An example of a fear conditioned by a single experience is that of a woman who was hurt in a car crash at an intersection where a truck driver ignored a red light and ran into her car. Subsequently she was afraid of any vehicles approaching at intersections from the side. An example of a fear conditioned by multiple events in a person's social fear of 'doing the wrong thing' conditioned from repeated chastisements by parents who could never be pleased. An example of a fear based on misinformation is that of people fearing masturbation because they have been brought up to believe that it will injure their health.

Practice

Reciprocal inhibition in counselling

Wolpe states that: 'The behavior therapist deliberately uses competing responses to overcome useless fears' (Wolpe & Wolpe, 1988, p. 27). In overcoming the neurotic reactions of clients or patients, Wolpe considers it vital to conduct a thorough behaviour analysis to determine which stimuli actually or potentially evoke them currently. Suffice it for now to say that Wolpe's method involves deciding which of a number of incompatible or competing responses can most appropriately be used to obtain reciprocal inhibition of neurotic anxiety responses. Wolpe (1958) listed eight incompatible responses at the disposal of counsellors, through which deliberate intervention for change may be made. These are:

1. assertive responses;
2. sexual responses;
3. relaxation responses;
4. respiratory responses;
5. 'anxiety-relief' responses;
6. competitively conditioned motor responses;
7. 'pleasant' responses in the life situation (with drug enhancement);
8. (a) interview-induced emotional responses;
   (b) abreaction.

Relaxation, as part of systematic desensitization, is probably the main incompatible response used in Wolpe's approach to counselling practice. Desensitization means that clients become less and less sensitive to whatever has been triggering their fears. Systematic means that only after counsellors have accomplished the desensitization at one level of anxiety do they move on to deal with the next level. The purpose of relaxation, achieved through the tensing and relaxing of various muscles, is to bring about a state of emotional calmness. In systematic desensitization progressively anxiety-evoking scenes on a hierarchy, for instance around the theme of fear of examinations, are presented by counsellors to the imaginations of relaxed clients. The idea is that the relaxation response progressively reciprocally inhibits the anxiety response. There is a close connection between the reduction of clients' anxiety in imagined and in real-life situations. Wolpe stresses that in a deconditioning procedure like systematic desensitization a client 'perceives the fact of change *secondarily, after the event*' (Wolpe & Wolpe, 1988, p. 123). This ordering of emotion changing before thinking is different from the need to correct thinking first when treating cognitively based fear. Systematic desensitization is discussed in much more detail in the next chapter.

Wolpe commonly uses assertive responses and sexual responses as competing responses, the former for interpersonal anxieties and the latter for sexual anxieties. Assertive training involves both mobilizing emotion, such as anger, which compete with and inhibit social anxiety, as well as teaching appropriate modes of verbal and motor expression. Wolpe has been a pioneering figure in a development of the behavioural approach to counselling.

EYSENCK'S INCUBATION THEORY

Hans Jurgen Eysenck (1916–), born and raised in Germany, was the son of actor parents whom he rarely saw. Called at school a 'white Jew' for sympathizing with their plight, in 1934 he refused to join the military forces and left Germany. After a period of study in France, Eysenck settled and continued his education in England. He became a psychology student at the University of London by default, lacking the qualifications to study physics. After obtaining his PhD in 1940, Eysenck became a research psychologist at the Mill Hill Emergency Hospital, a temporary psychiatric institution.

After the 1939–45 war, Eysenck became a senior research psychologist at the Maudsley Hospital in London. Soon he founded and became director of the psychology department in the hospital's Institute of Psychiatry. In 1955 he was appointed professor of psychology at the University of London, a position he held until his retirement from formal academic life. Eysenck continues to be active as a scholar, author and lecturer.

Eysenck has been a prolific writer and his many books include: *The Structure of Human Personality: Behaviour Therapy and the Neuroses; The Causes and Cures of Neurosis*, co-authored with S. Rachman; *The Biological Basis of Personality;* and *You and Neurosis*. He has extensively influenced the development of the theory and practice of the behavioural approach to counselling. As early as 1965 Wolpe wrote: 'The now popular term behavior therapy . . . owes its wide promulgation and acceptance to Eysenck' (Wolpe, 1965, p. vii).

Other theories of neurosis

Eysenck observed that neurotic behaviour, a distinctive feature of which is that behaviour followed by negative consequences is not eliminated, neither follows Skinner's law of reinforcement nor can be explained adequately in Skinnerian terms. Furthermore, he considered that Watson's view of neurosis as classically conditioned emotional responses was not elaborated in any detail. For instance, Watson never adequately explained the lack of extinction of neurotic responses. Another gap in Watson's work is that no explanation was offered for the phenomenon that, in many neuroses, not only does extinction fail to take place but there is an incremental enhancement effect, so the unreinforced conditioned stimulus (CS) may produced increases in anxiety (CR) with each presentation of the CS. This enhancement of the unreinforced CR, even more than the failure of extinction, is the central paradox of the neurotic reaction (Eysenck, 1976, 1977).

Innate and acquired sources of neurosis

Eysenck acknowledged four sources of neurotic fear/anxiety responses. First, they may be innate, for example when the degree of fear is strong on first encountering the stimulus object. Second, they may be attributed to 'preparedness', when the fear is weak, but the conditioning easy at the first encounter of the stimulus. Preparedness means that certain fears are highly 'prepared' to be learned by humans. Both innate fears and those to which the concept of preparedness applies reflect the evolutionary development of the species. Third, fears may be learned through modelling (imitation). Fourth, and the most important source of the learning of fear responses, is classical or Pavlovian conditioning. The main unconditioned stimulus (UCS) generating fear responses is neither pain nor the three stimuli suggested by Watson (loud noises, loss of support, and physical constraint), but frustration or 'frustrative non-reward', which can have physiological and behavioural consequences identical to those of pain. Eysenck's biological theory of personality states that introverts condition more readily than extroverts and are thus more likely to acquire neurotic fear responses.

Extinction and incubation

Eysenck tentatively proposed his incubation theory of neurosis, hoping to encourage the collection of relevant clinical and research data. He realized it went considerably beyond ascertained fact and was extrapolated heavily from animal experimentation. While a CS-only presentation always provokes a decrease in CR strength, it may also provoke an increase. Thus there are two possible consequences of CS-only presentation. The first is *extinction* of the CR, and the other is enhancement of the CR or *incubation* of the anxiety/fear responses. Extinction occurs if the decreasing exceed the increasing tendencies, while incubation takes place if the increasing exceed the decreasing tendencies. There are two classes of CR: those which have drive properties and those which do not, the former leading to enhancement and the latter leading to extinction. A CR leading to extinction, when the CS alone is presented, is a dog's salivation, since the salivation does not produce the hunger drive. However, giving rats a shock after a CS-only presentation does produce a CS-induced drive, or enhancement, and rats will learn new activities and practise established ones.

Eysenck proposed that fear/anxiety is a response which possesses drive properties and hence not only resists extinction but is enhanced by presentation of the CS. By definition, the initial position is that the UCS produces fear/anxiety, while the CS does not. Pairing the UCS with the CS leads to a situation in which, after conditioning the presentation of the CS alone produces a CR of fear/anxiety which is identical to the UCR. It is the drive properties of the CR which makes it functionally equivalent to the UCR, so providing reinforcement for the CS-only presentation. Thus where the CR, for example fear/anxiety, has drive properties, presentation of CS-only stimuli produces incubation (enhancement) of the CR. A positive feedback cycle is established in which the fear/anxiety associated with the CS-only presentation is itself a painful event, and the stimuli associated with the CS, by classical conditioning, come to evoke more fear. This process is responsible for not only the continuation but also the growth of neurotic responses.

Incubation has the effect of allowing the CR to exceed the strength of the UCR. Furthermore, it may account for the slow growth of neurotic responses over a period of time, with a few exposures to CS only. There is much evidence that the duration of the CS-only presentation is a critical factor, with short rather than long presentations favouring incubation of fear/anxiety responses. There is less evidence that a strong as opposed to a weak UCS presentation does so. Eysenck observed that stable extroverts extinguish more readily than other extroversion-neuroticism groupings, while neurotic introverts show most evidence of incubation.

Eysenck believed that his revision of the law of extinction made possible the acceptance of a conditioning model of neurosis. His theory demonstrates the interaction between theory and research in the search for a fuller understanding of the laws of behaviour. His incubation theory of neurosis is built on previous theory and research, and has generated further experimental work: for instance, a study by Sandin and Chorot (1989) which lends support to the theory. His work demonstrates that behavioural theory is still developing and should not prematurely be regarded as dogma, an attitude which conflicts with the behaviourists's scientific emphasis.

CHAPTER REVIEW AND SELF-REFERENT QUESTIONS
Pavlov

Chapter review questions

1. What does Pavlov mean by inborn reflex?
2. What is the function of the cerebral hemisphere in the organism's survival?
3. What is meant by classical conditioning?

Self-referent questions

1. Do you think you have acquired any of your behaviours through classical conditioning? If so, please illustrate.

2. What is Pavlov's influence on how you think about and practise counselling?

Watson

Chapter review questions

1. How does a Watsonian behaviourist view psychology?

2. How does Watson categorize stimuli?

3. How does Watson categorize responses?

4. How does Watson view the connection between stimulus and response?

5. How did Watson and his associates condition and uncondition emotional responses?

Self-referent questions

1. Can you think of an emotional response in your life that you could condition and uncondition? Describe how you might do this.

2. What is Watson's influence on how you think about and practise counselling?

Skinner

Chapter review questions

1. What does Skinner mean by each of the following terms?
   (a) operant conditioning
   (b) contingencies of reinforcement
   (c) positive reinforcement
   (d) negative reinforcement
   (e) primary reinforcers
   (f) conditioned reinforcers
   (g) non-intermittent schedules of reinforcement
   (h) intermittent schedules of reinforcement
   (i) extinction
   (j) shaping and successive approximation
   (k) stimulus discrimination and stimulus control
   (l) stimulus generalization
   (m) self-control

2. What is Skinner's view of psychotherapy?

3. What is the main difference between Pavlov's and Skinner's view of conditioning?

4. What is the main difference between Watson's and Skinner's view of conditioning?

Self-referent questions

1. Do you consider that your life is totally determined by the evolutionary history of the human species and by your environment? Give reasons for your position on this issue.

2. Give some examples from your own life of:
   (a) behaviours acquired and maintained through operant conditioning;
   (b) behaviours extinguished by lack of reinforcement.

3. What is Skinner's influence on how you think about and practise counselling?

Wolpe

Chapter review questions

1. How does Wolpe define the terms fear and anxiety?

2. How are neurotic fears learned?

3. Express in simple English what Wolpe means by the term reciprocal inhibition.

Self-referent questions

1. If possible, give examples from your own life of engaging in a competing response to inhibit the anxiety you experienced with an existing response.

2. What is the relevance of Wolpe's ideas to how you think about and practise counselling?

Eysenck

Chapter review questions

1. What does Eysenck consider to be the sources of neurotic fear/anxiety responses?

2. What is the difference between incubation and extinction?

3. How does incubation of a fear/anxiety response take place?

4. What influence does personality type have on conditioning, extinction and incubation?

Self-referent question

1. Can you think of any of your 'neurotic' behaviours which have not only failed to extinguish, but have actually been enhanced with the passage of time? If so, please describe them.

Annotated bibliography

Pavlov, I.P. (1927). *Conditioned Reflexes: An Investigation of the Physiological Activity of the Cerebral Cortex.* Oxford: Oxford University Press.
In this book Pavlov defines terms such as reflex, describes his experimental laboratory, and gives details of some of his pathfinding experiments into the functioning of the cerebral hemisphere of dogs.

Watson, J.B. (1931). *Behaviorism*. London: Kegan Paul, Trench & Traubner.
This book presents Watson's answer to the question 'What is behaviourism?' and includes his views on conditioning, instincts, thinking, memory, personality and ethics.

Skinner, B.F. (1938). *The Behavior of Organisms*. New York: Appleton-Century-Crofts.
In this book Skinner describes his seminal experiments in conditioning rats using a 'box' containing a food- or water-dispenser operated by a lever which could be depressed by a rat. His independent variables included deprivation and satiation, various categories of reinforcement and aversive consequences.

Skinner, B.F. (1953). *Science and Human Behavior*. New York: Macmillan.
This book presents Skinner's ideas on applying the science of behaviour to individuals and groups. In addition, Skinner examines controlling agencies such as government and law, religion, psychotherapy, economic control and education.

Skinner, B.F. (1957). *Verbal Behavior*. New York: Appleton-Century-Crofts.
This book presents Skinner's interpretation of language and the uses of language. Verbal behaviour results from the same principles of operant learning as found in other species. Skinner analyses the various controlling relationships in verbal behaviour.

Wolpe, J. (1958). *Psychotherapy by Reciprocal Inhibition*. Stanford, CA: Stanford University Press.
This is Wolpe's seminal book in which he describes his fundamental animal research and its counselling applications. The book is a classic in the behaviour therapy literature.

Wolpe, J. & Wolpe, D. (1988). *Life without Fear: Anxiety and its Cure*. Oakland, CA: New Harbinger Publications.
Written for the educated public and mental health professionals, this book attempts to present in non-technical language a clear and authoritative account of the essential features of behaviour therapy.

Eysenck, H.J. (1976). The learning theory model of neurosis – a new approach. *Behaviour Research and Therapy, 14*, 251–67.
This article represents Eysenck's major statement of his incubation theory of neurosis. Eysenck suggests shortcomings of Freud's, Skinner's, Watson's and Mowrer's models of neurosis. He presents his incubation model of anxiety and some empirical support for it.

Further references

Pavlov

Babkin, B.P. (1949). *Pavlov: A Biography*. Chicago, IL: University of Chicago Press.
Pavlov, I.P. (1928). *Lectures on Conditioned Reflexes*. New York: International Publishers Co.
Pavlov, I.P. (1955). *Selected Works*. Moscow: Foreign Languages Publishing House.
Kaplan, M. (Ed.) (1966). *Essential Works of Pavlov*. New York: Bantam.

Watson

Cohen, D. (1979). *J.B. Watson, The Founder of Behaviourism*. London: Routledge & Kegan Paul.
Jones, M.C. (1924). A laboratory study of fear: the case of Peter. *Pedagogical Seminary, 31*, 308–15.
Watson, J.B. (1903). *Animal Education*. Chicago, IL: University of Chicago Press.
Watson, J.B. (1913). Psychology as the behaviorist views it. *Psychological Review, 20*, 158–77.

Watson, J.B. (1914). *Behavior*. New York: Holt.
Watson, J.B. (1919). *Psychology from the Standpoint of a Behaviorist*. Philadephia: Lippincott. (2nd ed. 1924, 3rd ed. 1929)
Watson, J.B. (1928). *The Psychological Care of the Infant and Child*. New York: W.W. Norton
Watson, J.B. & Raynor, R.R. (1920). Conditioned emotional reactions. *Journal of Experimental Psychology, 3*, 1–14.

Skinner

Ferster, C.B. & Skinner, B.F. (1957), *Schedules of Reinforcement*. New York: Appleton-Century-Crofts.
Holland, J.G. (1992), B.F. Skinner (1904–1990). *American Psychologist, 47,* 665–67.
Holland, J.G. & Skinner, B.F. (1961). *The Analysis of Behavior*. New York: McGraw-Hill.
Skinner, B.F. (1948). *Walden Two*. New York: Macmillan
Skinner, B.F. (1958). Reinforcement today. *American Psychologist, 13,* 94–9.
Skinner, B.F. (1961). *Cumulative Record*. New York, Appleton-Century-Crofts.
Skinner, B.F. (1969) *Contingencies of Reinforcement*. New York: Appleton-Century-Crofts.
Skinner, B.F. (1971). *Beyond Freedom and Dignity*. Harmondsworth Penguin.
Skinner, B.F. (1974). *About Behaviorism*. New York: Alfred A. Knopf.
Skinner, B.F. (1976). *Particulars of My Life*. London: Jonathan Cape.
Skinner, B.F. (1989). The origins of cognitive thought. *American Psychologist, 44* 13–18.
Skinner, B.F. (1990). Can psychology be a science of the mind? *American Psychologist, 45,* 1206–10.

Skinner's influence on psychology continues in journals such as:
Journal of Applied of Behavior Analysis, first published in 1968, and *Journal of the Experimental Analysis of Behavior,* first published in 1958.

Skinner on video
Skinner's keynote address: *Lifetime scientific contribution remarks* (Item #4316150). Washington, DC: American Psychological Association.

Skinner on audio
The behavior of organisms at fifty (APA-88–035, 2 cassettes)
The operant side of behavior therapy (APA-88–089)
The origins of cognitive thought (APA-87–080)
Programmed instruction revisited (APA-87–080)
Whatever happened to psychology as a science of behavior? (APA-86–171)

All the above cassettes are available from the American Psychological Association, Washington, DC.

Wolpe

Wolpe, J. (1965). *The practice of Behaviour Therapy*. Oxford: Pergamon Press.
Wolpe, J. (1976) *Theme and Variations: A Behaviour Therapy Casebook*. Oxford: Pergamon Press.
Wolpe, J. (1982). *The Practice of Behaviour Therapy* (3rd ed.). Oxford: Pergamon Press.
Wolpe, J., Salter, A. & Reyna, L. (Eds.)(1964). *The Conditioning Therapies: The Challenge in Psychotherapy*. New York: Holt, Rinehart & Winston.

Eysenck

Eysenck, H.J. (1960). *Behaviour Therapy and the Neuroses*. Oxford: Pergamon Press.

Eysenck, H.J. & Rachman, S. (1965). *The Causes and Cures of Neurosis* London: Routledge & Kegan Paul.

Eysenck, H.J. (1967). *The Biological Basis of Personality*. Springhill, IL: C.C. Thomas.

Eysenck, H.J. (1968). A theory of the incubation of anxiety/fear responses. *Behaviour Research and Therapy*, 6, 309–21.

Eysenck, H.J. (1970). *The Structure of Human Personality* (3rd ed.). London: Methuen.

Eysenck, H.J. (1977). *You and Neurosis*. Glasgow: Fontana/Collins.

Sandin, B. & Chorot, P. (1989). The incubation theory of fear/anxiety: Experimental investigation in a human laboratory model of Pavlovian conditioning. *Behaviour Research and Therapy, 27*, 9–18.

Others

Hilgard, E.R. & Bower, G.H. (1966). *Theories of Learning* (3rd ed.) New York: Appleton-Century-Crofts.

Thorndike, E.L. (1932). *The Fundamentals of Learning*. New York: Teachers College Bureau of Publications.

TEN

Behavioural Counselling: Practice

PREVIEW

- *Behavioural counselling methods are based mainly on principles of learning, though also on counselling and clinical experience. Goals for behavioural counselling include: initiating and strengthening adaptive behaviours, weakening and eliminating maladaptive behaviours, and reducing unwanted fears and anxieties.*

- *Behavioural counselling starts with a behavioural assessment to specify treatment goals and methods. The assessment may include data collected both during interviews and from other sources, for instance client self-monitoring.*

- *Progressive relaxation, which consists of tensing and relaxing various muscle groupings, can be a treatment method in itself as well as part of more complex methods. Other relaxation procedures reviewed include: brief relaxation, differential relaxation, verbal relaxation and mental relaxation. Considerations for counsellors in conducting relaxation training are discussed.*

- *Systematic desensitization involves three elements: (a) training in deep muscular relaxation; (b) the construction of thematic hierarchies of anxiety-evoking stimuli; and (c) presentation of hierarchy items to the imagination of deeply relaxed clients. Variations of systematic desensitization involve real-life hierarchies, group desensitization, and different cognitive elements.*

- *Behaviour rehearsal involves the counsellor in shaping and rehearsing the client's behaviour for various target situations. Assertive training, or training in the accurate communication of positive and negative feelings without inhibition or aggression, is the main area for behaviour rehearsal.*

- *Reinforcement methods aim to modify behaviour by altering its consequences. Counselling may be seen as a process of social influence or reinforcement. Ways of identifying what clients find reinforcing are reviewed.*

- *Reinforcement programmes and token economies aim to change the behaviour of both individuals and groups, for example a classroom of children. Tokens are tangible conditioned reinforcers which may be exchanged for back-up reinforcers such as prizes and food. All reinforcement programmes should plan to overcome extinction of the target behaviours after removal of the reinforcers.*

- *Punishment procedures, which include presentation for an aversive event, time out and response costs, should always be used in conjunction with positive reinforcement of desirable or alternative behaviours. Time out involves removing clients from situations in which they receive reinforcement.*

- *Clients may be helped to increase the number and scope of reinforcers available to them, an approach which shows promise in treating depressed people. In addition, counsellors can train clients in how to control the stimuli associated with adaptive and maladaptive responses and in how to use positive and negative self-reinforcement.*

- *Aversive and flooding methods, both of which deliberately heighten clients' distress, are reviewed briefly.*

INTRODUCTION

This chapter provides an introduction to some basic methods of behavioural counselling. The terms 'behavioural counselling' and 'behaviour therapy' are both used to describe a series of counselling interventions which are based mainly on the principles of learning described in Chapter 9. However, Wolpe (1973) observes that the behavioural counsellor need not be confined to methods derived from principles, but may also employ methods that have been empirically shown to be effective.

Definitions of behavioural counselling differ according to whether the counsellor mainly emphasizes learning principles based on classical and operant conditioning, or emphasizes cognitive change as well. For instance, Wolpe (1973) defines behaviour therapy as a conditioning therapy involving 'the use of experimentally established principles of learning for the purpose of changing maladaptive behaviour. Unadaptive habits are weakened and eliminated; adaptive habits are initiated and strengthened' (p. IX). Wolpe's approach to behavioural counselling is based largely on classical conditioning (Wolpe, 1958, 1982; Wolpe & Wolpe, 1988). This chapter focuses predominantly on conditioning methods of altering observable behaviour rather than on approaches to altering cognitions.

GOALS FOR COUNSELLING

Krumboltz (1966) observed that behavioural goals for counselling; (a) should be capable of being stated differently for each client; (b) should be compatible with, though not necessarily identical to, the values of the counsellor; and (c) are such that the degree to which they are attained should be externally observable. He further suggested that there were three types of goals, albeit sometimes interrelated, which met his criteria and fell within the scope of counsellor responsibility. These were: altering maladaptive behaviour, e.g. increasing socially assertive responses; learning the decision-making process, e.g. making a list of possible courses of action; and preventing problems, e.g. implementing a system of helping young men and women to select compatible marriage partners. The goals of counselling are not always scientifically derived, since behaviourists recognize that there are many influences on clients' choice of goals and on counsellors' choice of methods.

At the risks of introducing a level of generality which behavioural counsellors, with their emphasis on specific goals for individual clients, might find uncongenial, there follows an attempt to derive a series of goals for counselling from the writings of the five behavioural theorists discussed in the preceding chapter. Such goals include:

1. overcoming deficits in behavioural repertoires;
2. strengthening adaptive behaviours;
3. weakening or eliminating maladaptive behaviours;
4. absence of debilitating anxiety reactions;
5. capacity to relax;
6. ability to assert oneself;
7. effective social skills;
8. adequacy at sexual functioning;
9. capacity for self-control

The above goals are for individuals. Of the behavioural theorists, Skinner in particular focused on the need for groups to design environments in which humans can behave in more reinforcing ways. Thus, further behavioural goals might focus on groups and include the capacity for group self-control, both by shaping environmental consequences and also by cognitive self-regulation.

BEHAVIOURAL ASSESSMENT

Behavioural counselling invariably begins with a behavioural assessment, sometimes known as a functional analysis of clients' problem areas. One of the main purposes of the assessment is to arrive at an informed specification of treatment objectives in behavioural terms to guide the choice of counselling methods. Thus behavioural assessment in initial counselling sessions has two foci: first, specification of the clients' problem areas; and second, specification of the most appropriate methods to be used by counsellors. Adequate behavioural assessments allow counsellors to identify the stimulus antecedents of the responses they wish to treat, while inadequate behavioural assessments may lead to the wrong methods being applied to the wrong problems. Beyond initial sessions, behavioural assessment aims to assist both in evaluating treatment effectiveness and in deciding whether to continue, discontinue or alter treatment (Galassi & Perot, 1992; Kazdin, 1993, 1994).

When clients make statements like 'I seem to be very depressed these days', 'I don't seem to have many friends' or 'I get very tense at work', behavioural counsellors attempt an analysis based on an SRC assessment, where S refers to the *stimulus* of *situational antecedents*, R to the *response variables* and C to the consequences or *consequent variables*. The purpose of the SRC analysis is to search for the key variables which control clients' behaviour. Sometimes these may be masked: for instance, aggression at work may reflect a poor marital relationship. Behavioural analysis aims for a high degree of specificity. For instance, in analysing a response, information on duration, frequency, generality, and strength of the response should be collected. Behavioural assessment may take place both within and outside counselling interviews. Furthermore, there is much scope for client self-assessment as part of or in addition to counsellor assessment.

Within interview assessment

Though a behavioural assessment interview tends to have a high degree of focus and counsellor direction, counsellor empathy plays an important role. This is because it helps to build rapport and facilitate clients' self-disclosure as well as ensuring that counsellors accurately listen to material. Apart from collecting basic information, such as clients' age, sex and marital and occupational status, two early objectives are to allow clients to convey their problem area or areas in their own words and to provide for them some minimal clarification concerning the goals of the initial behavioural assessment. At this stage some counsellors may also mention that much behaviour is learned and may be unlearned.

The interview may continue with the counsellor asking specific questions as part of an SRC analysis of presenting concerns. Behavioural counsellors rarely ask *why* questions: for example, 'Why do you get furious when she answers back?' Wilson (1989) states: 'Questions starting with *how, when, where,* and *what* are more useful in identifying relevant personal and situational variables currently maintaining the client's problems' (p. 258). Behavioural counsellors differ in the extent to which they gather historical material concerning how the presenting concerns were learned, though this may be important in obtaining an accurate picture. Wolpe (1982), for instance, gathers historical material on his clients' presenting concerns, family life, education and occupational development and sexual development. Wolpe also explores his clients' current social relationships. Potential pitfalls of a high degree of counsellor direction and questioning are that clients may feel threatened and also may become blocked from discussing areas not being focused on by their counsellors.

Other possible elements of initial assessments include counsellors' observations about clients' verbal and non-verbal behaviour. Socially awkward people may demonstrate at least part of their problems during the interview. Counsellors may explore emerging problem areas as the assessment proceeds. They note clients' personal assets and ways of either coping with or avoiding coping with problems. In addition, they may assess clients' motivation for change, any influences in their environments which are likely to hinder or help change, and their expectancies regarding the possibility of change. Counsellors are also likely to observe the kinds of things which clients find reinforcing, such as personal attention or praise, since these may be useful for eliciting behaviour change.

Additional sources of assessment data

There are a number of additional sources of assessment data, one or more of which behavioural counsellors may find useful both for generating more accurate hypotheses about treatment goals and for collecting baseline information against which to assess the progress and outcomes of counselling. These include the following.

Medical information

A medical examination is essential if there is any suspicion of a physiologically based problem or one with medical implications. For such clients, behavioural assessments are incomplete until such data have been collected and, even then, counsellors may further consult with physicians.

Previous record of psychological treatment

Counsellors may gain more information about the clients' concerns and the likely outcomes of treatment strategies from any available records of previous psychological or psychiatric treatment. Again, they may further consult with relevant psychologists or psychiatrists.

Self-report questionnaires

Clients may be asked to fill in self-report questionnaires. Such measures may focus on overt *behaviour*, or how the client acts, on *emotions*, or how the client feels, and on clients' perceptions of their environments. Perhaps the most commonly used type of questionnaire is the sort which asks clients to indicate the kinds of situations which cause them anxiety. One such questionnaire is Wolpe's (1982) *Fear Inventory* in which clients are asked to indicate on a five-point scale, ranging from 'not at all' to 'very much', how disturbed they currently feel in 87 situations, such as 'People in authority', 'Angry people', 'Darkness' and 'Airplanes'. A questionnaire focused on self-report of behaviour is Alberti and Emmons' (1990) *Assertiveness Inventory*, with such items as 'Do you speak out or protest when someone takes your place in line?'. Another kind of questionnaire, which focuses on activities, events and experiences which clients find rewarding, is MacPhillamy and Lewinsohn's *Pleasant Events Schedule* (Lewinsohn *et al.*, 1986). Such a questionnaire is useful in identifying actual and potential reinforcers which may be used in conjunction with treatment.

Client self-monitoring

Here clients are asked to collect baseline data by monitoring their current behaviour. The way to go about this is to ask clients to fill in daily diary sheets investigating the SRC elements of a specific behaviour being monitored. Table 10.1 illustrates such a behavioural monitoring diary, which might be kept for a week or however long it takes to obtain the relevant information. Such diaries imply that the assessment has arrived at the stage where further information is required about specific behaviours. Sharpe and Lewis (1976) provide examples of monitoring sheets across a wide range of behaviours based on a stimulus, response, consequence, 'what I would like to have done' format.

Direct observation in natural settings

Sometimes behavioural counsellors may go with clients into real-life settings to observe how they behave. An example of this might be going into pubs or restaurants with clients who experience difficulty drinking or eating in public, then observing and discussing their behaviour and emotions as they happen or shortly afterwards. However, when counsellors are present, clients may behave differently from usual.

Indirect observation in natural settings

Another form of observation in natural settings is to collect information from significant people who interact with clients in their everyday lives, such as teachers or parents in the case of children, or spouses in the case of married people. Counsellors need to bear in mind both the degree to which the reported behaviours may be representative of their clients' behaviours in particular situations and also potential contamination by observer bias. Again, if clients know they are being observed they may behave differently. However, there are ethical problems in observing and reporting on clients without their knowledge or consent. Sometimes valid indirect observations in natural settings may be made by using behaviour monitoring codes and making frequency counts of various categories of behaviour.

Direct observation in simulated settings

Role playing is one form of direct observation in simulated settings. Clients might be asked to enact with their counsellors pieces of behaviour as they would normally behave, and possibly various other roles in the situation. Such enactments might simulate pupils and students having difficulty talking to their parents, or marital partners who are failing to communicate. Another form of observation, either directly by counsellors or indirectly by other raters, is to observe behind one-way mirrors the behaviour of clients in a group. Lewinsohn and his colleagues have devised a behavioural rating schedule

Table 10.1 Example of an entry in a behavioural monitoring diary

Behaviour being monitored: Fear in public-speaking situations

Stimulus	Response	Consequences
3.30 p.m. Required to give a brief presentation to 15 colleagues concering a sales project I'm working on. The colleagues were seated round a conference table and I was standing at one end.	Felt anxious. Spoke too quickly and kept little eye contact with my audience. Managed to make all my main points. At the end of the talk I stumbled over my answers (for example, insufficiently clear and too many 'uhms').	Audience looked moderately interested. Asked questions that showed they had listened. Boss congratulated me on my performance. I felt relieved when talk was over. I think I am improving.

focused on the actions and reactions of each group member. This leads to a quantitative representation of aspects of social skill such as total amount of behaviour emitted by and directed towards each individual, use of positive and negative reactions, and range of interactions (Lewinsohn *et al.*, 1970).

Research on behavioural assessment

How do behavioural counsellors assess in practice? Swan and MacDonald conducted a national survey of the assessment procedures used by American behaviour therapists. The found that the top ten procedures they used were: (1) client interview (89%); (2) client self-monitoring (51%); (3) interview with client's significant others (49%); (4) direct observation of target behaviours (40%); (5) information from other professionals (34%); (6) role-playing (34%); (7) behaviour self-report measures (27%); (8) demographic questionnaires (20%); (9) personality inventories (20%); and (10) projective tests (19%) (Swan & MacDonald, 1978). Choice of assessment procedures is likely to vary according to which stage of treatment is involved.

Another insight into how behavioural counsellors assess in practice is Kazdin's conclusion based on studying the research evidence that 'the accumulating verdict regarding judgemental biases in decision making in general and, more specifically, within the context of clinical work has not been kind. . . . The collection of systematic information in the context of treatment does not eliminate bias' (Kazdin, 1993, p. 13). Along with all other counsellors, behavioural counsellors are not immune from interspersing subjectivity with objectivity. However, Kazdin (1993) also argues that systematic information improves client care more than impressionistic evaluation of treatment progress.

Specifying goals

A *behavioural analysis* needs to be conducted and formulated so that treatment goals can be selected and specified. Such an analysis entails descriptions of what the problems are, how they appear to have arisen, and what maintains them. These descriptions are in the form of hypotheses to be tested in counselling. The end product of the behavioural analysis is an exact specification of what variables are in need of modification be they situational antecedents, components of the problem behaviour itself, and/or consequent reinforcers. Frequently, the main goal or goals of treatment are called target behaviours (Kazdin, 1994). However, as indicated in the earlier discussion of goals, many behavioural counsellors go beyond stating goals in terms of observable behaviours to specifying anxiety reduction goals as well.

Selecting goals in turn leads to decisions about how to define them so that counsellors and clients can assess whether or not clients change (Cormier & Cormier, 1991). Clearly defined goals assist counsellors to select appropriate methods to attain them. Usually counsellors establish goals in consultation with their clients and elicit their co-operation for various treatment strategies. Clients tend to have more than one area of concern and, though it may be possible to deal with those simultaneously, sometimes an ordering of priorities is necessary. Here a prime consideration is the extent to which the problem behaviours interfere with clients' abilities to lead satisfactory lives. In most instances, client and counsellor will agree on goals and treatment procedures. Where disagreement exists, further discussion may be all that is necessary to resolve the issue. Referral to another counsellor may be indicated if disagreement persists.

Behavioural assessment and monitoring take place throughout a course of treatment and not just at the beginning. One function of such monitoring is to see whether treatment goals are being achieved. Another function is to see whether counsellors or clients feel that it is advisable to alter or revise their goals. Perhaps some new situation, such as getting married or acquiring a more responsible position at work, may precipitate changing goals. If goals are altered, treatment methods have to be amended accordingly. It is to some of the principal methods of behavioural treatment that I now turn.

RELAXATION PROCEDURES

Relaxation procedures may be used on their own or may form part of more complicated procedures, such as systematic desensitization. The acknowledged pioneer of relaxation training is Edmund Jacobson, the first edition of whose major work, *Progressive Relaxation,* appeared in 1929. Jacobson saw what he termed neuromuscular hypertension as a condition marked by reflex phenomena of hyperexcitation and hyperirritation. He was aware that symptoms or hypertension were very common and not restricted only to the severely disturbed. Jacobson hypothesized that his progressive relaxation treatment could bring absolute or relative rest to the neuromuscular system, including the mind. His term 'progressive relaxation' refers to the progressive cultivation of the relaxation response. Perhaps Wolpe is responsible for the present popularity of relaxation methods based on Jacobson's work, since they form a major part of his systematic desensitization technique (Wolpe, 1958, 1982; Wolpe & Wolpe, 1988). Relaxation procedures may be used as a complete or partial behavioural treatment approach to such problems as tension headaches, insomnia and general feelings of tension (Berstein & Borkovec, 1973; Tasto & Hinkle, 1973).

Progressive muscular relaxation

There are many variants to Jacobson's original progressive muscular relaxation procedures, including those described by Wolpe (1982; Wolpe & Wolpe, 1988), Vitalo (1969), Sharpe & Lewis (1976), Goldfried and Davison (1976) and Bernstein and Borkovec (1973). Although the latter's manual, *Progressive Relaxation Training,* provides a particularly clear introduction to the subject, the following description is drawn from a number of sources.

The physical setting of counsellors' offices should be conducive to relaxation. This involves absence of disruptive noise, interior decoration that is restful, and lighting which may be dimmed. Clients may be taught to relax in recliner chairs, on mattresses or, at the very least, in comfortable upright chairs with headrests. It is assumed that the behavioural assessment has indicated that relaxation training is a means towards one of the client's behavioural targets, such as a reduction in feelings of tension and irritability, or being able to get to sleep within a stipulated time of going to bed. Since a noticeable investment of time and effort is required for clients to learn relaxation, it is important that they clearly understand the relevance of the procedures to alleviating their problems.

At an early stage counsellors may explain that much tension is learned and that by training and practice it can be unlearned. From the start counsellors may endeavour to see that clients view relaxation training as learning a coping skill which can be used in daily life rather than just treating them as passive persons. Furthermore, clients should understand that success at learning relaxation, just like success at learning any other skill, requires practice and that relaxation homework will be required. Before starting relaxation, counsellors can suggest that clients wear loose-fitting, comfortable clothing both during interviews and when doing relaxation homework. Furthermore, clients should be told that it is helpful to remove items such as glasses and shoes.

Bernstein and Borkovec observe that in teaching muscular relaxation there is a succession of events which must be observed with each muscle group. This tension-relax cycle has five elements: (a) *focus*, focusing attention on a specific muscle group; (b) *tense*, tensing the muscle group; (c) *hold*, maintaining the tension for five to seven seconds; (d) *release*, releasing the tension in the muscle group; and (e) *relax*, focusing attention on the letting go of tension and further relaxation of the muscle group. Clients need to learn this *focus-tense-hold-release-relax* cycle so that they may apply it in their homework.

Having explained the basic tension-relax cycle, counsellors may then demonstrate it by going through the cycle in relation to their own right hand and forearm and at each stage asking their clients to do the same. Thus, 'I'm focusing all my attention on my right hand and forearm and I'd like you to do the same' progresses to 'I'm clenching my right fist and tensing the muscles in my lower arm . . .', then on to 'I'm holding my right fist clenched and keeping the muscles in my lower arm tensed . . .', followed by 'I'm now releasing as quickly as I can the tension from my right fist and lower arm . . .', ending with 'I'm relaxing my right hand and forearm, letting the tension go further and further and letting these muscles become more and more relaxed . . .' The final relaxation phase tends to last from 30 to 60 seconds, frequently accompanied by counsellor relaxation 'patter' about letting the tension go and acknowledging and experiencing feelings of deeper and deeper relaxation as they occur. Having been through the tension-relax cycle once, especially in the initial sessions, the client may be instructed to through it again, thus tensing and relaxing each muscle grouping twice.

Counsellors are then likely to take clients through the muscle groups, modelling them as necessary. Table 10.2 shows 16 muscle groups and suggested tensing instructions. The arms tend to be focused on at the beginning, since they are easy to demonstrate. For most clients the face is particularly important because, as Wolpe (1973) observes, 'the most marked anxiety-inhibiting effects are usually obtained by relaxations there' (p. 104).

Once clients have learned how to tense the various muscle groups, they are instructed to keep their eyes closed during relaxation training and practice. After the tension-relax cycle, counsellors may ask whether clients have relaxed completely and indicate that, if not, they should raise the index finger of the hand nearest to the counsellor. To facilitate genuine relaxation, counsellors should ensure that their clients

Table 10.2 Muscle groups and tensing instructions for muscular relaxation training

Muscle group	Tensing instructions*
Right hand and forearm	Clench your right fist and tense the muscles in your lower arm.
Right biceps	Bend your right arm at the elbow and flex your biceps by tensing the muscles of your upper right arm.
Left hand and forearm	Clench your left fist and tense the muscles in your lower arm.
Left biceps	Bend your left arm at the elbow and flex your biceps by tensing the muscles of your upper left arm.
Forehead	Life your eyebrows as high as possible.
Eyes, nose and upper cheeks	Squeeze your eyes tightly shut and wrinkle your nose.
Jaw and lower cheeks	Clench your teeth and pull the corners of your mouth firmly back.
Neck and throat	Pull your chin down hard towards your chest yet resist having it touch your chest.
Chest and shoulders	Pull your shoulder blades together and take a deep breath.
Stomach	Tighten the muscles in your stomach as though someone was about to hit you there.
Right thigh	Tense the muscles of the right upper leg by pressing the upper muscle down and the lower muscles up.
Right calf	Stretch your right leg and pull your toes towards your head.
Right foot	Point and curl the toes of your right foot and turn it inwards.
Left thigh	Tense the muscles of the left upper leg by pressing the upper muscle down and the lower muscles up.
Left calf	Stretch your left leg and pull your toes towards your head.
Left foot	Point and curl the toes of your left foot and turn it inwards.

* With left-handed people, tensing instructions for the left side of the body should come before those for the right.

feel safe to share any feelings of residual tension. Furthermore, counsellors should be observing their clients' body posture and breathing as a check on the extent of relaxation. Complete relaxation is not to be expected immediately. Consequently, counsellors should use their judgement about whether to repeat the tension–relax cycle. Given persistent failure to relax a muscle group, another approach is to alter the muscle group strategy. For instance, in the neck and throat muscle group, shrugging the shoulders by pulling the head down and the shoulders up may be an alternative to pulling the chin down hard towards the chest and resisting having it touch the chest. Clients differ in the muscle groups in which they experience much of their tension and counsellors may have to pay extra attention to such individual differences.

Towards the end of relaxation sessions, counsellors may ask clients for a summary of their relaxation, along the lines of 'Well, how was your relaxation today?' and discuss any issues that arise. Termination of relaxation sessions may be achieved by counsellors counting from five to one and when they get to one asking their clients to wake up pleasantly relaxed as though from a peaceful sleep. Bernstein and Borkovec advocate relaxation sessions ending with an 'enjoyment period' of a minute or two in which counsellors suggest that clients focus on the very pleasant state of relaxation prior to the counting procedure for terminating relaxation.

The importance of practising muscular relaxation may be further stressed at the end of the initial relaxation session. Clients are likely to be given the homework assignment of practising muscular relaxation for one or two 15 minute periods a day. Counsellors should ask their clients whether they anticipate any obstacles to practising, such as finding a quiet place, and help them to devise strategies for ensuring good homework. There is some evidence that clients who monitor their relaxation practice are much more likely to continue doing it (Tasto & Hinkle, 1973). Consequently, it may be helpful for counsellors to give clients logs for monitoring their relaxation homework. An example of an entry in such a monitoring log is provided in Table 10.3.

Brief muscular relaxation procedures

When the full muscular relaxation procedures have been learned and clients are able to attain deep relaxation, briefer muscular relaxation procedures may be introduced. The idea here is to learn to attain deep relaxation with less time and effort. This skill may be useful both within and outside counselling interviews. Brief muscular relaxation procedures may involve sequential or simultaneous application of the tension-relax cycle to various muscle groups, albeit interrelated.

Bernstein and Borkovec (1973) provide examples of sequential brief muscular relaxation procedures. One variation is to tense seven muscle groups: the right arm muscles, the left arm muscles and the facial muscles are each tensed as single groups; the neck and throat muscles are tensed as previously; and the chest, shoulder and stomach muscles, the right leg and foot muscles and the left leg and foot muscles are each tensed as single groups. The four muscle group variation, which, even more than the seven muscle group variation, involves simultaneous as well as sequential relaxation, refers to: arm muscles; face, neck and throat muscles; chest, shoulder and stomach muscles; and leg and foot muscles.

Table 10.3 Monitoring log for relaxation homework

Date	Time, place, length	Comments
3 Oct.	6 p.m., living room at home, 15 minutes	Started off feeling tense after day at work. Tensed and relaxed the 16 muscle groups. Distracting thoughts about work interfered with relaxation. Nevertheless, ended feeling considerably better.

Simultaneous muscular relaxation involves tensing virtually all muscles at once. An introductory counsellor statement might be 'When I give the signal, I would like you to close your eyes tightly, take a deep breath and simultaneously clench your fists and flex your biceps, frown very deeply, pull your shoulder blades together and tense your legs and feet. Now take a deep breath and tense everything . . . hold for five seconds . . . now release and relax as quickly and deeply as you can'. When using systematic desensitization procedures, simultaneous muscular relaxation may provide counsellors with useful economies in interview time. When ready, brief muscular relaxation procedures should be incorporated into clients' relaxation homework.

Verbal relaxation procedures

Verbal relaxation procedures can involve either counsellors instructing clients or the clients instructing themselves. The latter may be particularly useful where clients are in public situations, such as business meetings, where the tensing of various muscle groupings might appear rather incongruous, to say the least! Thus verbal procedures give clients a useful self-help strategy for stressful situations.

One verbal relaxation format is, without any further tensing, to ask clients to *focus* on the tension in a muscle grouping and then follow a *relax* procedure, with their attention being directed to letting go and experiencing relaxation replace tension as it leaves their body. This may be done with all or some muscle groupings. Again, for many clients attention to facial muscles may be particularly important.

Another verbal relaxation procedure involves counting. A simple version is to count for one to ten and instruct clients to notice the tension flowing out of their bodies. A variant of this is to count from one to ten but, for example after every two digits to draw the client's attention to noticing the tension leaving particular muscle groupings, such as the arms, legs, trunk of the body, face, and whole body. Again, when ready, clients should be encouraged to practise these verbal relaxation procedures as homework.

Mental relaxation

Often in conjunction with other relaxation procedures, clients are encouraged to engage in mental relaxation. Such relaxation usually involves imagining a peaceful scene, such as 'lying in a meadow on a nice warm summer's day, feeling a gentle breeze, watching the clouds'. Counsellors can discover which particular scenes clients find most conductive to relaxation. Frequently, mental relaxation is used after going through a muscular relaxation procedure.

Differential relaxation

Jacobson (1938) defined differential relaxation as 'a minimum of tension in the muscles requisite for an act along with the relaxation of other muscles' (p. 83). For instance, a golfer who gets inappropriately tense wrecks a shot, which frequently leads to further tension and further mistakes. Differential relaxation necessitates identifying the muscles requisite for an act and then relaxing all other muscles. Jacobson gives an example of a man sitting reading a book whose back, arms, head, legs and trunk are suitably relaxed rather than unnecessarily tense. Differential relaxation may involve muscular or verbal relaxation procedures to (a) get the appropriate tension level in certain muscle groups and (b) eliminate tension in all other muscle groups. Using differential relaxation may help clients handle tension in everyday life.

Conditioned relaxation

Another procedure which may be helpful in handling stress is conditioned relaxation. Here clients are conditioned to associate a cue word such as 'calm' or 'relax' with a deeply relaxed state which may have been attained by progressive muscular relaxation. Clients may then use the cue word to contain or reduce anxiety when faced with stressful situations.

Relaxed life-style

As well as the various relaxation procedures described above, counsellors need to be sensitive to whether or not their clients' life-styles are sufficiently relaxed. Straightforward precautions like proper holidays, leaving adequate time for meals, not taking on excessive commitments, keeping reasonably physically fit and having regular recreations may be very important relaxation goals for clients. Such areas should be identified in any adequate behavioural assessments.

Relaxation training considerations

Behavioural counsellors differ in the number of sessions they take for relaxation training. Also, clients differ in the speed with which they attain a capacity to relax. Wolpe (1982) teaches progressive muscular relaxation in about six lessons and asks his patients to practise at home for two 15–minute sessions per day. Wolpe and Wolpe (1988) write: 'It is crucial to realize that the aim of relaxation training is not muscle control per se, but emotional calmness' (p. 42). Bernstein and Borkovec (1973) suggest a ten-session relaxation training timetable, with the first three sessions devoted to training in relaxing all muscle groups, the next four sessions to brief muscular relaxation, and the final three sessions to verbal relaxation procedures. Again, daily homework practice is assigned. Counsellors may vary their relaxation training timetable according to their clients' needs and their own workload. Nevertheless, it is important that subjects have sufficient sessions to learn relaxation adequately.

Frequently, counsellors cassette-record relaxation instructions for their clients to play back during home practice. A risk here is that inadequate attention may get paid to muscle groupings which the client finds difficult to relax. One approach to this problem is to alert clients and ask them, if necessary, temporarily to switch off the cassette recorder and spend extra time relaxing a particular muscle grouping. Goldfried and Davison (1976) suggest there comes a time when clients should be weaned from their cassettes. One way to achieve this to encourage clients to relax for a stipulated period of time without their cassettes, then turn their cassettes on. As the difference in depth of relaxation diminishes between the periods when the cassette is off and when it is on, there is less need for the cassette.

Sometimes clients experience difficulties in getting deeply relaxed. I have already mentioned repeating the tension–relax cycle and altering the tensing strategy as ways of handling certain client difficulties. Also, some psychiatrists use tranquillizing drugs to induce relaxation. One way of dealing with the problem of interfering thoughts is to get clients engaged in mental relaxation. Sometimes clients are afraid of losing control and may be reassured by the counsellor's including in the relaxation instructions a statement to the effect that they will not lose control. Some clients have practice difficulties and I reiterate the desirability of counsellors' monitoring clients' relaxation homework and dealing with any issues that arise. One method of checking on the extent of the client relaxation both in interviews and at home is to ask them to rate themselves on a quantitative scale ranging from zero, representing maximum relaxation, to 100, representing maximum tension. A further point is that some relaxation difficulties may be more a matter or unrealistic expectations of the part of counsellors or clients rather than actual difficulties.

Borkovec and Sides (1979) reviewed 25 controlled studies using progressive muscular relaxation and found that 15 studies reported the superiority of the 10 studies its equivalence to control group outcomes. However, of the seven studies characterized by three or more training sessions, live rather than taped training, and clinical as contrasted with normal subjects, only one failed to prove progressive relaxation superior to control group conditions. The authors concluded 'In the case of progressive relaxation, we suggest that multi-session, live training with subjects for whom there is a relevant physiological response component involved in the target behavior represents a minimum requirement on both clinical and empirical grounds' (1979, p. 124).

SYSTEMATIC DESENSITIZATION

Systematic desensitization is a behavioural counselling method in which relaxation is an important component. Where behavioural assessments indicate that clients have certain specific anxiety or phobic areas, rather than just general tension, systematic desensitization may be the preferred treatment method. However, adequate behavioural assessments are essential. For instance, anxiety about tests or about occupational decisions may be the consequence of inadequate revision or poor decision-making skills. In such instances the anxiety is likely to be more effectively diminished by skills training than by systematic desensitization. There are numerous different theoretical explanations of the efficacy of systematic desensitization, some of which also have procedural implications (Thoresen & Coates, 1978).

Wolpe (1958, 1982; Wolpe & Wolpe, 1988) was the originator of systematic desensitization, a treatment he considered to be based on the reciprocal inhibition principle described in Chapter 9. He acknowledges that systematic desensitization may be conducted concurrently with other behavioural interventions. Systematic desensitization involves three elements: (a) training in deep muscular relaxation; (b) the construction of hierarchies of anxiety-evoking stimuli; and (c) asking the client, when relaxed, to imagine items from the anxiety-evoking hierarchies.

Rationale

Behavioural counsellors are likely to start systematic desensitization by presenting a rationale for its use in relation to clients' concerns identified in behavioural assessments. This may involve remarks about the reciprocal inhibition principle. Also, the three elements of systematic desensitization are likely to be briefly explained. Additionally, counsellors may mention learning relaxation as a coping skill to use in anxiety-evoking situations. Having already discussed relaxation training, I now turn to constructing hierarchies.

Constructing hierarchies

Wolpe (1982) writes: 'An anxiety hierarchy is a thematically related list of anxiety-evoking stimuli, ranked according to the amount of anxiety they evoke' (p. 145). There are a number of considerations in constructing desensitization hierarchies. First, suitable themes have to be identified around which anxiety-evoking stimuli can be clustered. Needless to say, themes or areas which most debilitate clients' functioning receive precedence. Such themes are likely to emerge from behavioural assessments and may concern any one of a number of stimulus situations, for example, public speaking, examinations, eating in public, being with a member of the opposite sex and sexual intercourse.

Second, clients have to be introduced to the notion of a subjective scale of anxiety or fear. A common way of checking on the anxiety-evoking potential of hierarchy items is to say that zero is a feeling of no anxiety at all, and 100 is the maximum anxiety possible in relation to a particular theme. Thus individual items can be rated according to their positions on this subjective anxiety continuum or scale.

Third, appropriate hierarchy items need to be generated around each theme. Since clients are going to be asked to imagine the items, the situations require being specifically and graphically described. Counsellors indicate the appropriate way for items to be formulated. Sources to hierarchy items may include data gathered in behavioural assessments, self-monitoring homework assignments, suggestions from counsellors or clients, and questionnaire responses.

Fourth, the items generated around a particular theme need to be ordered into a hierarchy (see Table 10.4). This involves rating the items on a subjective anxiety scale and ordering them accordingly. Some of this work may be done as homework assignments, but counsellors will need to check any hierarchy before starting treatment. Also, during treatment, hierarchy items may need to be re-ordered or reworded, or additional items introduced. Some counsellors write, or ask their clients to write, items on index cards to facilitate ordering. In general, gaps of over ten units on the subjective anxiety scale are to be avoided. Where they occur, counsellors and clients may spend additional time formulating an intervening item or items.

Presenting hierarchy items

During desensitization sessions counsellors ask clients to imagine various scenes when relaxed. A basic assumption is that clients are capable of imagining scenes in such a way that they represent real-life situations. Goldfried and Davison (1976) observe: 'It

Table 10.4 Hierarchy for a client with fear of examinations

1. (Rated 5)	Thinking about exams while revising at my desk three months before the exams.
2. (Rated 10)	Thinking about exams while revising at my desk two months before the exams.
3. (Rated 15)	Thinking about exams while revising at my desk one month before the exams.
4. (Rated 20)	Thinking about exams while revising at my desk one week before the exams.
5. (Rated 25)	Thinking about exams while revising at my desk on the night before the exams.
6. (Rated 30)	Being driven in a car on the way to the examinations.
7. (Rated 35)	Waking up on the morning of an examination.
8. (Rated 40)	Going up to the notice board to have a look at the exam results.
9. (Rated 50)	Waiting outside the exam room.
10. (Rated 60)	Going into the exam room.
11. (Rated 70)	Looking at the exam paper for the first time.
12. (Rated 80)	Sitting down in the exam room.
13. (Rated 90)	Sitting in the exam room thinking of the inescapability of three hours in a hall full of people.
14. (Rated 95)	Experiencing a panic attack during the exam with the feeling of wanting to leave.
15. (Rated 100)	Having to leave the exam room due to panic.

is therefore essential that one check whether a client can become anxious from an image even before considering this procedure' (p. 122). They suggest that clients' imaginal capacities should be tested by asking them, when not relaxed, to imagine a situation which, on the basis of their assessment data, causes them anxiety in real life. Sometimes clients can be helped to imagine scenes by being asked to verbalize what they can see in the situations. Also, counsellors may provide a fuller verbal description of scenes.

A desensitization session may start with counsellors verbally relaxing clients. After counsellors are assured that clients have attained states of deep relaxation, they may start presenting scenes along the lines of 'Now I want you to imagine that you are thinking about exams while revising at your desk three months before exams . . .'. Counsellors start with the least anxiety-evoking scene on hierarchies and ask clients to raise their index fingers if experiencing any anxiety. If no anxiety is experienced, after five to ten seconds counsellors ask clients to stop imagining that scene and go back to being pleasantly relaxed. After 30 to 50 seconds, clients may be asked to imagine the same scene again. If this causes no anxiety, counsellors withdraw the scene, possibly spend time further relaxing clients, and move on to the next hierarchy item.

In instances where clients raise their index fingers to indicate anxiety, the scene is immediately withdrawn and clients are encouraged to relax more deeply before one or more further presentations of the scene. If a scene repeatedly causes anxiety, counsellors may consult clients about presenting a less anxiety-evoking hierarchy item.

An important assumption underlying systematic desensitization is that once a low anxiety-evoking item, for example ten units, has ceased to cause anxiety, all the other items in the hierarchy become less anxiety-evoking by ten units. Thus the 100-unit item becomes a 90-unit item, and so on. In general, only weak anxiety-evoking stimuli are presented to clients during desensitization sessions.

Counsellors may work from more than one hierarchy during desensitization sessions. Indeed, time spent on desensitization may form only part of longer interviews in which counsellors focus on other problems using other methods. A record is kept of all scene presentations and their outcomes. Wolpe's desensitization sessions last 15–30 minutes and he observes that 'whereas at an early stage eight or ten presentations may be the total at a session, at an advanced stage the number may be 30 or even 50' (Wolpe, 1982, p. 161). Golfried and Davison (1976) indicate that it is more useful to cover from two to five items in a given session.

Variations of systematic desensitization

Ways in which the basic systematic desensitization procedure described above may be varied include the following.

In vivo desensitization

Two kinds of considerations may make *in vivo* or real-life rather than imaginal desensitization the method of choice. First, clients may have difficulty in imagining scenes, and second, the stimuli in clients' hierarchies may lend themselves to real-life presentation. Even using imaginal desensitization, it may be helpful, if not essential, to encourage clients to try out in reality the situations to which they have been desensitized in imagination.

Relaxation may be used as part of *in vivo* desensitization. For instance, a client with a fear of public speaking may be relaxed at the start of each session, then over a number of sessions be asked to give a short talk in front of increasingly large numbers of people, who may also ask increasingly demanding questions. The procedure differs from imaginal desensitization mainly in that the hierarchies are constructed out of real-life situations. Otherwise, many of the imaginal desensitization considerations, such as the level of anxiety within which to present items, apply.

Group desensitization

Systematic desensitization may be used as a group as well as an individual procedure. For instance, a counsellor might work with either test-anxious college students simultaneously rather than with one at a time, thus possibly saving resources. Group approaches tend to involve the construction of standard rather than individual hierarchies and thus assume some proximity of the ordering of members' anxieties to this standard hierarchy (Emery & Krumboltz, 1967). The standard hierarchy may be compiled from items previously collected or may be evolved in consultation with current group members. The counsellor may move the group through the hierarchy, ensuring that further scenes are not presented until all members do not experience anxiety with the present scene.

Cassette-recorded desensitization

Cassettes may be used not only for the relaxation training part of systematic desensitization, but also for imagination training and for presenting actual hierarchy scenes at home. Any number from one to five homework items may be placed on a cassette, with the assumptions being either that all of the items generate only a small amount of anxiety, or that the client will not move on to later, more anxiety-evoking items until comfortable with earlier items. Clients who find themselves getting very tense may be instructed to switch off the cassette-playback and relax themselves for a few minutes before going on. Like group desensitization, the use of cassettes may save interview time.

BEHAVIOUR REHEARSAL AND ASSERTIVE TRAINING

Often behavioural assessments highlight client deficits in the areas of assertion and other interpersonal skills, for instance, active listening, giving feedback and self-disclosing. Behaviour rehearsal is one counselling method used for such concerns. Although behaviour rehearsal involves dramatic enactment or role playing, it differs from Moreno's psychodrama in that clients are encouraged to role-play new appropriate responses rather than existing maladaptive responses. There are a number of stages in behaviour rehearsal, including: (a) assessment and analysis of the areas in which clients experience difficulty; (b) enlisting clients' motivation for the behaviour rehearsal method; (c) working with clients to define what might be appropriate behaviour in given situations; (d) giving clients practice in appropriate responding by means of role playing, with counsellors role-playing the other person in interactions and (e) encouraging clients to try out the rehearsed behaviours in real-life situations and offering appropriate praise and reinforcement when this is accomplished. Behaviour rehearsal involves counsellors in shaping clients' behaviour in certain situations. Counsellor behaviours while doing this may include modelling, coaching, constructing hierarchies of more difficult tasks, and sometimes specific cognitive interventions.

Assertive training

Assertiveness is probably the main target behaviour for behaviour rehearsal. Wolpe (1982) defines assertive behaviour as 'the appropriate expression of any emotion other than anxiety toward another person' (p. 118). He regards virtually all clients as inhibited from normal behaviours because of their neurotic fears. Assertive training deconditions unadaptive habits of responding with anxiety to other people's behaviour in two ways: by weakening clients' fears and by changing how they speak and act. Clients require encouragement to express legitimate emotions that are already present in problem situations. Legitimate expression of emotions 'can then successfully compete with the fear that has been inhibiting just this expression, and each time it does so, it weakens to some extent the fear habit' (Wolpe & Wolpe, 1988, p. 54).

An early trend in assertive training was that of standing up for one's rights or what might be termed *oppositional* behaviour. For some time now, assertive training has been extended to include the expression and accurate communication of *affectionate* behaviour, where appropriate. Thus assertive behaviour now encompasses the expression of positive as well as of negative feelings.

Alberti and Emmons (1990) distinguish between: (a) *non-assertive* or inhibited behaviour, in which people are self-denying; (b) *aggressive* behaviour, in which they are self-enhancing at the expense of others; and (c) *assertive* behaviour, in which the individual is self-enhancing in a way likely to enhance both parties in an interaction. They observe that lack of assertiveness or aggressiveness can be *general* traits or *specific* to particular situations.

After behavioural assessments, possibly including an assertiveness questionnaire, indicate a need for assertive training in general and/or in specific target areas, the next stage can be for counsellors to enlist clients' motivation for the behaviour rehearsal method. Sometimes counsellors may need to spend time reviewing the clients' religious or philosophical positions, which may foster effacement rather than assertion. For instance, some Christians may need help in understanding that they can be more effective both as people and as Christians if they allow themselves to become whole persons and not deny their needs and feelings, with the likely psychological toll that is entailed.

During the third stage counsellors and clients work together to define what may be appropriate behaviours in specific situations: for instance, asking a boss for a pay rise or a girl for a date. This stage involves the generation and consideration of alternative responses. Additionally, clients may be encouraged to observe effective models. Assertiveness must take into account the styles of individual clients and appropriate assertive behaviour should be as 'natural' for them as possible. Responses that might seem appropriate for counsellors may not be appropriate for particular clients. Timing is also important, in that clients should not be encouraged to engage in assertiveness tasks for which they are not ready. Consequently, it may be necessary to construct a hierarchy of progressively more difficult assertion tasks.

The fourth stage is that of the behaviour rehearsal of assertiveness. Alberti and Emmons (1990) stress that assertive training should not focus only on verbal behaviour, but also on other components such as eye contact, body posture, gestures, facial expression, voice tone, inflection and volume, and fluency and timing of assertion. Counsellors need to rehearse and coach their clients in these non-verbal and para-verbal aspects of assertiveness. Also, behaviour rehearsal can include rehearsing clients in handling the negative and positive consequences of their assertion.

The fifth stage is enactment in real life. Clients should be set appropriately difficult assertiveness homework assignments. Monitoring their between-session assertive behaviour attempts is likely to help them. Feedback from real-life attempts at assertive behaviour indicates the adequacy of the behaviour and where, if necessary, it might be improved. Furthermore, counsellors can draw clients' attention to any positive consequences of their assertive behaviour. If the consequences were negative, counsellors and clients can review the appropriateness of the behaviour.

Assertive training may be applied on an individual or group interview or on a self-help basis. An issue in the implementation of group assertive training is whether to have heterogeneous or homogeneous groups, such as women's groups, men's groups, etc. Without wishing to prejudge the issue, homogeneous groups seem increasingly common in non-clinical settings. Cassettes and video-recorders are used by some counsellors to provide feedback to clients about their assertive behaviours. Last, assertiveness may lead to conflict, and so counsellors and clients may need to focus on managing conflict as well as on assertion.

REINFORCEMENT METHODS

Reinforcement methods aim to modify behaviour by altering its consequences and, as such, reflect operant rather than classical conditioning principles. To recapitulate, both positive and negative reinforcement strengthen the probability of a response. Positive reinforcers involve presenting and negative reinforcers removing something in a situation. Punishment, or the presentation of a negative state of affairs, aims to weaken the probability of a response without necessarily increasing the frequency of other behaviours. Extinction also aims to weaken the probability of a response by withdrawal of customary reinforcers. Readers are referred to the section on Skinner in Chapter 9 for further discussion of reinforcement concepts, such as schedules of reinforcement.

Counselling as reinforcement

A reinforcement view of counselling sees the role of counsellors as that of controlling interviews by dispensing intentional and, sometimes, unintentional reinforcers. Thus counsellors are conceptualized as influencers or as social reinforcement machines who shape or manipulate client behaviour (Krasner, 1962). Inasmuch as social-influence processes exist anyway in counselling interviews, a behaviourist would argue that counsellors should be trained to maximize their efficiency in the influencing process. Also, they should become aware of ways in which clients may be reinforcing counsellors in maladaptive interview behaviours.

Counsellors may reinforce their clients with such variables as praise, attention, eye contact, empathy, warmth and genuineness. Truax (1966a) argues that counsellors offering high levels of empathy, non-possessive warmth, and genuineness are more effective than those offering low levels of these conditions because they become more potent positive reinforcers. Counsellors offering low levels of the conditions may be noxious stimuli who serve primarily as negative influences. Reasons why high levels of the 'therapeutic conditions' are important include reinforcement of human relating by clients, reinforcement of self-explanatory behaviour, and reinforcement of positive self-concepts and self-evaluations. Truax (1966b) conducted a study to explore whether Rogers was differentially using the core therapeutic conditions to reinforce certain categories of client behaviour. Counsellor-client-counsellor interaction units were selected randomly from the middle one-third of counselling hours from throughout an 85–interview, single, long-term, successful case handled by Rogers. Truax reported that Rogers significantly responded selectively with differential levels of empathy, warmth or directiveness to high and low levels of five out of nine classes of client behaviour. Furthermore, of the classes of client behaviour to which the counsellor selectively responded or reinforced, four out of five showed significant changes during counselling in the predicted direction.

Behavioural counsellors may sometimes reinforce their clients in very overt ways. For instance, during the behaviour rehearsal phase of assertion training, client behaviour will be shaped by reinforcement until it stands a reasonable chance of success when enacted in real life. Also, when clients report successful attainment of assertive training homework goals, they are likely to find that behaviour being reinforced by a counsellor comment like 'good'.

Identifying reinforcers

Many reinforcers, such as praise, affection and attention, are given out relatively unthinkingly during the course of everyday life. Reinforcement methods, however, involve the systematic application of reinforcement to initiate and strengthen adaptive behaviours and to weaken and eliminate maladaptive behaviours. In order to use reinforcement systematically, it is necessary to discover what is reinforcing for individual clients. Ways in which counsellors can find out what their clients consider reinforcing include asking them, asking others about them, observing what they say and do in the interview setting, and getting them to observe and monitor themselves outside interviews.

Some self-report questionnaires exist for assessing reinforcers. Cautela (1967) has devised a *Reinforcement Survey Schedule* to identify possible reinforcing stimuli together with their relative reinforcing values. The focus of the schedule is on identifying those stimuli which can be used to evoke adaptive responses. The schedule is divided into four major sections: (a) reinforcers that can be presented in many conventional settings: (b) reinforcers that can be presented only through facsimile or imagination; (c) situational contexts that 'I would like to be in'; and (d) a frequency count of frequently occurring daily behaviours and thoughts. Both counsellor and client can use the schedule for assessing the nature, range and strength of the client's reinforcers.

Another self-report questionnaire is MacPhillamy and Lewinsohn's *Pleasant Events Schedule* (Lewinsohn et al., 1986). This instrument consists of 320 events and activities generated after an extensive search of possible 'pleasant events'. Subjects rate each item in the schedule on a five-point scale of pleasantness. A shortened version of the *Pleasant Events Schedule* can be derived from those items associated with improved mood for a substantial proportion of people. Lewinsohn and Graf (1973) list 49 such items and suggest that they fall into three categories; social interactional, effects incompatible with depression, and ego supportive or activities leading to feelings such as adequacy and competence.

When working with children, pictures may be used instead of words to portray reinforcers. An example of this is the 'reinforcement menu' devised by Daley (1969) for finding effective reinforcers for eight- to eleven-year-old mentally retarded children. Twenty-two high-probability activities, such as talking, writing and colouring, were drawn in colour by an artist and enclosed in a single book or 'menu' with one activity per page. Children were encouraged to identify the activities in which they wanted to engage.

Reinforcement programmes and token economies

Positive reinforcement is the major method of changing behaviour in applied settings. Positive reinforcement programmes can be used both to increase desirable behaviours and to decrease undesirable behaviours. The second goal can be accomplished by positively reinforcing alternative or incompatible behaviours (Kazdin, 1994). Counsellors may design positive reinforcement programmes on their own or in consultation with significant others. In the latter cases, the significant others rather than the counsellors may administer the programme of rewards.

Hosford (1969) observes that four crucial elements are necessary in any counselling programme implementing operant reinforcement procedures. First, the reinforcements need to potent enough to motivate clients to continue performing the desired behaviours. Second, reinforcement must be applied systematically. Third, the contingency between the demonstration of the desired behaviour and the application of the reinforcement must be clear. Fourth, counsellors must be able to elicit the behaviours which they plan to reinforce. It is particularly important that, when a behaviour is initiated, the reinforcement contingent upon that behaviour is immediate, otherwise its differential effect may be lost. Acquisition of desired behaviours may initially involve reinforcement either of component behaviours or related behaviours and build up to the desired behaviours by successive approximation. Counsellors can use continuous reinforcement to establish behaviours initially. Afterwards, they can use intermittent reinforcement, since resistance to extinction is greater if fewer responses are reinforced.

Reinforcement may either be administered directly, by provision of actual reinforcers, or indirectly, by means of tokens which may later be exchanged for reinforcers. Furthermore, clients may be reinforced vicariously by observing models obtain rewards for desired behaviours. An example of direct reinforcement is Sanborn and Schuster's (1969) use of sweets to reinforce desired behaviours in a remedial reading class. For instance, the first boy to sit down was rewarded with a sweet and the contingency for the reward was verbally transmitted: 'This is for taking your seat'. As the class progressed pupils were rewarded for other specific behaviours.

Sometimes positive reinforcement can reward the wrong behaviours. For instance, institutionalized elderly people can receive the social reward of attention for dependency and helplessness behaviours whereas independence behaviours go unrewarded (Baltes, 1988). For such institutionalized elderly people, a positive reinforcement programme should target increasing the likelihood of appropriate independence responses.

Token are tangible conditioned reinforcers which may be exchanged for back-up reinforcers such as prizes, opportunities to engage in special activities, food or other purchases. Token reinforcement programmes need to establish clearly the rules of exchange that specify the number of tokens required to obtain back-up reinforcers (Wilson, 1989). Token economies or token reinforcement programmes have been used with school children, delinquents and hospital patients. Applications of token economies in elementary and secondary school settings have improved students' classroom performance in reading, writing, and arithmetic (Kazdin, 1989). In one American programme first-grade students received points at various intervals, depending on how well they were working, that they could exchange for prizes ranging in value from $0.05 to $1.50 at a 'good study store' in class (Breyer & Allen, 1975). In their review of token reinforcement programmes in the classroom, O'Leary and Drabman observe that different investigations repeatedly reported significant decreases in disruptive behaviour associated with token programmes and add 'the most obvious dramatic changes in token programs seem to have occurred in programs where non-academic behaviors served as the dependent variable' (O'Leary & Drabman, 1971, p. 385).

Kazdin and Bootzin (1972) suggest that extinction of the desired behaviours generally follows removal of token reinforcement. They state that generalization should be planned rather than depended on as an inadvertent consequence of the token economy. One way of enhancing resistance to extinction is to focus on teaching those behaviours which will continue to be reinforced after training. Another way involves gradually removing or fading the token reinforcement, possibly offering substitute kinds of reinforcement such as praise as the fading takes place. Yet another way of maintaining the behavioural gains is to encourage clients to use self-reinforcement by giving themselves reinforcers contingent upon the performance of desired behaviours.

Reinforcement programmes and token economies may involve the co-operation and training of significant others in the clients' environments. For instance, counsellors may need to work with teachers or parents in devising reinforcement procedures for individuals or groups of children. Furthermore, both teachers and parents may need to become aware of how they may inadvertently be reinforcing some of the behaviours they say they are trying to stop. Teaching the skills of effective reinforcement involves both theoretical learning and relevant practice. Furthermore, counsellors may need to support and guide teachers and parents as they apply their new skills in real-life settings.

Punishment

Goldfried and Davison (1976) observe that there are three basic punishment procedures, each of which attempts to reduce the frequency of a behaviour: presentation of an aversive event, time out and response costs. Anger, striking people, and threats if they perform a undesired behaviour are all aversive events which may reduce the probability of repetition of the behaviour.

Time out is a procedure frequently recommended by behavioural counsellors for use with disruptive children. It involves removal of clients from situations in which they might otherwise be receiving reinforcement. For instance, a child's attention-seeking behaviour in a classroom may be being reinforced by teacher attention and peer approval, neither of which is available when the child is made to leave the classroom for a set period of time. Time-out procedures involve a clear instruction, adequate warning that the time-out procedure is contingent upon the undesired behaviour and, if this goes unheeded, application of time out in a systematic and unemotional way. Nemeroff & Karoly (1991) observe: 'Most successful programmes with children employ TO durations of between 5 and 20 minutes, and for very young children, periods as short as 1 to 5 minutes may be effective' (p. 150).

Response costs involve deductions of certain amounts from clients' collections of reinforcers if they perform undesired behaviours. For instance, participants in a token economy may lose some of their tokens. As with all punishment procedures, response costs should be used in conjunction with positive reinforcement of desirable or alternative behaviours.

Helping clients to obtain reinforcement

A very important aspect of behavioural treatment may be that of helping clients to increase the number and scope of reinforcers available to them. Another way of saying this is that, instead of passively relying on others, clients can be helped to identify and actively seek out people, activities and situations that provide the desired reinforcements. Lewinsohn and Libet (1972) assert that a low rate of positive reinforcement is a critical antecedent of depressive behaviours and that improvement is likely to be accompanied by an increase of positive reinforcement. They report the findings of a study in which the 160 items from the *Pleasant Events Schedule* which a subject judged to be most pleasant were made into an activity schedule for that subject, who, for 30 consecutive days, was asked to indicate at the end of each day the activities in which he or she engaged. They found a significant association between mood and pleasant activities over their 30 subjects, though there were large individual differences. They see the clinical utility of activity schedules as including: (a) assessing which activities are potentially reinforcing; (b) illustrating to clients their low rates of emitting behaviours which bring positive reinforcement; (c) goal setting; and (d) monitoring behaviour change.

Another study by Turner and his colleagues in which the subjects were moderately depressed college students confirmed the effectiveness of using activity schedules and also instructing the subjects to increase their pleasant activities over their usual level (Turner *et al.*, 1979). A further study by Zeiss *et al.*, (1979) indicated that, with depressed outpatients, treatments focusing on interpersonal skills, cognitions, or activity schedules (with increasing frequency of target activities) all significantly alleviated depression. The authors concluded that all treatments ameliorated depression because they provided training in self-help skills which increased patients' feelings of self-efficacy regarding the obtaining of positive reinforcement as a result of their own skilfulness.

Training clients to use self-reinforcement

Behavioural counsellors often train clients in how to reinforce their own behaviours. Kanfer and Gaelick (1986) distinguish between an *administrative* and a *participant* model of treatment. In the administrative model, counsellors administer treatments to which clients submit. In the participant model, there is an emphasis on client responsibility and counsellors are viewed as transitory social support systems. Training clients in self-reinforcement assumes that they are active participants in their treatment.

Training clients to use self-reinforcement is often termed a self-control or self-management strategy. It can involve assisting clients to observe their behaviour, set goals for themselves, identify suitable reinforcers, plan graded steps to attain their goals and specify when to administer consequences (Watson & Tharp, 1993). In helping clients to design self-reinforcement programmes, it is important that they perceive both that they have chosen their goals or target behaviours and also that they have the confidence to complete tasks that will bring desired outcomes. Consequently, frequently counsellors design self-reinforcement programmes with graded steps to ensure that clients build up their confidence with success experiences. This enhances motivation both initially and later. Some clients may have to build up component skills prior initiating self-management programmes.

Self-observation

Behavioural counsellors encourage clients to observe and monitor themselves both to enhance their motivation and to clarify goals. However, as a treatment intervention, the effects of self-observation alone are often short-lived. Self-observation is important at the start of, during and after self-reinforcement programmes. Initially, it establishes a baseline and increases awareness. During a programme, it acts both as a reminder and also as a check on progress. Afterwards, it is relevant to maintaining gains, though at this stage self-observations are unlikely to be collected so systematically.

Counsellors request that clients collect quantative data. Charts and tally sheets may be used for this purpose, for example a daily weight chart or a daily tally of number of cigarettes smoked. Sometimes wrist counters and pocket counters are used; for instance, a shy adolescent may record the number of times she engages in conversations with peers. Self-observation can be expanded to include noting both the internal and external cues that come before actions and also the consequences of actions. Since clients may be poor observers of their own behaviour, counsellors often have to train them in self-observation and check their progress.

Stimulus control

Thoresen and Mahoney (1974) indicate that there are two general self-control strategies that clients can use to influence their actions. First, they can try modifying their environments to control target actions *prior to* their execution. Second, they can self-administer a reward *following* or *contingent upon* an action or series of actions that achieves either a goal or a subgoal.

Behavioural counsellors assist clients to use stimulus control as one form of environmental modification. Stimulus control entails either modifying in advance the stimuli or cues associated with maladaptive responses and establishing cues associated with adaptive responses. For example, ways in which behavioural counsellors might suggest that people on weight reduction programmes modify their environments to control their food intake include: ensuring that food is placed out of sight and out of easy reach; equipping their refrigerators with time locks; only keeping as much food in the house as can be consumed in a short period of time; and, where appropriate, avoiding contact with people associated with excessive eating. Stimulus control can also be used to enhance adaptive behaviours. For example, students can learn to associate their desks with work if they use them only for that purpose. Also, behavioural counsellors use stimulus control in treating sleep disorders by having insomniac clients associate their beds only with sleep (Morawetz, 1989).

Positive self-reinforcement

Behavioural counsellors assist clients to design programmes where they reinforce themselves on attaining a subgoal or goal. Self-reinforcers can be external or internal. External reinforcers include: (1) self-administration of new reinforcers that are outside clients' everyday lives, such as a new item of clothing or a special event; and (2) initial denial of some pleasant everyday experience and later administration of it contingent upon some desired action. Internal reinforcers include self-talk statements like 'That's great', or 'Well done', or 'I'm glad I made it' that clearly indicate the client's satisfaction with achieving target actions.

Behavioural counsellors planning positive self-reinforcement programmes with clients take into account a number of considerations. First they and their clients need to identify suitable rewards. Kanfer and Gaelick (1986) observe that wherever possible a positive self-reinforcer should be relevant to the target behaviour. An example might be the purchase of slimmer fitting clothes for those attaining weight reduction goals. As mentioned earlier, behavioural counsellors may break tasks down so that clients reward themselves for attaining progressively more difficult tasks. In addition, connections between achievement and reinforcement must be clear. Counsellors may encourage clients to draw up personal contracts which specify the relationship between positive self-reinforcement and desired actions. Alternatively counsellors and clients may draw up bilateral contracts. Such contracts should only be transitional phases in programmes designed to build clients' self-help skills.

When collaborating with clients to design self-reinforcement programmes, behavioural counsellors are mindful of external resources that clients can use. For instance, participating in activities of a social, educational, recreational or religious nature may provide opportunities for gaining confidence and skills. In addition, reading appropriate self-help books and manuals can be incorporated into a programme. Such material should be easily comprehensible to clients, but this is often not the case (O'Farrell & Keuthen, 1983).

Self-punishment

Above I have emphasized stimulus control and positive self-reinforcement. However, though less frequently used, behavioural counsellors encourage clients to self-administer aversive consequences. For example, weight loss programme clients can give to charity a specified sum of money for every 100 calories in excess of a daily intake limit or they can present themselves with a noxious odour after each extra snack (Thoresen & Mahoney, 1974). Furthermore, clients can imagine themselves experiencing aversive consequences in they perform undesirable actions: for instance throwing up if they eat a piece of chocolate cake. This process is known as covert sensitization (Cautela, 1967).

AVERSIVE AND FLOODING METHODS

This chapter has focused on basic behavioural counselling methods. Other less common and more controversial approaches exist, for example aversion therapy and flooding.

Both these methods deliberately heighten clients' levels of distress. They tend to be used in clinical rather than counselling settings and so are only briefly mentioned. Aversion therapy, which entails the presentation of an aversive event such as an electric shock contingent upon some undesired behaviour, might be viewed as a punishment technique. Though some of the assumptions behind what they did are out-dated, MacCulloch and Feldman (1967) used an aversion therapy procedure incorporating a special schedule of reinforcement in an attempt to decrease the homosexual and increase the heterosexual orientation of predominantly homosexually orientated patients.

Implosive therapy is an earlier term for flooding. Stampfl, the founder of implosive therapy, viewed the symptoms of his patients as 'conditioned fear reactions, and/or conditioned anger reactions, acquired from past experiences involving punishment, frustration and pain' (Stampfl, 1975, p. 68). Usually after two information-gathering clinical interviews, the counsellor presents scenes to the client's imagination which get progressively closer to what the patient finds most threatening. Some of the scenes are very gruesome. Stampfl's scenes aim to provide as good an approximation as possible to original conditioning events and may be highly anxiety-evoking. However, he hypothesized that continued repetition of these scenes should lead to a decrease in their anxiety-evoking potential through extinction (Stampfl & Lewis, 1968). Since many of the original conditioning events are associated with the patient's childhood, Stampfl found the psychodynamic literature, with its emphasis on toilet training, infantile sexuality and aggression, to be useful in indicating sensitive areas of early aversive conditioning. He stated that the single strategy of implosive therapy is for patients to confront and stare down their nightmares (Stampfl, 1975).

In current flooding techniques, counsellors arrange for clients to be exposed to relatively strong fear stimuli which, either real or imagined, are presented continuously. Presentations last until anxiety wanes, which frequently takes from 10 minutes to an hour. Sometimes clients are so distressed that they discontinue treatment. Nevertheless, flooding has been used with considerable success for a variety of phobias. However, Wolpe claims that, with few exceptions, desensitization has proved superior to flooding with the added advantage of being less stressful for clients (Wolpe & Wolpe, 1988).

CONCLUDING COMMENT

This chapter has presented a relatively traditional view of behavioural counselling. However, behavioural counselling has not remained static. Galassi and Perot (1992) observe that: 'Undoubtedly, the single most important change is the cognitive revolution that has swept through the behaviour therapy in the last dozen years or so' (p. 627). My view is that the cognitive revolution gained its momentum in the early 1970s. By 1990, 69 per cent and 27 per cent of American Association of Behavior Therapy members identified themselves as cognitive-behavioural and behavioural, respectively (Craighead, 1990). Now most counsellors, especially the younger ones, using the methods described above are more likely to view themselves as cognitive-behavioural rather than behavioural counsellors (Zook & Walton, 1989). Some of the assumptions of cognitive-behavioural counselling, for instance its emphasis on inner as well as outer behaviours, are uncongenial to traditional behaviourists. However, it is to the theory and practice of cognitive and cognitive-behavioural counselling that I turn in the next chapters of this book.

CHAPTER REVIEW AND SELF-REFERENT QUESTIONS
Goals

Chapter review question

1. What might behavioural counsellors view as appropriate goals for clients?

Self-referent question

1. Identify an area of your own behaviour that you wish to change. Formulate your goal(s) in behavioural terms.

Behavioural assessment

Chapter review questions

1. What are the functions of behavioural assessment?

2. How do behavioural counsellors collect behavioural assessment information?

3. Conduct a behavioural assessment, preferably on another person in class. Write out a report focusing on the following kinds of information: basic details of client (age, sex, marital status, occupation); interview observations about client; client's view of presenting concerns; SRC analysis of presenting concerns; relevant historical information; client's motivation, expectancies, likely co-operation; and treatment goals expressed in behavioural terms.

Self-referent question

1. For the behaviour that you wished to change above, for one week keep a behaviour monitoring diary collecting material in an SRC format.

Relaxation procedures

Chapter review questions

1. Describe the goals and methods of progressive muscular relaxation.

2. What are relaxation procedures other than progressive muscular relaxation?

3. If possible, role-play being a counsellor who is getting another person into a state of deep relaxation by means of progressive muscular relaxation.

Self-referent questions

1. Practise relaxing yourself for 15 to 20 minutes a day over a period of at least a week. Keep a monitoring log of your relaxation homework (Table 10.3). During your relaxation homework cover:
   (a) progressive muscular relaxation (Table 10.2);
   (b) brief muscular relaxation;
   (c) verbal relaxation;
   (d) mental relaxation; and
   (e) differential relaxation.
2. Assess your life-style to find out whether it is sufficiently relaxed regarding
   (a) the pace at which you lead your life; and
   (b) having sufficient relaxation outlets.

Systematic desensitization

Chapter review questions

1. Describe the goals and methods of systematic desensitization.

2. What are some of the ways of varying systematic desensitization?

3. If possible, work with another person in identifying and constructing hierarchies round anxiety-evoking themes in his or her life.

4. If possible, role-play being a counsellor who conducts systematic desensitization, including presentation of hierarchy items, with another person as client.

Self-referent questions

1. Identify themes in your own life which are appropriate for hierarchy construction and then, along the lines of Table 10.4, construct one or more hierarchies around them.

2. In one of the areas identified above, apply systematic desensitization to yourself.

Behaviour rehearsal and assertive training

Chapter review questions

1. What are the goals of assertive training?

2. How might a behavioural counsellor use behaviour rehearsal as part of assertive training?

3. If possible, role-play being a counsellor who works with a client to define goals for appropriate assertive behaviour in a specific situation, conducts the necessary behaviour rehearsals, then encourages the client to try out the new behaviours in real-life.

Self-referent questions

1. Assess yourself on the following dimensions:
   (a) general assertiveness, non-assertiveness, and aggressiveness;
   (b) assertiveness, non-assertiveness, and aggressiveness in one or more specific situations important to you;
   (c) oppositional and affectionate assertiveness.

2. Pick a specific situation in your life where you consider you could be more assertive. Set yourself behavioural goals for change and self-administer assertiveness training and behaviour rehearsal to attain your goals.

Reinforcement methods

Chapter review questions

1. In what ways do counsellors and clients use reinforcement during counselling interviews?

2. How can behavioural counsellors identify what clients find reinforcing?

3. Help another person to compile a list of at least 25 items that they find reinforcing. Then get them to rate each item using the following scale: 1, slightly reinforcing; 2, moderately reinforcing; 3, strongly reinforcing; 4, very strongly reinforcing.

4. What are some important considerations in establishing reinforcement programmes and token economies?

5. Design a token economy programme for an applied setting, such as an educational institution or a family. Specify:
   (a) the behavioural goals of the programme;
   (b) the population and setting for the programme;
   (c) the token and back-up reinforcers involved;
   (d) the precise contingency or contingencies for award of the tokens;
   (e) features in the programme designed to avoid extinction of the behaviours learned in the programme; and
   (f) steps to be taken in training and supporting any significant others.

5. What is meant by each of the following punishment procedures:
   (a) presentation of an aversive event;
   (b) time out; and
   (c) response costs?

6. How can behavioural counsellors assist clients in obtaining reinforcement in their daily lives?

7. What are the goals of stimulus control? Provide an example of stimulus control.

Self-referent questions

1. Make a list of at least 25 items which you personally find reinforcing. Rate each item using the following scale: 1, slightly reinforcing; 2, moderately reinforcing; 3, strongly reinforcing; 4, very strongly reinforcing.

2. Design a positive self-reinforcement programme. Specify:
    (a) your goal in behavioural terms;
    (b) how you intend to observe your behaviour, establish a baseline and monitor progress;
    (c) the positive reinforcer(s) you intend using;
    (d) the precise conditions for self-administering the positive reinforcer(s);
    (e) whether and how you intend using graded steps and subgoals to attain your goal; and
    (f) a time schedule for your programme.

Aversive and flooding methods

Chapter review questions

1. What are aversion therapy approaches to counselling?

2. What are the goals of and considerations in using flooding methods in counselling?

Self-referent questions

1. What are your personal reactions to the use of aversion methods in counselling? Are there instances where you would consider using them? If so, please describe.

2. Think of one or more areas in which you experience debilitating anxiety. For each area, how useful do you think flooding methods would be in helping you to cope better?

Annotated bibliography

Wolpe, J. (1982). *The Practice of Behavior Therapy* (3rd ed.). Oxford: Pergamon Press.
This book describes in detail the author's views on the causes of neurosis, behaviour analysis, and a range of treatment methods including assertiveness training, systematic desensitization and its variations, and operant conditioning. In addition, Wolpe presents some complex cases and provides an evaluation of behaviour therapy.

Kazdin, A.E. (1994). *Behavior Modification in Applied Settings* (5th ed.). Pacific Grove, CA: Brooks/Cole.
This book takes a scholarly, yet practical, approach to behavioural assessment and the design and evaluation of behaviour modification programmes. Chapters are included on positive and negative reinforcement punishment, extinction, self-control techniques, and response maintenance and transfer of training.

Kanfer, F.H. & Goldstein, A.P. (Eds.) (1991). *Helping People Change: A Textbook of Methods.* (4th ed.) New York: Pergamon Press.
This edited book covers current approaches to helping including: operant and aversion methods, modelling methods, fear reduction methods, self-management methods, cognitive change methods and cognitive behaviour modification.

Cormier, W.H. & Cormier, L.S. (1991). *Interviewing Strategies for Helpers: Fundamental Skills and Cognitive Behavioural Interventions* (3rd ed.). Pacific Grove, CA: Brooks/Cole.
This huge and extremely detailed book presents skills and strategies for four major stages of the helping process: relationship, assessment and goal setting, strategy selection and implementation, and evaluation and termination.

Watson, D.L. & Tharp, R.G. (1993). *Self-directed behavior: Self-modification for Personal Adjustment* (6th ed.). Pacific Grove, CA: Brooks/Cole.
This book acquaints readers with basic behavioural modification and cognitive-behavioural theory, provides exercises for developing skills of self-analysis and offers concrete information on how to achieve personal goals.

Further references

Alberti, R.E. & Emmons, M.E. (1975). *Stand Up, Speak Out, Talk Back!* New York: Pocket Books.

Alberti, R.E. & Emmons, M.E. (1990). *Your Perfect Right: A Guide to Assertive Living* (6th ed.). San Luis Obispo, CA: Impact Publishers.

Baltes, M.M. (1988). The etiology and maintenance of dependency in the elderly: Three phases of operant research. *Behavior Therapy, 19,* 301–19.

Bernstein, D.A. & Borkovec, T.D. (1973). *Progressive Relaxation Training: A Manual for the Helping Professions.* Champaign, IL: Research Press.

Borkovec, T.D. & Sides, J.K. (1979). Critical procedural variables related to the physiological effects of progressive relaxation: A review. *Behaviour Research and Therapy, 17,* 119–25.

Breyer, N.L. & Allen, G.L. (1975). Effects of implementing a token economy on teacher attending behavior *Journal of Applied Behavior Analysis, 8,* 373–80.

Cautela, J. (1967). A Reinforcement Survey Schedule for use in therapy, training and research. *Psychological Reports, 20,* 1115–30.

Craighead, W.E. (1990). 'There's a place for us: All of us'. *Behavior Therapy, 21,* 3–23.

Daley, M.F. (1969). The 'reinforcement menu': Finding effective reinforcers. In J.D. Krumboltz and C.E. Thoresen (Eds.), *Behavioral Counselling: Cases and Techniques* (pp. 42–5). New York: Holt, Rinehart & Winston.

Emery, J.R. & Krumboltz, J.D. (1967). Standard versus individualized hierarchies in desensitization to reduce test anxiety. *Journal of Counseling Psychology, 14,* 204–9.

Galassi, J.P. & Perot, A.R. (1992). What you should know about behavioral assessment. *Journal of Counseling & Development, 70,* 624–31.

Golfried, M.R. (1971). Systematic desensitisation as training in self-control. *Journal of Consulting and Clinical Psychology, 37,* 228–4.

Goldfried, M.R. (1976). Behavioral assessment. In I.B. Weiner (Ed.), *Clinical Methods in Psychology* (pp. 281–330). New York: Wiley.

Goldfried, M.R. & Davison, G.C. (1976). *Clinical Behavior Therapy.* New York: Holt, Rinehart & Winston.

Goldfried, M.R. & Trier, C.S. (1974). Effectiveness of relaxation as an active coping skill. *Journal of Abnormal Psychology, 83,* 348–55.

Hosford, R.E. (1969) Behavioral counselling – a contemporary overview. *The Counseling Psychologist, 1* (4), 1–33.

Jacobson, E. (1929) *Progressive Relaxation.* Chicago:, IL: University of Chicago Press.

Jacobson, E. (1938). *Progressive Relaxation* (2nd ed.). Chicago, IL: University of Chicago Press.

Kanfer, F.H. and Gaelick, L. (1986). Self Management Methods. In F.H. Kanfer and A.P. Goldstein (Eds.), *Helping People Change: A Textbook of Methods* (3rd ed.) (pp. 238–345) New York: Pergamon Press.

Kazdin, A.E. (1989). *Behavior Modification in Applied Settings* (4th ed.). Pacific Grove, CA: Brooks/Cole

Kazdin, A.E. (1993). Evaluation in clinical practice: Clinically sensitive and systematic methods of treatment delivery. *Behavior Therapy, 24,* 11–45.

Kazdin, A.E. & Bootzin, R.E. (1972). The token economy: An evaluative review. *Journal of Applied Behavior Analysis, 5*, 343–72.

Krasner, L. (1962). The therapist as a social reinforcement machine. In H.H. Strupp and L. Luborsky (Eds.), *Research in Psychotherapy* (Vol. 2, pp. 61–94). Washington, DC: American Psychological Association.

Krumboltz, J.D. (1966). Behavioral goals for counseling. *Journal of Counseling Psychology, 13*, 153–9.

Krumboltz, J.D. & Thoresen, C.E. (Eds.) (1976). *Counseling Methods.* New York: Holt, Rinehart & Winston.

Lewinsohn, P.M. (1976). Activity schedules in treatment of depression. In J.D. Krumboltz and C.E. Thoresen (Eds.), *Counseling Methods* (pp. 74–83). New York: Holt, Rinehart & Winston.

Lewinsohn, P.M. & Graf, M. (1973). Pleasant activities and depression. *Journal of Consulting and Clinical Psychology, 41*, 261–8.

Lewinsohn, P.M. & Libet, J. (1972). Pleasant events, activity schedules and depression. *Journal of Abnormal Psychology, 79*, 291–5.

Lewinsohn, P.M., Munoz, R.F., Youngren, M.A. & Zeiss, A.M. (1986). *Control Your Depression* (rev. ed.). New York: Prentice Hall.

Lewinsohn, P.M. Weinstein, M.S. & Alper, T. (1970). A behavioral approach to the group treatment of depressed persons: A methodological contribution. *Journal of Clinical Psychology, 26*, 525–32.

MacCulloch, M.J. & Feldman, M.P. (1967). Aversion therapy in management of 43 homosexuals. *British Medical Journal, 2*, 594–7.

MacPhillamy, D.J. & Lewinsohn, P.M. (1971). *Pleasant Events Schedule.* Mimeograph, University of Oregon.

Morawetz, D. (1989). Behavioral self-help treatment for insomnia: A controlled evaluation. *Behavior Therapy, 20*, 365–79.

Nemeroff, C.J. & Karoly, P. (1991). Operant methods. In F.H. Kanfer & A.P. Goldstein (Eds.), *Helping People Change: A Textbook of Methods* (4th ed., pp. 122–60). New York: Pergamon Press.

O'Farrell, T.J. & Keuthen, N.J. (1983). Readability of behaviour therapy self-help manual. *Behaviour Therapy, 14*, 449–54.

O'Leary, K.D. & Drabman, R. (1971). Token reinforcement programs in the classroom: A review. *Psychological Bulletin, 75*, 379–98.

Sanborn, B. & Schuster, W. (1969). Establishing reinforcement techniques in the classroom. In J.D. Krumboltz and C.E. Thoresen (Eds.), *Behavioral Counseling: Cases and Techniques* (pp. 131–52). New York: Holt, Rinehart & Winston.

Schmidt, J.P. & Patterson, T.E. (1979). Issues in the implementation of assertion training in applied settings. *Journal of Behavior Therapy and Experimental Psychiatry, 10*, 15–19.

Sharpe, R. & Lewis, D. (1976. *The Success Factor.* London: Souvenir Press.

Stampfl, T.G. (1975). Implosive therapy: Staring down your nightmares. *Psychology Today*, February, 66–73.

Stampfl, T.G. & Lewis, D.J. (1968). Implosive therapy – a behavioural therapy? *Behaviour Research and Therapy, 6*, 31–6.

Swan, G.E. & MacDonald, M.L. (1978). Behavior therapy in practice: A national survey of behavior therapists. *Behavior Therapy, 9*, 799–807.

Tasto, D.L. & Hinkle, J.E. (1973). Muscle relaxation treatment for tension headaches. *Behaviour Research and Therapy, 11*, 347–9.

Thoresen, C.E. & Coates, T.J. (1978). What does it mean to be a behavior therapist? *The Counselling Psychologist, 7*, 3–21.

Thoresen, C.E. & Mahoney, M.J. (1974). *Behavioral Self-Control.* New York: Holt, Rinehart and Winston.

Traux, C.B. (1966a). Some implication of behavior therapy for psychotherapy. *Journal of Counseling Psychology, 13*, 160–70.

Traux, C.B. (1966b). Reinforcement and nonreinforcement in Rogerian psychotherapy. *Journal of Abnormal Psychology, 71*, 1–9.

Turner, R.W., Ward, M.F. & Turner, J. (1979). Behavioral treatment for depression: An evaluation of therapeutic components. *Journal of Clinical Psychology, 35*, 166–75.

Vitalo, R. (1969). Systematic desensitization manual for helper instruction and treatment procedure. In R.R. Carkhuff, *Helping and Human Relations: Volume 1, Selection and Training* (pp. 271–90). New York: Holt, Rinehart & Winston.

Watson, D.L. & Tharp, R.G. (1993). *Self-directed Behavior: Self-modification for personal adjustment* (6th ed.). Pacific Grove, CA: Brooks/Cole.

Wilson, G.T. (1989). Behavior therapy. In R.J. Corsini & D. Wedding (Eds.), *Current Psychotherapies* (4th ed., pp. 241–82). Itasca, IL: Peacock.

Wolpe, J. (1958). *Psychotherapy by Reciprocal Inhibition.* Stanford: Stanford University Press.

Wolpe, J. (1973). *The Practice of Behaviour Therapy* (2nd ed.). Oxford: Pergamon Press.

Wolpe, J. & Lang, P.J. (1969). *Fear Survey Schedule.* San Diego, CA: Educational and Industrial Testing Service.

Wolpe, J. & Wolpe, D. (1988). *Life without Fear: Anxiety and its Cure.* Oakland, CA: New Harbinger Publications.

Zeiss, A.M., Lewinsohn, P.M. & Munoz, R.F. (1979). Nonspecific improvement effects in depression using interpersonal skills training, pleasant activity schedules, or cognitive training. *Journal of Consulting and Clinical Psychology, 47*, 427–39.

Zook, A. & Walton, J.M. (1989). Theoretical orientations and work settings of clinical and counseling psychologists: A current perspective. *Professional Psychology: Research and Practice, 20*, 23–31.

Journals

Behavior Therapy, ABBT, 15 West 36 Street, New York, NY 10018.
Published by the Association for Advancement of Behavior Therapy, this is an international journal devoted to the application of behavioural and cognitive sciences to clinical problems.

Behaviour Research and Therapy (incorporating *Behavioural Assessment*), Pergamon Press Ltd., Pergamon House, Bampflyde Street, Exeter EX1 2AH, England.
This journal publishes scientific papers pertaining to abnormal behaviour and experiences, and their modification, and to medical psychology. The journal devotes approximately one-quarter specifically to assessment.

PART SIX

Cognitive and
Cognitive-Behavioural

ELEVEN

Social Cognitive Theory

PREVIEW

- *Both social and cognitive processes are central to understanding motivation, emotions and action. Humans have five basic cognitive capabilities: symbolizing, forethought, vicarious, self-regulatory, and self-reflective. Humans are reciprocally determining and being determined by their environments.*

- *Most human behaviour is learned from observing models. Observational learning involves four main processes: attention, retention, production, and motivation.*

- *In enactive learning, learning from response consequences is mainly a cognitive process. Response consequences create expectations rather than stimulus-response connections. Further sources of predictive information are vicarious, observing others, and symbolic, hearing explanations.*

- *Three important regulatory incentive systems are those based on external, vicarious and self-produced outcomes. Self-regulation of behaviour involves self-observation, judgemental processes and self-reactive processes.*

- *Conceptions of personal efficacy are central to human agency. Perceived self-efficacy is a judgment about one's capability to accomplish a certain level of performance. Sources of efficacy information are enactive attainment, vicarious experience, verbal persuasion and physiological states. Efficacy information is cognitively processed with varying degrees of accuracy.*

- *People set goals that create states of disequilibrium which serve as motivators for action. Goals are also important for developing self-efficacy.*

- *Participant modelling, the distinctive counselling approach emanating from social cognitive theory, is described briefly. Applications of social cognitive theory include career counselling and development, fostering motivation and achievement in educational settings, and developing good health habits.*

INTRODUCTION

The designation social cognitive theory acknowledges both the social contribution to how people think and act and the importance of cognitive processes to motivation, emotions and actions. Though Bandura is primarily an academic psychologist, his work is included for the following reasons. First, he provides a chapter-and-verse challenge to the Skinnerian perspective on how reinforcement principles operate. Second, his work on observational learning has made a significant contribution to understanding how clients learn helpful and harmful ways of thinking and behaving. Third, he presents and elaborates the processes of cognitive concepts, such as self-efficacy and self-regulation, that merit serious consideration by all counsellors. Fourth, Bandura is an assiduous researcher and reader of others' research. He is an excellent example of how research findings can enlighten theorizing.

Albert Bandura

Albert Bandura (1925–) was born and raised in Mundare in northern Alberta, Canada. his entry into psychology was fortuitous. He commuted to the University of British Columbia in a car pool whose other members started each day early and he enrolled in a course in psychology because it filled his early time slot. In 1949 Bandura graduated from the University of British Columbia with a psychology major. In 1952 he received a doctorate in clinical psychology from the University of Iowa, followed by a one year postdoctoral internship at the Witchita Guidance Center. Afterwards he went to Stanford University in California as an instructor and, by 1964, had been appointed a full professor. In 1974 the university awarded him an endowed chair named the David Starr Jordan Professorship of Social Science in Psychology. Also, in 1974, Bandura was President of the American Psychological Association. Among his many honours and awards, in 1980 he received the American Psychological Association's Award for Distinguished Scientific Contributions.

During his Iowa years Bandura met his wife Virginia on the golf course. They have two daughters. His other interests in addition to golf include hiking in the high Sierras of California, visiting the opera and going to restaurants.

Bandura has published numerous journal articles on his experimental work on such topics as moral development, observational learning, fear acquisition, participant modelling treatment strategies, effects of the media and the cognitive regulation of behaviour, especially the mechanisms of human agency and people's perceptions of their efficacy to exercise influence over events which affect their lives. His books include: *Social Learning and Personality Development*, which he co-authored with Richard Walters; *Principles of Behaviour Modification; Aggression: A Social Learning Analysis; Social Learning Theory; Social Foundations of Thought and Action: A Social Cognitive Theory; Self-efficacy in Changing Societies* (edited by him); and *Self-efficacy: The Exercise of Control* (in preparation).

ASSUMPTIONS

Human nature

Except for elementary reflexes, people are not equipped with inborn repertoires of behaviour and hence must learn them. Biological factors, however, set limits to the learning process. For instance, genes and hormones affect physical development which, in turn, influences behavioural potentialities. Additionally, as in the case of speech, there is a rudimentary natural endowment on which new responses may be formed by learning. Often experiential and physiological influences are not easily separable and thus it may be more fruitful to analyse the determinants of behaviour rather than to try to categorize proportions of behaviour as learned or innate. Within biological limits, human nature possesses a vast potential to be fashioned by direct and vicarious experience into a variety of forms.

Thoughts are psychoneural processes. However, it is important to distinguish between psychological laws and biological laws. A simplistic reductionism is to be avoided in which psychology is reduced to biology, which is reduced to chemistry, which is reduced to physics and then to atomic particles. Focusing on psychological knowledge can address questions like how best to create belief systems and personal competencies. Such understanding cannot be derived just by studying the neurophysical mechanisms that subserve such activities. An interesting question is how people activate the cerebral processes that go beyond existing cognitive structures to generate new cognitive events and which characterize the exercise of personal agency.

Human capabilities

Whereas early classical and even operant conditioning may be viewed as an S → R or stimulus → response model, Bandura's social cognitive model is much more an S → O → R, or stimulus → organism's mediating cognitive processes → response, model. However, even this three-link chain does not do justice to his notion of the interaction of personal and environmental determinisms.

Following are five basic cognitive capabilities that characterize humans. First, humans possess a *symbolizing capability*. They have the capacity to transform their experiences into symbols and to process these symbols. They can create ideas that transcend their sensory experiences. The fact that humans have a symbolizing capability does not necessarily mean that they are rational. Thinking can be for good or ill, depending on the quality of people's thinking skills and the adequacy of the information available to them. Second, humans possess a *forethought capability*. Most of people's behaviour is regulated by forethought rather than reactions to their immediate environment. People anticipate the consequences of their actions and set goals for themselves. Forethought is not the sum of previous consequences but entails reflection.

Third, humans possesses a *vicarious capability*. Virtually all human learning does not result from direct experience but from observing other people's behaviour and its consequences. Vicarious learning shortens the time humans require to learn skills.

Some skills, such as language skills, are so complex that is unlikely they could learn them without the use of modelling. Fourth, humans possess a *self-regulatory capability*. They develop internal standards against which they evaluate their behaviour. Such self-evaluation influences subsequent behaviour. Fifth, humans possess a *self-reflective capability*. The capability for reflective self-consciousness is distinctly human. People can analyse their experiences and evaluate the adequacy of their thought processes. The most central and pervasive type of thought involved in self-reflection is people's judgements of their capability to deal with different realities.

Human agency and reciprocal determinism

Human agency is the capacity to exercise self-direction through control over one's own thought processes, motivation and action. Human agency has been conceptualized in three main ways: autonomous agency, in which people are totally independent agents of their actions; mechanical agency, where agency rests in environmental determinants; and emergent interactive agency, which is the model of social cognitive theory.

Emergent interactive agency is based on a model of triadic reciprocality. Reciprocal refers to mutual causation between the three factors. Behaviour (B), cognitive and personal factors (P), and environmental influences (E) each operate independently as determinants on one another. Figure 1 depicts this reciprocal determinism position. The 'influences vary in their selective strength and they do not occur simultaneously' (A. Bandura, personal communication, 1 February 1994).

Although environmental control has been minutely researched, personal control tends to have been neglected. Nevertheless, the fact remains that environments have causes as well as consequences. Environmental determinists, such as Skinner, are inconsistent when they assert that people are controlled by external events and, at the same time, advocate that they apply a technology of behaviour to obtain intentional control over their environments. Furthermore, psychological perspectives on determinism influence behaviour. For instance, personal determinists may be more likely to develop self-directed personalities. In the final analysis, human behaviour is the result of reciprocal interaction of external events and personal determinants such as genetic endowment, acquired competencies, reflective thought and self-initiative. People are free to the extent that they are able to exercise self-influence and determine their actions.

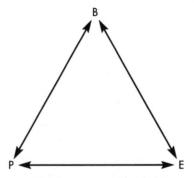

Figure 11.1 Schematic representation of triadic reciprocal determinism.

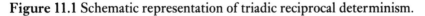

ACQUISITION

The two main modes of learning are observational learning and enactive learning, each of which is discussed in turn.

Observational learning

Functions

Most human behaviour and cognitive skills are learned by observing models. Modelling can instruct observers in the skills and rules of behaviour. Also, modelling can inhibit and disinhibit behaviour already in people's repertoires and facilitate responses. Modelled behaviour can serve as prompts and cues for people to perform behaviour already in their repertoires, and it can elicit emotional arousal. People can perceive and behave differently in states of heightened arousal. In addition, symbolic modelling shapes people's images of social realities by the way in which it portrays human relations and the activities they pursue.

Processes

Learning involves processing information. The power of modelling is derived from its ability to influence this. Observational learning entails four main processes.

1. *Attentional processes.* If people are to learn from modelling it is important that they pay attention to and accurately perceive the modelled behaviour. One set of attentional variables concerns characteristics of the modelling stimuli, such as availability, distinctiveness, personal attractiveness and the functional value of the modelled behaviour. Another set of attentional variables revolves around observer characteristics such as sensory capacities, arousal level, perceptual habits and past reinforcements.

2. *Retention processes.* To be effective modelling must be remembered. This involves either imaginal storing of information or, more frequently, coding of modelled events into readily usable verbal symbols. Material that is meaningful to observers and builds on their prior experience is more likely to be remembered. Further aids to retention include either imaginal rehearsal of the modelled behaviour or actually carrying it out. Observers' cognitive skills and structures can enhance retention. Motivation to learn also plays a part in retention, though motivational incentives are facilitative rather than necessary.

3. *Production processes.* At some stage, symbolic representations of modelled behaviour will probably need to be translated into effective action. Observers require accurate cognitive representations of modelled behaviours against which to compare sensory feedback from their enactments. Corrective modelling is an effective way of providing feedback when observers exhibit performance deficits. Observer variables influencing reproduction of behaviour include their physical capacities, whether their response repertoire already includes the necessary component responses, and their ability to make corrective adjustments when trying out the new behaviour.

4. *Motivational processes.* The distinction between learning and performance is highlighted by the fact that people are not motivated to enact everything they learn. The observer is more likely to adopt the modelled behaviour if it: (a) brings external rewards; (b) is internally positively valued; and (c) has been observed to bring rewards to the model. Anticipation of positive and negative outcomes affects which aspects of modelled behaviour are observed or ignored.

Modelling thought processes

People can learn thinking skills from observing models. However, often covert thought processes are inadequately conveyed by modelled actions. For instance, a model may solve a problem cognitively, but the observer only sees the resulting actions without gaining insight into the thought processes leading up to them. An approach to learning cognitive skills is to have models verbalize aloud how they think as they engage in problem-solving activities. Advantages of combining nonverbal with verbal modelling include the ability of nonverbal modelling to gain and hold attention and the chance of overt behaviour conferring added meaning to cognitive processes. Observers' cognitive skills are likely to improve more with models who demonstrate actions and thought processes rather than demonstrate actions alone.

Role of reinforcement

The social cognitive view is that observational learning does not necessarily require extrinsic reward. Such learning occurs through cognitive processing during modelling and before observers perform any responses. With Skinner's operant conditioning model, seemingly observational learning gets achieved when responses corresponding to the model's actions are reinforced, divergent responses are either unrewarded or punished, and others' behaviour becomes a stimulus for matching responses. However, this explanation of observational learning has shortcomings. Observers may not perform modelled behaviour in the same setting in which is was modelled. Neither the model nor the observer may be reinforced. The modelled behaviour may take place days or weeks later. Thus the operant model fails to explain how new response structures are acquired through observation.

The main role of incentives in observational learning is before rather than after modelling. For instance, observers' attention can be increased by anticipation of rewards from using modelled behaviours. Furthermore, anticipated rewards can motivate them to symbolize and rehearse modelled activities. Incentives are facilitative rather than necessary.

Enactive learning

Enactive learning or learning from experience is ubiquitous. A distinction exists between knowledge and skill. In many domains people need to go beyond knowledge structures to develop proficient actions. Developing performance skills requires people to have accurate conceptions of targeted skills against which to match their attempts to perform the skills. Enactment provides the vehicle to translate knowledge into skilled action. People use the information they gain from enactments to make adjustments in the spacial and temporal features of performance until what they do closely matches their cognitive conception of skilled performance.

Functions of response consequences

Research offers little support for the view that response consequences act as automatic shapers of human behaviour. Social cognitive theory views learning through response consequences as a largely cognitive process. Through enactments, people experience the positive and negative consequences of actions. However, the process of learning does not stop here, since people notice the effects of their responses. Thus reinforcement does not automatically strengthen a tendency to respond, but does so by altering informational and motivational cognitive variables. For instance, by examining patterns of response consequences performers can discern conceptions and rules of behaviour. Also, if the response consequences are highly valued, this mobilizes and strengthens behaviour. In other words, contrary to the mechanistic view, consequences determine behaviour largely through intervening thoughts. The term 'reinforcement' is misleading, since it has connotations of automatic responding and of 'strengthening' responses, like driving a car, which may not be able to be further strengthened. Regulation of behaviour is a concept preferable to reinforcement.

Efficiency of enactive learning

People are not equally adept at gaining knowledge from response consequences. They may differ in their knowledge and experience upon which to select or develop rules for enacting behaviour if the rules are not readily available. Learning is likely to be most efficient when consequences follow actions immediately, regularly and without confusing occurrences. Learning is more difficult in circumstances where the same actions do not always produce the same consequences. Learning from enactive experience does not guarantee that the best alternative ways of acting will be developed. If anything, learning from the consequences of enactive experience leads to developing sufficient rather than optimal skills. People tend to accept a sufficient solution rather than continue the search for an even better one.

Learning from the consequences of enactive experience can be inefficient on its own. If people lack competencies, they can be developed by means of verbal instruction that conveys which types of behaviour are most functional. In addition, people can be physically guided to perform behaviours and take part in graduated modelling procedures. As mentioned earlier, social cognitive theory views modelling, leading to observational learning through symbolic processes, to be the principal mode of transmitting new modes of behaviour.

Predictive knowledge and forethought

Effective functioning requires people to anticipate and evaluate the probable effects of different actions. Response consequences create expectations or beliefs rather than stimulus–response connections. Cues and stimuli acquire predictive value through their connections with response consequences. Humans attend closely to aspects of their environment that predict consequences, and ignore those that do not. For instance, children will behave more aggressively in the presence of their more lenient rather than their stricter parent. Knowledge of response consequences and of their predictive value permits foresightful action.

Three interrelated sources – enactive, symbolic and vicarious – provide information about consequences useful for predicting. Enactive information is derived from direct experience of response consequences. Symbolic information comes from explanations that describe the particular circumstances in which positive and negative response consequences will occur. Vicarious information is gained from observing what are the response consequences provided for others. Maintenance of the predictive value of cues learned verbally or symbolically normally requires periodic confirmation through direct experience.

Making accurate predictive judgements requires attention, memory and integrative cognitive skills. Often people need to sift through a bewildering variety of environmental cues to identify those that have predictive relevance. Then they need to form the relevant factors into generalizable rules of action. Most rules of action are imparted by instruction rather than discovered by direct experience. Explanatory feedback that provides information about the conditions under which certain consequences are likely to happen is very helpful in establishing predictive rules. People can lower their predictive accuracy by misreading events. For instance, they may misjudge threats, fail to notice or misperceive important aspects of their environments or overestimate the adequacy of their knowledge.

REGULATORY INCENTIVE SYSTEMS

Human behaviour is heavily influenced by the regulatory influence of response consequences. Outcomes influence behaviour largely through their informative and incentive value. Three important regulatory incentive systems are those based on external, vicarious and self-produced outcomes, each of which is reviewed in turn.

External motivators

Frequently external consequences are influential in motivating behaviour. Two broad classes of motivators are those which are biologically based and those which are cognitively based. Biologically based motivators include physical deprivation and physical pain. Cognitive motivators operate in two main ways. First, through people anticipating future outcomes. One category of outcome expectations is connected with material incentives, for instance food and physical pain. Another category is connected with sensory incentives, for instance new pleasant or unpleasant sensations. A further category focuses on social incentives, for instance approval and disapproval. Still another category is that of token incentives, for instance money and grades. In addition, people can be motivated by activity incentives, engaging in preferred activities, and by status and power incentives. The second main way that cognitive motivators operate is through people's internal standards and self-evaluations in relation to them.

Vicarious motivators

People's symbolic capability enables them to regulate their actions on the basis of knowledge gained from observing others' response consequences. Like directly experienced outcomes, observed outcomes can alter behaviour. In addition, observed outcomes can alter the value of external incentives. For instance, people observing others' similar performances more highly praised will experience praise for their own performances as less rewarding than if ignorant about the others' feedback.

Seeing others' behaviour rewarded increases the likelihood that observers will behave in a similar way. Furthermore, rewarded modelling is generally more effective in fostering similar patterns of behaviour than modelling alone. Seeing others' behaviour punished decreases the likelihood that observers will act similarly, though providing constructive alternatives is a more effective way of deterring undesirable behaviours.

Several mechanisms mediate the effects of observing others' response consequences on the observers' thoughts, feelings and actions. Observing vicarious consequences has an information function concerning the kinds of actions that are likely to have positive and negative consequences. The information function leads on to a motivation function in arousing expectations in observers that they will receive similar consequences for performing similar actions. Emotional arousal is a further function of observing vicarious consequences. Observers can learn what might cause pleasure or distress. However, many dysfunctional fears and avoidance behaviours stem mainly or partially from unpleasant vicarious experiences. Also, observers can acquire others' antipathies. Last, observing vicarious consequences can serve a valuational function. For instance, observers' values and internal standards of behaviour can be extensively altered by observing others' reactions to their own behaviour according to their personal standards.

Self-regulatory motivators

Much human behaviour is not performed under conditions of immediate reward. Many activities are directed towards future outcomes and people anticipate future gains and losses. They have to create guides and motivators for actions that lead to far off attainments. Human beings' symbolizing and self-reactive capabilities allow them to set internal standards for behaviour and evaluate themselves against these standards. Thus, these internal standards can acts as self-incentives.

Self-regulation of behaviour involves three subprocesses: self-observation, judgemental process and self-reaction.

1. *Self-observation*. Self-observation provides information for setting realistic performance standards and for evaluating behaviour. Self-observation is not always reliable since people's attention levels, mood states and preexisting self-conceptions can interfere with accuracy. There are a number of evaluative dimensions on which behaviour may be measured. For instance, writing may be measured in terms of quantity, quality and originality. Social behaviour may be measured on such dimensions as sociability or deviancy. These 'objective' evaluative dimensions vary according to the nature of the activity. Often when people observe their performances closely they set themselves progressive goals for improvement. Self-observation or

self-monitoring often elicits self-reactive influences and is not easily separable from the other subprocesses of self-regulation.

2. *Judgemental process.* Observation of one's behaviour is insufficient to do something about it. To change it requires making a judgement about the positiveness or negativeness of the behaviour. One aspect of the judgemental subfunction relates to the development of personal standards. Social influences on developing personal standards include direct tuition, others' evaluative reactions to one's behaviour and personal standards modelled by others. Among ways of establishing the adequacy of personal standards are comparisons with standard norms, social comparison with others' performances, and self-comparison with one's previous performances. People are more likely to make performance judgements in areas that they value than those that have little significance for them. How people judge their behaviour is influenced by their attributions concerning the causes of their performance. For instance, they are likely to take pride in accomplishment when attributing success to their own abilities and efforts.

3. *Self-reaction.* Personal standards and judgemental skills enable people to exert self-reactive influence over their behaviour. They pursue activities that lead to positive self-reactions and avoid those leading to negative self-reactions. Personal standards affect behaviour mainly through their motivational function in that people strive to attain the requisite performance. In several areas of behaviour, personal standards are relatively stable. However, when cultivating skills and seeking achievements, people tend progressively to raise their standards as earlier challenges are met. People also react to tangible self-motivators. For example, people can make free time, relaxing breaks and recreational activities contingent on performance attainments. For many people, self-incentives may be better motivators then externally arranged incentives. Dysfunctional self-evaluative systems tend to be those in which the individual has extremely harsh standards, thus giving rise to depression and feelings of worthlessness.

The ability of humans intentionally to influence their behaviour through self-produced consequences gives them a capacity for self-direction, albeit within the confines of reciprocal determinism. Through experience, people develop skills of monitoring their behaviour, for instance how and what to observe. Two sources of incentives are operative in the process of regulating behaviour through self-reactions. First, there are the conditional or short term incentives that provide guides for courses of action. Second, there are the more long-term incentives for adhering to internal standards. Personal benefits, for instance either gains from improved proficiency in a skill or avoidance of discomfort from regulating potentially aversive behaviour, provide one source of support for maintaining self-directedness. Receiving social rewards and observing others being socially rewarded provides another source of support. Yet another source of support is seeing others master tasks through adherence to personal standards. Negative sanctions, like criticism for lowering realistic performance standards, can also serve to maintain personal standards. Also, specific environmental contexts can support adherence to personal standards, for instance those valuing high performance standards. Self-inflicted punishment, for instance self-criticism, can also serve to maintain adherence to personal standards. Self-punishment can serve functions like providing a means to discontinue further negative ruminations and lessening the negative reactions of others.

SELF-EFFICACY AND GOALS
Defining self-efficacy

Conceptions of personal efficacy are central to human agency. It is not simply a matter of knowing what to do. To enact skilled performance people need both to possess the requisite skills and the self-beliefs of efficacy to use them. Judgements of personal efficacy are different from response outcome expectations. Perceived self-efficacy is defined as 'a judgement of one's capability to accomplish a certain level of performance' (Bandura, 1986, p. 391). Outcome expectations are judgements about the likely consequences such behaviour will produce. The judgement that one can jump six feet is an efficacy judgement. However, the anticipated social recognition from jumping six feet is an outcome expectation. Outcomes are consequences of acts, not the acts themselves.

Magnitude, generality and strength are three important dimensions of efficacy expectations (Bandura, 1977). Efficacy expectations can vary according to the magnitude or level of difficulty of tasks: for instance, being confident about performing well in easy rather than in difficult tasks. Generality refers to the degree of generalization of mastery expectations beyond the specific treatment situation. Strength refers to the persistence of personal mastery expectations despite disconfirming experiences.

Function and effects of self-efficacy

Efficacy beliefs contribute to how people operate in diverse ways. Conceptions of personal efficacy affect choice of behaviour: for instance, what to do. Perceived efficacy can foster engagement in activities, whereas perceived inefficacy can lead people to avoid potentially enriching experiences. Extreme misjudgements of efficacy are dysfunctional. However, the efficacy judgements that possibly are most functional are those that slightly exceed what one can do at any given moment.

Efficacy beliefs also influence how much effort to expend and how long to persist in face of setbacks and difficulties. Unlike self-doubt, strong self-efficacy beliefs strengthen people's resilience when engaging in difficult tasks. In addition, efficacy beliefs influence how people think and feel. Those judging themselves inefficacious in dealing with environmental demands tend to exaggerate their personal deficiencies, become disheartened more easily and give up in face of difficulties. Those with a strong sense of efficacy, though they may be temporarily demoralized by setbacks, are more likely to stay task-orientated and to intensify their efforts when their performances fall short of their goals. In endeavours where staying power is needed, it is resiliency of perceived self-efficacy that counts. Traditional behaviourist theory has to answer the question of how organisms capable of forecasting the future have no capacity for self-influence. People can produce their own futures rather than simply foretell it.

Perceived efficacy can influence the development of subskills necessary for complex tasks, whereas perceived inefficacy may retard their development. Perceived efficacy is subject to disincentives and performance constraints. People may possess the requisite subskills and self-efficacy, but have no incentives to use them. Also, efficacious people may lack adequate material and financial resources. Possessing accurate efficacy beliefs can be particularly difficult for cognitive skills, since frequently what is required is not readily apparent from what is easily observable. Sometimes people's efficacy beliefs are inaccurate because of faulty cognitive activities: for instance, deficits in perceiving feedback and in memory.

Sources of self-efficacy information

Four important sources of self-efficacy information are described below. Any method of treatment may work with one or more of these sources.

• *Enactive attainment.* Personal experiences of success provide the most fundamental source of efficacy expectations. Success raises efficacy expectations, whereas repeated failure lowers them. Once established, enhanced efficacy beliefs tend to generalize, especially to situations similar to those in which the beliefs were enhanced.

• *Vicarious experience.* Efficacy expectations may be altered by observing others and noting the positive and negative consequences of behaviour for them. Efficacy expectations induced by modelling are generally weaker than those induced by successful task performance. Modelling affects efficacy beliefs in two ways (A. Bandura, personal communication, 1 February 1994). First, observers make inferences from modelled successes and failures. Seeing people similar to themselves succeed by sustained effort raises observers' beliefs in their capabilities. However, seeing others fail despite high effort lowers observers' judgements of their own efficacy and undermines their motivation. Second, competent models transmit knowledge and teach observers effective skills and strategies for managing environmental demands. Acquisition of better skills raises perceived self-efficacy.

• *Verbal persuasion.* Verbal persuasion, such as suggestion and exhortation, may also influence self-efficacy. Persuasion may be most useful where it persuades people to try hard enough to succeed, which in turn enhances their efficacy beliefs. However, the raising of unrealistic efficacy beliefs that are not corroborated by successful enactment may do more harm than good.

• *Physiological state.* Physiological and affective states affect efficacy beliefs in three ways. First, when people are tense and anxious, their physiological state or level of emotional arousal can negatively influence their efficacy expectations. High arousal usually debilitates performance and thus lowered expectations of efficacy then become, in part, based on lowered performance. Approaches that lessen debilitating emotional arousal to subjective threats can enhance both efficacy beliefs and performance. Perceived self-efficacy to control thoughts beneficially influences cognitively generated arousal. When the extent of aversive cognitions can be controlled, perceived efficacy or inefficacy to control one's thoughts is strongly related to anxiety level.

Second, mood states affect people's judgement of their personal efficacy: positive mood enhances perceived efficacy, depressed mood diminishes it. Third, in activities involving strength and stamina, people judge their fatigue, aches and pains as signs of weak physical efficacy.

Efficacy information from enactive, vicarious, persuasive and physiological sources is cognitively processed. A distinction exists between information conveyed by environmental events and the information that is selected, weighted and integrated into self-efficacy judgements. The cognitive processing of efficacy information involves two separate processes: first, selecting efficacy-relevant information and, second, weighting and integrating this information. Regarding enactive information, there is no simple relationship between quality or performance and perceived self-efficacy. Even good performances may fail to enhance self-efficacy. Factors that affect how performance contributes to self-efficacy include task difficulty, amount of effort expended and amount of external aid received.

Regarding vicarious efficacy information, observers may consider that models similar or slightly higher in ability provide the most valid comparative information. Regarding persuasive efficacy information, its effect is related to how confident recipients are in the judgement of their persuaders. Physiological efficacy information is also cognitively processed. Salient considerations here include the sources and level of arousal, and past experiences of how arousal affects performance.

Functions of goals

Personal agency or international regulation of behaviour operates through two cognitively based sources of motivation: first, forethought and, second, goal-setting with self-evaluative reactions to one's behaviour. Bandura (1989) observes: 'Human motivation relies on *discrepancy production* as well as *discrepancy reduction*. It requires both *proactive control* and *reactive or feedback control*' (pp. 1179–80). Initially, people motivate themselves through setting standards or levels of performance that create a state of disequilibrium and then they strive to attain them. Feedback control involves subsequent adjustments of effort to achieve desired results. Goals act as motivators by specifying the conditions for self-satisfaction with performance.

In addition, goals are important for the development of self-efficacy. They provide people with standards by which to judge their capabilities. Particularly useful are progressively difficult short-term sub-goals. Such sub-goals provide both incentives for action and, when attained, produce efficacy information and confidence to persist. Perceived inefficacy can cause people to lower their goals and thus decrease their dissatisfaction with substandard performances.

PRACTICE
Participant modelling

Through highlighting the importance of observational learning and detailing the processes involved in it, Bandura's influence on counselling has been widespread.

Perhaps Bandura's most direct contribution to counselling has been his participant modelling approach. This approach emphasizes *in vivo* performance of feared tasks, with successful performance being viewed as the primary vehicle for psychological change. Participant modelling involves a number of stages. First, *counsellors repeatedly model* feared activities, for instance handling snakes or dogs, to show clients both how they can be successfully performed and that the feared consequences do not occur. Second, *joint performance with their counsellors* may enable clients to start engaging in activities which would be too threatening to engage in on their own. Counsellors, who function as guides and anxiety inhibitors, use hierarchies of increasingly difficult sub-tasks.

Third, *counsellors may introduce response induction aids* or protective conditions to reduce expectations of feared consequences and thus help clients to perform the desired tasks. For instance, when treating snake phobias, response induction aids might include the model holding the snake securely by the head and tail, use of protective gloves, and presenting a smaller snake. Fourth, *counsellors gradually withdraw performance supports* to ensure that clients can function effectively without assistance. Fifth, *clients may have a period of self-directed performance* in which they spend time interacting with the feared object on their own. During the initial period of self-directed performance, counsellors may stay in the room with clients. Later they may withdraw, possibly to observe clients behind one-way mirrors. The idea is that perceived self-efficacy is best strengthened by independent achievements in which it is clear that clients' successes are due to their ability to master feared situations on their own.

Other applications

Social cognitive theory shows promise in assisting understanding of and formulating interventions for career counselling and development. For instance, self-efficacy beliefs may be highly relevant with regard to how willing women are to consider non-traditional female occupations. Lent and Hackett (1987) observe that: 'self-efficacy beliefs are predictive of important indices of career entry behavior, such as college major choices and academic performance in certain fields. However, findings are not unanimously favorable' (p. 362). Taking into account the four sources of efficacy information, career counsellors can design more effective individual and group interventions for both sexes.

In educational settings, counsellors can work to develop perceived self-efficacy of students, teachers, faculties and parents to improve motivation and academic accomplishments. They may work with individual clients, groups or in a consultancy capacity. Guided mastery is the principal means for cultivating cognitive competences. Guided mastery is similar to the participant modelling approach described above. Steps in guided mastery include using cognitive modelling and instructive aids to convey relevant knowledge and skills in graduated steps, and guided practice in when and how to use the cognitive strategies to solve diverse problems (Bandura, 1986, 1993). Though frequently counsellors will have neither the knowledge nor time to teach instructional content, they can still assist teachers to design and implement curricula that develop students' perceived self-efficacy.

In health settings, counsellors can establish self-management approaches based on social cognitive theory. An example is that of assisting people to adopt and maintain habits conducive to health and to eliminate bad health habits. In sum, social cognitive theory provides counsellors with many insights into how they might increase their own and their clients' perceived self-efficacy and effectiveness.

CHAPTER REVIEW AND SELF-REFERENT QUESTIONS

Chapter review questions

1. Why does Bandura use the term social cognitive theory to designate his theoretical framework?

2. What are Bandura's five human cognitive capabilities and what is their significance?

3. What does the term triadic reciprocality mean?

4. What are the functions of observational learning?

5. Describe each of the processes of observational learning.

6. What is enactive learning and what functions do response consequences have in it?

7. What is the difference between biologically based and cognitively based motivators? Provide illustrations of each.

8. Describe each of the processes of self-regulation of behaviour?

9. What is the difference between a judgement of personal efficacy and a response outcome expectation? Illustrate with one or more examples.

10. What are the effects on humans of their efficacy beliefs?

11. Describe each of the sources of efficacy information.

12. Describe the role of cognitive processing in making judgements of personal efficacy.

13. How does goal-setting influence behaviour and self-efficacy?

14. Describe each of the steps in participant modelling.

Self-referent questions

1. Identifying a significant activity or cognitive skill that you have learned by observing one or more models. Describe the processes by which observational learning became an effective way of acquiring it.

2. Provide examples for (a) where your current internal standards are functional in helping you regulate your behaviour and (b) where they are dysfunctional in doing this.

3. Provide one or more examples from your own life of the distinction between an efficacy expectation and an outcome expectation.

4. For a significant area in your life, describe what have been the effects and consequences of your efficacy beliefs.

5. Provide an example from your own life of each of the sources of efficacy information.

6. Do you think that participant modelling could be applied to a problem in your life.? If so, how?

7. What is the relevance of Bandura's work to understanding your life?

8. What is Bandura's influence on how you think about and practise counselling?

Annotated bibliography

Bandura, A. (1986). *Social Foundations of Thought and Action: A Social Cognitive Theory.* Englewood Cliffs, NJ: Prentice-Hall.
This huge volume is the definitive statement of Bandura's position. In it he presents a theoretical framework for analysing human motivation, thought and action from a social cognitive perspective. This book was the main source for this chapter.

Bandura, A. (1977). *Social Learning Theory.* Englewood Cliffs, NJ: Prentice-Hall.
This book is an abbreviated and somewhat outdated version of issues discussed in much greater depth in *Social Foundations of Thought and Action.*

Bandura, A. (1989). Human agency in social cognitive theory. *American Psychologist, 44,* 1175–84.
This article examines the psychological mechanisms – such as self-belief of efficacy, goal representations and anticipated outcomes – through which people exercise personal agency. Issues of freedom and determinism are also discussed.

Further references

Bandura, A. (1969). *Principles of Behavior Modification.* New York: Holt, Rinehart & Winston.

Bandura, A. (1973). *Aggression: A Social Learning Analysis.* Englewood Cliffs, NJ: Prentice-Hall.

Bandura, A. (1976). Self-reinforcement: theoretical and methodological considerations. *Behaviorism, 4,* 135–55.

Bandura, A. (1977). Self-efficacy: Toward a unifying theory of behavioural change. *Psychological Review, 84,* 191–215.

Bandura, A. (1993). Perceived self-efficacy in cognitive development and functioning. *Educational Psychologist, 28 (2),* 117–48.

Bandura, A. (Ed.) (in press). *Self-efficacy in Changing Societies.* New York: Cambridge University Press.

Bandura, A. (in preparation). *Self-efficacy: The Exercise of Control.* New York: Freeman.

Bandura, A., Adams, N.E. & Beyer, J. (1977). Cognitive processes mediating behavioural change. *Journal of Personality and Social Psychology, 35,* 125–39.

Bandura, A., Jeffery, R.W. & Wright, C.L. (1974). Efficacy of participant modelling as a function of response induction aids. *Journal of Abnormal Psychology, 83,* 56–64.

Bandura, A., Jeffery, R.W. & Gadjos, E. (1975). Generalizing change through participant modeling with self-directed mastery. *Behaviour Research and Therapy, 13,* 141–52.

Bandura, A. & Walters, R. (1963). *Social Learning and Personality Development.* New York: Holt, Rinehart & Winston.

Others

Evans, R.I. (1989). *Albert Bandura: The Man and His Ideas: A Dialogue*. New York: Praeger.

Lent, R.W. & Hackett, G. (1987). Career self-efficacy: Empirical status and future directions. *Journal of Vocational Behavior, 30,* 347–82.

TWELVE

Rational Emotive Behaviour Counselling

PREVIEW

- *Rational emotive behaviour counselling (REBC) is not a purely intellectual approach, but strongly emphasizes the interplay of feeling, behaviour and cognition.*

- *Humans' fundamental goals are survival, freedom from pain, and happiness. Their cognitions can be hot, warm or cool and their feelings can be appropriate or inappropriate. People have biological tendencies for both actualizing themselves and being irrational, as well as some degree of free choice.*

- *Ellis has expanded his ABC theory of personality to a GABCDE theory with: G, goals; A, activating events; B, beliefs, both rational and irrational; C, consequences, both emotional and behavioural; D, disputing irrational beliefs; and E, effective new philosophy.*

- *In pursuit of their goals (G), people create their inappropriate emotions and self-defeating behaviours at C because they have demanding, as contrasted with preferential, beliefs at B in relation to activating events at A. In addition, they have derivatives of their demanding beliefs, for instance, awfulizing, I can't-stand-it-itis, feelings of worthlessness and predictions of continuous failure.*

- *As well as their innate tendencies to irrationality, humans acquire irrational beliefs partly by social learning but also because they do not develop and exercise their capacity for rational choice.*

- *Reasons why people persist in maintaining irrational beliefs include: biological tendencies to irrationality, the emotional strength of their beliefs, insufficient scientific thinking, reinforcing consequences, emphasizing their 'Godawful' pasts, unrealistic beliefs about change, and insufficiently challenging their beliefs through action.*

- *REBC has two goals: helping clients overcome emotional blocks and disturbances and helping them become more fully functioning or self-actualizing. It aims to help people change from rigid and demanding to preferential thinking. Treatment and change can be inelegant, consisting of symptom removal, or elegant, producing an effective new philosophy.*

- *The REBC counsellor is a teacher who uses a variety of cognitive, emotive and behavioural techniques to assist clients to dispute (D) their irrational beliefs and their derivatives so that they can develop an effective new philosophy (E).*

- *Scientific questioning is the main cognitive disputing technique. Emotive disputing techniques include vigorous disputing and rational-emotive imagery. Behavioural disputing techniques include assignments that challenge demandingness, shame attacking exercises, and skill training. Also counsellors help clients to solve genuine problems in their lives.*

- *REBC aims to assist clients to maintain their changes through stressing work and practice, assigning homework, and teaching clients, if they backslide, to go back to their ABCs and then dispute irrational beliefs that cause them to revert to previous behaviours.*

- *Other applications of REBC include group counselling, marital and family counselling and psychological education.*

INTRODUCTION

When first developed in 1955, Ellis termed his approach rational therapy (RT). In 1961 he changed its name to rational-emotive therapy (RET). In 1993 Ellis (1993a) further changed its name to rational emotive behaviour therapy (REBT). What Ellis means by 'rational' is cognition that is effective in self-helping rather than cognition that is empirically and logically valid. He wishes that he had used the word cognitive from the start since many people narrowly restrict the word rational to mean intellectual or logico-empirical. People's rationality rests on judging soundly which of their desires or preferences to follow and, therefore, is based on their emotions and feelings (Ellis, 1990).

Ellis introduced 'behaviour' into his approach's name for the sake of accuracy. From its start, the approach has strongly emphasized behaviour along with cognition and emotion. Ellis writes: 'So, to correct my previous errors and to set the record straight, I shall from now on call it what it has really always been – rational emotive behavior therapy (REBT)' (Ellis, 1993a, p. 258).

Ellis (1989a) distinguishes between general REBT and preferential REBT. General REBT is virtually the same as cognitive-behaviour therapy and aims to teach clients rational or appropriate behaviours. Preferential REBT includes general REBT but also teaches clients how to dispute irrational ideas and self-defeating behaviours and how to use powerful cognitive-emotive-behavioural methods as self-helping skills. This chapter focuses on preferential REBT, which from now on will be referred to as rational-emotive behaviour counselling (REBC).

Albert Ellis

Albert Ellis (1913–) was born in Pittsburgh, Pennsylvania, and grew up in New York City. He had a brother and sister who were 19 months and 4 years younger than him, respectively. His father was physically absent much of the time. His Jewish mother was benignly neglectful and 'was much more immersed in her own pleasures and ego-aggrandizing activities than she was in understanding and taking care of her children' (Ellis, 1991a, p. 3). Aged 12, he discovered that his parents had divorced. Another childhood trauma was that, aged 4½, Ellis almost died of tonsilitis and nephritis and for the next few years was frequently hospitalized. During childhood and adolescence Ellis was unusually shy and introverted and very afraid of public speaking. However, he did very well at school and developed problem solving skills to make the most of his difficult childhood. For instance, when 19, to overcome his shyness with women, he forced himself to talk to a hundred girls in a row in the Bronx Botanical Gardens (Dryden, 1989).

In 1934, despite an early ambition to become the Great American Novelist, he received a bachelor's degree in business administration from the City University of New York. Early occupations included a business matching trousers to still usable jackets and being personnel manager of a gift and novelty firm. Ellis devoted much of his spare time to writing fiction. Partly because of difficulties getting his fiction published, Ellis turned exclusively to writing non-fiction, especially focusing on the 'sex-family revolution'.

Discovering that he liked counselling as well as writing, in 1942 Ellis entered the clinical psychology programme at Columbia University, receiving a master's degree in 1943. Soon afterwards Ellis began a small private practice in marital and sex counselling. In 1947 Ellis received his doctorate from Columbia University with a thesis on personality questionnaires, an earlier thesis on love having been censored before it got off the ground. Ellis's ambition was to become an outstanding psychoanalyst and so he completed a training analysis with an analyst from the Karen Horney group and began to practise psychoanalysis under his teacher's direction. From 1948 to 1952 Ellis worked for the New Jersey Mental Hygiene Clinic, first as chief psychologist of the New Jersey State Diagnostic Center and then as chief psychologist of the entire state of New Jersey. He also continued his private practice in New York.

For some time Ellis had employed active-directive methods in his marital and sex counselling Also, before undergoing analysis, Ellis had worked through many of his own problems by reading and practising and philosophies of Epictetus, Marcus Aurelius, Spinoza and Bertrand Russell, and so he started teaching clients the philosophic principles that had helped him. Between 1953 and 1955 Ellis increasingly rebelled against psychoanalysis and began calling himself a 'psychotherapist' rather than a 'psychoanalyst'. He writes: 'I finally wound up, at the beginning of 1955, with RET' (Ellis, 1991a, p. 15). He presented his first paper on RET at the American Psychological Association's annual meeting in Chicago on 31 August 1956.

In 1959 Ellis founded The Institute for Rational Living, Inc., now called the Institute for Rational-Emotive Therapy, as a non-profit-making scientific and educational organization to teach the principles of rational living. Since then, Ellis has donated all his royalties and income from clients and workshops to the Institute. In 1964 the Institute bought a large New York townhouse, where it is still headquartered. Currently the Institute has branches in several cities in the United States and in other countries, all devoted to disseminating the rational emotive behaviour approach.

Ellis is a man of boundless energy, probably a genetic inheritance from his 'two highly energetic parents who both lived reasonably long lives and were active until the last day of their lives' (Dryden, 1989, p. 545). He spends most of his time working. Although in his eighties, during a typical week in New York he sees about 70 individual clients (mainly for half hour sessions) and leads five therapy groups. In addition, he holds a two-hour Friday night workshop, where he interviews people in public, and on the weekend he devotes time to working on his books, research and letters (Palmer, 1993a). Ellis also gives numerous workshops and seminars in America and overseas and uses the travel time to write and read.

Ellis's work is his main priority. However, he has been married and divorced twice, as well as having relationships with a number of other women. Since 1964 he has been in a stable relationship with Janet Wolfe and comments that his life 'would be greatly bereft of laughter, warmth, and intimacy without her' (Dryden, 1989, p. 541). Albert and Janet have no children, since they thought it would be unfair that, due to the heavy demands of his work, he would not have been able to spend much time with them.

Ellis's work has been controversial. His REBC ideas challenged psychoanalytic and Rogerian orthodoxies. His ideas on sex challenged conventional morality. In addition, Ellis has not been afraid to speak his mind. However, over the past 20 years or so, cognitive behavioural ideas have become increasingly fashionable and Ellis now regards himself as the father of REBC and the grandfather of cognitive-behavioural counselling. Ellis has received numerous honours and awards, including the American Psychological Association's major award for Distinguished Professional Contributions to Knowledge and the American Counselling Association's major Professional Development Award.

Ellis has always been a prolific writer, even before entering the field of psychology. He had published over 600 papers in psychological, psychiatric, and sociological journals and anthologies. In addition, he has authored or edited over 50 books and monographs including: *Sex without Guilt, Reason and Emotion in Psychotherapy, Humanistic Psychotherapy: The rational-emotive approach, A New Guide to Rational Living* (with Robert Harper), *Overcoming Resistance: Rational-emotive Therapy with Difficult Clients, The Practice of Rational-emotive Therapy* (with Windy Dryden), and *How to Stubbornly Refuse to Make Yourself Miserable about Anything – Yes, Anything!* Ellis is also well known for his rational-humorous songs such as 'Beautiful Hangup', sung to the tune of Stephen Foster's 'Beautiful Dreamer', the first two lines of which are (Ellis, 1988, p. 123): Beautiful hangup, why should we part, When we have shared our whole lives from the start? Apart from humour, the guiding principles of Ellis's work have been 'science, efficiency, honesty, revolutionism, and passionate skepticism' (Ellis, 1991a, p. 30).

ASSUMPTIONS
Fundamental and primary goals

Virtually all humans have three fundamental goals (FG): to survive, to be relatively free from pain, and to be reasonably satisfied or content. As sub-goals or primary goals (PG), humans want to be happy:

- when by themselves

- gregariously with other humans

- intimately, with a few selected others

- informationally and educationally

- vocationally and economically

- recreationally (Ellis, 1991b).

REBC sees these basic goals as choices or preferences rather than needs or necessities. Rational living consists of thinking, feeling and behaving in ways which contribute to the attainment of the chosen goals, whereas irrationality consists of thinking, feeling and behaving in ways which block or interfere with their attainment. Living rationally consists of striking a sensible balance between short-range and long-range hedonism, or between the pleasures of the here-and-now and the longer-range pleasures gained through present discipline. Thus rationality may be defined as the use of reason in pursuit of chosen short-range and long-range hedonism.

Emotion, cognition and behaviour

In an early paper on 'Rational psychotherapy' Ellis (1958b) proposed three fundamental hypotheses. First, thinking and emoting are closely related. Second, thinking and emoting are so closely related that they usually accompany each other, act in a circular cause-and-effect relationship and in certain (though hardly all) respects are essentially the same thing, so that one's thinking becomes one's emotion and emoting becomes one's thought. Third, both thinking and emoting tend to take the form of self-talk or internalized sentences and, for all practical purposes, the sentences that people keep saying to themselves are or become their thoughts and emotions. Thus people's internal self-statements are capable of both generating and modifying their emotions.

In addition, Ellis (1988, 1989, 1991b) stresses that thinking and emotion interact with behaviour. For instance, people usually act on the basis of thoughts and emotions and their actions influence how they think and feel. In sum, cognitions, emotions and behaviours are rarely, if ever, totally separable and pure.

Cool, warm and hot cognitions

Ellis's (1988, 1991b) breakdown of cognitions into cool, warm and hot illustrates how feelings are integrated into cognitions. Hot cognitions influence and create more intense feelings than do warm or cool cognitions. Cool cognitions are descriptive and may include little or no feelings. Warm, cognitions are preferential thoughts or rational beliefs. They include evaluations of cool cognitions, ranging from weak to strong evaluations, influencing and creating weak to strong feelings. Hot cognitions contain hot or high evaluative thoughts and usually include strong to very strong feelings. Ellis gives the example of a husband having three kinds of choices if his wife is violently angry:

- *Cool cognition* 'I see that my wife is violent.'

- *Warm or preferential cognitions-feelings* 'I don't like her violence, I wish she didn't act that way. How annoying that she does.'

- *Hot cognitions-feelings* 'I utterly loathe her attacks! She must not assault me! She's no damned good for acting that way! I'll kill her!' (Ellis, 1991b, p. 154.).

Hot thoughts can vary on many dimensions of heat. These dimensions include being held occasionally or always, loosely or devoutly; mildly or intently, blandly or vividly, softly or loudly, and limited to one situation or held more generally (Ellis, 1988).

Appropriate and inappropriate emotions

REBC is not an approach of no emotions; rather, it emphasizes appropriate emotions. Inappropriate emotions are those which interfere with achieving a sensible balance between short-range and long-range hedonism. For instance, it may be appropriate for people in an alien and difficult world to be fearful, cautious or vigilant so that they may take any necessary steps for realistic protection. However, anxiety and overconcern are inappropriate emotions, since they are based on irrational thinking or unsane beliefs and, in fact, may interfere with or block attaining goals. Similarly, hostility may have a sane and an unsane part. The sane part of hostility involves acknowledging discomfort or annoyance as a basis for action designed to overcome or minimize the irritation. The unsane part of hostility may involve blaming others and the world in such a way as to block effective action and possibly generate even more unhappiness for oneself and further hostility from others. Thus emotions are appropriate when they are accompanied by rational or sane beliefs which are functional in that they do not block the possibility of effective action and attaining fundamental and primary goals.

Pleasurable and enjoyable emotions can also be appropriate or inappropriate. For example, people may feel excessive pride when praised by others because they possess an unsane belief about the necessity of others' approval. A sensible balance between achieving short-range and long-range hedonistic goals involves a balance between achieving short-range and long-range appropriate pleasurable emotions.

Biological tendencies

In all people a tension exists between two opposing innate creative tendencies (Ellis, 1993b). On the one hand, people have tendencies to create, develop and actualize themselves as healthy goal-attaining human beings. They have a great potential to be rational and pleasure-producing. On the other hand, they have tendencies to create, develop and implement irrational cognitions, inappropriate emotions and dysfunctional behaviours. REBC theorizes that often people are 'biologically predisposed to strongly, passionately, and rigidly construct and hold on to their disturbance-creating musts and other irrational beliefs' (Ellis, 1993b. p. 199). Thus, they possess a huge potential to be destructive of themselves and of others, to be illogical and continually to repeat the same mistakes.

Ellis believes that the major human irrationalities exist in virtually all humans, regardless of culture and educational level. Human fallibility has an inherent source. The fact that people seem so easily conditioned into dysfunctional thinking and behaviour and that it is so hard to modify are both viewed as evidence for an innate tendency to irrationality (Ellis, 1980). People's failure to accept reality almost always causes them to manifest the characteristics of emotional disturbance. However, differences exist in genetic predisposition to irrationality.

It is helpful for counsellors to acknowledge people's powerful innate tendencies to irrationality. Their expectations about clients' progress should become more realistic. Client insight on its own is insufficient. Counsellors need to persuade clients to work and practise hard, both to change and to maintain their gains.

Biological basis of choosing

People are not only born and raised to be irrational, they also possess an element of free choice in whether or not and how much they make themselves emotionally disturbed. Heredity, environment and choice interact. Ellis recalls how he and his sister coped with their father's absences and their mother's neglect. His sister failed to develop the same problem-solving skills that he did partly because 'she was born with a whiny, demanding, injustice-collecting temperament and . . . consequently she *chose* to make the worst of her childhood conditions' (Ellis, 1991a, p. 4). Thus, his sister was partly responsible for her misery by consciously or unconsciously choosing to victimize herself in relation to 'what is going on (WIGO) in the world' (Ellis, 1988, p 29).

People can use their biological tendency to have some degree of free choice to help as well as to damage themselves. First, they can choose to think differently and more effectively about what is going on. Second, because they possess the capacity to think about how they think, they can choose to acquire and maintain the cognitive skills for containing and counteracting their tendencies to irrationality.

ABC theory of personality

Defining the ABCs

Ellis has an ABC theory of personality to which he has added D and E to cover change and the desirable result of change. In addition, the letter G can be placed first to provide a context for people's ABCs.

G Goals, both fundamental and primary

A Activating events in a person's life

B Beliefs, both rational and irrational

C Consequences, both emotional and behavioural

D Disputing irrational beliefs

E Effective new philosophy of life

The ABCs of rational thinking and living

When thinking rationally about activating events (As) that either aid or confirm or block or sabotage their goals (G), people engage in preferential thinking. Preferential as contrasted with demanding thinking involves either explicitly and/or tacitly reacting with their belief systems (Bs) in realistic ways and experiencing appropriate emotional and enacting goal-oriented behavioural consequences (Cs). Following are ABCs for goal enhancing and for goal blocking activating events (Ellis, 1991b, p. 143).

A Activating event perceived as aiding or confirming goals.

B Belief system involving preferential thinking: 'This is good! I like this activating event.'

C Consequences: emotional – pleasure or happiness; behavioural – approaching and trying to repeat this activating event

A Activating event perceived as blocking or sabotaging goals.

B Belief system involving preferential thinking: 'This is bad! I dislike this activating event.'

C Consequences: emotional – frustration or unhappiness; behavioural – avoiding or trying to eliminate this activating event.

The ABCs of irrational thinking and emotional disturbance

Ellis (1977, 1991b) divides belief systems into two basic categories: rational beliefs (rB) and irrational beliefs (iB). When people's goals are blocked or sabotaged by activating events, they have a conscious or unconscious choice of responding with appropriate or inappropriate emotional and behavioural consequences. In reality, people's responses to activating events usually result from a combination of rational and irrational beliefs, though often one becomes the 'winning' mode. In the case of emotional self-disturbance, people choose to allow irrational beliefs to predominate.

Often irrational belief systems operate on at least four levels: primary demanding belief(s), derivatives of the primary demanding belief(s), secondary demanding belief(s), and derivatives of the secondary demanding belief(s).

1. *Primary demanding belief(s)*. The primary demanding belief or beliefs involves people's main demands and commands in relation to the activating event. Ellis (1989) has coined the term 'musturbation' to indicate that these beliefs are usually expressed as musts, shoulds, ought to's, have-to's and got-to's. He has identified three major clusters of irrational beliefs that create inappropriate emotional and behavioural consequences (1980):

(a) '*I must* do well and win approval for all my performances . . .' (p. 5),

(b) 'Others *must* treat me considerately and kindly . . .' (p. 6), and

(c) 'Conditions under which I live *must* be arranged so that I get practically everything I want comfortably, quickly and easily . . .' (p. 7).

An ABC example how to create emotional disturbance is as follows:

A Activating event perceived as blocking or sabotaging goals.

B Belief system involving demanding thinking: 'I absolutely must have my important Goals unblocked and fulfilled!'

C Consequences: emotional – anxiety and/or excessive hostility; behavioural – self-defeating overreaction or underreaction to this activating event.

2. *Derivatives of the primary demanding belief(s)*. People usually create highly unrealistic and overgeneralized inferences and attributions as derivatives of their musturbatory and absolutistic demands. Following are common irrational derivatives that often accompany their musturbatory beliefs (Ellis, 1988, 1991b).

Awfulizing, horribleizing, terribleizing
'If I don't have my important Goals unblocked and fulfilled as I must, it's awful!' In this context, 'awful' means totally bad or more than bad.

I can't stand-it-itis
'If I don't have my important Goals unblocked and fulfilled as I must, I can't stand it!'

Feeling of worthlessness and self-hatred
'If I don't have my important Goals unblocked and fulfilled as I must, I'm a stupid, worthless person.'

Predictions of continuous failure
'If I don't have my important Goals unblocked and fulfilled as I must, I'll always fail to get what I want and only get what I don't want both now and in future.'

Ellis (1988) proposes that neurotic problems can be grouped in two main headings according to the three main musturbatory beliefs and their derivatives: (1) ego disturbance (self-damning) and (2) low frustration tolerance (LFT) or discomfort disturbance. Ego disturbance arises from the belief '*I must* do well and win approval for all my performances . . .' because it leads to people thinking and feeling that they are inadequate and undeserving persons when they do not do as well as they believe they must. He regards this as godlike grandiosity since people demand that they be special, perfect, outstanding, superhuman.

Low frustration tolerance arises from the ego disturbance belief that people think they are so special and perfect. They then progress to holding either or both the irrational beliefs 'Others *must* treat me considerately and kindly . . .' and 'Conditions under which I live *must* be arranged so that I get practically everything I want comfortably, quickly and easily . . .'. Awfulizing and I can't-stand-it-itis and derivatives of such beliefs. Basically in ego disturbance and low frustration tolerance what people are insisting is that 'I must have an easy life, I must be perfect, and people and conditions should always cater to *me, me, me, me!*' (Ellis, 1988, p. 119).

3. *Secondary demanding belief(s)*. Once people make themselves miserable at C, they tend to exacerbate their misery by making themselves miserable about being miserable. In other words, they transform the negative consequences (C) of the primary demanding belief ABC into an activating event (A) for a secondary level demanding belief ABC. Following is an example (Ellis, 1989, p. 207):

Primary ABC

A1 'I did poorly on my job today.'

B1 'Since I must do well, isn't that horrible!'

C1 'I feel anxious, depressed and worthless.'

Secondary ABC

A1(C1) 'I feel anxious, depressed and worthless.'

B2   'Since I must not feel anxious, depressed and worthless, isn't that horrible!'

C2   'I feel even more anxious, depressed and worthless.'

Frequently, people make themselves anxious about being anxious, depressed about being depressed, guilty about feeling guilty and so on.

4. *Derivatives of secondary demanding belief(s)*. People can now choose to create and derive awfulizing, I can't-stand-it-itis, feelings of worthlessness and predictions of failure from their secondary as well as their primary musturbatory beliefs. They now have two negative consequences and their derivatives for the price of one. Also, in an ever spiralling cycle, they can intensify the unhappiness they create with their beautiful hang-ups.

Interactions of Gs, As, Bs and Cs

Just as cognitions, emotions and behaviours interact with each other and are virtually never entirely pure, so do the ABCs of REBC. Goals (G), activating events (A), beliefs (B) and consequences (C) 'all seem to be part of a collaboration with one another' (Ellis, 1991b, p. 145).

Regarding the goal of survival, Ellis gives the example of the urge to eat having a cognitive component ('Food is good and nourishing so I had better obtain it'), an emotive component (the pleasure of eating good food and the displeasure of eating bad food), a behavioural component (for instance, cooking food), and a physical component (for instance, sensations of touch, taste, smell and sight) (Ellis, 1991b, p. 145).

The relationship between activating events (As) and beliefs (Bs) is interactional and reciprocal. For instance, people who perceive an activating event (A) as a loss of approval may perceive it as a slight affront if they have the belief (B) 'I prefer to be approved but I don't have to be.' However, they may perceive the same event (A) as a cruelly intended assault if they have the belief (B) 'I must be approved and I'm worthless if I am not!' (Ellis, 1991b, 146–7). Ellis sees humans as almost always adding or constructing cognitive, emotive and behavioural elements to A. Once people construct their irrational beliefs many times they are made into 'Basic Philosophies' that seem and feel absolutely right. As one of Ellis's clients observed: 'B starts off following A, but then it becomes before A and is brought into new As' (Ellis, 1991b, 160).

The relationship between Bs and Cs is also reciprocal and interactional. For instance preferential or musturbatory beliefs (Bs) lead to different consequences (Cs). Also, consequences (Cs) reciprocally influence beliefs (Bs). Ellis gives the example of people who perceive a rejection (A) and feel depressed (C), then avoiding potential rejectors (also C) because they have chosen to create beliefs such as 'So-and-So is stupid and is not worth approaching' or 'I can easily find better people than So-and-So to approach' (Ellis, 1991b, p. 149). When beliefs strongly interact with emotional and behavioural consequences they are 'cognitive-emotive' (Ellis, 1991b, p. 153).

ACQUISITION

How do people acquire rational and irrational cognitions? This section mainly emphasizes acquiring demanding and musturbatory beliefs and their derivatives. Ellis stresses that musturbatory beliefs are highly emotive and behavioural as well as cognitive. Furthermore, these musts are 'an integral part of people's Goals, Activating Events, Beliefs, and disturbed Consequences when they become – or make themselves – neurotic' (Ellis, 1991b, p. 164).

Ellis's emphasis is much more on how people sustain their irrationality than on how they initially acquire it. The past cannot be undone and it is counterproductive to focus excessively on how people feel about the past. Ellis advises people to 'Forget your "Godawful" past' (Ellis, 1988, p. 69). He believes that psychology has focused too much on people originally become illogical and that this by no means indicates how people maintain or perpetuate their illogical behaviour, or what they should do to change it. Consequently, Ellis's treatment of the development of irrational cognitions and musturbatory beliefs is cursory. However, three main strands may be identified: biology, social learning and choosing irrational cognitions. Since biological or innate tendencies to irrationality have been previously discussed, the main focus here is on social learning and choosing.

Social learning

Given that human beings are born with a distinct proneness to irrationality, this tendency is frequently exacerbated by their environment, especially early in life when people are most vulnerable to outside influences. Ellis sees humans as basically highly suggestible, but a acknowledges innate differences (Ellis, 1977b). Irrational ideas, which once might have been appropriate in view of the helpless state of the child, are acquired for a number of reasons (Ellis, 1989; 1991b; Ellis & Harper, 1961, 1975). First, young children are unable to think clearly. They have a strong tendency to insist on immediate rather than on future gratification and they are unable accurately to distinguish real from imagined fears. However, as they grow older, normal children become less insistent on having their desires and demands immediately gratified. Second, frequently childish demands can be assuaged by magic, for instance parents saying that a fairy godmother will satisfy them. Third, children are dependent on the planning and thinking of others. Fourth, parents and members of the family group themselves have irrational tendencies, prejudices and superstitions which they inculcate into their children. Fifth, this process is exacerbated by the indoctrinations of the mass media. Sixth, cultures and religions can impart irrational, self-defeating and society-defeating views.

Choosing irrational cognitions

The process of acquiring irrationality is not simply a matter of how others behave. Humans largely create their own emotional disturbances through not developing and exercising their capacity for rational choice. Negative social learning experiences do not in themselves lead to people acquiring irrational cognitions. Many people who have had negative upbringings choose not to disturb themselves unduly. Still others, with or without support, work through their problems. The reverse is also true. Favourable social learning experiences do not in themselves lead to rational cognitions. Many people who have had favourable upbringings develop significant irrational beliefs. While social learning experiences influence people for good or ill, they still have the capacity to choose how they react to them.

MAINTENANCE

Why do people persist in holding their irrational beliefs and their derivatives? People not only become irrational, they stay irrational. In fact, often they become even more irrational. Staying rational in an irrational world is a struggle. Once their irrational beliefs are acquired, people tend to repeat them again and again and again. Ellis continually stresses that people have strong tendencies to reindoctrinate themselves with their self-defeating ideas. Numerous reasons exist why people stay irrational.

Biological tendencies

People's biological tendencies to irrationality do not go away with maturation but are part of their life-long genetic inheritance. Ellis stresses that humans: 'are powerfully predisposed to unconsciously and habitually prolong their mental dysfunctioning and to fight like hell to give it up' (Ellis, 1987, p. 365). Rather than strike a realistic balance between short-range and long-range hedonism, humans mostly embrace short-range hedonism. This preference for the pleasures of the moment is the main source of resistance to change.

Emotional contributions

Absolutistic musts are often 'hot' cognitions that have a strong evaluative-feeling component in them. Such cognitions are held strong and powerfully and, as such, can be difficult to change. In addition, people then not only develop derivatives of their primary irrational beliefs but also secondary irrational beliefs and their derivatives. As a result they raise the level of their emotionality and then may think even more irrationally. They may fail to see how upset they are. Furthermore, they are now so upset that they fail to reality-test and dispute their irrational beliefs in ways that they might otherwise do. A 'catch 22' situation develops in which unrealistic beliefs (Bs) create disruptive feelings (Cs) which in turn perpetuate, fan the flames of, and enhance the unrealistic beliefs (Bs). In addition, unrealistic beliefs (Bs) create dysfunctional behaviours (Cs) which in turn also augment and exacerbate the unrealistic beliefs (Bs). Instead of the consequences of irrational beliefs making people better, they make them worse.

Insufficient scientific thinking

People continue to disturb themselves because they fail to think scientifically about what is going on in the world (WIGO). To think scientifically people need constantly to observe and check the 'facts' and thus see the extent to which they are 'true' and whether or not they have changed. Scientific thinking is flexible and requires evidence to uphold or negate viewpoints. Also, the scientific method is sceptical that the universe has any absolute standards of 'good' and 'bad'. Science does not have absolute rules in regard to human behaviour. However, once people establish goals, for instance to survive and be happy, to some extent science can study whether people meet these goals. People persist in irrational beliefs because they fail to use the scientific method to dispute them with such questions as 'Is this belief realistic and factual?', 'Is this belief logical?' (For instance, is it logical to think that people must always act competently?), and 'Can this belief be falsified?' (Ellis, 1988a).

Reinforcing consequences

People can emotionally, cognitively and behaviourally reinforce their irrational beliefs. Emotionally, absolutistic musturbatory beliefs lead to strong negative feelings – such as severe anger and depression – that make them seem true. Cognitively and behaviourally, people reinforce their beliefs in different ways according to the belief. For instance, people who seek social approval avoid taking social risks, and by doing so convince themselves that it is too difficult and dangerous to do otherwise. Furthermore, when avoiding social situations they may feel a sense of emotional relief. The combination of their emotional, cognitive and behavioural reactions makes them more rather than less socially anxious.

People who get extremely angry exaggerate the negative qualities of their 'enemies', thus justifying and reinforcing the original self-disturbing beliefs. Furthermore, their behaviour may create hostile reactions in others which then gives their beliefs validity and turns them into self-fulfilling prophesies. Once these self-disturbing and redisturbing processes occur over a period of time and people vainly try to correct their emotional disturbances, often they conclude it is not worth trying any more. Ellis (1987) regards this as the unkindest cut of all. People give in to their emotional disturbances.

Emphasizing one's 'Godawful' past

Ellis states as an REBC insight: 'Your early childhood experiences and your past conditioning did not originally make you disturbed. You did' (Ellis, 1988, p. 70). People maintain their emotional disturbance by looking for causes in their pasts. Focusing on the past interferes with people focusing on the present in which they still may be upsetting themselves with the same irrational beliefs with which they upset themselves in their pasts. People cannot undo their pasts, but they can change their presents and futures. Furthermore, often focusing on the past leads to an overemphasis not only on the past relative to the present, but also to an overemphasis on other people's behaviour relative to one's own. Focusing on the past can obscure rather than bring into focus people's responsibility for their own cognitions, emotions and behaviour. Ellis (1989) believes that many counselling approaches, for instance psychoanalysis, collude in people's tendencies to avoid dealing with their presents by focusing on their pasts.

Unrealistic beliefs about change

People's low frustration tolerance can be both cause and consequence of unrealistic beliefs about working to change, with or without professional assistance, their thoughts, feelings and actions. Irrational beliefs about change include (Ellis, 1987, 1993b):
• 'I must be able to change with little discomfort, work and practice on my part.'
• 'Changing how I think, feel and behave shouldn't be so hard.'
• 'I must change quickly and profoundly.'
• 'When changing, I must not have any setbacks.'
• 'I must not be able to change any more, therefore I will settle for how I function now.'

Other cognitive factors

Ellis (1987) lists a number of other factors and processes whereby people maintain and worsen their irrational beliefs and emotional disturbances.

• *Ignorance.* People, including counsellors, can believe that it is statistically normal and healthy for them to be unnecessarily upset. They fail to distinguish between appropriate and inappropriate thoughts, feelings and behaviours.

• *Stupidity.* Many people are too unintelligent to work effectively on their emotional problems. They fail to gain sufficient insight into the fact that they create their own disturbances.

• *Unperceptiveness.* Without counselling, many disturbed people rarely look at their irrational beliefs and ideas and how these create and drive their upsetness. Even when pointed out to them in counselling, many disturbed people are still incapable of grasping how they upset themselves.

• *Rigidity.* Even when they acknowledge their self-defeating irrational beliefs, many people rigidly stick to their musturbatory beliefs and their derivatives, for instance awfulizing and I can't-stand-it-itis. Some such people may be psychotic or have borderline personality disorders, whereas others are plain rigid thinkers.

• *Defensiveness.* Humans are prone to avoid facing and dealing directly with their problems. They use various methods of distorting and denying problems. For instance, they may not wish to perceive that they are hostile, paranoid or withdrawn. Also, they may fail to disclose behaviours of which they are ashamed.

• *Pollyannaism and indifference.* Some people who are prone to extreme anxiety and suffer from a serious illness, such as heart disease or cancer, may deal with it by denying its seriousness. Sometimes, such defensive manoeuvres may help people to cope. However, on many occasions such thinking may block efforts to attain physical health and psychological change.

• *Changing the situation.* For many, the easy way out is to change the situation, for instance, obtain a divorce rather than try to change themselves and then consider whether or not to change the situation. For every neurotic who really tries to have a fundamental shift in the way they think, there are probably ten times as many trying to *feel* better by changing the situations in which they behave self-defeatingly rather than *get* better. This ratio holds true whether or not people come for counselling.

• *Other palliative means.* People and their would-be helpers resort to many palliative means to deal with emotional disturbances rather than get to the root of them. Many clients and potential clients use distraction techniques such as progressive relaxation, biofeedback, meditation and yoga. Some try superficial positive thinking. Many people lose themselves in political, religious and mystical cults. Short-term feel-good remedies like alcohol and drugs are very common. In brief, many disturbed people seek low level and palliative remedies rather than more rigorous and long-lasting solutions. In addition, many people either resist entering counselling or, once in counselling, resist changing. Ellis stresses that the main reason for client resistance is that 'most clients are natural resisters who find it exceptionally easy to block themselves from changing and find it unusually hard to resist their resistances' (Ellis, 1987, pp. 370–1).

Insufficiently challenging beliefs through action

As mentioned earlier, people may reinforce their beliefs through unwillingness to change their actions. Their 'tried and true' self-defeating ways may bring short-term relief at the expense of long-term gain. An Ellis insight is: '*You can change irrational beliefs (iBs) by acting against them: by performing behaviours that contradict them*' (Ellis, 1988, p. 109). Why then don't people change their actions to challenge their beliefs? One reason is that they may not have insight into their irrational beliefs, their derivatives, and their emotional and behavioural consequences. Another reason is that people resist the risk and effort involved in taking action. Some people may not be clear what to do. Still others may know what to do but lack the skills, confidence and support to do it. Another category is people who change their actions but lack the staying power to maintain them, especially when faced with difficulties and setbacks.

PRACTICE
Goals

REBC has dual goals: 'first, to help people overcome their emotional blocks and disturbances; second, to help them become more fully functioning, more self-actualizing, and happier than they would otherwise be' (Ellis, 1991f, p. 7). The approach aims to 'help clients make – or, rather, give themselves – a profound philosophic change, and especially to change their rigid musturbatory to preferential thinking' (Ellis, 1991b, p. 164). REBC focuses on changing clients' cognitions, emotions and behaviour (Ellis & Bernard, 1986). Cognitively, REBC aims to help them become more rational and to give up 'childish demandingness – the main element of emotional disturbance' (Ellis, 1989, p. 214). Emotionally, it aims to help them feel more appropriately. Behaviourally, it aims to help them act more effectively to achieve their fundamental and primary goals.

Inelegant and elegant counselling goals

Earlier in this chapter I presented Ellis's GABCDE outline and more fully described goals (Gs), activating events (As), beliefs (Bs) and consequences (Cs). Though D stands for disputing irrational beliefs, it is also a shorthand way to describe all REBC's cognitive, emotive and behavioural techniques. There are two meanings to E, depending on whether the goals of REBC are inelegant or elegant.

Ellis (1980) writes: 'Inelegant change largely consists of some kind of symptom removal' (p. 13). Here, at D, REBC targets the cognitions, emotions and behaviours that accompany self-defeating feelings, like anxiety and depression, and dysfunctional behaviours, like avoiding social and public-speaking situations. The goal of focused or inelegant REBC is that of focused or inelegant change. Here the letter E stands for an effective new philosophy focused on one or more specific symptoms or problems. Effectiveness in relation to these symptoms can be cognitive (similar to rational beliefs), emotional (appropriate feelings), and behavioural (desirable behaviours).

In contrast to inelegant change, Ellis states: 'Elegant change in RET goes much beyond this kind of symptom removal, and aims at a significant lessening (rather than a complete removal) of clients' *disturbability*' (Ellis, 1980, p. 13). In elegant change, E goes further than an effective new philosophy that supports removal of specific symptoms to assisting clients to develop and implement an effective philosophy of life. Thus E stands for the goal of effective new philosophies for specific symptoms in inelegant REBC and for the goal of an effective philosophy of life (which includes effective new philosophies for specific symptoms) in elegant REBC.

REBC stresses the interactions of activating events (As), beliefs (Bs) and emotional and behavioural consequences (Cs). Ellis regards this profound basic change to an effective philosophy of life as extremely cognitive, emotive and behavioural. This philosophic change has the following characteristics. First, those making it genuinely and much of the time choose to think in flexible and preferential rather than in rigid and musturbatory ways. People with effective philosophies keep working on disciplined, goal-oriented reactions to everyday obnoxious activating events (As), so that such reactions become somewhat automatic. Second, strongly and quite emotionally, they think scientifically and fight and act against 'narrow-mindedness and arbitrary intellectual-emotional-behavioural restriction!' (Ellis, 1991b, p. 166).

Length of counselling and goals

Most clients are seen by counsellors for weekly individual sessions. Ellis's own counselling sessions usually last for 30 minutes. Clients normally have 5 to 50 sessions. Brief counselling of one to ten sessions is used for clients who have specific problems or for those only prepared to stay in counselling for a short time. Individuals who are not too generally disturbed can usually attain the inelegant change of symptom removal in brief counselling. Preferably, individuals with severe problems come for individual and/or group counselling for at least six months so that they can practise what they learn.

Uses and limitations of REBC

REBC can be used with most kinds of clients, ranging from those who are mildly disturbed to juvenile delinquents, borderline personality disorders, psychotics when they have some contact with reality and individuals with higher grade mental deficiency. Normally, Ellis does not consider REBC suitable for clients who are 'out of contact with reality, in a highly manic state, seriously autistic or brain injured, and in the lower ranges of mental deficiency . . .' (Ellis, 1989, p. 222).

REBC is significantly more effective with mildly disturbed clients and with those who have a single major symptom, say sexual inadequacy, than with strongly disturbed clients. Counsellors find it much more difficult to assist the latter to change since REBC theory hypothesizes that the causes of musturbatory thinking and emotional disturbance are largely innate.

Characteristics of self-actualizing persons

Where possible, REBC goes beyond helping people overcome their emotional blocks to helping them become more self-actualizing and happy. Ellis (Ellis, 1980; Ellis & Bernard, 1986; Ellis, 1991f) has listed several important characteristics of fully functioning or self-actualizing people.

Self-interest. Primarily valuing their own interests, though being prepared to sacrifice them to *some* degree for those for whom they care, but not completely.

Social interest. Because most people choose to live in groups or communities, being interested in the needs of others and in social survival.

Self-direction. Assuming primary responsibility for their lives.

Tolerance. Giving themselves and others the right to be wrong. Even when disliking someone's behaviour, refraining from damning them as persons.

Flexibility. Thinking flexibly and being open to change. Not making rigid rules for self and others.

Acceptance of uncertainty. Acknowledging that we live in a world of probability and chance. Enjoying a good degree of order, without demanding it.

Commitment. Being committed to something outside of themselves. Achieving maximum fulfilment and happiness by throwing themselves into a long-term, vital, absorbing interest.

Creativity and originality. Being innovative and creative about both commonplace and artistic problems. Often possessing at least one major creative interest.

Scientific thinking. Being rational and objective by applying the rules of logic and scientific method in how they think.

Self-acceptance. Choosing to accept themselves unconditionally. Not measuring their intrinsic worth extrinsically or by what others think of them. Attempting to enjoy rather than to prove themselves.

Acceptance of human animality. Accepting their own and others' animal nature.

Risk taking. Being prepared to take calculated risks to do what they want to do. Being adventurous rather than foolish.

Long-range hedonism. Being hedonistic in seeking happiness and avoiding pain, yet balancing long-range with short-range considerations. Not being obsessed with immediate gratification.

Non-utopianism. Accepting the likelihood that utopias and perfection are probably unachievable. Refusing to strive unrealistically for total happiness or total absence of negative emotions.

High frustration tolerance. Changing obnoxious conditions that they can change, accepting those that they cannot, and discriminating the difference between the two.

Self-responsibility for disturbance. Accepting much of the responsibility for their upsets rather than defensively blaming others or social conditions.

Counsellor–client relationship

In REBC, the main role of the counsellor is that of a teacher who strives to impart to clients self-helping skills conducive to thinking rationally, feeling appropriately and behaving effectively so that they can attain their goals. Ellis writes 'Rational-emotive practitioners often employ a fairly rapid-fire active-directive-persuasive-philosophic methodology' (Ellis, 1989, p. 215). What kind of a counselling relationship best supports this active-directive teaching role? Counsellors try to build rapport with clients by using empathic listening, including reflecting feelings. Dryden and Ellis (1986) distinguish between *affective* empathy, understanding how clients feel, and *philosophic* empathy, understanding the philosophies or thinking underlying these feelings. Counsellors attempt to offer both kinds of empathy. In addition, counsellors accept their clients as fallible human beings and do not judge the goodness or badness of their personhood against predetermined moral standards.

Rational emotive behaviour counsellors do not show undue warmth to most of their clients. They are wary of colluding in clients' dire needs for approval. Also, they try to encourage clients to confront their own problems and assume responsibility for finding their own warmth and happiness rather than seeking it from counsellors. Often clients perceive rational emotive behaviour counsellors as warm and caring because of their commitment to their welfare and tolerance for all individuals.

Particularly during early sessions, rational emotive behaviour counsellors do most of the talking. They do not hesitate to confront clients with how they contribute to their own distress. They forcefully dispute and debate their clients' illogical thinking as well as helping clients to do this for themselves. They freely share their opinions and self-disclose, so long as this is not detrimental to clients. Furthermore they use humour, but never at their clients' expense, since they consider that many of them take themselves and their problems far too seriously. Also, counsellors use humour to attack disturbance-producing ideas.

A distinction exists between REBC content and the counsellor's style of working with clients. Ellis's counselling style, like that of many of his followers, is hard-hitting and forceful. However, either with specific categories of clients or with all of their clients, some rational emotive behaviour counsellors choose more passive and gentle styles (Dryden & Ellis, 1986).

The counsellor as teacher

Ellis views the role of the rational emotive behavioural counsellor as that of 'an authoritative (but not authoritarian!) and encouraging teacher who strives to teach his or her clients how to be their own best therapist once formal therapy sessions have ended' (Dryden & Ellis, p. 143). As early as the first session, counsellors try to explain to clients the ABCs of how humans disturb themselves and also the process of rational-emotive behaviour counselling (Ellis, 1992a). As counselling progresses, counsellors not only dispute their clients' beliefs, but they teach and practise them in how to dispute their own beliefs. Thus throughout rational emotive behaviour counselling, however brief, counsellors strive to give clients insights, philosophies and skills that they can use both between sessions and afterwards.

REBC counsellors as teachers do not treat all clients the same. Realizing that people have both similarities and differences, they vary how forceful they are, how much homework they use, and the mix between cognitive, emotive and behavioural techniques.

Detecting irrational beliefs and their derivatives

Counsellors as teachers detect clients' irrational beliefs, their musturbations, and their derivatives, for instance awfulizing. Furthermore, they teach clients how to do this for themselves. In order to relinquish their demandingness, it helps if clients can acknowledge that they may possess this characteristic. Ellis teaches them his ABC system. Within the ABC system, irrational beliefs can be traced cognitively, emotionally and behaviourally. Cognitively, irrational beliefs can be detected through overt or implicit signs of demandingness. In particular, Ellis looks for 'musts', 'shoulds', 'oughts', 'have tos' and 'got tos' that signal clients' musturbatory absolutistic beliefs. In addition, he looks for explicit and implicit phrases such as 'That is horrible!' and 'I can't stand it' that indicate derivatives of possession primary and secondary irrational beliefs

Emotionally, irrational beliefs are signalled by inappropriate feelings. Behaviourally, self-defeating actions offer clues to irrational beliefs. Sometimes the cognitive, emotional and behavioural clues are obvious to both counsellors and clients. On other occasions, though obvious to counsellors, clients may resist acknowledging the evidence. In still other instances clients may hold irrational beliefs in subtle and tricky ways that make them seem natural (Ellis, 1987). Such beliefs can challenge counsellors' powers of detection.

Disputing irrational beliefs and their derivatives

It is insufficient for musts and their derivatives to disappear just to acknowledge them. Instead, counsellors and clients combine to fight them by disputing them. The technique of disputing is the most typical and perhaps the most often used method of REBC (Ellis, 1980). Disputing involves challenging and questioning unsubstantiated hypotheses that clients hold about themselves, others and the world. In most instances, rational emotive behaviour counsellors quickly pin clients down to a few central irrational ideas and their derivatives that they then challenge and dispute. In addition, they teach clients how to dispute their own beliefs. Cognitions, feelings and behaviours interact in how people create and maintain irrational beliefs. Therefore, when disputing irrational beliefs and their derivatives, counsellors are likely to be more effective if they work in all three of the cognitive, emotional and behavioural modalities rather than in one or two. However, no modality is entirely pure or free form the others.

Disputing: Cognitive techniques

Scientific questioning

The main cognitive technique in disputing is that of scientific questioning. Clients are required to use reason, logic and facts to support their beliefs. The purpose of this questioning is to show clients how and why their irrational beliefs do not hold water. Disputing questions for counsellors to ask clients and for clients to ask themselves include the following: These questions are stated in the first person singular to emphasize the teaching self-help skills nature of REBC.

'What irrational belief do I want to dispute and surrender?'

'Can I rationally support this belief?'

'What evidence exists for the truth of this belief?'

'What evidence exists for the falseness of this belief?'

'Why is it awful?'

'Why can't I stand it?'

'How does this make me a rotten person?'

'Why must I always do poorly in future?'

'What is an effective new belief (philosophy) with which to replace my irrational belief?'

The desired cognitive outcome of disputing specific irrational beliefs and their derivatives is a sound set of preferential beliefs or effective new philosophies (E) related to each belief. Desirable emotional and behavioural effects should stem from and interact with the effective new philosophies. For clients seeking elegant change, the desirable effect of learning how to dispute irrational beliefs is an Effective New Philosophy that can be applied both now and in future.

The following is an example (Ellis, 1988).

A   I go for an interview and fail to get the job.

B   'I must never get rejected.'
    'How awful to get rejected!'
    'I can't stand the rejection!'
    'This rejection makes me a rotten person.'
    'I'll always do poorly in job interviews.'

C Undesirable emotional consequences: depression, worthlessness, anxiety, anger.
   Undesirable behavioural consequences: Refusing to go for other job interviews.
   Functioning poorly on job interviews through anxiety.

D 'Why must I never get rejected?'
   'Why is it awful to get rejected for a job?'
   'Why can't I stand this rejection?'
   'How does this rejection make me a rotten person?'
   'Why must I always do poorly on job interviews?'

E 'I'd prefer to have got this job, but there is no evidence that I absolutely must have
   it.'
   'Nothing makes it awful to get rejected, though I find it highly inconvenient.'
   'I can stand rejection, though I'll never like it.'
   'Rejection never makes me a rotten person, but a person with some unfortunate
   traits.'
   'I don't have to do poorly on job interviews always, especially if I try to learn from
   my errors.'
   Illustrative emotional effect: feeling sorrowful, but not depressed.
   Illustrative behavioural effect: I went for some more job interviews.

Discussion

Counsellors can discuss with clients various aspects of their irrational thinking. For
instance, with Roger a 24-year-old computer programmer afraid of public speaking,
Ellis discussed the harm of self-rating and how he could choose unconditionally to
accept himself whether or not he failed at speaking and whether or not he was anxious
about failing and showed his anxiety to others (Ellis, 1991e).

Homework techniques

Clients need repeatedly to challenge their irrational beliefs and to practise their
disputing skills both to learn them and also to reinforce their new rational philosophies.
REBC uses various homework techniques to develop disputing skills.

• *Cassettes of sessions.* Counsellors encourage clients to record sessions and listen to each
one several times.

• *Self-help forms.* Clients are encouraged to fill out self-help forms. Counsellors check
the forms to see how accurately clients dispute their irrational beliefs. For instance in
Sichel and Ellis's (1984) form, clients identify an activating event (A) and the
consequences or conditions (C) they would like to change. Then the form consists of
three columns. In the first column, clients circle which of 13 irrational beliefs (B), for
instance 'I MUST do well or very well!' and 'People MUST live up to my expectations
or it is TERRIBLE!', lead to their consequences (C). In addition, they can add other
relevant irrational beliefs. In the second column, there is space for them to dispute (D)
each circled irrational belief. In the third column, they write in effective rational beliefs
(E) to replace their irrational beliefs. After the columns there is a space (f) where they

can write in feelings and behaviours experienced after arriving at their effective rational beliefs. The form ends with the following self-statement about the necessity of work and practice: 'I WILL WORK HARD TO REPEAT MY EFFECTIVE RATIONAL BELIEFS FORCEFULLY TO MYSELF ON MANY OCCASIONS SO THAT I CAN MAKE MYSELF LESS DISTRUBED NOW AND ACT LESS SELF-DEFEATINGLY IN THE FUTURE' (Sichel & Ellis, 1984, p. 2).

Another self-help form is known as DIBS (Disputing irrational beliefs). DIBS consists of six questions about: the belief I want to dispute, whether the belief can be rationally supported, existing evidence for the belief, existing evidence against the belief, the worst that could happen to me if I never achieved what I wanted in respect to the belief, and good things that might happen if I never achieved what I wanted (Dryden & Ellis, 1986).

• *Reminder cards.* Clients can write out rational self-statements on 3×5 cards and repeat them at various times between sessions.

• *Listing disadvantages.* Clients can be asked to list ten disadvantages of continuing to avoid a certain behaviour, for instance public speaking, and review them every day (Ellis, 1991e).

• *Practising REBC on others.* Encouraging clients to practise talking their friends and relatives out of their disturbances.

• *Visualizing.* Clients can be shown how to visualize themselves competently performing situations that they currently fear.

• *Bibliotherapy.* Assigning clients self-help books to read, for instance Ellis (1977a, 1988), Ellis & Becker (1982), and Ellis and Harper (1975). Ellis (1993d) is keenly aware of the advantages and disadvantages of self-help materials.

• *Self-help cassettes.* Ellis has made innumerable audio and video cassettes, including *Solving Emotional Problems* (1982b), *How to be Happy though Human* (1984) and *How to Stop Worrying and Start Living* (1987b). Many clients find these cassettes helpful.

Discriminating irrational beliefs

Counsellors can show clients how to discriminate irrational from rational beliefs. Also, they can help clients to show themselves how the former lead to inappropriate feelings and self-defeating behaviours and the latter to positive results. Homework reports may be used to build this skill. For example, in the above example of 'I went for a job interview and I failed to get the job', clients can be asked to list rational beliefs (rB) based on preferential thinking (wants and desires) in one box and irrational beliefs (iB) based on demands or commands in another box. Then they can be asked to cite desirable consequences stemming from their rational beliefs as well as undesirable consequences stemming from their irrational beliefs. Above I presented irrational beliefs and their consequences for the 'failing to get a job' activating event. Consequently, here I only present rational beliefs and their consequences (Ellis, 1976, 1988).

A I went for a job interview and failed to get the job
rB 'How unfortunate to get rejected!'
   'I don't like getting rejected'
   'I wish I had gotten accepted.'
   'How annoying!'
   'Looks like I'll have difficulty getting the job I want.'

C Desirable emotional consequences: sorrow and regret, frustration and irritation, determination to keep trying.
   Desirable behavioural consequences: continued search for a job; attempt to upgrade my skills.

Disputing: Emotive techniques

REBC emotive disputing techniques include the following.

Vigorous disputing

Vigorous disputing may be performed both by counsellors on clients and by clients on themselves (Ellis, 1993e). Since many irrational beliefs involve hot cognitions that possess a large emotional component, they require forceful and vigorous disputing. Often counsellors need to argue, persuade and point out strongly the shaky logic of their clients' beliefs. Weak or moderately strong disputing may be insufficient. Ellis showed Roger, the computer programmer, how to create strong anti-worrying statements about public speaking and say them to himself forcefully: for example 'I NEVER, NEVER, NEVER have to speak well or unnervously in public, though it would be nice if I did!' (Ellis, 1991e, p. 454). In addition, Ellis worked out with Roger a dialogue with himself in which he recorded some of his potent irrational beliefs, e.g. 'I'm a nervous slob who deserves to be mute rather than risk making a fool of myself in public!', and in which he vigorously, forcefully and heatedly disputed them. Clients can make, and remake more powerfully, such cassettes for themselves as homework. Then they can play them back to themselves, their counsellors and, if in counselling groups, to the other group members.

   Reverse role play is another REBC vigorous disputing technique. For example, Ellis role played Roger tenaciously holding on to some of his irrational beliefs so that Roger could practise forcefully attacking them (Ellis, 1993e).

Rational-emotive imagery

In rational-emotive imagery (Ellis, 1993f), clients are encouraged to imagine one of the worst activating event adversities (A) that could happen to them, for instance, rejection by someone whose approval they really want. They vividly imagine this adversity occurring and bringing a host of problems into their life.

   Then they are encouraged to get in touch with the undesirable negative emotional consequence triggered by this adversity (A) – for instance, anxiety, depression, rage, self-hatred or self-pity – and really, really feel it (C1). They should spontaneously feel what they feel and not what they are supposed to feel. Once they feel inappropriately upset at Cl, they should hold on to this feeling for a minute or two. Then, keeping the same activating adversity (A) in their imagination, they should work on changing their disturbed negative feeling to a prescribed appropriate negative feeling consequence (C2), such as sorrow, disappointment, regret, frustration, irritation or displeasure. The way to do this is by telling themselves strongly and repetitively sensible rational beliefs or coping statements: for example, 'Yes, they really did treat me shabbily and unfairly, which I wish they wouldn't have done. But there is no reason why they must treat me fairly, however preferable that would be . . .' (Ellis, 1993f, p. 11–9). Clients should persist with their imagery and rational statements until they change their inappropriate feeling (C1) to an appropriate feeling (C2). It usually takes only a few minutes. They should have the homework assignment of carrying out this imagery procedure daily for about 30 days for each disturbed feeling they are trying to change.

Other emotive disputing techniques

Following are other emotive REBC techniques.

• *Unconditional acceptance.* The counsellor's basic acceptance of them as persons helps clients feel and think that they are acceptable, despite any negative characteristics.

• *Humour.* The judicious use of humour can help reduce clients' irrational beliefs and self-defeating behaviours to absurdity. Counsellors frequently exaggerate clients' nutty ideas and use 'various kinds oᶠ puns, witticisms, irony, whimsy, evocative language, slang, and deliberate use of sprightly obscenity . . .' (Ellis, 1980, p. 26). For example, Ellis said to Roger, his public-speaking phobia client: 'You really should feel ashamed of avoiding making speeches. Every other person your age speaks fluently and has no anxiety. What a unique jerk you are!' (Ellis, 1991e, p. 454). Encouraging clients to sing to themselves rational humorous songs (Ellis, 1977d). and telling amusing anecdotes are further methods to counteract clients' tendencies to not take themselves, others and the world too seriously.

• *Rational role playing.* Ellis uses role playing as a way of showing clients what their false ideas are and how they affect relating to others. For instance, Roger role played giving a difficult talk in front of Ellis and the counselling group he had joined as an adjunct to individual sessions. When Roger appeared anxious during the role-play, Ellis stopped the performance to let Roger ask himself 'What am I telling myself right now to *make* myself anxious? And what can I do right now to think and feel away this anxiety?' (Ellis, 1991e, p. 454).

Disputing: Behavioural techniques

Ellis doubts whether people ever truly change their irrational beliefs until they act many times against them. When young, Ellis suffered from severe fears of public speaking and meeting new women. He forced himself to engage repetitively in activities, giving political talks and talking to women on a park bench in the Bronx Botanical Garden, that challenged his fears. In both instances his actions helped rid him of his irrational fears (Ellis, 1988). Following are some REBC behavioural techniques.

Assignments that challenge demandingness

Clients who have musturbatory beliefs about approval and derivatives of these beliefs about the awfulness of rejection may be encouraged to ask someone for a date or force themselves to socialize. Simultaneously they convince themselves that it is not awful, but only inconvenient to get rejected. Clients who have perfectionist beliefs may have the assignment of deliberately making a real attempt to speak badly in public.

Clients are encourage to do their assignments *repetitively*. For instance Roger, the speech anxious client, was asked to speak in public as often as he could, once or twice a week (Ellis, 1991e). Often clients are asked to do their assignments *floodingly*, staying in situations they perceive as highly dangerous until they see that their 'danger' is largely imagined. For instance, clients afraid of riding on buses or underground trains are urged to do this immediately, many times a day in rush hours, if that is what they most fear (Ellis, 1980). Concurrently, in all instances where clients dispute their musturbatory beliefs behaviourally, they can dispute them cognitively too.

Shame attacking exercises

Ellis hypothesizes that ego anxiety is highly related to feelings of shame, guilt, embarrassment and humiliation. Consequently, the more people confront the irrational beliefs behind these feelings, the less they are likely to disturb themselves. Clients are encouraged to do things in public that they regard as particularly shameful or embarrassing. Examples are yelling out the stops on elevators, buses or underground trains or asking for sex-related items in loud voices in chemist shops. The purpose of these exercises is to prove that these behaviours in themselves are really not shameful and that they can be done with relative comfort and self-acceptance (Ellis, 1980). In addition, clients are urged to attack feelings of shame through greater self-disclosure of what they perceive, or what they perceive others perceive, as shameful.

Skill training

The distinction between behavioural skills and cognitive skills is imprecise. Always, when counsellors assist clients with behavioural skills – for instance assertion and communication skills – they train clients cognitively in disputing the accompanying irrational beliefs and derivative self-statements. Sometimes clients are asked to seek additional training experiences to acquire relevant skills. For instance, Ellis thought that speech-anxious Roger showed insufficient assertion skills at work, for instance not refusing to do presentations when genuinely unprepared. Ellis encouraged Roger to attend a six week assertion course at his Institute as well as take a five month public speaking course at a local college (Ellis, 1991e).

Use of rewards and penalties

REBC uses rewards and penalties to encourage clients to do homework and implement self-change programmes (Ellis, 1980; Dryden & Ellis, 1986). For instance, every time Roger filled out an RET Self-Help Report or gave a public speech, he would reward himself by listening to one of his favourite CDs. Whenever he failed to carry out an assignment he would talk to his boring aunt for 30 minutes. Two doses of this excruciating penalty cured Roger of not doing assignments! (Ellis, 1991e).

Problem-solving

Clients bring their goals (G) to the activating events (A) in their lives. These goals present many practical or reality problems for them to try to solve: for instance, obtaining a good education, finding a mate, getting a job, succeeding at work. Clients have a choice about whether they solve these reality problems or choose to upset themselves about them. If clients upset themselves, then they have an emotional problem about their reality problem. In such cases, counsellors can assist them to detect and actively dispute the relevant irrational beliefs. Sometimes it is better that clients do not address practical difficulties until they have worked through related emotional difficulties. For instance, an individual or couple might defer a decision to divorce until they have given themselves sufficient chance to see whether or not, with a lessening of their irrational beliefs, they might happily live together.

Counsellors willingly assist clients to solve reality problems. However, where necessary, they also insist on vigorously detecting and disputing accompanying irrational beliefs. In assisting problem solving, counsellors help clients to state problems and goals clearly, generate and evaluate alternative strategies, outline the steps to attain goals, identify resources and supports and develop the requisite practical skills for success.

Overcoming resistance

When clients resist following counselling procedures and doing homework assignments, they mainly do so because of the following irrational beliefs (Ellis, 1986a): (1) '*I must* do well at changing myself'; (2) 'You (the counsellor and others) *must* help me change'; and (3) 'Changing myself *must* occur quickly and easily'. Stemming from such beliefs (B), resisters have negative feelings consequences, for instance depression and self-pity, and behavioural consequences, for instance procrastination and withdrawal. In addition, they employ derivatives of irrational beliefs, such as awfulizing. The main REBC approach to resistant clients is to teach them to find and vigorously dispute the main irrational beliefs contributing to their resistance. Other techniques to resistance include:

• *Rational and coping self-statements.* Clients can keep telling themselves statements like: 'Therapy doesn't have to be easy. I can, in fact, enjoy its difficulty and its challenge' (Ellis, 1986a, p. 262).

• *Referenting.* Referenting means listing the disadvantages of resisting and the advantages of working at counselling and then regularly reviewing and thinking about these lists.

• *Proselytizing others.* Encouraging resistant clients to use REBC on friends and relatives.

Maintaining change

REBC is committed to assisting clients to maintain their changes. However, Ellis (1988) acknowledges the likelihood of backsliding. Right from the start, clients are taught that they can only change and maintain change with work and practice. Throughout counselling, homework assignments are used to help clients build skills for both outside and after counselling. When clients find themselves backsliding, they are told to go back to the ABCs and see what they did to fall back into their old patterns. Then they are encouraged vigorously to dispute (D) these irrational beliefs. They are advised to try and try again until they genuinely replace their irrational beliefs with their effective new philosophies (E)

Other applications

Other applications of REBC include group counselling, either along with individual counselling or instead of it (Ellis, 1992b). In REBC groups, members are taught to apply detecting and disputing irrational beliefs on one another (Ellis, 1989). They also get practice at attacking their ego disturbance irrational beliefs through disclosing material that they perceive as risky. In addition clients in groups, while working on assertion and other communication skills, can partake in role plays.

Ellis has a major interest in the application of REBC to marital, couples and family relationship problems (Ellis, 1986b, 1991b, 1991d, 1993c). Counsellors usually see marital or love partners together, listen to their complaints, and then teach them that even though their complaints actively describe behaviour at A, their upsetness at C is not justified. In particular, work focuses on musturbatory beliefs generating hostility. Also, counsellors frequently teach partners compromising and relating skills. In REB family counselling tolerance for oneself and others, independent of how obnoxious specific behaviours may be, is taught repeatedly to both parents and children.

Ellis, through his books and cassettes, has made a major contribution to educating the public in America and elsewhere on how to live more effectively. Also, he has influenced numerous other writers of self-help books. Possibly Ellis is the most influential English-speaking psychological educator of the twentieth century in terms of helping ordinary people learn how to overcome their emotional disturbances and become more self-actualizing.

CHAPTER REVIEW AND SELF-REFERENT QUESTIONS

Chapter review questions

1. Why does Ellis now call his approach rational emotive behaviour therapy?

2. What are humans' fundamental and primary goals?

3. Describe the difference between cool, warm and hot cognitions and provide an example of each.

4. Describe the differences between appropriate and inappropriate emotions.

5. What does Ellis consider to be the biological basis of personality?

6. Give an example of Ellis's ABC theory where B represents preferential thinking.

7. Give an example of Ellis's ABC theory where B represents demanding musturbatory thinking.

8. Critically discuss Ellis's ideas of the derivatives or irrational beliefs.

9. Why does Ellis consider that Gs, As, Bs and Cs reciprocally interact with one another? Give an example of a B influencing a subsequent A.

10. Discuss the roles of social learning and free choice in acquiring irrational beliefs.

11. Describe the contribution of each of the following factors to maintaining, and possibly strengthening, irrational beliefs:
    (a) biological tendencies
    (b) emotional contributions
    (c) insufficient scientific thinking
    (d) reinforcing consequences
    (e) emphasizing one's 'Godawful' past
    (f) unrealistic beliefs about change
    (g) insufficiently challenging beliefs through action.

12. What are the differences between inelegant and elegant counselling goals?

13. What is the nature of the counsellor–client relationship in REBC?

14. What is the role of the counsellor in REBC?

15. How can counsellors and clients detect irrational beliefs and their derivatives?

16. How can counsellors and clients use scientific questioning to dispute irrational beliefs? Provide an example.

17. Apart from scientific questioning, what other cognitive techniques does REBC use?

18. Describe vigorous disputing and give reasons why Ellis advocates it.

19. Describe and critically discuss rational-emotive imagery.

20. What is the role of humour in REBC?

21. Provide two examples of behavioural assignments that challenge musturbatory demanding beliefs.

22. Describe and critically discuss the use of shame attacking exercises.

23. What is the role of skill training in REBC?

24. What is the role of problem-solving in REBC?

25. Critically discuss the issue of overcoming resistance in REBC.

26. Critically discuss Ellis's views about the difficulties of maintaining change and what counsellors and clients can do about them.

27. What are some applications of REBC other than individual counselling?

Self-referent questions

1. Identify at least two irrational beliefs based on absolutistic demanding thinking in relation to each of the following:

(a) yourself;

(b) others;

(c) the conditions under which you live.

2. For one of the irrational beliefs you identified above state

(a) how you acquired it;

(b) how you maintain it.

3. From your own life, given an example of each of the following:

(a) the ABCs of rational thinking;

(b) the ABCs of irrational thinking.

4. Choose one of your irrational beliefs (B) that you wish to change. How could you dispute (D) it by:

(a) cognitive techniques?

(b) emotive techniques?

(c) behavioural techniques?

What effective new philosophy (E) would you arrive at?

5. What relevance, if any, has the theory and practise of rational emotive behaviour counselling for how you counsel?

6. What relevance, if any, has the theory and practice of rational emotive behaviour counselling for how you live?

Annotated bibliography

Ellis, A. (1989). Rational-emotive therapy. In R.J. Corsini & D. Wedding (Eds.). *Current Psychotherapies* (4th ed., pp. 197–238). Itasca, IL: Peacock.
This chapter overviews the theory and practice of REBC. The chapter's content includes: basic concepts, historical development, theory of personality, and theory and process of counselling. In addition, the chapter contains over four pages of transcript and a review of applications of REBC in such areas as group counselling and marriage and family counselling.

Ellis, A. (1991b). The revised ABC's of Rational-emotive therapy (RET). *Journal of Rational-Emotive & Cognitive Behaviour Therapy, 9*, 139–72.
An important article in which Ellis discusses: basic human goals and values; the ABCs of emotional disturbance; interactions of As, Bs and Cs; the ABCs of interpersonal relationships; and using the ABCs in counselling. Ellis emphasizes and explains the interactions of cognitions, emotions and behaviours in the theory and practice of his approach.

Ellis, A. (1962). *Reason and Emotion in Psychotherapy*. Secaucus, NJ: Citadel.
The classic text in the early development of REBC. Ellis presents the theory and practice of his approach. He discusses the treatment of problems such as frigidity, impotence and schizophrenia. The book also contains material on group counselling, comparisons with other counselling approaches and objections to and limitations of the approach.

Ellis, A. & Grieger, R. M. (Eds.) (1977e, Vol. 1; 1986, Vol. 2). *Handbook of Rational-emotive Therapy*. New York: Springer.
These sourcebooks contain authoritative accounts of REBC theory, the dynamics of emotional disturbance and the main techniques used in the approach. In addition, the books contain chapters on specific applications of REBC, for instance to love problems.

Ellis, A. (1988). *How to Stubbornly Refuse to Make Yourself Miserable about Anything, Yes Anything.* Sydney: Pan Macmillan.

Every counselling practitioner is at risk of crooked thinking. An excellent way to learn about REBC is to apply it to yourself. This entertaining self-help book presents Ellis's views on emotional disturbance and on the importance of scientific thinking. Readers are then presented with a series of chapters showing them in simple language 'how to' take and maintain more control of their thoughts, feelings and actions. The book contains a number of self-help exercises.

Ellis, A. (1977a). *Anger: How to Live With and Without it.* Sydney: MacMillan Sun Books.

This self-help book takes the position that people are responsible for creating their anger because of difficulties in relinquishing childish demandingness. Readers are encouraged to dispute their self-angering philosophies and shown ways to think, feel, and act their way out of disturbing themselves with anger.

Further references

Ellis

Dryden, E. & Ellis, A. (1986). Rational-emotive therapy (RET). In W. Dryden & W. Golden (Eds.), *Cognitive-behavioural Approaches to Psychotherapy* (pp. 129–68). London: Harper & Row.

Dryden, W. (1989). Albert Ellis: An efficient and passionate life. *Journal of Counseling and Development, 67,* 539–46. (Interview with Albert Ellis)

Ellis, A. (1958a). *Sex without Guilt.* New York: Lyle Stuart.

Ellis, A. (1958b). Rational psychotherapy. *Journal of General Psychology, 59,* 35–49

Ellis, A. (1973). *Humanistic Psychotherapy: The Rational-emotive Approach.* New York: McGraw-Hill.

Ellis, A. (1976). *Homework Report.* New York: Institute for Rational-Emotive Therapy.

Ellis, A. (1977b). The basic clinical theory of rational-emotive therapy. In A. Ellis & R.F. Grieger (Eds), *Handbook of Rational-emotive Therapy* (pp. 3–34). New York: Springer.

Ellis, A. (1977c). Personality hypotheses of RET and other modes of cognitive-behaviour therapy. *The Counseling Psychologist 7(1),* 2–42.

Ellis, A. (1977d). *Irrational Ideas* (handout). New York: Institute for Rational-Emotive Therapy.

Ellis, A. (1980). Overview of the clinical theory of rational-emotive therapy. In R. Grieger & J. Boyd (Eds.) *Rational-emotive Therapy: A Skills-based Approach* (pp. 1–31). New York: Van Nostrand.

Ellis, A. (1985). *Overcoming Resistance: Rational-emotive Therapy with Difficult Clients.* New York: Springer.

Ellis, A. (1986a). Rational-emotive therapy approaches to overcoming resistance. In A. Ellis & R.M. Grieger (Eds.), *Handbook of Rational-Emotive Therapy* (Vol. 2, pp. 246–74). New York: Springer.

Ellis, A. (1986b). Application of rational-emotive therapy to love problems. A. Ellis & R.M. Grieger (Eds.) *Handbook of Rational-Emotive Therapy* (Vol. 2, pp. 162–82). New York: Springer.

Ellis, A. (1987). The impossibility of achieving consistently good mental health. *American Psychologist, 42,* 364–75.

Ellis, A. (1990) Is Rational-Emotive Therapy (RET) "Rationalist" or "Constructivist"? In A. Ellis & W. Dryden, *The Essential Albert Ellis* (pp. 114–41). New York: Springer.

Ellis, A. (1991a). My life in clinical psychology. In C.E. Walker (Ed.), *The History of Clinical Psychology in Autobiography*, (Vol. 1, pp. 1–37). Pacific Grove, CA: Brooks/Cole.

Ellis, A. (1991c). Using RET effectively: Reflections and interview. In M.E. Bernard (Ed.), *Using Rational-emotive Therapy Effectively* (pp. 1–33). New York: Plenum.

Ellis, A. (1991d). Rational-emotive family therapy. In A.M. Horne & J.L. Passmore (Eds.), *Family Counselling and Therapy* (2nd ed., pp. 403–34). Itasca, IL: Peacock.

Ellis, A. (1991e). Rational-emotive treatment of simple phobias. *Psychotherapy, 28*, 452–6.

Ellis, A. (1991f). Achieving self-actualization: The rational-emotive approach. In A. Jones & R. Crandall (Eds.), *Handbook of Self-Actualization* (Special Issue). *Journal of Social Behavior and Personality, 6(5)*, 1–18.

Ellis, A. (1992a). Brief therapy: The rational-emotive method. In S.H. Budman, M. F. Hoyt & S. Friedman (Eds.), *The First Session in Brief Therapy* (pp. 36–58). New York: Guilford Press.

Ellis, A. (1992b). Group rational-emotive and cognitive-behavioral therapy. *International Journal of Group Psychotherapy, 42*, 63–80.

Ellis, A. (1993a). Changing Rational-Emotive Therapy (RET) to Rational Emotive Behavior Therapy (REBT). *The Behavior Therapist, 16*, 257–8.

Ellis, A. (1993b). Reflections on rational-emotive therapy. *Journal of Consulting and Clinical Psychology, 61*, 199–201.

Ellis, (1993c). The rational-emotive therapy (RET) approach to marital and family therapy. *The Family Journal: Counselling and Therapy for Couples and Families, 1*, 292–307.

Ellis, A. (1993d). The advantages and disadvantages of self-help therapy materials. *Professional Psychology: Research and Practice, 24*, 335–9.

Ellis, A. (1993e). Vigorous RET disputing. In M.E. Bernard & J.L. Wolfe (Eds.), *The RET Resource Book for Practitioners* (p. II 7). New York: Institute for Rational-Emotive Therapy.

Ellis, A. (1993f). Rational-emotive imagery: RET version. In M.E. Bernard and J.L. Wolfe (Eds.), *The RET Resource Book for Practitioners* (pp. II 8–11). New York: Institute for Rational-Emotive Therapy.

Ellis, A., & Becker, I.M. (1982). *A Guide to Personal Happiness*. Hollywood, CA: Wilshire Book Co.

Ellis, A. & Bernard, M. (1986). What is rational-emotive therapy? In A. Ellis & R. M. Grieger (Eds.), *Handbook of Rational-emotive Therapy* (Vol. 2, pp. 3–30). New York: Springer.

Ellis, A. & Dryden, W. (1987). *The Practice of Rational-emotive Therapy*. New York: Springer.

Ellis, A. & Dryden, W. (1990). *The Essential Albert Ellis*. New York: Springer.

Ellis, A. & Dryden W. (1991). *A Dialogue with Albert Ellis*. Stony Stratford, UK: Open University Press.

Ellis, A. & Harper, R.A. (1961). *A Guide to Rational Living in an Irrational World*. Englewood Cliffs, NJ: Prentice-Hall.

Ellis, A. & Harper, R.A. (1975). *A New Guide to Rational Living*. Hollywood: Wilshire Book Co.

Ellis, A., Sichel, J., Yeager, R., DiMattia, D. & DiGuiseppe, R. (1989). *Rational Emotive Couples Therapy*. New York: Pergamon

Palmer, S. (1993a). In the counsellor's chair: Stephen Palmer interviews Dr. Albert Ellis. *Counselling, 4*, 171–4.

Palmer, S. (1993b). Rational emotive behavior therapy and counselling psychology: Stephen Palmer interviews Albert Ellis. *Counselling Psychology Review, 8* (4), 34–40.

Sichel, J. & Ellis, A. (1984). *RET Self-help Form*. New York: Institute for Rational-Emotive Therapy.

Others

Dryden, W. & Yankura, J. (1993). *Counselling Individuals: A Rational-emotive Handbook* (2nd ed.), London: Whurr.

Dyer, W. (1976). *Your Erroneous Zones.* London: Sphere Books.

Grieger, R.M. (1986). The process of rational-emotive therapy. In A. Ellis & R.M. Grieger (Eds.), *Handbook of Rational-emotive Therapy* (Vol. 2, pp. 203–12). New York: Springer.

Walen, S., DiGuiseppe, R. & Dryden, W. (1992). *A Practioner's Guide to Rational-emotive Therapy.* New York: Oxford University Press.

Ellis on cassette (illustrative)

Ellis, A., (1977d). *A Garland of Rational Songs* (with songbook). New York: Institute for Rational-Emotive Therapy.

Ellis, A. (1982b). *Solving Emotional Problems.* New York: Institute for Rational-Emotive Therapy.

Ellis, A. (1984). *How to be Happy though Human.* New York: Institute for Rational-Emotive Therapy.

Ellis, A. (1987b). *How to Stop Worrying and Start Living.* Washington, DC: Psychology Today Tapes.

For further details of REBC self-help materials, contact: Institute for Rational-Emotive Therapy, 45 East 65th Street, New York, NY 10021–6593, USA. Telephone: (212) 535–0822. Fax: (212) 249–3582.

Ellis on film

Ellis, A. (1965). Rational-emotive therapy. In E. Shostrom (Ed.). *Three Approaches to Psychotherapy.* Santa Ana, CA: Psychological Films.

Journal

Each quarter the *Journal of Rational-Emotive & Cognitive-Behavior Therapy* publishes articles on REBC theory, research and practice. Subscription details are available from: Human Sciences Press, Inc., 72 Fifth Avenue, New York, NY 10011–8004, USA.

THIRTEEN
Cognitive Counselling

PREVIEW

- *Beck's cognitive counselling views clients as faulty processors of information. People have the capacity for primal and higher level cognitive processes. As well as voluntary thoughts, people possess schemas and automatic thoughts. Schemas are relatively stable cognitive patterns that influence people's beliefs. When activated, dysfunctional schemas and beliefs can lead people to bias information systematically.*

- *Automatic thoughts, which occur very rapidly and at the fringe of awareness, are not so deeply buried as schemas and reflect schema content. Dysfunctional beliefs can lead to systematic cognitive errors. Four fundamental emotions – sadness, joy, anger and anxiety – are reflected in basic cognitive themes. A continuity exists between normal emotions and emotions and behaviour found in psychiatric disorders.*

- *Evolutionary and genetic causes contribute to how people think and behave. People acquire cognitive vulnerability through childhood traumas, negative treatment in childhood, social learning and inadequate experiences for learning coping skills. Cognitive vulnerability can be activated by perceived losses, increased demands and stress.*

- *Factors maintaining psychological disorders include failure to turn off hypervalent modes, inability to reality-test dysfunctional interpretations, resistances to change, and unhelpful influences in people's daily lives. Beck's cognitive models of depression, anxiety disorders, distressed couple relationships and personality disorders are overviewed.*

- *The main goal of cognitive counselling is to re-energize the client's reality-testing system. Cognitive counselling teaches clients how to evaluate and modify their thinking. In addition, counselling focuses on symptom relief and on helping clients to develop adaptive behaviours.*

- *Cognitive counselling, which tends to be highly structured and short-term, starts with defining problems and case conceptualization. Counsellors perform a number of roles: offering accepting relationships, collaborating with clients to investigate problems, assisting clients to question the validity of their thinking and acting as guides in helping clients to reality-test their possible errors in logic. Questions are the cognitive counsellor's main verbal tool.*

- *Cognitive techniques focus on eliciting and identifying automatic thoughts, reality-testing and correcting automatic thoughts, identifying and underlying beliefs and modifying underlying beliefs.*

- *Behavioural techniques may be used to support both cognitive and behavioural change. Behavioural techniques include activity scheduling, conducting experiments to test thinking, and rehearsing behaviour and role-playing.*

- *Cognitive counselling emphasizes relapse prevention and has wide applicability.*

INTRODUCTION

Cognitive counselling, better known as cognitive therapy, was initially developed in the early 1960s by Dr Aaron Beck of the University of Pennsylvania in America. Cognitive counselling takes an information-processing approach to clients based on the premise that the way people interpret their experience determines the way that they feel and act. During clients' cognitive development they learn incorrect habits of processing and interpreting information. Cognitive counselling aims to correct specific habitual errors in how clients think. Counsellors attempt to unravel clients' distortions and help them to learn different and more realistic ways of processing information.

Beck acknowledges the influences on the theory and practice of cognitive counselling of many philosophers, psychologists and psychiatrists (Beck & Weishaar, 1989; Beck & Rush, in press). Regarding cognitive theory, the Greek stoic philosophers, philosophers such as Kant and Heidegger, and psychiatrists like Adler and Sullivan had previously emphasized the importance of individuals' views of themselves and their personal worlds in influencing behaviour. Freud's theory contributed to Beck's structuring cognition into primary and secondary processes. Kelly's concept of personal constructs is similar to Beck's idea of schemas (Beck et al., 1990).

Influences on the practice of cognitive counselling include Rogers, Ellis and the behaviour therapists. The gentle style of questioning and emphasis on unconditional acceptance owes much to person-centred counselling. The emphasis on finding solutions to conscious problems resembles rational emotive behaviour counselling. Setting goals and session agendas, testing hypotheses, using specific behaviour change procedures and assigning homework are among the contributions of behaviour therapy.

Aaron Beck

Aaron Temkin 'Tim' Beck was born on 18 July, 1921 in Providence, Rhode Island, the fourth, but third surviving, son of Russian Jewish immigrant parents. In 1919 Beck's parents lost their only daughter in an influenza epidemic, an event that precipitated a deep depression in his mother which lasted off and on for the rest of her life. Aged seven, Beck had a near fatal illness which reinforced his mother's over protectiveness. While his father was tranquil, Beck did not like his mother's moody, inconsistent and excitable behaviour. Beck's father, who ran a printing business, encouraged his interest in science and nature. At high school Beck edited the school paper and graduated first in his class. While growing up Beck developed many anxieties and phobias, including fears of abandonment, surgery, suffocation, public speaking and heights (Weishaar, 1993).

In 1942 Beck graduated from Brown University, having majored in English and political science. Beck took pre-medical courses both before and after graduating and, in 1946, he received his M.D. from Yale University School of Medicine. From 1946 to 1948 he served a rotating internship and a residency in pathology at the Rhode Island Hospital. In 1950 he started a neurology residency at the Cushing Veterans Administration Hospital in Framingham, Massachusetts. Due to a shortage of psychiatry residents Beck was forced, against his wishes, to complete a six month rotation in psychiatry. He decided to remain in psychiatry and from 1950–2 he was a Fellow in psychiatry at the Austen Riggs Center in Stockbridge, Massachusetts. In 1953 the American Board of Psychiatry and Neurology certified Beck in psychiatry, and in 1958 Beck graduated from the Philadelphia Psychoanalytic Institute.

Since 1954 Beck has been a faculty member in the Department of Psychiatry of the University of Pennsylvania Medical School, becoming an assistant, associate and full professor in 1959, 1967 and 1971, respectively. The period from 1960–3 saw the development of cognitive therapy. Beck was researching and re-examining psychoanalytic theory and ended by discarding it. Beck observes: 'There's nothing that I've been associated with since 1963 the seeds of which were not in the 1963 and 1964 articles. That was the critical period: changing from psychoanalysis to developing a new theory of therapy' (Weishaar, 1993, p. 21). Beck's process of developing theory is that (a) he observes patients, (b) he develops ways of measuring these observations, (c) he formulates a theory if the observations are validated by a number of cases, (d) he designs interventions congruent with the theory, and (e) over time and through further experimentation he continues to asses whether the theory is confirmed or negated. When developing theory Beck also uses self-observation.

Beck has authored or co-authored over 300 articles. His books include *Cognitive Therapy and the Emotional Disorders; Cognitive Therapy of Depression,* co-authored with Rush, Shaw and Emery; *Anxiety Disorders and Phobias,* co-authored with Emery and assisted by Greenberg; *Love Is Never Enough;* and *Cognitive Therapy of Personality Disorders,* co-authored with Freeman and associates. Tests and measures that Beck has developed with colleagues include the Beck Depression Inventory, the Beck Hopelessness Scale, the Suicide Intent Scale, the Suicide Ideation Scale, and the Beck Self-Concept Test.

In 1979 Beck was awarded the American Psychiatric Association's Foundation Fund Prize for Research in Psychiatry for his research in depression and the development of cognitive therapy and, in 1989, the American Psychological Association's Distinguished Scientific Award for Applications of Psychology. In 1987 Beck was elected a Fellow of Britain's Royal College of Psychiatrists.

Beck continues to be highly active in writing, research and training. In 1950 Beck married his wife Phyllis, a continuing source of strength and support, who developed her own career by becoming a Pennsylvania Superior Court Judge. The Becks have four adult children and many grandchildren.

ASSUMPTIONS
Primal and higher level cognitive processing

The distinction between primal and higher level cognitive processing resembles Freud's distinction between primary and secondary processes. People possess primal cognitive processes that mediate both normal and pathological reactions. Thinking based on primary cognitive processing tends to be 'primitive' and to conceptualize situations in global and relatively crude ways (Beck & Rush, in press). In addition, humans are capable of higher levels of cognitive processing that are more specific and refined. When functioning properly, higher level processes test reality and correct primal, global conceptualization. However, in psychopathology these corrective functions become impaired and primary responses can escalate into full-blown psychiatric disorders.

Schemas

Sometimes the terms schemas, rules and basic beliefs are used more or less interchangeably. However, Beck observes that: 'More strictly, "schemas" are the cognitive structures that organize experience and behaviour; "beliefs" and "rules" represent the content of the schemas and consequently determine the content of the thinking affect and behavior' (Beck *et al.*, 1990, p. 4). Schemas are relatively stable cognitive patterns that influence through people's beliefs how they select and synthesize incoming data. Schemas are not pathological by definition – they may be adaptive or maladaptive. They are analogous to George Kelly's (1955) formulation of 'personal constructs'. People categorize and evaluate their experiences through a matrix of schemas.

Schemas may be general or specific. People may even have competing schemas. Schemas are organized by both content and functions. The content of schemas ranges from personal relationships to inanimate objects. Five main categories of schemas by their functions are:

1. *cognitive* schemas, concerned with such activities as abstracting, interpreting, recalling and evaluating self and others;

2. *affective* schemas, responsible for generating feelings;

3. *motivational* schemas, dealing with wishes and desires;

4. *instrumental* schemas, that prepare people for action; and

5. *control* schemas, that involve self-monitoring and inhibiting, modifying and directing actions.

Systems of interlocking schemas are responsible for the sequence extending from receiving a stimulus to responding to it. Once incoming data are selected, the psychological sequence moves from evaluating them to arousing affect and motivation and then to selecting and implementing a relevant strategy. For example, exposure to a danger stimulus triggers the 'danger schema', which begins processing the information. The person uses the cognitive schema to interpret the situation as dangerous, then activates the affective schema by feeling anxiety. This activates the motivational schema, compelling the person to get away, which in turn activates the action or instrumental schema of becoming mobilized to run. The person can then use the control schema to inhibit or direct the action of running away.

Schemas possess structural qualities such as degree of breadth, flexibility, and relative prominence in a person's cognitive organization. Also, according to the degree of energy invested in them at any time, schemas can range from latent to hypervalent. When schemas are hypervalent, they are prepotent and easily triggered. Psychopathology is characterized not only by the activation of inappropriate schemas but, in all probability, by their crowding out or inhibiting more adaptive schemas.

Information processing and schemas

Information processing is based on fundamental beliefs embedded in schemas. The term *cognitive vulnerability* refers to humans' cognitive frailty. (Beck & Weishaar, 1989). Because of their schemas, each person has a set of unique vulnerabilities and sensitivities that predispose them to psychological distress. People's schemas and beliefs influence the way they process data about themselves. When they possess any of the disorders appearing in the revised third edition of the *Diagnostic and Statistical Manual of Mental Disorders* (American Psychiatric Association, 1987), their dysfunctional schemas and beliefs lead them systematically to bias information in unhelpful ways.

Beck (Beck *et al.*, 1990) gives the example of Sue, who heard noises coming from the next room where her boyfriend Tom was working on some chores. Sue's first thought was that 'Tom is making a lot of noise'. However, Sue's information processing continued and she made the following interpretation of her experience: 'Tom is making a lot of noise *because he's angry at me.*' Her attribution of causality was produced by a conditional schema or belief that 'If an intimate of mine is noisy, it means he is angry at me.' Further down her hierarchy were the beliefs that 'If people reject me, I will be all alone' and 'Being alone will be devastating'. At the most basic level Sue had the belief of schema that 'I am unlovable'. When activated, Sue's basic belief (or schema) 'I am unlovable' acted as 'feed-forward' mechanism moulding the information about Tom's behaviour in a way to fit the schema. Beck provides an alternative explanation that might have better fitted the information available to Sue, namely that 'Loud hammering is a sound of exuberance.'

Automatic thoughts

Automatic thoughts are less accessible to awareness than voluntary thoughts, but not so deeply buried as beliefs and schemas. These thoughts are similar to what Freud termed 'preconscious' thinking and what Ellis terms 'self-statements'. People's self-evaluations and self-instructions appear to be derived from deeper structures – their self-schemas. Automatic thoughts reflect schema content – deeper beliefs and assumptions. In normal functioning self-appraisals and self-evaluations operate more or less automatically to help people stay on course. However, in psychopathology certain automatic thoughts operate to steer people off course. Most psychological disorders are characterized by specific systematic biases in processing information. For example, depressive disorders are characterized by a negative view of self, experience and the future, and anxiety disorders by fear of physical or psychological danger.

What are some salient characteristics of automatic thoughts? First, automatic thoughts are part of people's internal monologue – what and how they talk to themselves. Second, these thoughts can take the form of words, images or both. Third, such thoughts occur very rapidly and usually at the fringe of awareness. Fourth, automatic thoughts precede emotions, including feeling and inhibitions. For instance, people's emotional responses to each other's actions follow from their interpretations rather than from the actions themselves. Fifth, these thoughts are generally plausible to people who assume that they are accurate. Sixth, these thoughts have a recurring quality, despite people trying to block them out. Seventh, even though they may not be expressed verbally, automatic thoughts affect tone of voice, facial expression and gestures. Eighth, automatic thoughts can be linked together with more subtle thoughts underlying more obvious thoughts. For instance, a husband boasts about his wife's cooking. The wife's secondary obvious automatic thought is 'He's fishing for a compliment', while the primary subtle automatic thought is 'They'll think that's all I'm good for' (Beck, 1988). Ninth, though automatic thoughts are often hard to identify, counsellors can train clients to pinpoint these thoughts with great accuracy.

Cognitive errors

Dysfunctional beliefs embedded in cognitive schemas contribute to systematic cognitive errors, more accessible in automatic thoughts, that both characterize and maintain psychopathology. Following are some of the main information processing errors that interfere with logical thinking (Beck & Rush, in press; Beck & Weishaar, 1989).

• *Arbitrary interference.* The process of drawing specific conclusions without supporting evidence and sometimes in the face of contradictory evidence. An example of arbitrary inference is that of the working mother who after a busy day concludes, 'I am a terrible mother'.

• *Selective abstraction.* Selectively attending to a detail taken out of context at the same time as ignoring other more salient information. An example of selective abstraction is that of the boyfriend who becomes jealous at seeing his girlfriend tilt her head towards a man at a noisy party in order to hear him better.

• *Overgeneralization.* Drawing a general rule or conclusion from one or a few isolated incidents. Applying the rule too broadly and to unrelated situations. An example of overgeneralization is the woman who concludes after a disappointing date, 'All men are alike. I'll always be rejected.'

• *Magnification and minimization.* Evaluating particular events as far more or far less important than they really are. An example of magnification is the student who catastrophizes 'If I appear the least bit nervous in class it will mean disaster.' An example of minimization is that of a man describing his terminally ill mother as having a 'cold'.

• *Personalization.* Having a tendency without adequate evidence to relate external events to oneself. For instance concluding, when an acquaintance walking down the opposite side of a busy street does not acknowledge a wave of greeting, 'I must have done something to offend him/her.'

• *Dichotomous thinking.* Black-and-white, either-or, and polarized thinking are other terms for dichotomous thinking. Thinking in extreme terms, for instance, 'Unless I do extremely well on this exam, I am a total failure.'

In his book on the problems of distressed couples, *Love Is Never Enough*, Beck (1988) lists a further five cognitive errors or distortions.

• *Tunnel vision.* Related to selective abstraction, in tunnel vision people perceive only what fits their state of mind, even though this may be only part of a much larger situation. An example of tunnel vision is the husband who cannot think of a single positive thing done for him by his wife, even though this is far from the case.

• *Biased explanations.* People in distressed relationships tend to make negative attributions about each other. They can too readily assume that there are malicious or unworthy motives behind their partner's 'offensive' actions. For instance, one partner may attribute their marital problems to the other's defective character.

• *Negative labelling.* Stemming from biased explanations, partners proceed to attach critical labels to each other's actions. Then they react to the labels they have attached to each other, for instance 'inconsiderate' or a 'bully', as though they were the real thing. At worst, they may 'devilize' their partner, to use Ellis's term.

• *Mind reading.* Mind reading can be divided into two further errors: 'I can tell what my partner is thinking' and 'My partner should be able to tell what I am thinking'. Partners can damage their relationships by making assumptions based on either error.

• *Subjective reasoning.* Subjective reasoning relates to the belief that if one feels an emotion strongly enough, then it must be justified.

Relation of cognition to emotion

Four fundamental emotions – sadness, joy, anxiety and anger – are reflected in basic cognitive themes. Sadness and joy relate to failing to attain or attaining positive goals. People experience sadness when they perceive a loss – for instance, of a loved one, of status, or of disconfirmed positive expectations. The disruption of a valued personal relationship can also evoke sadness. A common consequence of sadness is that people withdraw their investment and energy from the source of disappointment. Joy or elation is evoked when people perceive a gain, for instance expressions of affection or attaining a goal.

Anxiety and anger are responses to perceived threats either to oneself or to people and things that one values. Anxiety (Beck & Emery, 1985) serves to draw attention to concerns about physical vulnerability, being hurt or killed, and psychological vulnerability, being devalued. Anxiety may lead to withdrawal or appeasement in face of the threat. Anger, on the other hand, focuses on the offensive qualities of the threat and may lead to aggressive self-defence or to counterattack.

The four emotions are linked to the mobilization and maintenance of basic cognitive structures and strategies through their attachment to people's pleasure and pain centres. Activities directed towards survival and reproduction lead to pleasure when successfully enacted and to 'pain' when thwarted. Expecting and experiencing pleasure strengthens behaviours directed towards survival and bonding. Experiencing anxiety serves to lessen the changes of potentially dangerous or self-defeating actions.

Continuity hypothesis

A continuity exists between 'normal' emotions and behaviours and the emotions and behaviours found in psychiatric disorders. The highly dysfunctional emotions and behaviours found in such disorders are exaggerations of normal adaptive processes (Beck, 1976, 1991). For example, in depression, sad feelings and withdrawal behaviours are intensifications of usual reactions to loss, deprivation and failure. In mania, there is an excess of euphoria and goal-directed activity. In anxiety disorders, a heightened sense of vulnerability to a wide variety of threats and perceived dangers elicits debilitating anxiety feelings and self-defeating avoidance behaviours.

Beck believes that much can be learned about normal psychological functions from the study of psychopathology. For example, the overconcern about physical danger in phobias, such as heights, crowded places and in relation to small animals, points to similar sources of anxiety in the psychology of normal people.

Evolutionary origins of cognition and behaviour

The cognitive structures and schemas relevant to depression, anxiety disorders and personality disorders reflect our evolutionary history (Beck, 1991; Beck et al., 1990). Beck writes: 'It is reasonable to consider that the notion of long-standing cognitive-affective motivational processes influence our automatic processes: the way we construe events, what we feel, and how we are disposed to act' (Beck et al., 1990, p. 24). Much animal behaviour is regarded as programmed, with underlying processes reflected in overt behaviour. Though there are risks in extrapolating from animal to human ethology, similar developmental processes may be operative in humans. Animal analogies may clarify many aspects of normal and abnormal human behaviour. For instance, observations or primate behaviour seem highly relevant to depressed behaviour in humans.

'Strategies' are forms of programmed behaviour designed to serve biological goals. By means of natural selection humans evolved strategies and programmes to maintain life and promote reproduction. However, humans have altered their environment more rapidly than nature has altered their automatic adaptive strategies. Consequently, in a highly individualized and technological culture, certain evolutionary-derived strategies become problematic. Variability in the gene pool may account for individual differences in programmed strategies.

Regarding anxiety and anger, Beck (Beck & Emery, 1985) suggests four 'primal' survival strategies – fight–flight–freeze–faint – to perceptions of threat. Also, he proposes that strategies associated with traditional personality disorders may have possible antecedents in our evolutionary past (Beck *et al.*, 1990). The dramatic strategy of the histrionic personality may have roots in the display rituals of non-human animals. The attack strategy of the antisocial personality may have roots in predatory behaviour.

Human strategies may be adaptive or maladaptive depending on their circumstances. The strategies adopted by people with personality disorders are maladaptive exaggerations of normal strategies. For instance, with the dependent personality disorder the cognitive substrate or basic belief is 'I am helpless' which leads to a strategy of attachment based on fear of abandonment. With the avoidant personality disorder, the basic belief is 'I may get hurt', which leads to strategy of avoidance.

Role of genetic factors

Mention was made of the role of evolution in laying the foundations for cognitive schemas and behavioural strategies. In addition, biological factors, such as variation in the gene pool, differentiate individuals in terms of their vulnerability to different kinds of distress. For instance, predisposing factors in depression are hereditary susceptibility and diseases that cause persistent neurochemical abnormalities.

Beck (Beck *et al.*, 1990) regards the evidence as strong for relatively stable temperamental and behavioural differences being present at birth. These innate 'tendencies' can be strengthened or weakened by experience. For instance, because of the quality of their interpersonal interactions and learning experiences, not all shy children become shy adults. Furthermore, mutually reinforcing cycles can be established between people's innate tendencies and others' reactions to them. For instance, individuals with innate care-eliciting tendencies can elicit care-producing behaviour in others, even beyond the age when such behaviour is adaptive.

ACQUISITION

This section on acquisition seeks to answer two main, yet interrelated, questions. First, how are cognitive schemas, automatic thoughts and cognitive errors initially acquired? Second, how are symptoms of psychiatric and other disorders activated? Here my focus is on dysfunctional cognitions and behaviour, though much that follows is relevant to acquiring adaptive cognitions and behaviour.

Acquisition of vulnerability

Cognitive counselling views the acquisition of the potential for psychological distress as the result of many interacting factors: evolutionary, biological, developmental and environmental. Though many of the factors are common across individuals, each individual has his own unique variations and way of attaching personal meaning to events. Below are some ways in which people acquire vulnerabilities.

Childhood traumas

Specific affect-laden incidents in childhood may create the potential for later distress by generating dysfunctional underlying beliefs (Beck & Emery, 1985). On example is the client who suffered a sense of doom and dread every Christmas season. His earliest memory of this feeling was when, aged seven, he saw his mother taken away to a tuberculosis sanatorium. His underlying belief became 'Something bad is going to happen over the Christmas holidays'. Another example is the five-year-old, who went away on a trip and returned to find the family dog dead, developing the belief 'When I'm not physically close to others, something bad will happen to them'. A further example is that of the seven-year-old, whose father left the family permanently after a marital fight, developing the underlying belief 'If I make others angry they will leave me'.

Negative treatment in childhood

Children can be subject to ongoing negative treatment which affects their self-esteem and later makes them vulnerable to psychological distress. Furthermore, parents and significant others can model abusive behaviour which their children later use against others. Beck (Beck, 1988; Beck *et al.*, 1990) provides the example of Gary, who had periodic violent outbursts against Beverly, whom he perceived as needling him all the time for not doing chores. Gary had suffered from being brought up in a household where people controlled each other through power and might. His father and older brother intimidated him and Gary developed a core schema 'I am a wimp'. To compensate for this belief, Gary adopted an interpersonal strategy of intimidation to control other people's inclination to dominate him as his family had done earlier.

Another example of childhood psychological abuse is that of a 28-year-old single woman who suffered from panic disorder (Beck *et al.*, 1990). One day when she had come home from school early her mother had screamed at her for waking her up, 'How dare you interrupt my sleep!'. Despite the fact that her mother drank a lot and was irritable and unpredictable, the woman developed the beliefs 'I am a bad kid' and 'I am wrong because I upset my mother'.

An instance of parental behaviour influencing later dysfunctional behaviour is that of the female client who kept criticizing herself unnecessarily. She lessened her self-criticism when she re-experienced childhood scenes of criticism and obtained the insight 'I criticize myself now not because it's right to do so, but because my mother always criticized me and I took this over from her' (Beck *et al.*, 1990, p. 91).

Social learning

Beck (Beck & Weishaar, 1989) endorses social learning theory. However, he also stresses that individuals have unique learning histories and idiosyncratic ways of attaching meanings to earlier events. Many reasons exist for personality disorders – for example, obsessive-compulsive and paranoid behaviour may develop either as a compensation or as the result of fear. However, the reinforcement of relevant strategies by parents and significant others is among the reasons for specific personality disorders. For instance, the dependent personality's help-seeking and clinging strategies may have been rewarded and attempts at self-sufficiency and mobility discouraged. Identification with other family members can be important in what personality disorder strategies get developed. In addition, negative life experiences may worsen an initial predisposition so that, for instance, the shy child turns into an avoidant personality.

Modelling is a key process in social learning theory. For example, marital partners have memories about how their parents behaved. Parental modelling provides a basis for rules, shoulds and should nots, that they bring into their own marriages. Beck (1988) provides the example of Wendy and Hal, who married very young and had trouble freeing themselves from parental modelling and reinforcement. Wendy had absorbed her mother's traditional rule that 'That role of a wife is to take care of her husband'. When Wendy failed to live up to the rule, she disparaged herself. Hal's father had stressed and rewarded perfectionism so much that Hal had developed the belief 'I can never do anything right'. His mother reinforced his self-doubts because she had a negative attitude towards men: 'Men can't do anything – they're weak and helpless'. Hal's rules and beliefs made him vulnerable both to creating and dealing with difficulties in his marriage.

Inadequate experiences for learning coping skills

People may have been inadequately provided with personal experiences to learn coping skills. For example, an element in the anxious person's assessment of a threat is their ability to cope with the threat. A boy who has developed the coping skills of dealing with a bully is likely to feel less anxious about the bully because of this. People who fail to develop adequate assertion skills may be more prone to depression because, first, they may lose self-esteem through others' actions and, second, they may then disparage themselves for lack of assertion. Most couples have learned insufficient skills in marital communication 'and so unwittingly produce continual abrasions, misunderstandings, and frustrations' (Beck, 1988, p. 275). The following are rules of conversation etiquette that may have been inadequately learned: tuning in to your partner's channel, giving listening signals, not interrupting, asking questions skilfully, and using diplomacy and tact. Boys may be especially prone to learning poor conversational skills since, more often than girls, they use words to gain status and dominance rather than to build bridges.

Activation of vulnerability

The term *cognitive shift* describes the shift of energy away from normal or higher level cognitive processing to a predominance of processing by pathological primal schemas. According to the disorder, energy is used to activate and inhibit unconscious patterns. For instance, in depression, generalized anxiety disorders, and panic attacks, the depressive, danger and panic modes are energized, respectively. The concept of mode reflects the manner in which a schema is expressed. For example, a schema such as 'I'm inadequate' may lead to a predominance of catastrophizing cognitions when the anxiety mode is activated and to a predominance of self-blame and hopelessness cognitions when the depressed mode is activated.

Thinking and behaving in ways that indicate vulnerability is a matter of degree. The continuity hypothesis suggests that anxiety depression and personality disorders are exaggerated mechanisms of normal functioning. People can acquire dysfunctional schemas, rules, automatic thoughts and behaviours and not have them activated so that they become full-blown disorders or highly damaging factors in marital relationships.

The cognitive shift gets triggered when people perceive their vital interests are at stake or have been affected. Often, initially, the shift into psychopathology is activated in response to major life stressors. Later the shift may be activated by less severe stressors (A. Butler, personal communication, 8 April 1994). With repeated activations over the life span, people become increasingly sensitive to triggers so that it takes subjectively less severe or salient stressors to precipitate a shift.

An example of the development of vulnerability to activation of the cognitive shift is that of a person with recurrent depression whose first episode may have been precipitated by a severe life stressor (e.g. being made redundant). Later episodes may be precipitated by relatively minor and less directly relevant stressors (e.g. hearing a friend in another field being made redundant) that take on inordinate meaning due to prior experiences.

Beck believes that in nonendogenous unipolar depression, people have a cognitive vulnerability that is triggered by stressful life events or a series of traumatic experiences. Beck (1983, 1991) suggests that there are two types of people – sociotropic and autonomous – prone to depression after experiencing a perceived loss. Socially dependent or sociotropic people highly value closeness and sharing. Their cognitive vulnerability is prone to be activated by social deprivation, disruptions in relationships and rejection. For example, for a sociotropic person who has lost a parent during childhood, the disruption of a close relationship may activate the schema of irreversible loss implanted by the earlier experience. Autonomous people value independent achievement, mobility and solitary pleasures. Their cognitive vulnerability is more likely to be activated after defeat, failure, immobilization or enforced conformity.

Three activating or precipitating factors are proposed for generalized anxiety disorders (Beck & Emery, 1985). First, people may face increased demands, for instance after the birth of a child or a job promotion. Second, there may be increased threat in an area of a person's life, for example, a new mother having a baby susceptible to infections, or an employee getting a hostile new boss. Third, stressful events and reversals may undermine confidence. An example is that of a young lawyer who failed his bar examination and, about the same time, was told by his girlfriend that she did not love him. Fearing for his future as a lawyer and family man, he became chronically anxious. Often precipitating factors interact with previous problems. The activating stressors gain their force from striking at people's specific vulnerabilities. For example, the mother who was chronically anxious after the birth of her child had experienced longstanding feelings of inadequacy. The young lawyer was already afraid that he lacked charm and now worried that he might never find a good mate.

MAINTENANCE

When people's cognitive vulnerabilities get activated and their cognitive processes go awry, why do they stay that way? Many people cope with the activation of their cognitive vulnerabilities by instigating adaptive cognitive and behavioural strategies. However, those with psychopathological disorders and those with deeply distressed marriages may remain stuck in faulty patterns of information processing and behaviour, to their own and other people's great disadvantage. There is no single cause why people continue to process information inefficiently. The evolutionary history of the species and genetic influences play a part. Also, the extent and depth of people's experiences of childhood traumas, negative treatment in childhood, faulty social learning and inadequate experiences of learning coping skills play their parts too.

Failure to turn off hypervalent modes

Beck develops the concept of 'mode' which he defines as 'a subsystem of the cognitive organisation . . . designed to consummate certain adaptational principles relevant to survival, maintenance, breeding, self-enhancement, and so on' (Beck & Emery, 1985). Among others, there are depressive, narcissistic, hostility, fear (or danger) and erotic modes. The type of schema that is evoked may be determined by the mode that is active at any given time. Normally there is a balance between modes so that when one is hypervalent for a long time, an opposing mode is activated. For instance, during a period of elation a person may become aware of negative feedback, or hostility may be counterbalanced by anxiety. In psychopathological disorders there seems to be an interference in the turn-off of the dominant mode. This results in systematically biased interpretations of negative events in depression, of positive events in mania and of dangerous events in anxiety disorders. Beck believes the reasons are obscure as to why the opponent mode remains relatively inactive, thus failing to contribute to a more balanced view of reality. One possibility is that neurochemical disturbances either stimulate a prolonged overactivity of the dominant mode or fail to stimulate sufficient activity in the opposing mode.

Inability to reality-test dysfunctional interpretations

Since clients accept their dysfunctional beliefs so readily during anxiety and depression, Beck believes that they have temporarily lost their ability to reality test their interpretations. Their information processing, based on dysfunctional schemas and beliefs, is permeated with automatic thoughts containing cognitive errors. (As a reminder, six of the main cognitive errors are: arbitrary inference, selective abstraction, overgeneralization, magnification and minimization, personalization and dichotomous thinking.) Cognitive errors are not only manifestations of psychopathology but also serve to maintain it by interfering with clients' ability to test the reality of their thinking. Clients think in rigid, stereotypical terms. They fail to distinguish adequately between fact and inference. Instead of viewing the content of their thoughts as testable hypotheses, they jump to cognitive conclusions on inadequate evidence and then view their conclusions as facts. They insufficiently take into account any feedback that might modify or negate their thoughts and perceptions. Thus information processing systems become closed, instead of remaining open to assessing new data as they become available.

Already I've mentioned the notion of each pathological disorder containing its own cluster of systematic biases in information processing. The notion of bias also applies in distressed marriages. Partners move from altruism to egocentricity and along the way either or both partners develop a 'negative cognitive set' about the other consisting of biased expectations, observations and conclusions. In short, virtually everything their partner says, does, thinks or feels is interpreted negatively. People with low self-esteem can also become systematically biased against themselves and continually make unjustified negative observations about how their partner regards them.

Resistances to change

Many reasons exist for why people resist the notion of change. For instance, people may be fearful of the negative effects of their changing on others. Martha was a 42-year-old woman living with her mother and diagnosed as having a dependent personality disorder. Whenever she thought of moving she feared that this would kill her mother – and her mother reinforced this thinking (Beck *et al.*, 1990). Many highly anxious, depressed and suicidal people fear change as an unknown. Sometimes people fear the positive as well as the negative consequences of change, for instance having to deal with the added responsibility of a promotion or marriage.

Beck (1988) believes that partners in distressed relationships may need to confront many beliefs, possibly expressed in the form of automatic thoughts, that weaken their motivation for change. He divides these dysfunctional and exaggerated beliefs into the following clusters.

• *Beliefs about change.* Illustrative beliefs are: 'My partner is incapable of change', 'Nothing can improve our relationship', and 'Things will only get worse'.

• *Self-justifying beliefs.* For instance: 'It's normal to behave the way I do', 'It feels right to think the way I do', and 'He/she hurt me. He/she deserves to be hurt'.

• *Reciprocity arguments.* For instance, 'I won't make an effort unless my partner does', 'It's not fair for me to have to do all the work', and 'My partner hurt me badly in the past, so now he/she must do a lot to make up for it'.

• *The problem is my partner.* For instance: 'I had no problems in my life until we were married'. 'My partner is impossible', 'My partner doesn't care about improving our relationship'.

Other factors

Many other factors in daily life can maintain dysfunctional cognitions and behaviour. Children, adolescents and even adults may continue to live with significant others who provide them with negative experiences, model inefficient thinking and behaviour, and do not provide them with sufficient opportunities to develop coping skills. People may continue to be faced with external stressors, for instance a hostile boss. However, once people become depressed or develop anxiety disorders, they can find it even harder to deal with external stressors. In addition, there may be a reciprocal interaction effect in which depressed and anxious people trigger negative behaviours in others. For instance, people either slipping into depression or who are depressed may withdraw from others who in turn may reject or criticize them, thus exacerbating their tendencies to self-rejection and self-criticism. Also, people in distressed relationships can find it hard to reality-test their own interpretations of events when feeling highly threatened by their partner's anger and accusations.

COGNITIVE MODELS

Overviews of Beck's cognitive models of depression, anxiety disorders, distressed couple relationships and personality disorders are now presented.

Cognitive model of depression

Beck (1987) elaborated his basic model of depression into six separate but overlapping models which he named: cross-sectional, structural, stressor-vulnerability, reciprocal-interaction, psychobiological and evolutionary. For space reasons, only his basic formulation is presented here (Beck, 1991; Beck *et al.*, 1979). Key concepts include the following.

• *Cognitive triad.* Beck views depression not just as a mood state but as a cognitive state as well. Depression entails the activation of three major cognitive patterns known as the cognitive triad. The first component relates to clients' negative views of themselves as unlovable, worthless, helpless and lacking in ability to attain happiness. The second component relates to clients' negative views of their past and present experiencing of the world. Their personal world is extremely demanding and presents huge obstacles to achieving goals. The third component is a negative view of the future which is viewed as hopeless and unlikely to improve. This hopelessness may bring about ideas of suicide. These cognitive patterns lead to the motivational, behavioural and physical symptoms of depression. An illustrative motivational symptom is paralysis of the will. Inertia and fatigue are illustrative behavioural and physical symptoms, respectively.

• *Predisposing schemas.* Depressive schemas are formed early in life. Situations of loss similar to those originally embedding the schema may trigger a depression. Sociotropic and autonomous people can differ in what triggers their depression. Series of traumatic events may also activate depressions. As the depression worsens, depressive schemas become hypervalent to the point where clients may become unable to view their negative thoughts objectively and find themselves completely preoccupied with repetitive negative thoughts. Absolute beliefs related to depressed clients' schemas include 'I am worthless', 'I am unlovable' and 'I can't do anything right' (Beck, 1991).

• *Cognitive deficits and distortions.* The hypervalent depressive schemas and beliefs interfere with normal cognitive processing and impair perception, recall, inferences and long-term memory. Clients lose their ability to reality-test their interpretations of events. In addition, they become less efficient at problem solving. As dysfunctional schemas become more activated, so does the incidence of systematic cognitive errors, for instance arbitrary inference and selective abstraction. Dysfunctional automatic thoughts evolve from underlying schemas and beliefs. Following are the main characteristics of depressive thinking: a predominant emphasis on the negative aspects of life events; self-attribution of responsibility for problems across all situations; self-devaluation for falling short of one's own standards; overgeneralization of specific deficiencies into pervasive and lasting deficiencies; and a 'blind alley' view that problems cannot be resolved or ameliorated (Beck, 1987).

Cognitive model of anxiety disorders

The main cognitive theme in anxiety disorders is danger. Anxiety is a strategy in response to threat. In anxiety disorders the normal evolutionary survival mechanism of anxiety becomes exaggerated and malfunctioning. Beck (Beck & Emery, 1985) adopts Lazarus' (1966) distinction between primary and secondary appraisal. Primary appraisal is the first impression of a situation that suggests the situation is noxious. Then successive reappraisals are made concerning the nature and relevance of the threat to a person's vital interests, including physical and psychological injury. Secondary appraisal involves the person assessing his or her resources for dealing with the threat. The process takes place at the same time as evaluating the nature of the threat. As with depression, dysfunctional schemas and beliefs may predispose to anxiety. These dysfunctional beliefs may be activated by increased demands, threats and stresses which may interact with previous problems. Cognitive errors reflecting dysfunctional schema include overestimating the probability and severity of the threat, magnification of the negative consequences (catastrophizing), underestimating one's resources for dealing with the threat, and insufficiently taking into account support factors, for instance the presence of others who might help. In brief, anxious individuals maximize the likelihood of harm and minimize their ability to cope (Beck & Weishaar, 1989).

Cognitive model of distressed couples' relationships

Beck observes 'what attracts partners to each other is rarely enough to sustain a relationship' (Beck, 1988, p. 46). Poor communication skills are one reason for marital difficulties. In addition, partners bring much personal baggage into the relationship in terms of hidden expectations of each other and the relationship. The expectations in marriage are less flexible than in uncommitted relationships. Furthermore, much behaviour in marriage has idiosyncratic symbolic meanings attached to it revolving around symbols of love or rejection, security or insecurity.

When disappointment in a relationship sets in and emotions run high, partners lose some or virtually all of their ability to reality-test their interpretations of their own and each other's thoughts, feelings and actions. Instead they react to their 'invisible reality' which is likely to be based more on their internal states, fears and expectations than on what actually happens. Dysfunctional schemas and beliefs can be triggered leading to a negative cognitive set about the other person. A distressed couple's voluntary and automatic thinking contains numerous cognitive errors. Partners tend to fixate on what is wrong in their relationship rather than on what is right. They can develop a tendency to think in black and white terms about each other. They attach negative labels to each other, like insensitive, inconsiderate, selfish and rude, and then react to them. Furthermore, they can develop a tendency to regard these as permanent traits. They misperceive and misinterpret what the other says or does. They engage in mind reading and attribute undesirable and malicious motives to each other. They fail to check out the accuracy of their negative explanations and illogical conclusions.

In addition, partners send each other barbed messages that trigger hurt and anger. They perceive they have been wronged, get angry, feel impelled to attack, and attack. Hostility is part of a primitive fight-flight survival mechanism. However, acting on the primitive urge to attack is often destructive to the relationship. It increases the level of threat in the relationship and hence partners' tendencies to think in rigid and erroneous ways. Furthermore, hostility can increase partners' resistance to working on their relationship. Included among resistances to working on relationships are defeatist beliefs about change and seeing each other as the problem.

Cognitive model of personality disorders

Personality disorders, along with other kinds of psychopathology, partly represent evolutionary strategies that have been insufficiently adapted to today's individualized and technological society (Beck *et al.*, 1990). Also, genetic predispositions and differing learning experiences influence which disorders different individuals develop. Each personality disorder is characterized by a basic belief and a corresponding overt behavioural strategy. Different overt responses represent important structural differences in basic beliefs (or schemas). The dependent personality disorder has the basic belief, 'I am helpless' and the overt strategy of attachment. The corresponding beliefs and strategies in the other personality disorders are: avoidant disorder, 'I may get hurt', avoidance; passive aggressive disorder, 'I could be stepped on', resistance; paranoid disorder, 'People are potential adversaries', wariness; narcissistic disorder, 'I am special', self-aggrandizement; the histrionic disorder, 'I need to impress', dramatics; obsessive–compulsive disorder, 'Errors are bad. I must not err', perfectionism; antisocial disorder, 'People are there to be taken', attack; and schizoid disorder, 'I need plenty of space', isolation. Another way of looking at strategies is that each personality disorder reflects both overdeveloped and underdeveloped strategies: for example, in the paranoid disorder 'mistrust' is overdeveloped and 'trust' is underdeveloped. A fuller cognitive profile may be drawn for each personality disorder.

When particular schemas are hypervalent, their constituent schemas are readily triggered. In personality disorders a cognitive shift occurs in which there is a redirection or energy away from normal cognitive processing into the different schemas that constitute the disorders. As part of this process more adaptive schemas may get inhibited. Because of the tenacity of their dysfunctional schemas, cognitive counselling with clients with personality disorders is generally longer-term and involves a fuller exploration of the origin of schemas than for clients with depression or anxiety disorders.

PRACTICE
Goals

Cognitive counselling 'aims explicitly to "reenergize" the reality-testing system' (Beck *et al.*, 1990, p. 37). In varying degrees, clients with psychopathological disorders and couples in distressed relationships have lost the ability to reality-test dysfunctional interpretations. Cognitive counselling 'teaches patients to self-correct faulty cognitive processing and to bolster assumptions that allow them to cope' (Beck & Weishaar, 1989,

p. 288). While cognitive counselling may initially address symptom relief, its ultimate goal is to remove systematic biases in how clients think. In addition, cognitive counselling aims to impart behavioural skills relevant to clients' problems, for instance, listening and communication skills for distressed couples or assertion skills for shy people.

When working with clients' cognitions, goals include teaching them to: (1) monitor their negative automatic thoughts; (2) recognize the connections between cognition, affect and behaviour; (3) examine and reality-test the evidence for and against distorted automatic thoughts; (4) substitute more realistic interpretations for biased cognitions; and (5) learn to identify and alter the beliefs that predispose them to distort their experiences (Beck et al., 1979). Clients need not be highly intelligent to gain from cognitive counselling – in fact Beck's researches show no relationship between intelligence and cognitive counselling outcomes (Beck & Rush, in press).

Uses and limitations

Beck (Beck & Rush, in press) has listed five uses of cognitive counselling, which can also be viewed as goals. First, removing the symptoms of disorders, either by counselling on its own or in combination with medication. Second, reducing the likelihood of relapse once formal treatment, counselling or medication has stopped. Third, increasing compliance to taking recommended medication. Fourth, addressing specific psychosocial difficulties, such as marital discord and low self-esteem, that either preceded or were caused by the illness episode or psychopathologic syndrome. Fifth, modifying the underlying psychological beliefs (schemas) contributing to psychopathology and dysfunctional thinking and behaviour.

Cognitive counselling works best with clients who can focus on their automatic thoughts and take some responsibility for self-help. It is not recommended for clients with impaired reality testing, such as hallucinations and delusions, or for clients with impaired memory and reasoning abilities, such as with organic brain syndromes. For some disorders, such as recurrent major depressive episodes, a combination of cognitive counselling and medication is recommended.

Length of treatment

Cognitive counselling tends to be highly structured and short-term. The standard treatment for cognitive counselling for depression is 15 to 20 visits over 12 weeks. Clients with anxiety disorders generally receive from 5 to 20 sessions (Clark & Beck, 1988). Cognitive counselling is discontinued gradually with clients usually receiving booster sessions one or two months after termination. The treatment of personality disorders generally takes longer and may last for a year or more. Cognitive counselling sessions generally last for 45 minutes.

Problem definition and case conceptualization

At Beck's Center for Cognitive Therapy in Philadelphia, clients undergo a three hour intake protocol consisting of a clinical interview and psychological tests. The clinical interview provides a thorough history of the background factors contributing to the client's distress. The interview also assesses current level of functioning, prominent symptoms and expectations for counselling. The Beck Depression Inventory (Beck *et al.*, 1961), the Anxiety Checklist (Beck, 1978), and the Dysfunctional Attitudes Scale (Weissman, 1979) are prominent among psychological tests used during the intake protocol.

The initial interview has many purposes: initiating a relationship, providing a rationale for cognitive counselling, producing symptom relief and eliciting important information. Counsellors start to define problems. Definitions of problems entail both functional and cognitive analyses. The functional analysis seek to answer questions such as: 'What are the component parts of the problem?', 'How is it manifested?', 'In what situations does it occur?', 'What is its frequency, intensity and duration?', and 'What are its consequences?'. The cognitive analysis identifies the client's thoughts and images when emotion is triggered, the extent to which the client feels in control of thoughts and images, and predictions about the likelihood of the problem occurring and what will happen. From the beginning, counsellors train clients to monitor their feelings, thoughts and behaviour and to recognize the connections between them. An example of an early homework assignment might be asking clients to record their automatic thoughts when distressed.

During initial sessions, counsellors and clients draw up problem lists. Problem lists can consist of specific symptoms, behaviours or pervasive problems. Their function is to assign treatment priorities. Considerations in prioritizing treatment include magnitude of distress, symptom severity, and pervasiveness of theme. Counsellors approach each problem by choosing the appropriate cognitive and behavioural techniques to apply. Counsellors always offer a rationale for each technique. Also, both when suggesting and implementing techniques, counsellors elicit feedback from clients. While the early stages of counselling may focus on symptom removal, middle and later stages are more likely to emphasize changing how clients think.

In this book on personality disorders, Beck (Beck *et al.*, 1990) talks of a tentative conceptualization of the case as the first step in making a treatment plan. Counsellors need understand both the cognitive profile of clients' disorders and their unique beliefs. The case conceptualization contains the counsellor's hypotheses about the client's idiosyncratic dysfunctional beliefs and core schemas, their underlying goals, their specific vulnerabilities, and the particular stresses that interact with these vulnerabilities to activate the present pattern of symptoms. As new information becomes available, counsellors can drop, modify or add hypotheses into their formulation. Case conceptualizations are shared and discussed with clients. Some counsellors use blackboards or flip cards to demonstrate how clients' misinterpretation of reality is derived from their beliefs. Treatment plans based on case conceptualizations are tailored to the needs of individual clients.

An example of beliefs stemming from a core schema is that of Gary, who had a narcissistic personality disorder (Beck *et al.*, 1990). Gary used to have violent outbursts against his partner Beverly, whom he accused of needling him all the time for not doing certain chores. Gary's beliefs contained: a should, 'Beverly should show me more respect'; a must, 'I must control others' behaviour'; a special conditional belief, 'If I give them a chance, people will dump on me'; a fear, 'I will be dumped on'; emanating from a core schema 'I am a wimp'. The formulation contained a similar analysis of Beverly's beliefs emanating from her core schema, 'I am a helpless baby'.

Counsellor roles

In cognitive counselling, counsellors perform a number of roles.

Counsellors as offerers of relationships

In cognitive counselling the quality of the counsellor-client relationship is an important medium for improvement. Cognitive counselling is not an impersonal approach but one in which counsellors seek to understand their clients as individuals. Beck regards his counselling style as somewhat Rogerian (Beck & Rush, in press). Counsellors strive to create an emotional climate of genuine warmth and non-judgemental acceptance. They attempt to demystify counselling by using language that clients can understand. They treat clients with respect by offering rationales both for their overall approach and for each technique that they propose. In addition, they share responsibility for what happens in counselling by discussing case conceptualizations and involving clients in setting goals and session agendas. Also, cognitive counsellors elicit feedback from clients about both their suggestions and their behaviour. Counsellors are sensitive to signs of transference and allow reactions to them to be aired. They use transference reactions to identify and work with clients' automatic thoughts and interpersonal distortions.

With most personality-disordered clients, cognitive counsellors offer a closer and warmer relationship than in acute disorders, such as anxiety and depression. Counsellors can face problems of noncollaboration from clients, especially those with personality disorders (Beck *et al.*, 1990).

Counsellors as co-investigators with clients – collaborative empiricism

In addition to offering accepting and warm relationships, cognitive counsellors play an active role in the counselling process. Counsellors encourage clients to play an active role too. All the client's cognitions are viewed as testable hypotheses. Counsellors and clients collaborate together in the scientific endeavour of examining the evidence to confirm or negate the client's cognitions. Based on what clients say and how they say it, counsellors develop hypotheses that can identify cognitive errors as well as underlying beliefs. Counsellors then ask clients to comment on whether their hypotheses fit the facts. By this means, clients are encouraged both to view their thoughts as personal constructs of reality and to build their skills in evaluating their validity. Throughout the process of identifying and exploring the evidence for biased thinking, either the counsellor or the client take the more active role, as needed.

Counsellors as questioners – Socratic dialogue

Questions comprise the largest category of counsellor verbal statements. Questions reflect the basic empirical orientation of the approach and have the immediate goal of converting clients' closed belief systems into open systems. More specifically, questions seek to help clients: become aware of what their thoughts are; examine them for cognitive distortions; substitute more balanced thoughts; and make plans to develop new thought patterns. A basic awareness raising question is to ask clients 'What is going through your mind right now?'.

Counsellors use questioning rather than indoctrination and disputation. Conducted in an emotional climate of warmth and acceptance, the Socratic style of questioning assists clients to expand and evaluate how they think. Typical questions are 'Where is the evidence?', 'What is the logic?', 'What do I have to lose?', 'What do I have to gain?', 'What would be the worst thing that could happen?', and 'What can I learn from this experience?' (Beck & Emery, 1985).

Clients learn to ask themselves the same questions that their counsellors have asked. For instance, however plausible their automatic thoughts may 'feel', clients in distressed relationships can question their validity by asking themselves the following series of questions: 'What is the evidence in *favour* of my interpretation?', 'What evidence is *contrary* to my interpretation?', 'Does it *logically follow* from my spouse's actions that my spouse has the motive that I assign to him or her?', and 'Is there an *alternative* explanation for his or her behaviour?' (Beck, 1988).

Counsellors as guides – guided discovery

There are a number of different facets to guided discovery. Counsellors can operate as guides to assist clients to discover the themes that run through their present automatic thoughts and beliefs. This can be taken one stage further where counsellors and clients link the beliefs to analogous experiences in the past and collaboratively piece together the developmental history of the beliefs. Another use of guided discovery is that counsellors act as guides in assisting clients to reality-test their possible errors in logic by designing new experiences that involve the client experimenting with different behaviour. Counsellors do not use cajoling, disputation and indoctrination to assist clients to reality-test their thinking and adopt new beliefs. Instead they encourage clients to develop their own skills of using and assessing information, facts and probabilities in order to obtain more realistic perspectives than sometimes offered by their initial thoughts.

Cognitive techniques

Following are some of the main cognitive techniques used by cognitive counsellors to assist clients to replace their distorted automatic thoughts and beliefs with more realistic ways of processing information.

Eliciting and identifying automatic thoughts

In order to change their thinking, clients need first become aware of their thought processes. Included below are some specific techniques for eliciting and identifying automatic thoughts.

• *Providing a rationale.* Counsellors can provide a rationale for the importance of examining the connections between how clients think, feel and act. Furthermore, they can introduce the concept of automatic thoughts and provide an example of how underlying perceptions influence feelings: for instance, the feelings consequences of hearing a loud noise in the middle of the night would differ according to whether its cause was perceived as a burglar breaking in or as a window banging. They can communicate that a major assumption of cognitive counselling is that clients are experiencing difficulties in reality-testing the validity of their interpretations.

• *Questioning*. Clients may be questioned about automatic thoughts that occur during upsetting situations. Where clients experience difficulty recalling thoughts, imagery or role playing may be used. When questioning, counsellors observe clients carefully for signs of affect that may offer leads for further questioning.

• *Using a chalkboard*. When clients see their initial thoughts written up on the board, this may trigger them to reveal less obvious and more frightening thoughts.

• *Encouraging clients to engage in feared activities*. Frequently during sessions, clients are encouraged to engage in anxiety-evoking activities: for instance, making phone calls or writing letters they had been putting off. As they perform the activity, counsellors can ask the question 'What is going through your mind right now?'. Counsellors can also go with clients into real-life situations where they experience difficulty, for instance crowded places, and get them to verbalize what they think.

• *Focusing on imagery*. Gathering information about imagery can be an important way of accessing automatic thoughts. Though individual differences exist, clinical observations suggest that many people visualizing scenes react to them as though they were real.

• *Self-monitoring of thoughts*. Clients may be set homework in which they record their thoughts. They may complete a Daily Record of Automatic Thoughts log in which they record in their respective columns: (1) date; (2) situation leading to negative emotion(s); (3) emotion(s) felt and their degree on a 0–100% scale; and (4) automatic thought(s) and belief in automatic thought(s) on a 0–100% scale. Wrist counters may be used to help some clients learn to recognize automatic thoughts as they occur.

Reality-testing and correcting automatic thoughts

Techniques for assisting clients to treat their thoughts as hypotheses that require testing against reality and, if necessary, discarding, modifying or replacing include the following.

• *Socratic questioning*. Counsellors can frame a series of questions that lead clients to challenge the validity of their thinking and to learn that they can choose among alternative interpretations those which best fit the facts. A useful question in this loosening up process is: 'What's another way of looking at it?'.

• *Identifying cognitive errors*. Counsellors can teach clients what the common cognitive errors are, for instance arbitrary inference and magnification. Both during counselling and as homework, clients can be challenged to identify the errors in how they think.

The three-column technique may be used for this. In the first column clients describe a situation that elicits negative emotions; in the second, their automatic thoughts; and in the third, the types of errors in these thoughts.

• *Decatastrophizing.* In decatastrophizing the basic question is, 'So what if it happens?'. Areas covered in this technique include: the event's probability and severity, the client's coping capacity and support factors, and the client's ability to accept and deal with the worst possible outcomes.

• *Reattribution.* Reattribution techniques test automatic thoughts and underlying beliefs by considering alternative ways of assigning responsibility and cause. Clients can be encouraged to rate on a 0–100 scale the degree of responsibility they feel for negative events and feared outcomes. By means of questioning, the counsellor attempts to loosen them up by generating and evaluating alternative explanations.

• *Redefining.* Redefining problems entails making them more concrete and stating them in terms of what the client might do. For example, a lonely person who feels uncared for may redefine his or her problem as 'I need to reach out to other people and be caring' (Beck & Weishaar, 1989, pp. 309–10).

• *Decentring.* Decentring involves assisting clients to challenge their belief that everyone is focusing on them. Clients can be encouraged to evaluate more closely what others are doing: for instance, other students may be daydreaming, looking at their lecturer, or taking notes. In addition, clients can be asked to observe closely how frequently they attend to others. This may help them to realize how limited their observations are, and thus to infer that other people's observations are the same.

• *Rational responses.* Cognitive counsellors train clients in how to formulate more rational responses to their automatic thoughts. Again, questioning is an important way to assist clients in learning to use their inner monologue for rather than against themselves. An example is that of Wendy who was phoned by her husband Hal to say he was tied up at the office. Wendy's feeling was anger; her automatic though was, 'It's not fair – I have to work too. If he wanted to, he could be home on time'; her rational response to this automatic thought was, 'His job is different. Many of his customers come in after work.' (Beck, 1988, p. 264).

• *Daily recording of rational responses.* When ready, clients can be encouraged to fill out rational response and outcome columns on their Daily Record or Automatic Thoughts. In the outcome column, clients (1) re-rate their belief in their automatic thought(s) on a 0–100% scale and (2) specify what their subsequent emotions are and rate them on a 0–100% scale.

• *Imagery techniques.* Numerous imagery techniques are discussed by Beck and Emery (1985). Among these techniques are assisting clients to gain more realistic perspectives through repeated visualizations of fantasies, through projecting themselves into the future and looking back on their present situations, and by getting them to exaggerate images, for instance of harming others.

Identifying underlying beliefs

Underlying beliefs may be harder for counsellors and clients to access than automatic thoughts. Often they fall into one of three main belief clusters centring on issues of acceptance – for instance, 'I'm flawed and therefore unacceptable', competence – for instance, 'I'm inferior', and control – for instance 'I have no control'. Underlying beliefs are signposted by the themes in clients' automatic thoughts. Clients' behaviour, coping strategies and personal histories are additional sources for counsellors to form belief hypotheses. Most clients find it difficult to articulate their beliefs without assistance. Generally counsellors present hypotheses to clients for verification. Where clients disagree, counsellors can work with them to form more accurate statements to their beliefs.

Modifying underlying beliefs

Following are some cognitive techniques for modifying beliefs.

• *Socratic questioning.* Counsellors can use questions that encourage clients to examine their beliefs: for instance: 'Does the belief seem reasonable?', 'Can you review the evidence for it?', and 'What are the advantages and disadvantages of maintaining the belief?'.

• *Conducting cognitive experiments.* Together counsellors and clients can set up cognitive experiments that encourage clients to test the reality of their beliefs. Beck provides the example of Marjorie, who was afraid to make a mental commitment to her spouse, Ken, because she was afraid she might find out that she could not trust him. Her underlying belief was 'I must never allow myself to be vulnerable'. A consequence of her distorted thinking was that her aloof behaviour and fault finding created distance in their relationship. Beck set up a three-month experiment for her to test the hypotheses: 'If I totally commit myself to the relationship, look for the positive instead of the negative, I will feel more secure' (Beck, 1988, p. 224). As a result of the experiment Marjorie discovered that she was more secure and had fewer thoughts about leaving Ken.

• *Using imagery.* Imagery can be used to assist clients to 'relive' past traumatic events and so restructure their experiences and the beliefs derived from them.

• *Reliving childhood memories.* Beck (Beck *et al.*, 1990) believes that with chronic personality disorders it is crucial to use childhood material to assist clients in reviewing and loosening their underlying beliefs. By recreating 'pathogenic' developmental situations through role-playing and role reversal, clients have an opportunity to restructure or modify beliefs formed during this period.

• *Refashioning beliefs.* Counsellors can assist clients to refashion their beliefs. Beck gives the example of M.K., a director of a research institute at a major university who suffered from a major depressive disorder and generalized anxiety disorder. The client had strong beliefs of inadequacy and rejection which he crystallized as 'I must be the best at everything I do.' One of M.K.'s beliefs was refashioned thus: 'It is rewarding to succeed highly, but lesser success is rewarding also and has no bearing on my adequacy or inadequacy. In am adequate no matter what' (Beck & Rush, in press, p. 48).

Behavioural techniques

Behavioural techniques have many purposes in cognitive counselling. First, behavioural techniques can lay the foundation for later cognitive work. An issue arises whether to focus on behaviour first, cognition first, or both concurrently. Behavioural techniques may sometimes be used before cognitive techniques to promote symptom relief and enhance motivation. For instance, severely depressed clients may be encouraged to perform small tasks to counteract their withdrawal, get them involved in constructive activities, and open their mind to the possibility of gaining satisfaction from previously pleasurable activities. However, in contrast to normal people, depressed clients can change their behaviour markedly but do not necessarily change their negative hypervalent cognitions (Beck *et al.*, 1979). In working with couples, Beck (1988) concentrates on changing behaviour first since he regards it as easier to change actions than thinking patterns. Also, spouses may immediately reward each other's changes in behaviour.

Second, behavioural techniques can be used to assist clients in reality-testing their automatic thoughts and beliefs. A third use of behavioural techniques is, along with cognitive techniques, to assist clients to engage in feared activities. A fourth use is to train clients in specific behavioural skills. Since the uses of behavioural techniques overlap, they are not categorized according to purpose. Following are some of the main behavioural techniques used by cognitive counsellors.

• *Activity scheduling.* Activity scheduling is a form of timetabling. Planning specific activities with clients can be important in helping clients to realize that they can control their time. A principle of activity scheduling is to state what activity the client agrees to engage in rather than how much they will accomplish. Clients can set aside time each evening to plan their activities for the next day.

• *Rating mastery and pleasure.* Using 0–10 scales, clients can rate the degree of mastery and the degree of pleasure they experienced in each activity during the day. Mastery and pleasure ratings can give depressed clients an insight into the activities that reduce their dysphoria.

• *Conducting behavioural experiments.* Especially later in counselling, behavioural experiments may be designed to provide information that may contradict existing automatic thoughts, faulty predictions and underlying beliefs. A young man about to cancel a date because of the fear 'I won't know what to say' was encouraged to go on the date and treat not knowing what to say as an experimental hypothesis. The findings of this particular experiment disproved his hypothesis (Beck & Emery, 1985). In the earlier example of Marjorie, assuming she changed her behaviour along with her cognitions, she engaged in a behavioural as well as a cognitive experiment to test her underlying belief 'I must never allow myself to be vulnerable.'

• *Rehearsing behaviour and role-playing.* Behaviour rehearsal can be used to develop clients' skills for specific social and stressful situations. Demonstration and video feedback can be used as part of skills training. Behaviour rehearsals should have a number of trials and rehearse clients in a variety of responses. Also, clients can rehearse situations by using their imaginations.

• *Assigning graded tasks.* Often clients fail at tasks because they try to do too much too soon. Counsellors and clients can develop hierarchies of feared or difficult situations. Then clients can perform less threatening activities before moving on to more threatening ones.

• *Using diversion techniques.* Clients may be encouraged to engage in activities that divert them from their strong negative emotions and thinking. Such activities include work, play, socializing and doing something physical.

• *Assigning homework.* Homework forms an important part of cognitive counselling. Its purpose is both to shorten the time spent in counselling as well as facilitate the development of cognitive and behavioural skills for use after counselling. Homework assignments include self-monitoring, activities designed to reality-test automatic thoughts and underlying beliefs, implementing procedures for dealing with specific situations, and activities for developing cognitive skills such as identifying cognitive errors, rational responding and refashioning beliefs.

Termination and relapse prevention

Because it is generally a short-term structured approach, cognitive counselling tends to have its ending built into its beginning. From the outset counsellors discuss with clients criteria and expectations for termination. There are a number of ways of assessing progress including: relief from symptoms, changes in reported and observed behaviour, and changes in thinking both inside and outside counselling. Performance in homework assignments, such as filling in the Daily Record of Automatic Thoughts and carrying out specific tasks and experiments, also assists in assessing progress. In particular, counsellors look out for clients' ability to reality-test and, if necessary, modify or discard distorted interpretations. Often termination is gradual, say from weekly to biweekly sessions, followed by booster sessions one and two months after termination.

Cognitive counselling lays great stress on relapse prevention. Clients are taught to reality-test their interpretations as a self-help skill. Homework assignments not only build their skills for real life during counselling but prepare them to manage on their own afterwards. Clients are assisted in anticipating and developing strategies to deal with future difficulties and setbacks. Also, the availability of booster sessions encourages clients to use and maintain their enhanced information processing abilities after counselling.

Other applications

Cognitive counselling has been used with all ages, from children to the elderly. Beck (Beck & Rush, in press) reports that several controlled studies have shown it to be at least as effective as antidepressant medication in treating elderly depressed clients. Cognitive counselling has been used for group work with families. Some new applications of cognitive counselling include working with clients with schizophrenia, post-traumatic stress disorders, substance abuse problems, hypertension and dissociative disorders as well as with clients who have committed sexual offences, such as exhibitionism and incest. Beck and Weishaar (1989) observe that, with the current emphasis on containing costs, cognitive counselling's short-term approach will be increasingly popular with both third-party payers and clients.

CHAPTER REVIEW AND SELF-REFERENT QUESTIONS

Chapter review questions

1. What is the difference between primal and higher level cognitive processing?

2. What are schemas and why are they so important?

3. What are automatic thoughts and why are they so important?

4. What are cognitive errors and why are they so important?

5. What is the relation of cognition to emotions?

6. What is the continuity hypothesis?

7. What are Beck's views on (a) the evolutionary and (b) the genetic causes of cognitions and behaviour?

8. What is the nature and role of each of the following factors in helping people acquire cognitive vulnerability: childhood traumas, negative treatment in childhood, social learning, and inadequate experiences for learning coping skills?

9. What does the term cognitive shift mean?

10. What are some factors activating cognitive vulnerability?

11. What is the nature and role of each of the following factors in helping people maintain cognitive vulnerability: failure to turn off hypervalent modes, inability to reality-test dysfunctional interpretations, resistances to change, and other factors in clients' daily lives?

12. Outline the main points of the cognitive model of depression.

13. Outline the main points of the cognitive model of anxiety disorders.

14. Outline the main points of the cognitive model of distressed couple relationships.

15. Outline the main points of the cognitive model of personality disorders.

16. Critically discuss the goals of cognitive counselling.

17. How do cognitive counsellors define problems and conceptualize cases?

18. Describe the nature of the counsellor-client relationship in cognitive counselling.

19. What does the term collaborative empiricism mean?

20. In the context of cognitive counselling, what does the term Socratic dialogue mean?

21. What does the term guided discovery mean?

22. What are some of the main cognitive techniques for eliciting and identifying automatic thoughts?

23. What are some of the main cognitive techniques for reality-testing and correcting automatic thoughts?

24. How do cognitive counsellors approach identifying underlying beliefs?

25. How do cognitive counsellors approach modifying underlying beliefs?

26. What are the purposes of using behavioural techniques in cognitive counselling?

27. Describe each of the following behavioural techniques: activity scheduling, rating mastery and pleasure, conducting behavioural experiments, rehearsing behaviour and role-playing, assigning graded tasks, using diversion techniques, and assigning homework?

28. How do cognitive counsellors deal with relapse prevention?

Self-referent questions

1. List any significant factors when you were growing up that may have contributed to your acquiring faulty ways of processing information.

2. Think of a specific problem in your life. Elicit and identify some of your automatic thoughts regarding it.

3. Identify characteristic cognitive errors, if any, in the way you process information.

4. Identify an automatic thought in a problem area and challenge it by means of Socratic questioning.

5. In a problem area, identify a thought that lends itself to being reality-tested through changing your behaviour. Design and implement a behavioural experiment to reality-test your thought.

6. What relevance, if any, has the theory and practice of cognitive counselling for how you counsel?

7. What relevance, if any, has the theory and practice of cognitive counselling for how you live?

Annotated bibliography

Beck, A.T., Rush, A.J., Shaw, B.F. & Emery, G. (1979). *Cognitive Therapy of Depression.* New York: John Wiley.
This book presents Beck's cognitive model of depression. The bulk of the book is a clinical handbook devoted to practical aspects of treating depressed clients, for instance the counselling relationship, the application of both cognitive and behavioural techniques, and problems related to termination and relapse.

Beck, A.T. & Emery, G. (1985). *Anxiety Disorders and Phobias: A Cognitive Perspective.* New York: Basic Books.
Part 1 of the book, written by Beck, is entitled 'Theoretical and clinical aspects' and presents his cognitive model of anxiety. Part 2 of the book, written by Emery, is entitled 'Cognitive therapy: Techniques and applications' and has chapters on the principles of cognitive therapy, techniques for cognitive restructuring, modifying imagery, affect and behaviour, and on restructuring assumptions.

Beck, A.T. (1988). *Love Is Never Enough: How Couples Can Overcome Misunderstandings, Resolve Conflicts, and Solve Relationship Problems through Cognitive Therapy.* New York: Harper & Row.
This book describes the power of negative and biased thinking in couple relationships. Beck shows how partners can improve their relationship by identifying and modifying their maladaptive automatic thoughts and underlying beliefs.

Beck, A.T., Freeman A. and Associates (1990). *Cognitive Therapy of Personality Disorders*. New York: Guilford Press.

Part 1 of this book, written by Beck and Freeman, presents Beck's cognitive model of personality disorders as well as the history of and research of cognitive therapy for personality disorders. Part 2 of the book, written by a series of associates, focuses on clinical applications of cognitive therapy for each of the personality disorders.

Weishaar, M.E. (1993). *Aaron T. Beck*. London: Sage.

Weishaar has been both a student and collaborator of Beck's, so she writes with authority. The five chapters in the book cover: Beck's life, his theoretical contributions, his practical contributions, some criticisms and rebuttals, and Beck's overall influence.

Further references

Beck

Beck, A.T. (1963). Thinking and depression. 1. Idiosyncratic content and cognitive distortions. *Archives of General Psychiatry, 9*, 324–33.

Beck, A.T. (1964). Thinking and depression. 2. Theory and therapy. *Archives of General Psychiatry, 10*, 561–71.

Beck, A.T. (1976). *Cognitive Therapy and the Emotional Disorders*. New York: New American Library.

Beck, A.T. (1978). *Anxiety Checklist*. Philadelphia, PA: Center for Cognitive Therapy.

Beck, A.T. (1983). Cognitive therapy of depression: New perspectives. In P.J. Clayton & J.E. Barnett (Eds.). *Treatment of Depression: Old Controversies and New Approaches* (pp. 265–84). New York: Raven Press.

Beck, A.T. (1987). Cognitive models of depression. *Journal of Cognitive Psychotherapy, 1*, 5–37.

Beck, A.T. (1991). Cognitive therapy: A 30–year retrospective. *American Psychologist, 46*, 368–75.

Beck, A.T., Epstein, N. & Harrison, R. (1983). Cognitions, attitudes and personality dimensions in depression. *British Journal of Cognitive Psychotherapy, 1*, 1–16.

Beck, A.T. & Haaga, D.F. (1992). The future of cognitive therapy. *Psychotherapy, 29*, 34–8.

Beck, A.T., Kovacs, M. & Weissman, A. (1979). Assessment of suicide intention: The scale for suicide ideation. *Journal of Consulting and Clinical Psychology, 47*, 343–52.

Beck, A.T., Laude, R. & Bohnert, M. (1974). Ideation components of anxiety neurosis. *Archives of General Psychiatry, 31*, 456–9.

Beck, A.T. & Rush, A.J. (in press). Cognitive therapy. In H.I. Kaplan & B.J. Sadock (Eds). *Comprehensive Textbook of Psychiatry (Vol. VI)*. Baltimore, MD: Williams & Wilkins.

Beck, A.T., Steer, R.A., Kovacs, M. & Garrison, B. (1985). Hopelessness and eventual suicide: A ten-year prospective study of patients hospitalized with suicidal ideation. *American Journal of Psychiatry, 147*, 190–5.

Beck, A.T., Ward, C.H., Mendelson, M., Mock, J.E. & Erbaugh, J.K. (1961). An inventory for measuring depression. *Archives of General Psychiatry, 4*, 561–71

Beck, A.T. & Weishaar, M.E. (1989). *Cognitive Therapy*. In R.J. Corsini & D. Wedding (Eds.)., *Current Psychotherapies* (4th ed, pp. 285–320). Itasca, IL: Peacock.

Beck, A.T., Young, J.E. & El Shamma, K. (1979). *Competency Checklist for Cognitive Therapists*. Philadelphia, PA: Center for Cognitive Therapy.

Clark, D.M. & Beck, A.T. (1988). Cognitive approaches. In C.G. Last & M. Hersen (Eds.). *Handbook of Anxiety Disorders* (pp. 362–85). New York: Pergamon.

Kendall, P.C., Hollon, S.T., Beck, A.T., Hammen, C.L. & Ingram, R.E. (1987). Issues and recommendations regarding use of the Beck Depression Inventory. *Cognitive Therapy and Research, 11,* 289–99.

Scott, J., Williams, J.M.G. & Beck, A.T. (Eds.) (1989). *Cognitive Therapy in Clinical Practice: An Illustrative Casebook.* London: Routledge.

Weishaar, M.E. & Beck, A.T. (1986). Cognitive therapy. In W. Dryden & W. Golden (Eds). *Cognitive-Behavioural Approaches to Psychotherapy* (pp. 61–91). London: Harper & Row.

Others

American Psychiatric Association (1987). *Diagnostic and Statistical Manual of Mental Disorders* (3rd ed., rev.). Washington, DC: APA.

Burns, D.D. (1980). *Feeling Good: The New Mood Therapy.* New York: Signet.

Burns, D.D. (1989). *The Feeling Good Handbook: Using the New Mood Therapy in Everyday Life.* New York: William Morrow.

Emery, G. (1982). *Own Your Own Life: How the New Cognitive Therapy Can Make You Feel Wonderful.* New York: Signet.

Emery, G., Hollon, S. & Bedroisan, R.C. (Eds.). (1981) *New Directions in Cognitive Therapy.* New York: Guilford Press.

Kelly, G. (1955). *The Psychology of Personal Constructs.* New York: Norton.

Lazarus, R.S. (1966). *Psychological Stress and the Coping Process.* New York, McGraw-Hill.

Weissman, A. (1979). *The Dysfunctional Attitudes Scale.* Philadelphia, PA: Center for Cognitive Therapy.

Beck on cassette

All the following cassettes are available from The Guilford Press, 72 Spring Street, New York, NY 10012.

Cognitive Therapy of an Avoidant Personality (2 cassettes), Cat. #2966.

Cognitive Therapy of Depression Demonstration of an initial interview (1 cassette), Cat. #2837.

Cognitive Therapy of Anxiety and Panic Disorders First interview (1 cassette), Cat. #8740.

PART SEVEN

Eclectic and Integrative

FOURTEEN
Multimodal Counselling

PREVIEW

- *Multimodal counselling is a technically eclectic approach which uses a range of techniques selected on the basis of empirical evidence and client need rather than theoretical predisposition.*

- *Physiologically, people have different thresholds for tolerating negative symptoms such as pain, frustration and stress. Human personality can be divided into seven discrete, yet interacting, dimensions that form the acronym BASIC I.D.: behaviour, affect, sensation, imagery, cognition, interpersonal, and drugs/biology. People tend to respond to situations according to their favoured modalities.*

- *Multimodal counselling is not atheoretical and is broadly based on social cognitive learning theory without being shackled to it. Misinformation and missing information lie behind the acquisition and maintenance of many emotional problems. Much learning occurs through nonconscious processes. Through social learning people acquire defensive reactions. People's personalities are acquired and maintained through the interaction of genetic endowment, social learning and environmental influences.*

- *Multimodal counselling goals are tailored to the BASIC I.D. needs of individual clients, though sometimes a thorough assessment of all seven modalities is unnecessary.*

- *The counsellor is an 'authentic chameleon' who varies the style of the counselling relationship to provide goodness-to-fit with individual clients. When bridging, counsellors deliberately tune into clients' preferred modalities before moving into other modalities.*

- *Frequently, on the basis of initial interviews and the clients responses to the Multimodal Life History Questionnaire, multimodal counsellors draw up Modality Profiles. Modality Profiles are BASIC I.D. charts listing problems and interventions within each modality.*

Structural Profiles illustrate how clients see themselves on each of the BASIC I.D. dimensions.

• *Tracking refers to how clients order modalities when they generate particular negative affects, for instance sensations may 'fire' cognitions. When impasses occur in treatment, counsellors can perform second-order BASIC I.D. assessments that allow a more detailed review of each dimension in the problem area proving difficult.*

• *When selecting techniques, multimodal counsellors pay great attention to empirical evidence. Counsellors start with the most logical and obvious techniques. They attempt to implement techniques taking into account clients' unique characteristics. Principal multimodal techniques for each of the seven modalities are reviewed.*

• *The BASIC I.D. provides a framework for evaluating client progress. Beyond individual counselling, other applications of multimodal counselling include couples work, group work, and parent training.*

INTRODUCTION

Multimodal counselling is an approach developed by Arnold A. Lazarus, a clinical psychologist, in response to the constraints of traditional behavioural counselling. He writes: 'the multimodal orientation transcends the behavioral tradition by adding unique assessment procedures and by dealing in great depth and detail with sensory, imagery, cognitive, and interpersonal factors and their interactive effects' (Lazarus, 1989a, p. 503). Clients' needs are often better served if counsellors work in multimodal rather than unimodal or bimodal fashions. Multimodal counselling rests heavily on multimodal assessment to choose the most appropriate treatment techniques for particular clients with their unique psychological profiles and circumstances. Lazarus observes about the term multimodal therapy, 'It might have been better to call it "multimodal assessment and comprehensive psychotherapy" or something like that' (Dryden, 1991, p. 107).

Arnold A. Lazarus

On 27 January 1932 Arnold Lazarus was born in Johannesburg, South Africa, the youngest of four children. His father ran a small retail business. At the time of his birth his two sisters were 14 and 17 and his brother was 8. Lazarus grew up feeling that as the youngest family member 'I was typically ignored and my opinion was considered unimportant' (Dryden, 1991, p. 101). This contributed to his feeling shy, inadequate and hypersensitive. Lazarus was a 'skinny kid who was bullied a lot' (Dryden, 1991, p. 1) and, consequently, spent much time on body building activities. He exhibited an early interest in writing and while in his teens had some stories published in local newspapers. He also was Associate Editor of a South African body building magazine. When Lazarus was growing up, broadening experiences included: attending several high schools, spending time on a farm, working in a department store and selling houses.

Lazarus started university with a view to becoming a journalist and writer. However, on discovering that he could be a psychotherapist without going through a formal medical education, he became seriously interested in psychology and psychotherapy. In 1956 Lazarus received a BA in psychology and sociology. This was followed in 1957 by a BA Honours in Psychology and an MA in Experimental Psychology, and in 1960 by a PhD in Clinical Psychology, all degrees conferred by the University of the Witwatersrand in Johannesburg. His PhD research on 'New group techniques in the treatment of phobic conditions' used group systematic desensitization. Joseph Wolpe was chairperson of his dissertation committee.

Lazarus's occupational history started with a part-time psychologist position in 1958–9 with the Mental Health Society in Johannesburg. From 1959–63 and from 1964–6 he was in private practice as well as being a part-time lecturer at Witwatersrand Medical School. Albert Bandura, on the basis of seeing a write-up of Lazarus' PhD findings in the *Journal of Abnormal and Social Psychology* (Lazarus, 1961), invited him to Stanford University, where he was a Visiting Assistant Professor in the Psychology Department in 1963–4. Uneasy with apartheid and the South African political situation, in 1966 Lazarus and his family returned to the United States, where in 1976 he became a naturalized American citizen. From 1966–7, Lazarus directed the Behavior Therapy Institute in Sausalito, California. From 1967–70 he was a Professor of Psychology in the Department of Behavioural Science in Temple University Medical School, Philadelphia. Joseph Wolpe, his former supervisor, was also at Temple University but he and Lazarus had an acrimonious falling out when Wolpe perceived Lazarus's views on the broadening of behaviour therapy to include cognition and 'technical eclecticism' as heretical and threatening to what he was propounding.

From 1970–2 Lazarus was Visiting Professor and Director of Clinical Training in Yale University's Department of Psychology. In 1972 he moved to Rutgers University in New Jersey where from 1972–4 he was Chairman of the Psychology Department and, from 1974 onwards, a Distinguished Professor in the Graduate School of Applied and Professional Psychology. Lazarus has held numerous consultant positions and editorial board appointments. His professional awards include the American Board of Professional Psychology's 'Distinguished Service to the Profession of Psychology Award' in 1982 and the American Psychological Association's Division of Psychotherapy's Distinguished Psychologist Award in 1992.

Lazarus's early interest in writing has continued unabated. He has published numerous journal articles and book chapters. His books include: *Behavior Therapy Techniques* (with Joseph Wolpe), *Behavior Therapy and Beyond*, *Clinical Behavior Therapy* (as editor and contributor), *Multimodal Behavior Therapy* (with 11 contributors), *In the Mind's Eye: The Power of Imagery for Personal Enrichment*, *Marital Myths*, *Don't Believe It for a Minute!* (with Clifford Lazarus and Allen Fay) and *The Practice of Multimodal Therapy*.

Lazarus values his humanity and works in order to live. In 1956 he married Daphne, and in 1959 their daughter Linda was born, followed in 1961 by their son Clifford. His priorities are: first, wife and family; second, meaningful friendships and the pursuit of fun (plays, music, tennis etc.); and third, work. By work he means intellectual stimulation, making a social contribution and surviving economically. Given another life he has a fantasy that he would like to direct and create movies like Steven Spielberg. The question Lazarus always asks when someone dies is, 'Did this person have enough fun on this earth?' (Dryden, 1991, p. 14). If not, he feels they have had wasted lives.

Regarding his professional work, Lazarus mentions three contributions: first, showing that behavioural counselling can be more humanistic; second, in Ellis's footsteps, broadening behavioural counselling's horizons to include cognitions; and third, developing 'an even broader and more systematic framework in my writings on multimodal methods' (Dryden, 1991, p. 112). Lazarus's son Clifford is a clinical psychologist and his proud father now derives 'infinitely more pleasure from helping his ideas grow than from reiterating my own' (Dryden, 1991, p. 113).

ASSUMPTIONS
Technical eclecticism

Eclecticism is not a unitary construct (Lazarus, 1989b). Instead there are many different kinds of eclecticism. Lazarus distinguishes unsystematic eclecticism, where counsellors require neither a coherent rationale nor empirical validation for the techniques they use, and systematic (technical) eclecticism, where counsellors are guided by a preferred theory but also draw techniques from other orientations. Bandura's social and cognitive learning theory is the main preferred theory for multimodal counsellors (Lazarus, 1989b, 1992, 1993b).

Lazarus distinguishes theoretical eclecticism from technical eclecticism. Unlike their theoretically eclectic counterparts, technically eclectic counsellors 'use procedures from different sources without necessarily subscribing to the theories or disciplines that spawned them' (Lazarus, 1989a, p. 503). Systematic technical eclectics neither choose techniques that 'feel right' nor hop from theory to theory. Lazarus writes 'The hallmark of technical eclecticism is the use of prescriptive treatments based on empirical evidence and client need, rather than theoretical and personal predisposition' (Lazarus, 1989b, p. 252). Technical eclectics mainly use cognitive-behavioural ideas and techniques. In addition, they may draw from Adlerian, Rogerian, Eriksonian, psychodrama, Gestalt, reality and transactional analysis schools, but without embracing any of these diverse theories. They regard as excess baggage the needless addition or multiplication of explanatory principles.

Unlike eclectics, integrationists not only employ techniques from various sources but try to combine different theoretical positions. Lazarus sees technical eclecticism as a step towards eventual integrationism. However, he urges caution in proceeding with integrationism. There is the danger of superficially merging theoretical tenets that are intrinsically incompatible (Lazarus *et al.*, 1992). Furthermore, counsellors can become more intent on attaching theoretical labels to what they do than on stating precisely both what they do with each client and how they select what they do.

Thresholds

Physiologically, people react to a variety of arousing stimuli with differing and distinctive patterns of autonomic nervous system activity. Lazarus (1989a) uses the term threshold to describe people's differing capacities to tolerate negative stimuli. People innately differ in their abilities to tolerate pain, frustration and stress. People whose autonomic nervous systems are stable are less anxiety prone than those whose autonomic reactions are labile. Innate thresholds can limit the effectiveness of psychological interventions. Lazarus gives the example of the limitations of hypnosis and other psychological techniques on a person with extremely low pain tolerance. While their pain tolerance may be raised, their innate tendency to overreact to pain stimuli nevertheless remains.

The seven modalities: BASIC ID

The concept of modalities in the bedrock of multimodal counselling assessment and treatment. Human personality can be divided into seven discrete, yet interacting, modalities or dimensions. Lazarus writes: 'These modalities exist in a state or reciprocal transaction and flux, connected by complex chains of behavior and other psychophysiological processes' (Lazarus, 1992, p. 236). Following are the seven modalities, each illustrated by its description in the Structural Profile, a multimodal self-assessment questionnaire (Lazarus, 1992, pp. 244–5).

• *Behaviour.* 'Some people may be described as "doers" – they are action oriented, they like to busy themselves, get things done, take on various projects. How much of a doer are you?'

• *Affect.* 'Some people are very emotional and may or may not express it. How emotional are you? How deeply do you feel things? How passionate are you?'

• *Sensation.* 'Some people attach a lot of value to sensory experiences, such as sex, food, music, art and other "sensory delights". Others are very much aware of minor aches, pains, and discomforts. How "tuned in to" your sensations are you?'

• *Imagery.* 'How much fantasy or daydreaming do you engage in? This is separate from thinking or planning. This is "thinking in pictures", visualizing real or imagined experiences, letting your mind roam. How much are you into imagery?'

• *Cognition.* 'Some people are very analytical and like to plan things. They like to reason things through. How much of a "thinker" and "planner" are you?'

• *Interpersonal.* 'How important are other people to you? This is your self-rating as a social being. How important are close friendships to you, the tendency to gravitate toward people, the desire for intimacy? The opposite of this is being a "loner".'

• *Drugs/biology.* 'Are you healthy and health-conscious? Do you avoid bad habits like smoking, too much alcohol, drinking a lot of coffee, overeating etc.? Do you exercise regularly, get enough sleep, avoid junk foods, and generally take care of your body?'

The acronym BASIC I.D. is formed by using the first letter of each modality. This provides a useful shorthand descriptor of the seven modalities. Also, the acronym serves as a memory aide.

Lazarus acknowledges people's behaviour is specific to situations, other people and when it occurs. Nevertheless, people have tendencies, usually evident in the first decade of their lives, to favour some BASIC I.D. modalities over others. People's BASIC I.D.

tendencies determine the tone and quality of how they function. For instance, to call someone an 'imagery reactor' means that their most highly valued and predominant modality is visual. Though they may not do so all the time, they are inclined to respond to and organize the world in terms of mental images. On the other hand, 'cognitive reactors' respond to the world from their intellects. In terms of brain research, the right hemisphere is probably dominant for imagery reactors and the left dominant for cognitive reactors. Sensory reactors may be subdivided according to the predominance of each of the five basic senses. Lazarus observes: 'To "know" or to "understand" another person is to have full access to his or her BASIC I.D. Self-knowledge implies an awareness of the content of one's own BASIC I.D. as well as insight into the interactive effects therein' (Lazarus, 1989c, pp. 16–17).

Thresholds and preferred modalities interact. For example, the person with low pain tolerance, high frustration tolerance, high activity and vivid imagery is very different from a person with low frustration tolerance, moderate activity, highly analytical (cognition) and capable of only forming fleeting images (Lazarus, 1989a).

ACQUISITION

Lazarus has never developed a full theoretical statement of his own regarding how people acquire and maintain their BASIC I.D. modalities and their personality strengths and weaknesses. Instead he prefers to be more of an empiricist and leave the theorizing to others. Nevertheless, he endeavours to understand other theorists' frameworks and principles to see which are the best scientifically proven ideas upon which he can draw. Lazarus has studiously avoided theoretical integration and writes: 'It cannot be overstated that multimodal therapy is not a conglomeration of psychoanalysis, behavior therapy and many other systems' (Lazarus, 1989a, p. 519).

People's personalities stem from their genetic endowment, physical environment and social learning history. Multimodal counselling is not atheoretical: instead 'its technically eclectic stance operates within a consistent *social cognitive learning theory* (Bandura, 1986)' (Lazarus, 1989c, p. ix). However, when dealing with dyadic, family, and other complex interactions, Lazarus adds explanatory concepts from communication and systems theory (Kwee & Lazarus, 1986).

Social learning

Association, in the form of events occurring simultaneously or in close succession, is important in all learning processes. Much human behaviour is the result of classical and operant conditioning. For instance, many aversions appear to originate from *classical conditioning*. Lazarus (1989a) provides the example of the client who had experienced post-operative nausea a few years previously and been in a hospital bed next to a man who kept playing a cassette of Beethoven's *Moonlight Sonata*. Later the client became sick to his stomach any time he heard that music. *Operant conditioning*, where the probability of behaviour recurring is mediated by its consequences, is another major social learning process. For instance, a depressed woman can reinforce her depression by locking herself up in her bedroom and avoiding rewarding social contacts (Kwee &

Lazarus, 1986). Another example is that of a woman who states 'I now realize that my headaches were in large part due to the fact that the only time my husband showed me any real caring was when I was in pain' (Lazarus, 1989a, p. 516). *Modelling and vicarious processes* are also important in learning. People learn from observing and imitating what other do. Furthermore, they learn from perceiving the positive and negative consequences of others' behaviour.

People filter and can override their conditioning and modelling because of their intervening thoughts about these stimuli. They do not respond to the real environment, but to their *perceived* environment. Factors influencing their perceptions include: personalistic use of language, expectancies, selective attention, problem-solving competencies, goals, performance standards, and their values, attitudes and beliefs.

Nonconscious processes

Much learning is neither conscious nor deliberate. Nonconscious processes are not to be confused with the Freudian notion of the unconscious. What Lazarus means by nonconscious processes is that 'people have different levels and degrees of awareness, and that unrecognized – subliminal – stimuli can influence one's thoughts, feelings, and behaviors . . .' (Lazarus, 1992, p. 235). Frequent demonstrations have illustrated that, during altered states of consciousness, people have access to memories and skills that are unavailable to conscious recall.

Defensive reactions

Through their social learning experiences people may acquire a variety of unnecessary defensive reactions. Defensive reactions avoid pain, discomfort and 'negative emotions like anxiety, depression, guilt and shame' (Lazarus, 1981, p. 38). People lessen their awareness, deny or distort their perceptions and mislabel their feelings. Included among defensive reactions are: denial; over intellectualization and rationalization; projection, wrongly attributing one's feelings to others; and displacement, for instance of aggression on to other people, animals or things.

Misinformation and missing information

Lazarus sees misinformation and missing information as two of the major means through which emotional problems and disorders arise (Dryden, 1991).

Misinformation

With misinformation, people have learned incorrect assumptions and beliefs about life and living. One area of misinformation encompasses the perfectionist beliefs held in Western society, for instance that lifelong happiness results from fame and fortune. Other areas of misinformation include: the inability of people to realize that their lives are mainly controlled by their own thoughts and perceptions rather than by external events; the belief that it is good to ventilate anger; the belief in the importance of pleasing others; and the idea that it is better to play safe by leading a life where there are no risks. Marital misinformation includes the myths that 'Romantic love makes a good marriage' and 'If you feel guilty, confess.' (Lazarus, 1985).

Missing information

With misinformation, people have acquired erroneous ideas. With missing information, people do not possess the information to enact basic skills required for successful living. Social skills provide an important area of missing information about such matters as eye contact and how to converse. In addition, many people lack information on how to handle job interviews and present themselves favourably.

Lazarus regards as terrifying the amount of ignorance pervading the world. Even events such as international terrorism and drug smuggling can be 'tied into extreme misinformation and missing information that people have about the sort of values and skills that could make for a happier world' (Dryden, 1991, p. 15).

MAINTENANCE

People's personalities are not only acquired but also maintained through the interaction of genetic endowment, social learning and environmental influences.

Genetic endowment

People's genetic endowment persists in the form of different thresholds and favoured BASIC I.D. modalities.

Social learning

Social learning influences the maintenance of personality in a number of ways. People learn maladaptive habits or conditioned emotional reactions 'though various associations and unfortunate connections of events' (Dryden, 1991, p. 9). Such habits may be simple or complex and persist in interfering with their happiness. In addition, through conditioning and modelling they learn not only behaviours but perceptions of self-efficacy, performance standards, and goals that they maintain for good or ill. In addition, people's environments can continue to offer reinforcements and models that contribute to maintaining their thoughts, feelings and behaviours.

Nonconscious processes

Nonconscious processes influence maintenance of personality. People may remain unaware of what they have learned and keep learning from others. Consequently, such thoughts, feeling and behaviours are less easy to change.

Defensive reactions

Once learned, defensive reactions act as habits that block people from full awareness of how they and others behave. Defensive reactions make it harder for people to work on their problems since they lack insight both into their defensive reactions and into their negative consequences. Consequently, defensive reactions are both part of and serve to maintain unhelpful aspects of people's BASIC I.D.s.

Misinformation and missing information

Lazarus assigns a pivotal role to misinformation and missing information in maintaining behaviour and in causing people to become counselling clients. He writes that 'gaps in people's repertoires – they were never given necessary information and essential coping processes – render them ill-equipped to deal with societal demands' (Lazarus, 1989a, p. 517).

Other factors

Following are other factors, interacting with those already mentioned, that can contribute to people maintaining dysfunctional thoughts, feelings and behaviours (Dryden, 1993).

• *Conflicting or ambivalent feelings or reactions.* People can possess approach-approach or avoidance-avoidance conflicts resulting in extreme indecisiveness. Their prior learning experiences have contributed to their indecision and inertia. Their indecisiveness may be both self-maintaining and also contribute to their inability to change aspects of how they function.

• *Interpersonal inquietude.* Many people remain upset because of undue dependencies, excessive hates and misplaced loves. Lazarus sees such interpersonal inquietude stemming from skills deficits and from unrealistic demands that people impose upon each other.

• *Poor self-acceptance.* People maintain negative feelings about themselves because they do not understand the difference between accepting their totality as human beings and functionally evaluating specific shortcomings and personal limitations. Self-acceptance means 'Don't put your ego on the line, accept yourself, your totality, even though there might be lots of little "i's" as part of the big "I", that are less than exemplary' (Dryden, 1991, p. 13). For instance, people can make mistakes and possess skills deficits without feeling totally crushed as persons.

PRACTICE

The practice of multimodal counselling possesses six distinctive features:

'1. The specific and comprehensive attention given to the entire BASIC I.D.

2. The use of Second-Order BASIC I.D. assessments

3. The use of Modality Profiles

4. The use of Structural Profiles

5. Tracking the modality firing order

6. Deliberate bridging procedures (Lazarus, 1992, p. 250).'

Though not in the order listed above, this section reviews how each of these distinctive features form part of multimodal counselling.

Goals

Long-range hedonism is a guiding philosophy (Dryden, 1991). Though Lazarus does not define fun, a major goal for most humans is to have fun while alive. However, people need attain a good balance between long-range and short-range hedonism.

Though individuals differ in their predominant modalities, the BASIC I.D. suggests illustrative sub-goals for effective functioning:

• *Behaviour.* Taking effective actions in pursuit of realistic goals

• *Affect.* Acknowledging, clarifying and recognizing feelings; coping with negative feelings and enhancing positive feelings

• *Sensation.* Being in touch with and enjoying one's senses

• *Imagery.* Being in touch with one's imagination; using coping images

• *Cognition.* Possessing sufficiently accurate and complete information; thinking realistically

• *Interpersonal.* Possessing good relating skills, for instance assertion and conversational skills; capacity for healthy interdependency

• *Drugs/biology.* Taking good care of one's body and physical health; eating and drinking in moderation

People can have deficits in one or more of the above modalities and still be happy. Humans are fallible, with a biological penchant sometimes to be self-defeating. However, people can feel self-acceptance and accept their fallibility at the same time as attempting to be less fallible.

Multimodal counselling goals are tailored to particular clients and take into account their 'goals, coping behaviours, situational contexts, affective reactions, "resistances", and basic beliefs' (Lazarus, 1992, p. 237). Rigidity is to be avoided in all aspects of counselling, including assessment and goal-setting. In some instances, clients' main problems are obvious and a thorough assessment of all seven BASIC I.D. modalities is unnecessary. However, in most cases multimodal counselling rests on a thorough assessment of the BASIC I.D. which leads to constructing a Modality Profile listing salient problems and recommended treatments within each modality. Outcome goals, namely overcoming or coping with the problem, are implicit for each problem listed by modality in the profile. For instance, depression is one of the problems listed in the Affect section of a client's modality profile. An outcome goal for this problem relates to a lessening of the client's depressed feelings, preferably in some measurable way. Inasmuch as Modality Profiles also list recommended interventions, decision and process goals are implicit in them. A counsellor decision goal is to select the most effective treatments of choice for each problem. Could the counsellor have selected better treatments of choice for the client's depression problem that the recommended interventions fo coping imagery and increasing rewarding activities? Once chosen, to what extent does each intervention, on its own or in combination, contribute to the problem or outcome goal of lessening the client's depression?

The counselling relationship

The counselling relationship can be divided into relationship behaviours that are universal and those that differ for specific clients. One universal relationship behaviour is the attempt to develop a collaborative alliance whenever possible. Multimodal counsellors endeavour to work together with clients. A second relationship universal is never to attack to a client's sense of dignity as a person, though their maladaptive behaviours may be assailed.

'"Relationships of choice" are no less important than "techniques of choice" for effective psychotherapy' (Lazarus, 1993a, p. 404). For most clients the purpose of the counselling relationship is to provide 'the soil that enables the techniques to take root' (Dryden, 1991, p. 17). Unlike Rogers, who would offer the same kind 'carefully cultivated warmth, genuineness and empathy to all his clients' (Dryden, 1991, p. 18), Lazarus tries not only to match the relationship to the client, but also to the client's observed needs at different times in counselling. For some clients, good listening is sufficient. However, many clients require counsellors to select and use specific techniques to help them develop coping skills for problems identified in their Modality Profiles. Thus, counsellors need offer relationships that go beyond good listening.

Lazarus emphasizes flexibility and versatility and uses the metaphor of the 'authentic chameleon' (Kwee & Lazarus, 1986; Dryden, 1991; Lazarus, 1993a) to indicate that multimodal counsellors vary their relationship styles to provide a goodness-of-fit with clients' expectancies, personalities, problems and goals. He describes four different, yet overlapping, ways of varying relationships with clients.

• *The relationship continuum.* Multimodal counsellors view helping relationships on a continuum from 'a very close-knit, dependent bonding at the one end, to a rather formal, businesslike involvement at the other' (Kwee & Lazarus, 1986, p. 333). Throughout counselling, the relationship is used flexibly to fit each client's expectancies and preferred modalities. For instance, some people do not respond well to counsellor warmth and empathy and like a more businesslike approach.

• *Matching counsellor styles.* Counsellor styles that Lazarus seeks to match to individual clients include: 'whether and when to be cold, warm, or tepid; when and when not to be confrontational; when and whether to be earthy, chummy, casual and informal rather than "professional"; when to self-disclose or remain enigmatic; when to be soft-nosed, gentle and tender, and when to come on like a tough army sergeant; and how to adjust my levels of supportiveness and directiveness' (Lazarus, 1993a, p. 405).

• *Supportiveness and directiveness dimensions.* During counselling, multimodal counsellors continually ask themselves how supportive and how directive they need be with their clients. Four possibilities are: high direction-high support, low direction-low support, low direction-high support and high direction-low support. Effective counsellors switch among and between all four modes 'in the chameleon sense' (Dryden, 1991, p. 19). Lazarus works mostly in the high direction–high support mode, since he sees counselling as an educational process in which the counsellor's main role is that of a clinical teacher. Furthermore, clients change most rapidly when ready for high direction and high support.

• *Relationships differing with selected techniques.* Lazarus uses techniques that draw upon the work of Freud, Rogers, Perls, Ellis, Adler, Haley and the behaviourists, among others. As part of tailoring his interventions to the needs of each client, he also flexibly utilizes the kind of relationship implicit in these techniques (Lazarus, 1989c). For instance, he may use Rogerian reflection, Gestalt psychodrama and imagery techniques, or behavioural assertiveness training, and accordingly adjust the kind of relationship he offers.

The two *client* variables that most influence Lazarus's relationship style are his perceptions of their readiness for change and their reactance level. Ongoing counselling interactions play a dominant part in selecting the relationship of choice. For instance, Lazarus adopted an extremely gentle stance in which he was almost whispering to a very timid and shy young woman who expressed strong reactions about her dealings with 'loud, pushy, or obnoxious people' (Lazarus, 1993a, p. 406). The outcome was that the client, who had poor relationships with her two previous counsellors, cooperated well with him.

Bridging

Bridging is a rapport enhancement technique that illustrates the flexibility of the multimodal counselling relationship. When bridging, counsellors deliberately tune into the clients' preferred modalities before gently helping them cross bridges into their modalities that may prove more productive (Lazarus, 1989a, 1992). Clients are more likely to feel understood by counsellors who first respond within their preferred representational system. Other ways of describing bridging are that counsellors first 'talk their clients' language' or 'start from where they are' before moving into less preferred modalities. An advantage of doing this is that clients then become less resistant to working in those other modalities.

Lazarus gives the example of the counsellor asking 'How did you feel about your father's decision to leave home?' to which the client replied 'My father tended to put his needs first, and neither my mother nor I were factored into the equation' (Lazarus, 1992, p. 247). Rather than pressure him into the affective modality the multimodal counsellor first joined with him in the cognitive modality. Then after about five minutes, the counsellor could bridge into a modality that was less threatening than the affective modality, for instance the sensory modality with a question like 'By the way, can you tune into some sensations anywhere in your body?'. Then, after discussing sensations, the counsellor could bridge into the affective modality with a question such as 'I really wonder how you feel about the things your father has done?' (Lazarus, 1992, p. 248). By now the client should be much less defensive about revealing feelings.

Multimodal assessment

Initial interviews

Initial sessions follow no rigid format. Counsellors may meet with individuals, couples or families. They may begin with small talk and collecting basic information, for instance address and phone number, before embarking on a more detailed inquiry. Two main questions relating to clients' presenting complaints are: 'What has led to the current situation?' and 'Who or what is maintaining it?' (Lazarus, 1989c, 1992). In addition, counsellors look for signs of psychosis, organic problems and depression. From the start, counsellors are attuned to noting information about which modalities of the BASIC I.D. their clients' complaints apply to. In addition, they try to assess clients' expectations about counselling and the most appropriate kind of counselling relationship style to adopt. Furthermore, they look for clients' strengths and positive attributes. Quite often in initial interviews counsellors use specific interventions, for instance cognitive disputation. At the end of the initial interview, counsellors give most adult clients the 15–page Multimodal Life History Inventory (Lazarus & Lazarus, 1991a). This inventory asks numerous questions about antecedent events and maintaining factors with the answers being divided into BASIC I.D. categories.

An important multimodal counselling principle is 'Know your own limitations and other clinicians' strengths' (Dryden, 1991, p. 30). Referrals should be made where other counsellors have skills that the counsellor does not possess or more appropriate personal styles for particular clients. Lazarus does not consider himself particularly good at working with seriously disturbed people – for instance schizophrenics and substance abusers – or with adolescents. He seeks out more expert or gifted people for such clients. Often referrals to other counsellors are best made before bonding with the original counsellor occurs. Lazarus also refers clients to self-help groups such as Alcoholics Anonymous, Overeaters Anonymous and Parents without Partners.

The Modality Profile

Lazarus (1992) writes: 'the mainstay of multimodal assessment centers on Modality Profiles and Structural Profiles' (p. 246). A Modality Profile is a BASIC I.D. chart listing problems and interventions within each modality. Lazarus only draws up such profiles when counselling is not going quickly enough and unforeseen problems arise. Around the start of the third session, counsellors have usually gleaned enough information from interviews and the life history inventory to spend 15 to 20 minutes drafting a preliminary Modality Profile for the client. Sometimes clients are asked to draft their own Modality Profiles separately from their counsellors and then the two compare notes (Lazarus, 1989c). Multimodal counsellors treat their clients' Modality Profiles as sets of hypotheses. Modality Profiles are shared and discussed with clients.

Table 14.1 provides an example of a Modality Profile for a 37-year-old man in counselling for generalized anxiety (Lazarus, 1992, p. 242).

Table 14.1 Example of a Modality Profile

Modality	Problem	Intervention
Behaviour	Procrastination	Contingency contracting
	Tends to pout or withdraw when frustrated	Modelling and role playing of assertiveness skills
	Volatile and explosive	Relaxation and communication training
Affect	Anxiety	Breathing and deep muscle relaxation; stress inoculation training
	Depression	Coping imagery; increase rewarding activities
Sensation	Tension (esp. in jaws and neck)	Relaxation training
	Lower-back pain	Orthopaedic exercises
Imagery	Lonely images	Picturing various coping responses
	Images of failure	
Cognition	Perfectionism	Cognitive restructuring
	Negative scanning	
	Dichotomous thinking	
	Self-downing	
Interpersonal relationships	Passive-aggressive	Social skills and assertiveness training
	Unassertive	
	Has few friends	
Drugs/biology	Insufficient exercise	Healthy lifestyle programme
	Overweight	

The Structural Profile

The Structural Profile comes towards the end of the Multimodal Life History Inventory. Here clients are asked to rate themselves across each of the BASIC I.D. modalities on a 7-point scale with 1 being the lowest and 7 being the highest. The descriptions for each modality were provided earlier in this chapter when introducing the seven BASIC I.D. modalities. The Structural Profile provides useful additional information to both counsellor and client about how the client interacts with the world. It can be easily depicted on a bar graph.

In addition to the 7 questions that form part of the Multimodal Life History Inventory, Lazarus has developed a 35-item standardized instrument called the Structural Profile Inventory (SPI), which forms Appendix 4 in Lazarus (1989c). The SPI has proved very useful when counselling couples. The profiles pinpoint reasons for misunderstanding and can lead to fruitful discussions of what to do about them. Sometimes the profiles may indicate that divorce counselling is a more realistic prospect than marriage counselling – for instance, where one partner values affective expression and interpersonal intimacy and is low on behaviour and cognition, whereas the other partner has the opposite profile.

Tracking

Clients have fairly reliable patterns or orderings of modalities in how they generate negative affect, though on occasion these patterns may vary. Tracking refers to the careful assessment of the 'firing order', the ordering of the chain reaction of the different modalities. For instance, one client may generate negative emotions through dwelling first on sensations (S) (e.g. heart palpitations) which 'fire' cognitions (C) (e.g. 'I must get very ill or die') which 'fire' aversive images (I) (e.g. pictures of catastrophic disease) which 'fire' maladaptive behaviour (B) (e.g. extreme withdrawal) (Lazarus, 1989a). Another client, instead of the SCIB firing order outlined above, may display a CISB pattern (cognitive-imagery-sensation-behaviour).

One purpose of tracking is to provide clients with insight into the precise processes by which they generate negative affect so that they can intervene appropriately. Another purpose is to assist counsellors in selecting and prioritizing treatment techniques. Lazarus (1989a) provides the example of an agoraphobic woman who tracked in herself a CISA firing order. An illustrative cognition (C) was 'What if I pass out?', followed by mental images (I) of herself hyperventilating and fainting, which fired sensations (S) of light-headedness and sweaty palms, which fired feelings (A) of tension and anxiety.

Following her firing order, her counsellor first provided the client with self-instructional training (Meichenbaum, 1977) to counteract her self-defeating cognitions. Next, she was taught coping imagery in which she vividly imagined herself remaining calm and controlled in feared situations (such as shopping in a supermarket). In the sensory modality, her counsellor taught her slow abdominal breathing and differential muscle relaxation. The client was instructed to practise her training in real life. When shopping in a supermarket, she was to follow the sequence of using positive self-instructions (C), then adding coping imagery (I), and then using abdominal breathing while deliberately relaxing muscles not in use at the time (S). Had the client a different firing order, the counsellor would have trained her in a different sequence and encouraged her to use this different sequence in real life.

Second-order BASIC I.D. assessments

When impasses occur in treating clients, counsellors may perform second-order BASIC I.D. assessments. Such assessments allow a more detailed review of behaviours, affective responses, sensory reactions, images, cognitions, interpersonal factors, and drugs and biological factors in relation to the area in which change is proving difficult. For instance, unassertive behaviours may persist, despite role playing, behaviour rehearsal, modelling and other relevant training. When, as part of her second-order assessment, one client was asked for her BASIC I.D. associations to the concept of assertiveness, her answers were as follows: *behaviour*, attacking; *affect*, angry; *sensation*, tension; *imagery*, bombs bursting; *cognition*, get even; *interpersonal*, hurting; and *drugs/biologicals*, high blood pressure (Lazarus, 1989a). Although the counsellor had attempted to convey to her the difference between assertion and aggression, the second-order BASIC I.D.

showed that she still regarded assertive responses as tantamount to vicious attacks. In another case where a male client was failing to respond to assertiveness training, his second-order BASIC I.D. assessment revealed that he did not feel entitled to certain rights and privileges (Lazarus, 1992).

Selection of techniques

Lazarus writes: 'A fundamental premise of the multimodal approach is that clients are usually troubled by a multitude of specific problems that should be dealt with by a multitude of specific treatments' (Lazarus, 1989a, p. 519). How do multimodal counsellors select treatment techniques? Table 14.1 provides, as part of a Modality Profile, the techniques selected for a male client being counselled for generalized anxiety. Multimodal counsellors need to be aware of and skilled in a wide repertoire of techniques. If unaware of or unskilled in certain techniques that are unlikely to help clients with certain conditions. The first or main requirement for selecting techniques is the extent to which there are research data to support them. Empirical data exist for documenting treatments of choice across a variety of conditions including 'bulimia nervosa, compulsive rituals, social skill deficits, bipolar depression, schizophrenic delusions, focal phobias, tics and habit disorders, pain management, hyperventilation, panic disorders, autism, enuresis, vaginismus and other sexual dysfunctions, and a variety of stress-related disorders . . .' (Lazarus *et al.*, 1992). However, probably some 'grey areas' will always exist. Practising counsellors should familiarize themselves with the research outcome literature.

Multimodal counsellors take a number of other factors into account in selecting and prioritizing techniques. Such factors include clients' priorities, firing orders, and the desirability of early success experiences. Careful consideration is given to answers to the following three items on page 4 of the Multimodal Life History Questionnaire: 'In a few words, what do you think therapy is about?', 'How long do you think your therapy should last?', 'What personal qualities do you think the ideal therapist should possess?' (Lazarus, 1992, pp. 242–3). For instance, clients thinking the ideal counsellor is an active listener may take unkindly to active-directive, task-oriented counsellors.

Multimodal counsellors start 'with the most obvious and logical procedures' (Kwee & Lazarus, 1986, p. 335). Once selected, counsellors still need to accommodate their chosen techniques to the unique characteristics of each client in order to promote adherence and compliance. While the initial selection of techniques may be relatively straightforward, their implementation 'requires clinical experience, acumen, and artistry' (Kwee & Lazarus, 1986, p. 337). If the initially selected techniques do not work, Lazarus may draw on other well-researched techniques. Sometimes he goes beyond well-researched techniques to try other techniques that may help specific clients: for example the technique of shrinking the feared object down to size from neurolinguistic programming (NLP) or using the conceptualization of Parent, Adult and Child from Transactional Analysis (Dryden, 1991). In addition, second-order BASIC I.D. assessments may be conducted to look for significant factors that may have been overlooked in initial assessment procedures.

Principal multimodal techniques

Following are principal multimodal techniques for each BASIC I.D. dimension (Kwee & Lazarus, 1986; Lazarus, 1989c). Frequently, these techniques are used in combination. Techniques should be used sparingly according to the assessed needs of individual clients.

Behaviour

• *Behaviour rehearsal.* Counsellors, who start by playing the other person, repeatedly rehearse clients in how to behave in specific situations. Dialogues are either cassette- or video-recorded and played back. When ready, clients enact their skills in the actual situations.

• *Modelling.* Counsellors provide role models for specific behaviours clients are encouraged to imitate. Counsellors may model behaviours in real-life settings: for instance assertively returning faulty goods to a shop.

• *Nonreinforcement.* By not attending to specific client behaviours, counsellors and others in clients' social environments can facilitate their extinction.

• *Positive reinforcement.* To strengthen specific client behaviours, counsellors can dispense social reinforcers such as praise, recognition and encouragement. With children and adolescents counsellors may use tangible reinforcers, such as food and money. Counsellors may also use tokens that may be exchanged for tangible rewards.

• *Recording and self-monitoring.* Counsellors encourage clients to engage in the systematic recording, charting and/or counting of targeted behaviours.

• *Stimulus control.* The absence or presence of certain stimuli is related to the frequency of behaviours. For example, people trying to lose weight can keep snacks and desserts out of their homes. Students trying to increase study behaviours can arrange their desks without distracting stimuli and only sit at them when studying.

• *Systematic exposure.* Counsellors encourage clients to expose themselves step-by-step to their feared situations. Many additional techniques, for instance *goal rehearsal* or *coping imagery*, may be used to overcome avoidances in conjunction with systematic exposure.

Affect

• *Anger expression.* Anger-expression means assisting clients to own and express their anger. It is not an end in itself and clients may require *behaviour rehearsal* in how to express anger assertively. Techniques to get clients in touch with angry feelings include coaxing them to say louder and louder 'I am angry' and getting them to pummel and kick foam rubber cushions, pillows and inflatable objects.

• *Anxiety management training.* First counsellors teach clients general *relaxation training* and *goal-rehearsal* or *coping imagery*. Then they teach clients to generate anxiety evoking cognitions and imagery and immediately after to relax and dwell on calm sensations, picture serene images, dispute irrational ideas and concentrate on optimistic and relaxing thoughts.

• *Feeling-identification.* Labelling feelings accurately is one area of feeling-identification: for instance, clients may say they are 'depressed' when their symptoms are more those of 'anxiety'. The main focus of feeling-identification is on exploring the client's affective domain to help identify significant feelings that might be unclear or misdirected.

• *The empty chair.* The client faces an empty chair and imagines it occupied by a significant other. The client starts a dialogue with this other person and then switches chairs back and forth to conduct both parts of the dialogue. Counsellors may offer prompts about what to say, for instance, 'Ask her to tell you exactly how she would have wanted you to respond.' As well as assisting clients to own and express feelings, the empty chair helps them appreciate others' viewpoints.

Sensation

• *Biofeedback.* There are biofeedback devices that can help clients to monitor and modify physiological functions like muscular tension, heart rate, brain wave activity, galvanic skin response and skin temperature. For example, for a client suffering from painful tension in the jaw, the counsellor can attach electrodes to the jaw muscles that are wired to a machine that provides tonal feedback (the more tension the louder the sound) according to the degree of muscular tension. Clients can learn to maintain a low decibel level or eliminate the tone altogether.

• *Focusing.* Counsellors encourage clients in contemplative and relaxed states to tune into their spontaneous thoughts and feelings until one major felt bodily expression emerges. After several minutes of intense focusing, clients are asked to extract something new from their sensations, images and emotions.

• *Hypnosis.* Counsellors can usefully learn several methods for inducing trances to maximize their chances of success with individual clients. Hypnotic-induction techniques mostly involve sensory fixation (e.g. focusing on a spot on the ceiling) and monotonous repetitions, such as 'calm and relaxed'.

• *Meditation.* Counsellors can teach clients meditation, for instance sitting down, gradually closing their eyes, and inwardly repeating a 'mantra' such as the word 'in' on inhaling and the word 'out' on exhaling. As thoughts float in and out of awareness, the meditator continues to think the words 'in' and 'out'. Often two daily 20-minute sessions are advocated. However, some clients gain most from mini-meditations of two or three minute sessions several times daily.

• *Relaxation training.* Clients can learn total relaxation and/or differential relaxation. Total relaxation is another term for progressive muscular relaxation involving alternate tensing and letting go of each major muscle area. Differential relaxation entails learning to relax those muscles not in use when performing various tasks. For instance, a person tensing their jaw, shoulders and neck and holding their breath when sitting and writing can deliberately relax the tense muscles and breathe abdominally in a slow and rhythmic fashion.

• *Sensate focus training.* Usually prescribed for sexually dysfunctional couples, sensate focus refers to sensual rather than to sexual pleasuring The pleasuring partner is forbidden to touch the genitals or female breasts and no pressures for sexual performance are permitted. Instead the pleasuring partner massages, touches and stimulates parts of the body that the recipient enjoys having stimulated. Afterwards partners can reverse roles.

• *Threshold training.* Threshold training is a common technique for the treatment of premature or rapid ejaculation. The female manually stimulates the man's penis. When he feels a preorgasmic sensation he says 'stop' and/or removes her hand until the sensation abates. This procedure is repeated. Later more advanced variations can be added: for instance manual stimulation using a lubricant, and effecting vaginal entry and withdrawing on feeling a preorgasmic urge. Within a few weeks, many males can delay ejaculation for long periods.

Imagery

• *Anti-future shock imagery.* This technique helps prepare clients for changes likely to happen in the coming months or years: for instance, becoming a parent, being promoted or moving to a new location. Clients are encouraged to visualize themselves coping with these changes.

• *Associated imagery.* When clients experience unwanted emotions for which they are unable to account, counsellors can ask them to focus immediately on any image that comes to mind and see it as vividly as possible. New images that emerge are to be visualized as clearly as possible. If no new images emerge, the original image is to be examined as if through a zoom lens, with this process often eliciting other images for tracking. Frequently clients report significant insights from using this technique.

• *Aversive imagery.* Clients can learn to associate unpleasant images with behaviour that is unwanted yet self-reinforcing (e.g. alcoholism, sexual deviations, overeating). For instance, clients on diets can be trained to imagine that someone has vomited over the rich food they wish to eat.

• *Goal-rehearsal or coping imagery.* Clients are trained to break down the steps involved in difficult upcoming events. For each step, they visualize themselves faltering, but coping. For instance, a woman with an aversion to hospitals had the goal of visiting and supporting a sick friend. She imagined herself coping with the difficulties involved in the hospital visit and her sense of achievement for helping her friend.

• *Positive imagery.* Positive imagery entails visualizing a pleasant scene, real or imagined, past, present or future. Beneficial effects of positive imagery include: reducing tension, inhibiting anxiety and enhancing enjoyment.

• *The step-up technique.* Clients unduly anxious about upcoming events, for instance a public speech, are asked to picture the worst thing imaginable and then imagine themselves coping with the situation and surviving the most negative outcomes. Some clients require *self-instructional training* along with the step-up technique.

• *Time projection (forward or backward).* Time projection or 'time tripping' can be used to help clients relive and work through past events. In addition, clients can imagine both what might happen in the future, for instance depressed clients picturing themselves engaging in more and more rewarding activities, and how the present might look from the vantage point of the future, for instance picturing an event after a few months and realizing the temporary nature of some current problem.

Cognition

• *Bibliotherapy.* A well-chosen self-help book 'can be worth more than a dozen sessions' (Lazarus, 1989c, p. 243). Books should be thoroughly read, even summarised in notebooks, and readings discussed during sessions.

• *Correcting misconceptions.* Counsellors can provide clients with factual information to correct misconceptions about society, other people and themselves. Sexual misconceptions are common. Counsellors should learn the relevant facts and realities. Bibliotherapy can form an important component of correcting misconceptions.

• *Ellis's A-B-C-D-E paradigm.* Counsellors can teach clients Ellis's A (activating event), B (beliefs), C (consequences), D (disputing) and E (effects) paradigm. Clients can learn to identify their irrational beliefs (B) about activating events (A) which lead to negative consequences (C). Disputing these irrational beliefs (D) can result in the effect (E) of the diminution or elimination of negative consequences.

• *Problem-solving.* Clients can learn to apply the rudiments of scientific methodology to problems. Problem-solving involves generating plausible hypotheses that can be strengthened or weakened by gathering relevant information. Decisions are made on the basis of facts and probability rather than by mysticism or chance.

• *Self-instructional training.* Counsellors can train clients to replace negative self-statements with positive, task-oriented statements that facilitate coping. For instance, clients anxious about a forthcoming event could instruct themselves to: develop a plan; handle the situation one step at a time; if anxious, to pause and take a few deep breaths; remind themselves that they only have to keep fear manageable rather than eliminate it; focus on what they need to do; acknowledge the link between controlling self-talk and controlling fear; and recognize that it gets easier each time they use their self-instructions.

• *Thought-blocking.* Thought-blocking is a technique to combat obsessive and intrusive thoughts. Clients can be taught to subvocally scream 'STOP!' over and over again. A variation of thought-blocking is for clients to flick their wrists with a rubber band when they scream 'STOP!'. Some clients find it helps to picture huge neon signs flashing the letters 'S T O P' on and off.

Interpersonal

• *Communication training.* Counsellors can train clients in how to send and receive communications. Sending skills include eye-contact, body posture, voice projection and the use of simple concrete terms. Receiving skills include active listening and rewarding senders for communicating. Role playing and behaviour-rehearsal are especially useful in communication training.

• *Contingency contracting.* Clients agree to make rewards or negative consequences (usually self-imposed) contingent upon increasing, decreasing or maintaining a specific behaviour.

• *Friendship training.* In friendship training, counsellors identify and train clients in how to interact in prosocial and affectionate ways. Skills that counsellors emphasize include empathy, showing caring and concern, self-disclosing, positive reinforcement and give-and-take. Clients are taught to avoid competitiveness and self-aggrandizement.

• *Graded sexual approaches.* Partners are advised to engage in sensual and sexual activities only so long as pleasurable feelings predominate. They terminate such activities when anxious feelings erupt. With each encounter anxieties can recede and greater sexual arousal and intimacy become possible.

• *Paradoxical strategies.* Symptom prescription, for instance counsellors telling compulsive clients to increase their checking and ritualistic behaviours, is a common paradoxical strategy. Clients may decrease their unwanted behaviours if their counsellors prescribe that they exaggerate symptoms. Another common paradoxical strategy is that of forbidding a desired response. An example is that of counsellors forbidding men with erectile difficulties to have intercourse until they get specific permission. Clients whose desired responses are forbidden may be more likely to enact them, for instance by engaging in sexual intercourse.

• *Social skills and assertiveness training.* Four specific assertive response patterns or abilities that counsellors can train clients in are: saying 'no'; asking for favours and making requests; expressing positive and negative feelings; and initiating, continuing and terminating conversations. *Behaviour-rehearsal* and *modelling* are two major techniques employed in social skills and assertiveness training.

Drugs/biology

Multimodal counsellors encourage clients to take responsibility for their health and to develop good habits of eating nutritionally, exercising, and engaging in recreational activities. Counsellors refer clients to physicians where they suspect organic problems or consider biological interventions, such as anti-depressant medication, are indicated.

Evaluating multimodal counselling

Ongoing evaluations of progress are integral to multimodal counselling. Since Modality Profiles are commonly drawn up, counsellors can evaluate progress for each problem within each of the seven BASIC I.E. dimensions. Lazarus provides the following example of how a multimodal counsellor specifies a client's gains and achievements (Lazarus, 1989a, p. 528):

'Behaviour:	Less withdrawn; less compulsive; more outspoken
Affect:	More warm, less hostile; less depressed
Sensation:	Enjoys more pleasures; less tense, more relaxed
Imagery:	Fewer nightmares; better self–image
Cognition:	Less self-downing; more positive self-statements
Interpersonal:	Goes out on dates; expresses wishes and desires
Drugs/biologicals:	Stopped smoking; eats well; exercises regularly.'

Other applications

Multimodal counselling, with its BASIC I.D. assessment and interventions, has been applied in many areas in addition to individual personal counselling. Multimodal counselling has been used in marital work and in group work. In addition, multimodal counselling has provided a framework for career counselling and for Employee Assistance Program (EAP) counselling. Other areas of application of multimodal principles include: working with children in classroom settings; developing gifted adolescents; parent training; working with inpatients in mental hospitals; and counsellor education. Thus multimodal counselling, at the same time as espousing breadth in how counsellors assess and treat clients, has broad applicability to a wide range of areas.

Lazarus concludes the epilogue to the 1989 edition of the practice of multimodal therapy by stressing that he views psychotherapy as coping skills training and stating that he offers 'the BASIC I.D. as a systematic and comprehensive framework to ensure that significant issues are less likely to be overlooked' (Lazarus, 1989c, p. 224).

CHAPTER REVIEW AND SELF-REFERENT QUESTIONS

Chapter review questions

1. Why does Lazarus call his approach multimodal?

2. What does the term technical eclecticism mean?

3. What does Lazarus mean by thresholds?

4. What are modalities?

5. Describe each of the seven modalities of the BASIC I.D.

6. Critically discuss dividing human personality into the BASIC I.D. modalities.

7. To what extent does multimodal counselling have a theoretical base? Why is Lazarus afraid of his approach being too closely tied to any theory?

8. What do the terms nonconscious processes and defensive reactions mean?

9. What does Lazarus mean by misinformation and missing information? Why does he attach such importance to information deficits in how people acquire and maintain emotional disorders?

10. What are goals for multimodal counselling?

11. Critically discuss the role of the counselling relationship in multimodal counselling.

12. What does Lazarus mean by bridging? Provide an example.

13. What is the role of assessment in multimodal counselling and how do counsellors go about it?

14. What are Modality Profiles and what are their uses?

15. What are Structural Profiles and what are their uses?

16. What does Lazarus mean by tracking? Provide an example.

17. What are second-order BASIC I.D. assessments?

18. How do multimodal counsellors select techniques?

19. What are some principal multimodal techniques for changing behaviour?

20. What are some principal multimodal techniques for changing affect?

21. What are some principal multimodal techniques for changing sensation?

22. What are some principal multimodal techniques for changing imagery?

23. What are some principal multimodal techniques for changing cognition?

24. What are some principal multimodal techniques for the interpersonal dimension?

25. What are some principal multimodal techniques for the drugs/biology dimension?

26. How do multimodal counsellors evaluate clients' progress?

Self-referent questions

1. Identify a specific problem area in your life. To what extent do missing information and misinformation contribute to your acquiring and maintaining it?

2. Develop your Structural Profile by rating yourself, by using a 1 to 7 point scale, on each of the BASIC I.D. modalities?

3. Develop a Modality Profile for yourself.

4. Select and implement techniques to help you with one of your problems.

5. What relevance, if any, has the theory and practice of multimodal counselling for how you counsel?

6. What relevance, if any, has the theory and practice of multimodal counselling for how you live?

Annotated bibliography

Lazarus, A.A. (1989c). *The Practice of Multimodal Therapy: Systematic, Comprehensive and Effective Psychotherapy* (Rev. ed.). Baltimore, MA: Johns Hopkins University Press.
This book is exactly the same as the 1981 version apart from a 1989 epilogue and the addition of the 35–item Structural Profile Inventory as Appendix 4. The book includes chapters on multimodal counselling's basic rationale, its basic concepts for practice, the initial interview, multimodal assessment-counselling connections, relationship factors and the selection of

techniques. In addition, there are chapters on multimodal marriage therapy, multimodal sex therapy and multimodal therapy in special situations, for instance working with children. In addition to the Structural Profile Index appendix, the book has appendices containing a glossary of 37 principal techniques, the Multimodal Life History Questionnaire, and the Marital Satisfaction Questionnaire.

Lazarus, A.A. (1992). Multimodal therapy: Technical eclecticism with minimal integration. In J.C. Norcross & M.R. Goldfried (Eds.), *Handbook of Psychotherapy Integration* (pp. 231–63). New York: Basic Books.

This chapter presents Lazarus's ideas on systematic (technical) eclecticism and the risks of integration. Lazarus describes the distinctive features of the multimodal approach and how it differs from other eclectic approaches. Research findings are reviewed and suggestions made for clinical training and desirable future directions for psychotherapy. The chapter includes a case example.

Lazarus, A.A. (1989a). Multimodal therapy. In R.J. Corsini & D. Wedding (Eds.), *Current Psychotherapies* (4th ed, pp. 503–44). Itasca, IL: Peacock.

This chapter includes material on multimodal counselling's basic concepts, history and current status, theory of personality, theory of psychotherapy, process and mechanisms of therapy, applications and evaluation. A case example is provided.

Lazarus, A.A. (1984). *In the Mind's Eye: The Power of Imagery for Personal Enrichment.* New York: Guilford Press.

This is a well-written book of imagery techniques that counsellors can use with clients and people can use for self-help. The book is divided into four parts: the power of imagery; using imagery to build confidence and skill; using imagery to overcome problems; and some additional imagery exercises.

Further references

Lazarus

Dryden, W. (1991). *A Dialogue with Arnold Lazarus: 'It Depends'.* Milton Keynes: Open University Press.

Kwee, M.G.T. & Lazarus, A.A. (1986). Multimodal therapy: The cognitive-behavioural tradition and beyond. In W. Dryden & W. Golden (Eds.), *Cognitive-behavioural Approaches to Psychotherapy* (pp. 320–55). London: Harper & Row.

Lazarus, A.A. (1961). Group therapy of phobic disorders by systematic desensitization. *Journal of Abnormal and Social Psychology, 63,* 505–10.

Lazarus, A.A. (1967). In support of technical eclecticism. *Psychological Reports, 21,* 415–16.

Lazarus, A.A. (1971). *Behavior Therapy and Beyond.* New York: McGraw-Hill.

Lazarus, A.A. (Ed.) (1972). *Clinical Behavior Therapy.* New York: Brunner/Mazel.

Lazarus, A.A. (1976a). *Multimodal Behavior Therapy.* New York: Springer.

Lazarus, A.A. (1981). *The Practice of Multimodal Therapy.* New York: McGraw-Hill.

Lazarus, A.A. (1985). *Marital Myths.* San Luis Obispo, CA: Impact Publishers.

Lazarus, A.A. (1977). Toward an egoless state of being. In A. Ellis & R. Grieger (Eds.), *Handbook for Rational-emotive Therapy* (pp. 113–18). New York: Springer.

Lazarus, A.A. (1989b). Why I am an eclectic (not an integrationist). *British Journal of Guidance and Counselling, 17,* 248–58.

Lazarus, A.A. (1989d). The case of George. In D. Wedding & R.J. Corsini (Eds.), *Case Studies in Psychotherapy* (pp. 227–38). Itasca, IL: Peacock.

Lazarus, A.A. (1990). Can psychotherapists transcend the shackles of their training and superstitions? *Journal of Clinical Psychology, 46*, 351–8.

Lazarus, A.A. (1993a). Tailoring the therapeutic relationship, or being an authentic chameleon. *Psychotherapy, 30*, 404–7.

Lazarus, A.A. (1993b). Theory, subjectivity and bias: Can there be a future? *Psychotherapy, 30*, 674–7.

Lazarus, A.A. Beutler, L.E. & Norcross, J.C. (1992). The future of technical eclecticism. *Psychotherapy, 29*, 11–20.

Lazarus, A.A. & Fay, A. (1975). *I Can if I Want to*. New York: William Morrow.

Lazarus, A.A. & Lazarus, C.N. (1991a). *Multimodal Life History Inventory*. Champaign, IL: Research Press.

Lazarus, A.A. & Lazarus, C.N. (1991b). Let us not forsake the individual nor ignore the data: A response to Bozarth. *Journal of Counseling and Development, 69*, 463–5.

Lazarus, A.A. Lazarus, C.N. & Fay, A. (1993). *Don't Believe It for a Minute!* San Louis Obispo, CA: Impact Publishers.

Lazarus, A.A. & Mayne, T.J. (1990). Relaxation: Some limitations, side effects and proposed solutions. *Psychotherapy, 27*, 261–6.

Wolpe, J. & Lazarus, A.A. (1966). *Behaviour Therapy Techniques*. Oxford: Pergamon Press.

Zilbergeld, B. & Lazarus, A.A. (1987). *Mind Power*. Boston: Little Brown.

Others

Bandura, A. (1977). *Social Learning Theory*. Englewood Cliffs, NJ: Prentice-Hall.

Bandura, A. (1986). *Social Foundations of Thought and Action: A Social Cognitive Theory*. Englewood Cliffs, NJ: Prentice-Hall.

Meichenbaum, D.H. (1977). *Cognitive-behavior Modification*. New York: Plenum.

Lazarus on cassette

Lazarus, A.A. (1976b). *Learning to Relax*. New York: Institute for Rational Living.

Lazarus, A.A. (1982). *Personal Enrichment through Imagery* (3 cassettes plus workbook). New York: BMA Audio Cassette Publications.

Lazarus, A.A. (1984a). *Mental Imagery: Your Hidden Potential*. Washington, DC: American Psychological Association (Psychology Today).

Lazarus, A.A. (1984b). *Mental Imagery: Techniques and Exercises*. Washington, DC: American Psychological Association (Psychology Today).

FIFTEEN
Lifeskills Counselling

PREVIEW

- *Lifeskills counselling is an integrative approach for assisting clients to develop self-helping skills. The approach distinguishes between biological and psychological life. Lifeskills are sequences of choices affirming psychological life that people make in specific skills areas.*

- *The theory and practice of lifeskills counselling is expressed in skills language. Skills language consistently uses the concept of skills to describe and analyse how people think and act. In each skills area people can possess skills strengths and skills deficits.*

- *There are three forms of self: The Natural Self; the Learned Self, consisting both of self-concept and of lifeskills; and the Executive Self, or choosing self. All people possess an energizing drive towards surviving, maintaining and developing themselves.*

- *Survival anxiety is a normal part of life, though it may become transformed into debilitating anxiety. People are personally responsible for making their psychological lives. They require courage to confront and relinquish lifeskills deficits and to acquire, maintain and develop lifeskills strengths.*

- *Lifeskills theory focuses on the acquisition of both lifeskills and skills language. Processes by which people acquire lifeskills strengths and deficits include supportive relationships, learning from example and consequences, instruction and self-instruction, information and opportunity, and experiences of anxiety and confidence.*

- *Processes by which people maintain lifeskills deficits include insufficient use of skills language, various thinking skills deficits, and unchanged environmental circumstances.*

- *Lifeskills counselling has dual goals: developing the skills to cope with specific problems now and in future, and developing skilled persons. The skilled person possesses significant lifeskills strengths in each area of the five Rs of affirming psychological life: responsiveness, realism, relating, rewarding activity, and right-and-wrong.*

- *The practice of lifeskills counselling is structured around DASIE, a systematic five stage model of the counselling process. DASIE's five stages, each of which are described, are: (1) Develop the relationship, identify and clarify problem(s); (2) Assess problem(s) and redefine in skills terms; (3) State working goals and plan interventions; (4) Intervene to develop self-helping skills; (5) End and consolidate self-helping skills.*

- *Other applications of the lifeskills counselling framework include confronting existential concerns and group approaches to counselling and lifeskills training. Above all, lifeskills counselling is an approach to self-helping.*

INTRODUCTION

Lifeskills counselling, otherwise known as lifeskills helping (LSH) or lifeskills therapy, is a counselling approach that integrates many of the insights and strengths of the theoretical and practical approaches presented in this book. Lifeskills counselling is integrative because it combines and reworks ideas from other approaches into a coherent theoretical whole. In addition, the approach possesses some distinctive features. Lifeskills counselling assumes that theory is as much for clients' benefit as for that of their counsellors. Where possible, lifeskills counsellors transmit lifeskills theory to clients.

Lifeskills counselling owes much to others' work. For example, the emphasis on the important of supportive helping relationships and on sensitively attending to clients' feelings shows the influence of Carl Rogers' person-centred approach. The emphasis on thinking skills is derived from the writings of Albert Ellis, Aaron Beck, Arnold Lazarus and Donald Meichenbaum, among others. The emphasis on action skills represents the influence of the behaviourists. The emphasis on personal responsibility, choice and courage has origins in the work of Viktor Frankl, Irvin Yalom, Rollo May, William Glasser, Abraham Maslow, Hobart Mowrer and the theologian Paul Tillich. Harry Stack Sullivan, Gerard Egan and Robert Carkhuff were forerunners in presenting stage models of counselling sessions and the counselling process.

Though still in process of development, lifeskills counselling fulfils each of the three main functions of counselling theories outlined in Chapter 1. First, it provides a conceptual framework in which counsellors can think systematically about human development and counselling practice. Second, it offers a language or vocabulary in which the counselling conversation can take place. Third, lifeskills counselling may be viewed as a series of research hypotheses. For instance, research may be conducted on the processes and outcomes of counsellors and clients using lifeskills language during counselling and of clients using it after counselling to maintain self-helping skills.

Richard Nelson-Jones

Richard Nelson-Jones was born in London on 2 December 1936, though the act of conception took place in Hong Kong where his father was a medical practitioner.

Fearing the outcome of war in the East, his parents settled in Britain, though they were soon to separate. From 1940–5, with his mother and older brother, Nelson-Jones was a refugee in the San Francisco Bay Area of the United States. In 1945, returning to postwar Britain from relatively affluent and much more relaxed California, he received an early experience of culture shock. His parents reunited but never consistently found happiness together, which adversely affected the emotional climate at home. Nelson-Jones had a traditional middle-class British education and was sent away to boarding schools until the age of 18.

After two years a national service officer in Malaya, Singapore and Germany, Nelson-Jones completed an economics undergraduate degree at Cambridge University. In 1960 Nelson-Jones returned to San Francisco for a summer vacation before joining a London merchant bank, which he left after six months to go back to America. There he worked in a San Francisco stockbroking house for a year. Then, in 1962, he went to Stanford University Business School. The next six months were a turning point leading to Nelson-Jones enrolling in the counselling and guidance programme in the Stanford University School of Education. Three important factors influenced his decision to become a counsellor. First, at Business School he did poorly in economics and extremely well in organizational psychology; second, he had a part-time job as a counsellor in an undergraduate residence hall; and third, he increasingly realized his own need for counselling. Nelson-Jones received his MA and PhD from Stanford in 1964 and 1967, respectively. During his Stanford years Nelson-Jones received numerous hours of individual client-centred counselling from Dr John Black, the then Director of the Counseling and Testing Center. In addition, he was a member of three Standford University Medical Center therapy groups, one of which was co-led by Irvin Yalom.

In August 1966 Nelson-Jones moved to Boston where he was Associate Director and Acting Director of the New England Board of Higher Education, a coordinating body for public higher education. In Boston he resumed individual counselling, this time with Dr Stanley Estes, recently retired from the Harvard University Psychology Department. He left the New England Board shortly after it moved to Durham, New Hampshire, and from spring 1968 to autumn 1969 he worked in Ottawa as a full-time Research Associate for the Association of Canadian Medical Colleges.

Returning to Britain in 1969, from 1970–82 he was lecturer and then Senior Lecturer in the Department of Educational Studies at the University of Aston in Birmingham. At Aston he set up a Postgraduate Diploma in Counselling in Educational Settings course and also worked as a counselling psychologist for the University Health Service. In 1982, as part of government cuts as Aston, Nelson-Jones took voluntary redundancy with compensation for loss of office. Moving to London, he established the London Centre for Counselling Psychology, a private training and consultancy business.

In March 1984 Nelson-Jones joined the Department of Social Science of the Royal Melbourne Institute of Technology, Australia, where, as a Senior Lecturer, Principal Lecturer and Associate Professor, he has been responsible for counselling psychology training. In 1994, as part of a reorganization, he joined RMIT's Department of Psychology and Intellectual Disability Studies. In recent years Nelson-Jones has run workshops and given seminars on his lifeskills helping approach in Australia, Britain,

Hong Kong, Malaysia, Thailand (where he has been Visiting Professor in the University of Chaing Mai) and at Stanford and Virginia Commonwealth Universities in the United States.

Nelson-Jones has written numerous scientific and professional articles in American, Australian, British and Canadian journals. His books include *The Theory and Practice of Counselling Psychology, Personal Responsibility Counselling and Therapy, Human Relationship Skills, Effective Thinking Skills: Preventing and Managing Personal Problems, Practical Counselling and Helping Skills: How to Use the Lifeskills Helping Model, Training Manual for Counselling and Helping Skills* and *You Can Help!: Introducing Lifeskills Helping.* In addition to Britain, his books are published in Australia, America and India.

ASSUMPTIONS

Lifeskills counselling's theory and practice is based on Albert Einstein's dictum 'Everything should be made as simple as possible, but not simpler'. Following are some assumptions.

Psychological education approach

Lifeskills counselling is a people-centred approach for assisting clients to develop self-helping skills. This approach spurns psychological jargon in favour of a simple, direct, educational framework. Geared to the needs of the vast majority of ordinary people, lifeskills counselling assumes that *all people* have acquired and sustain lifeskills strengths and deficits. Following are four key concepts of this approach.

1. Most problems brought to counsellors reflect clients' learning histories.

2. Though external factors contribute, clients sustain problems by possessing deficits in how they think and in how they act (in their thinking skills and in their action skills).

3. Counsellors are most effective when, within supportive helping relationships, they train clients in relevant thinking and action skills.

4. The ultimate goal of lifeskills helping is self-helping, whereby clients maintain and develop thinking skills and action skills strengths, not just to cope with present problems but to prevent and handle future problems.

Biological and psychological life

Life is generally regarded as a biological concept. However, the main concern of lifeskills counselling is with psychological rather than biological life. The two concepts overlap and psychological existence takes place within biological life. Also, biological life can influence psychological life, for instance the effects of fatigue on feelings of well-being, and psychological life can influence biological life, an extreme example being suicide. In addition, with physical illnesses such as cancer, treatment frequently needs to focus on both biological and psychological lives.

Having noted a few areas of overlap, what are some distinguishing characteristics of psychological as contrasted with biological life? Figure 15.1 summarizes some of these differences.

The following discussion elaborates the distinctions made in Figure 15.1. Most often, despite the use of the word versus, the differences are of degree rather than either-or distinctions.

• *Body versus mind.* The primary focus of psychological life is the mind rather than the body.

• *Animate existence versus awareness and choice.* By definition any form of biological life has animate existence. From birth, people's vital organs exist at a sufficient level to sustain this existence. They can obtain energy by breathing and eating. However, human psychological life goes beyond animate existence in that humans have a unique capacity for self-awareness and choice. They can remember their pasts, make choices in their presents and plan their futures. Psychological life is a continuous process of struggling to make life-enhancing rather than life-constricting choices. A psychological life-against-death struggle permeates biological life.

• *Health versus attaining human potential.* The primary goal of biological life is good physical health. The primary goal of psychological life is attaining human potential. Psychological life concerns people's ability to use their minds for the purpose of enhancing the quality of their existence by fulfilling their unique potentials.

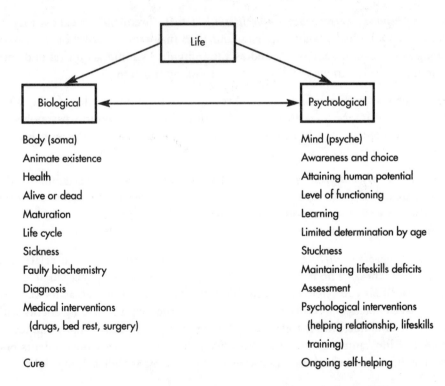

Figure 15.1 Some differences between biological and psychological life.

• *Alive/dead versus level of functioning.* The opposite of biological life is death, ceasing to exist in animate form, or non-being. There are some debatable areas regarding when people are clinically dead. However, for most humans, even when sick, the issue is polarized into being either alive or dead. The purpose of psychological life is to enhance existence rather than survival. People are at different levels of functioning in terms of their ability to affirm their psychological lives. Psychological life is relative (there are varying degrees of it) rather than dichotomous (such as being alive or dead).

• *Maturation versus learning.* Maturation is an important concept in acquiring biological abilities, for instance the ability to reproduce. The quality of psychological life is based more on learning rather than maturation, on nurture rather than nature. However, there are areas of overlap: for instance, cognitive capacities biologically mature and people possess biological tendencies to sabotage their psychological lives.

• *Life cycle versus limited determination by age.* There is a biological human life cycle of conception, birth, growing up, maturity, decline and death. However, there is no fixed relationship between psychological life and biological age. Young people's potentials can be stunted and old people can be actively in control of their lives.

• *Sickness versus stuckness.* Though a simplification, when people come to see medical doctors they are physically or biologically sick and do not know how to get better. When they come to see counsellors they are psychologically stuck and do not know how to think and act better.

• *Faulty biochemistry versus maintaining lifeskills deficits.* Frequently, sickness may be viewed as the individual's body acquiring and then maintaining faulty biochemistry. Psychological stuckness may be viewed as the individual's mind acquiring and then maintaining lifeskills deficits or faulty ways of thinking and acting.

• *Diagnosis versus assessment.* Sickness requires medical diagnosis to identify the faulty biochemistry that interferes with biological health. Stuckness requires psychological assessment to identify the lifeskills deficits that interfere with attaining human potential.

• *Medical versus psychological intervention.* Medical interventions for attaining health include drugs, bed rest and surgery. Counselling interventions for attaining psychological lifeskills include offering supportive helping relationships and training clients in relevant lifeskills.

• *Cure versus ongoing self-helping.* Often the concept of cure is used in relation to overcoming sickness. The concept of cure is inappropriate to psychological life. Psychological life is reversible in that people can go backwards as well as forwards in ability to make choices. Lifeskills counselling is concerned with providing clients with the skills to enhance and maintain psychological life. Because maintenance of psychological life cannot be assumed and given the certainty that most clients end counselling, lifeskills counselling's prime objective is to impart self-helping skills.

Skills language

What are skills?

One meaning of the word skills pertains to *areas* of skill: for instance, listening skills or disclosing skills. Another meaning refers to *level of competence*, for instance, skilled or unskilled in a particular area. A third meaning of skill relates to the *knowledge and sequence of choices* entailed in implementing the skill. The essential element of any skill is the ability to make and implement sequences of choices to achieve objectives. For instance, if clients are to be good at asserting themselves or managing stress, they have to make and implement effective choices in these lifeskills areas.

The concept of skill is best viewed not as an either/or matter in which people either possess or do not possess a skill. Rather, it is preferable to think of people as possessing *skills strengths* or *skills deficits* or a mixture of the two. Good choices in skills areas are skills strengths. Poor choices are skills deficits. The criterion for good or poor client choices is whether or not they affirm psychological life. In all lifeskills areas people are likely to possess skills strengths and deficits in varying degrees. For instance, in the skills area of listening they may be good at understanding talkers but poor at showing their understanding. The object of lifeskills counselling is to help clients, in one or more skills areas, move more in the direction of skills strength rather than skills deficits.

What are lifeskills?

Apart from such obviously biological functions as breathing, virtually all human behaviour is viewed in terms of learned lifeskills. The term lifeskills in itself is a neutral concept. Lifeskills may be strengths or deficits depending on whether or not they help people to survive and to maintain and develop potentials. A neutral definition of the term is: *lifeskills are sequences of choices that people make in specific skills areas.* A positive definition of the term is: *lifeskills are sequences of choices affirming psychological life that people make in specific skills areas.*

What is skills language?

Skills language means consistently using the concept of skills to describe and analyse people's behaviour. In regard to counselling, skills language means conceptualizing and conversing about clients' problems in terms of lifeskills strengths and deficits. Skills language provides a relatively simple way that both counsellors and clients can analyse and work on problems. Many clients find it easier to look at their problems in terms of the skills they need to work on them rather than having to admit personal inadequacy or blame. In particular, skills language involves identifying the specific thinking skills and action skills deficits that maintain clients' problems. Feelings too are important. However, feelings represent people's animal nature and are not skills in themselves. People can influence their feelings for good or ill through their use of thinking and action skills.

A difference exists between the vernacular, the descriptive language of ordinary conversation, and the functional language required for people trying to help themselves. Since the goal of counselling is to help people adopt a life-long philosophy of self-helping, the language of counselling needs to lend itself to client self-instructing. However, counselling's language should still be as close as possible to the vernacular to help clients understand and use it. Skills language provides a psychologically functional way of communicating that is close to the vernacular.

In any helping contact, at least four possible languages are involved: namely helper and client private and public talk (Nelson-Jones, 1986). Lifeskills counselling is based on an educational theoretical framework, expressed in skills language, that counsellors can use both for private and public talk. Counsellors do not need to talk one language to themselves and another to clients. Lifeskills counsellors use their own and their clients' public talk to develop clients' private talk so that the latter can understand their own problems and instruct themselves through sequences of choices to cope with them.

Figure 15.2 illustrates public and private talk in counselling. Much counselling is educationally inefficient. It focuses insufficiently on moving beyond counsellor and client public talk at points B and C. In lifeskills counselling, counsellors use public talk at points B and C not just to develop a helping relationship but actively to work from helper private self-talk at point A to influence client private self-talk at point D. By communicating from an educational framework expressed in skills language, counsellors can help clients acquire relevant private self-talk to monitor, maintain and develop targeted skills. Hence, the language of lifeskills helping becomes the people-centred language of self-instructing and self-helping.

Three forms of self

A person's self is what she or he calls 'I' or 'me'. It is the centre of her or his personal universe. As depicted in Figure 15.3, the self has three major components.

(a) *The Natural Self.* Each person has a fundamental biological inner nature, or inner core of genetic aptitudes, drives, instincts, instinct remnants and human potentialities.

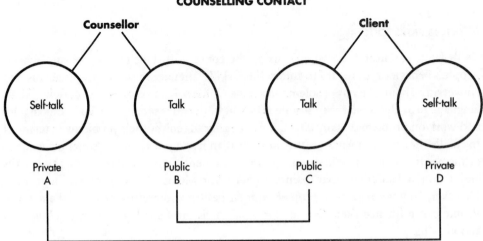

Figure 15.2 Public and private talk in counselling.

This is their animal nature. The Natural Self incorporates characteristics such as energy, sexuality, feelings and anxiety. It possesses needs shared by the entire human species; for instance, for food, shelter, physical safety, belonging and love. However, the Natural Self is also unique to each individual in terms of their specific aptitudes, inner valuing process, energizing drive and thresholds for conditioning and anxiety. The Natural Self is a person's inner nature or the biological core of their personhood. Unfortunately, this inner nature can work against as well as for the person: for instance, in terms of a universal biological propensity to think irrationally as well as rationally (Ellis, 1989).

(b) *The Learned Self.* The Learned Self is the product of people's learning experiences. The self-concept is the traditional way of viewing the learned self. In Figure 15.3 it is depicted as the LC or Learned Self-Concept. The LC consists of people's self-conceptions in numerous different areas: relationships sexuality, work, leisure, tastes and preferences, values and so on.

Another way of looking at the Learned Self is in terms of people's lifeskills strengths and deficits in different areas. In Figure 15.3 this is depicted as the LS or Learned Self-Skills. People's self-concepts (LC) do not necessarily reflect their lifeskills strengths and deficits (LS). First, they may not think about themselves in

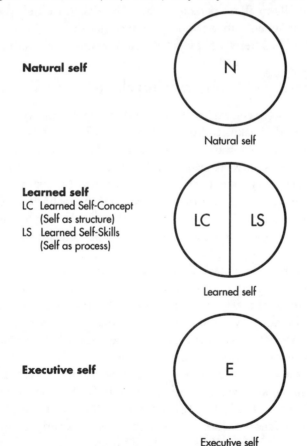

Natural self

Natural self

Learned self
LC Learned Self-Concept
　　(Self as structure)
LS Learned Self-Skills
　　(Self as process)

Learned self

Executive self

Executive self

Figure 15.3 The three forms of self.

skills language. Second, they may not know the different specific lifeskills they require. Third, they may inaccurately perceive their strengths and deficits in various lifeskills areas.

Viewing the Learned Self in skills terms has advantages. The LC relates to the self as structure, whereby people describe their self-concepts in static terms; for instance 'I'm depressed'. The LS relates to the self as process, whereby people are in process of using, maintaining, developing or losing skills; for instance 'I'm using certain skills that contribute to my being depressed'. The LS has the advantages of skills language in that counsellors and clients can then try to pin-point the skills for becoming less depressed. Furthermore, once clients know what the sequences of choices are for the skills of becoming less depressed, they can use these skills again when on their own.

(c) *The Executive Self.* Whereas people's Natural and Learned Self represents their biological endowment and their Learned Self reflects their past learning history, their Executive Self represents their capacity to *make* their lives through their choices in the present and future. Thus people not only have selves but also continuously create selves. People can choose those aspects of their Natural and Learned Selves that they wish to develop. This is particularly important in lifeskills helping where clients choose to develop specific skills to attain personal goals. The Executive Self provides a means whereby people can choose to work on relinquishing the misperceptions and skills deficits of their Learned Selves that block the fulfilment of their Natural Selves.

Energizing drive

Ordinary people may have difficulty understanding terms like 'the organism's actualizing tendency' (Raskin & Rogers, 1989, p. 169) or self-realizing. All people possess an energizing drive towards surviving, maintaining and developing themselves. However, humans possess weak instinctual remnants (Maslow, 1970): unlike other animals, human behaviour is not strongly programmed by instincts. Consequently, people can have fortunate or unfortunate experiences in both acquiring and also learning how to maintain and develop lifeskills. The long human learning process and human's ability for symbolic thought offer much scope for acquiring and maintaining lifeskills deficits as well as strengths.

The energizing drive is neither good nor bad: nature does not operate in such terms. Humans are animals first and people second. If anything, instinctually people are more likely to operate in ways that protect themselves and the species than not. However, biologically, both as individuals and as a species, humans have predispositions for both life affirming and life destructive behaviours. Consequently, both for biological reasons and as a result of faulty learning, the energizing drive may turn against itself.

The goals of the energizing drive may be viewed on at least three dimensions: first, the basic animal survival dimension; second, the pleasure dimension or what Ellis terms 'short-range hedonism' (Ellis, 1989, p. 209); and third, the dimension of higher level and often more socially oriented involvements and commitments. Terms life 'self-actualizing' (Maslow, 1962, 1970) and 'propriate striving' have been used to describe 'the integrity that comes only from maintaining major directions of striving' (Allport, 1955, p. 51). Lifeskills are required for each of the above three ways of expending energy. However, most humans are probably more spontaneously driven by survival and short-range hedonism than by longer-term and higher level strivings, although they can learn to forgo short-term goals in the pursuit of longer-term goals.

Meanings of anxiety

Survival anxiety

The existential counselling viewpoint is that fear of biological death, non-being or destruction is the underlying fear from which all other fears are derived (May & Yalom, 1989; Yalom, 1980). The term survival anxiety seems preferable to that of death anxiety. The notion of survival anxiety focuses more than death anxiety on the continual fears of the living. Survival anxiety relates both to people's fear of biological death itself and also to their fears of not being competent to meet their survival needs, which they perceive in psychological as well as biological terms.

Survival anxiety can be conscious, preconscious and unconscious. In varying degrees people can be aware of their anxiety as it happens. Preconscious anxiety may surface in relatively safe situations, such as counselling or in loving relationships. Much anxiety is repressed because it is too threatening to the organism and because other people collude in the repression. For instance, repressed fears of death may appear in disguised form in dreams and nightmares.

Normal and debilitating anxiety

Anxiety is viewed as a normal part of life in a number of ways. First, anxiety is a basic animal survival mechanism that signals some danger or threat to the organism. Second, humans cannot escape the anxiety connected with confronting the givens of existence: death, suffering, freedom, isolation and meaninglessness. Third, anxiety is part of learning, deciding and changing, each activity requiring relinquishing something to gain something. For example, a degree of psychological independence from parents is a developmental task of all humans, yet most often this entails giving up some security to become, ultimately, more secure.

For many reasons, humans learn skills deficits that contribute to normal anxiety being transformed into debilitating anxiety (Alpert & Haber, 1960). In varying degrees, all humans acquire and maintain an exaggerated sense of danger and threat, either general or in relation to specific situations, that interferes with full psychological life. This view is echoed by Beck, who viewed anxiety disorders as characterized by 'excessive functioning or malfunctioning of normal survival mechanisms' (Beck & Weishaar, 1989, p. 297). Debilitating anxiety can be both cause and effect of lifeskills deficits. People with anxiety disorders can maximize the chances of negative and minimize the chances of positive outcomes instead of realistically appraising situations and having an optimal level of anxiety. As part of this process, they may distort their sense of competence to bring about desired outcomes or, to use Bandura's term, their self-efficacy beliefs (Bandura, 1986).

Personal responsibility

Focusing on personal responsibility is almost like focusing on one's nose. Though right in front of the face, the concept is not always easy to observe (Nelson-Jones, 1984). Lifeskills counselling adopts the existential notion of people as responsible for the authorship of their lives (Sartre, 1956; May & Yalom, 1989; Yalom, 1980). Another metaphor is that people are responsible for inventing their lives. Authorship or invention requires a continuous process of choosing. Personal responsibility is an inner process in which people work from 'inside to outside'. This process starts with people's thoughts and feelings and leads to their observable actions. Furthermore, especially as people grow older, many if not most of the significant barriers to assuming responsibility are internal rather than external. However, both inside and outside of helping, people 'differ enormously in the degree of responsibility they are willing to accept for their life situation and in their modes of denying responsibility' (May & Yalom, 1989, p. 377).

Courage

The word courage is derived from the Latin word *cor*, meaning heart. Paul Tillich, in his inspiring book *The Courage to Be* (1952), wrote: 'The courage to be is the ethical act in which man affirms his own being in spite of those elements of his existence which conflict with his essential self-affirmation' (p. 3). May, a long-standing friend of Tillich's, distinguishes between physical, moral, social and creative courage (May, 1975).

Here I distinguish between three different, yet overlapping, kinds of courage. First, there is the courage to confront and relinquish lifeskills deficits. Though lifeskills deficits may offer the illusion of security, by definition they constrict psychological life. It can take courage to acknowledge one's human frailty. Second, there is the courage to develop lifeskills strengths. Frequently people need to develop lifeskills strengths despite many personal and environmental factors that make it hard for them to do so. Such 'despite' factors include the work involved and anxieties about learning and change. Third, there is the courage to maintain and develop lifeskills. There is no magic or concept of cure. Nor is there any automatic 'pat on the back' for good use of lifeskills. Instead, counsellors and clients need to work on the skills of having the courage to be 'centred' and authentic people. Inner strength is another term to describe the sort of courage to which I refer.

ACQUISITION

The lifeskills approach to human development seeks to answer two important and interrelated questions. First, how do people acquire lifeskills strengths and deficits? In particular, how do they acquire thinking skills and action skills strengths and deficits? Second, how do people acquire skills language, the ability to think about and analyse their behaviour in skills terms? In this section, the focus is more on the processes of acquiring lifeskills strengths and deficits, though the same processes apply to learning skills language. I start by describing what I mean by thinking skills and action skills.

Inner and outer games

If humans are to control their behaviour, they need to think and act effectively. A simple way of highlighting the distinction is to talk about people's inner and outer games of living. The inner game relates to what goes on inside them, how they think, or their thinking skills. The outer game relates to what goes on outside them, how they act, or their action skills. Thinking is covert, action is overt. Feelings are not ignored. Humans need to be able to experience, express and manage their feelings. However, as mentioned earlier, feelings represent humans' animal nature and are not skills in themselves.

Thinking skills

Below are brief descriptions of ten thinking skills areas. By using skills language, counsellors can draw upon the insights of different cognitive theorists, such as Beck and Ellis, without getting trapped in the different languages of their theoretical positions. The thinking skills are presented in 'you' language both to heighten readers' awareness of their meaning and to make the point that counsellors and clients require the same lifeskills.

• *Owning responsibility for choosing.* You are aware that you are the author of your existence and that you can choose how you think, act and feel. You are aware of the limitations of existence, such as your death.

• *Using coping self-talk.* Instead of talking to yourself negatively before, during and after specific situations, you can make self-statements that calm you down, coach you in how to cope, and affirm the skills you possess.

• *Choosing realistic personal rules.* Your unrealistic personal rules make irrational demands on yourself, others, and the environment: for instance, 'I must be liked by everyone', 'Others must not make mistakes', and 'Life must be fair'. Instead you can develop realistic rules: for instance, 'I prefer to be liked, but its unrealistic to expect this from everyone.'

• *Choosing to perceive accurately.* You avoid labelling yourself and others either too negatively or too positively. You distinguish between fact and inference and make your inferences as accurate as possible.

• *Explaining cause accurately.* You explain the causes of events accurately. You avoid assuming too much responsibility by internalizing, 'It's all my fault', or externalizing, 'It's all their fault'.

• *Predicting realistically.* You are realistic about the risks and rewards of future actions. You assess threats and dangers accurately. You avoid distorting relevant evidence with unwarranted optimism or pessimism. Your expectancies about your level of competence to perform tasks are accurate.

• *Setting realistic goals.* Your short- medium- and long-term goals reflect your values, are realistic, are specific and have a time frame.

- *Using visualizing skills.* People think in pictorial images as well as in words. You use visual images in ways that calm you down, assist you in acting competently to attain your goals and help you to resist giving in to bad habits.

- *Realistic decision-making.* You confront rather than avoid decisions and then make up your mind by going through a rational decision-making process.

- *Preventing and managing problems.* You anticipate and confront your problems. You assess the thinking and action skills you require to deal with them. You set goals and plan how to implement them.

Action skills

Action skills involve observable behaviours. They are what you do and how you do it rather than what and how you feel and think. Action skills vary by area of application: for instance, relating, study, work, leisure, health and social participation.

There are five main ways in which people can send action skills messages. Again, I list these in 'you' language.

- *Verbal messages.* Messages that you send with words.

- *Voice messages.* Messages that you send through your voice volume, articulation, pitch, emphasis and speech rate.

- *Body messages.* Messages that you send with your body through your gaze, eye contact, facial expression, posture, gestures, physical proximity and clothes and grooming.

- *Touch messages.* A special category of body messages. Messages that you send with your touch through the part of your body that you use, what part of another's body you touch, how gentle or firm you are, and whether or not you have permission.

- *Action messages.* Messages that you send when you are not face-to-face with others, for example sending flowers or a legal writ.

After this brief introduction to viewing how people think and act in skills terms, below are some processes by which people acquire lifeskills strengths and deficits.

Supportive relationships

Children require supportive relationships. Bowlby (1979) talks of the concept of a secure base, otherwise referred to as an attachment figure. He notes accumulating evidence that humans of all ages are happiest and most effective when they feel that standing behind them is a trusted person who will come to their aid should difficulties arise. Rogers has also stressed the need for supportive parent-child relationships characterized by high degrees of respect, genuineness and empathic understanding whereby children can feel sensitively and accurately understood (Rogers, 1951, 1959). Supportive relationships can be provided by many people other than parents; for instance, relatives and teachers. When growing up, most people seem to need at least one primary supportive relationship.

Many reasons exist why presence of supportive and absence of unsupportive or hostile relationships can help children to develop lifeskills strengths. First, supportive relationships provide children with the security to engage in exploratory behaviour and risk trial-and-error learning. Such exploratory behaviour represents a series of personal experiments in which children collect information about themselves and their environments. Second, supportive relationships help children listen better to themselves. By feeling prized and accurately understood, children can get more in touch with their wants, wishes and personal meanings. Third, children may feel freer to bring out into the open and show others emerging lifeskills without risk of ridicule. Fourth, instruction in specific skills is frequently best conducted in the context of supportive relationships in which the anxiety attached to learning is diminished. Fifth, the presence or absence of supportive relationships can either affirm or negate children's sense of worth. They may either be helped to become confident to face life's challenges or they may become inhibited, withdrawn and afraid to take risks. Alternatively, they may mask their insecurity by excessive attention-seeking.

Learning from example

Learning from observing is a major way in which people acquire lifeskills strengths and deficits (Bandura, 1986). How to think, feel and act can be learned from others' examples. Frequently people remain unaware of behaviours they demonstrate to children. If either or both parents are emotionally unexpressive, children miss opportunities for observing how to express emotions. If parents and others use ineffective thinking skills, for example blaming and overgeneralizing, children may be quick to do likewise. In addition, children may acquire from parents' examples poor action skills for relationships, work, leisure and health care. The converse is also true in that lifeskills strengths in how to feel, think and act may be acquired from the role-modelling of parents and significant others. Significant others may include peers, teachers, siblings, other relatives and even the media.

Just as teaching by example is often unintentional, so is learning by example. For instance, the effects of modelling are less direct when thinking skills rather than action skills are involved. Not only are thinking skills not observable in the sense that action skills are, but they are seldom clearly verbalized. People may absorb from example deficient skills for thinking, feeling and action and then possess the added barrier of remaining unawares that this has happened.

Learning from consequences

Lifeskills learning from observing role models is frequently intermingled with learning from rewarding or unrewarding consequences. For example, parents poor at showing emotions may also be poor at receiving children's emotions. Rewarding consequences can be either primary or secondary. Primary rewarding consequences are ones that people find rewarding independent of their learning histories: for instance, food, shelter, sex and human warmth. Skinner considers that all rewards eventually derive their power from evolutionary selection and that it is part of human nature to be rewarded by particular things (Skinner, 1971). However, only a small part of behaviour is immediately reinforced by rewards of evident biological significance. Most behaviour is emitted in response to secondary rewards, such as approval or money, that have become associated with or conditioned to primary rewards.

People receive consequences in two main ways. First, there is *classical conditioning* where consequences are independent of operating on the environment. For example, a person who has been in a serious car accident may feel anxious either about being in a car or about other characteristics of the accident, for instance its location. Many aversions appear to result from classical conditioning (Lazarus, 1989). Second, there is *operant conditioning* where consequences result from behaviours that operate on the environment. For example, the behaviour of requesting dates may lead to acceptance or rejection. However, people do not just receive consequences, they think about past consequences they have received, present consequences they are receiving, and make rules and predictions to guide their future behaviour (Bandura, 1986). Thus, people's cognitive processes may strengthen, weaken or otherwise alter the impact of rewarding consequences. In addition, there are biological differences in people's propensity to be conditioned by rewarding consequences.

Rewarding consequences play a large part in helping or hindering people in acquiring lifeskills strengths. Virtually from birth, humans receive messages about how 'good' or 'bad' their actions are. Usually with the best of intentions, adults try to reward children for developing the skills necessary to cope with the world. However, often adults provide rewards in deficient ways. For example, most people learn their relationship skills and thinking skills from a mixture of observing others, unsystematic feedback and trial-and-error. Rarely, either inside or outside the home, are people systematically rewarded as they develop these lifeskills. Furthermore, sometimes children are rewarded for exhibiting skills deficits rather than strengths. For instance, they may find that they are more likely to get their way if they shout aggressively rather than take a more reasonable approach. In addition, skills deficits can be acquired by people becoming too dependent on the need for external rewards rather than trusting their own judgement and skills. Also, skills deficits can be developed by people receiving the message that their whole personhood is bad rather than a specific behaviour being insufficiently skilled. Last but not least, many people acquire skills deficits through receiving negative consequences because of their biological sex, race, social class or culture.

Instruction and self-instruction

Psychologists researching animal behaviour stress the importance of learning from example and consequences. However, humans possess the capacity for symbolic thought and communication. Consequently, instruction is a major transmitter of lifeskills strengths and deficits. Much lifeskills instruction takes place informally in the home. Some of this instruction is very basic: for, instance, asking children to say 'please' and 'thank-you'. Children are frequently being told by their parents how to relate, how to study, how to look after their health and so on. Relatives and peers are other providers of instruction outside educational settings.

Much informal lifeskills instruction takes place in schools and colleges. However, systematic attempts to train children in a range of relationship skills are probably still more the exception than the rule. Nevertheless, lifeskills programmes are run in many schools in such areas as career education and drug and alcohol education. In addition, a range of lifeskills programmes may be offered in colleges and universities inside or outside the formal curriculum. The lifeskills targeted include: relationship skills; study skills, managing test anxiety, career development skills, anxiety and stress management skills, and effective thinking skills. Most often participation in such programme is voluntary.

Instruction can be for better or worse. Skills deficits as well as strength can be imparted. For various reasons, those instructed may resist instructors. Sometimes instructors are poor at drawing out the learner rather than just telling them what to do. Frequently instruction contains sex bias: for instance teaching only girls cooking and parenting skills. In addition, lifeskills may not be communicated clearly enough for learners to instruct themselves afterwards. If learners are unable to talk themselves through the relevant sequences of choices, many lifeskills have been inadequately imparted and learned. Much instruction falls far short of this self-instructional objective.

Information and opportunity

People require adequate information to develop lifeskills. For example, keeping children in ignorance about basic facts of sexuality and death impedes self-awareness and emotional responsiveness. Intentionally or unintentionally, adults often relate to their children on the basis of lies, omissions of truth and partial truths (Steiner, 1974). Furthermore necessary information may not be readily available outside the home. For instance, schools differ greatly in the adequacy of the career information they provide.

Children, adolescents and adults alike need available opportunities to test out and develop lifeskills. Ideally such opportunities are in line with their maturation and state of readiness. People may have different opportunities on account of their sex, race, culture, social class, financial position and schooling, to mention but some barriers. Furthermore, people can be fortunate or unfortunate in having parents who open up rather than restrict learning opportunities. Children and adults also have a role in seeking out information and opportunities. Some have better skills at this than others.

Anxiety and confidence

Children grow up having both helpful and harmful experiences for developing self-esteem. The fortunate acquire a level of anxiety that both protects against actual dangers and also motivates them towards realistic achievements. Those less fortunate may acquire debilitating anxieties through role modelling, instruction and provision of faulty consequences. Even parents who communicate carefully can bruise children's fragile self-esteem. Far worse are parents who communicate hostilely and then become defensive. Here children's feelings and perceptions are doubly discounted: first by the initial aggression and second by being subjected to further aggression when they react. However, children differ both biologically in the extent to which they are vulnerable to negative parental behaviour and also in terms of the coping skills they possess.

Deficient behaviours resulting from as well as manifesting anxiety include: unwillingness to take realistic risks; tense and nervous rather than relaxed learning; a heightened tendency to say and do the wrong things; unnecessary aggression; excessive approval seeking; and underachieving, with or without overstriving. Inadequate performance in different skills may further raise anxiety and make future lifeskills learning even more difficult. However, people who are helped or who help themselves to acquire anxiety management skills may learn lifeskills more easily than those without such skills.

MAINTENANCE

People can maintain both lifeskills strengths and deficits. This section focuses only on how people maintain lifeskills deficits. Especially for children, *acquiring* lifeskills strengths and deficits is more a matter of 'what the environment does to me' than 'what I do to myself'. Young people are frequently at the mercy of their elders. However, *maintaining* lifeskills strengths and deficits is a different matter. Here, partly because lifeskills are maintained into adulthood, cause shifts more in the direction of 'what I do to myself' than 'what the environment has done or does to me'. Following are processes which maintain lifeskills deficits.

Insufficient use of skills language

Though offered as a hypothesis, a contributing factor or people maintaining skills deficits is that they insufficiently think about their behaviour in lifeskills terms. Already, drawbacks of not using lifeskills language have ben indicated. People can go round in circles talking about their problems in descriptive language rather than analysing them in skills language. Few people think rigorously about how they think, including being familiar with the various thinking skills. In addition, most people do not know how to redefine everyday problems in skills terms so that they can work for change.

Thinking skills deficits

Lifeskills counselling focuses on stuckness rather than sickness. Thinking skills deficits are a major reason why people maintain poor lifeskills. Too much anxiety tends to be a common theme in faulty thinking. Below are some illustrative thinking skills deficits.

Explaining cause deficits

How people explain cause influences the degree to which they maintain lifeskills deficits. The following are possible explanatory errors that may sustain lifeskills deficits. A common theme is that these explanations of cause tend to convert partial truths into whole truths by missing out relevant aspects of personal responsibility.

• 'It's my nature.' Such as explanation inadequately acknowledges the large learned component in most lifeskills deficits.

• 'It's my unfortunate past.' For people who have left home, explanations of inadequate pasts are largely irrelevant to how they maintain their skills deficits in the present.

• 'It's my bad luck.' People often make their luck by developing relevant skills.

• 'It's my poor environment.' Many people have learned to overcome the skills deficits contributed to by their poor environments.

• 'It's all your fault.' Why bother to change when negative events are someone else's fault?

• 'It's all my fault.' Quite apart from being inaccurate, overinternalizing causes may erode the confidence people require to deal with difficulties in their lives.

Unrealistic personal rules

Personal rules are the 'do's' and 'dont's' by which people lead their lives. Each person has an inner rulebook of standards for themselves and for others. Sometimes these standards are realistic and appropriately flexible. On other occasions the standards may be unrealistic and inappropriately rigid. Ellis has coined the term 'musturbation' to refer to rigid internal rules characterized by 'musts', 'oughts' and 'shoulds' (Ellis, 1980, 1989). These unrealistic rules are not only lifeskills deficits in themselves but may help maintain other lifeskills deficits. Below are illustrations of musturbatory personal rules in different lifeskills areas.

Feeling. 'I must never get angry.'
Sex. 'I must always perform at a high level.'
Thinking. 'All women are less smart than men.'
Relationships. 'I must always win an argument.'
Study. 'I must write the perfect essay.'
Work. 'I must always be stimulated by my job.'
Leisure. 'I must always earn my leisure time.'
Health. 'I must always push myself to the limit of my endurance.'

Possessing unrealistic personal rules about change – that it always should be easy, effortless and painless – contributes to low tolerance of the frustrations entailed in changing. People's low frustration tolerance can contribute to their maintaining their lifeskills deficits.

Perceiving inaccurately

A Chinese proverb states: 'Two-thirds of what we see is behind our eyes.' People erroneously maintain lifeskills deficits if they rigidly perceive their skills to be either better or worse than they are. They may find it difficult to accept contrary feedback if they overestimate how intelligent, affectionate, competent at work or good in bed they are. Also, people may misperceive positive feedback to sustain a negative self-picture as well as negative feedback to sustain a positive self-picture (Rogers, 1959). In both instances, the faulty perceiving contributes to maintaining lifeskills deficits as well as being a lifeskills deficit in itself.

'Defence mechanisms', 'defences' or 'security operations' are terms for the way that people operate on incoming information that differs from their existing self-pictures

(Freud, 1936; Sullivan, 1953; Yalom, 1980). Defensive processes involve people diminishing awareness for short-term psychological comfort. Defensive processes range from denying incoming information to distorting it in various ways: for example rationalizing, making excuses when your behaviour causes you anxiety, or projecting, externalizing thoughts and feelings on to others rather than owning them.

Negative self-talk

Negative self-talk may be contrasted with coping self-talk (Meichenbaum, 1986; Meichenbaum & Deffenbacher, 1988). Negative self-talk statements inhibit people from working on a range of lifeskills deficits. Such negative statements include: 'I'm never going to be able to do it', 'I'm starting to feel anxious and this is a signal that things may get out of control', and 'The future is hopeless'.

Coping self-talk has three main functions: calming, coaching and affirming. A sample calming self-instruction might be 'Keep calm.' A sample coaching self-instruction might be 'Break the task down.' A sample affirming self-instruction is 'I have some skills to deal with this situation.' Frequently, calming, coaching and affirming statements are combined: 'Keep calm. Break the task down. I have some skills to deal with the situation.'

Unrealistic predictions about change

Once acquired, lifeskills deficits can become well-established habits resistant to change (Ellis, 1987). Possible areas for unrealistic predictions about changing include the following.

Fear of the unknown.
Fear of discomfort in making the effort to change.
Fear of losing the payoffs from existing behaviours.
Fear of inner conflict between the old and the emerging self.
Fear of conflict with others arising from changing.
Fear of failure.
Fear of the consequences of success.

Especially if unrealistic, perceived self-inefficacy or lack of confidence in being able to enact the level of performance necessary to produce a desired outcome can be a major prediction that blocks change (Bandura, 1986). Many people fail either to try out changed behaviours, or, if tried, to persist in them in face of setbacks. All learning involves giving up the safety of the known to develop new or different skills. Some people are better able to confront fears about change and setbacks than others. Some of the thinking skills mentioned earlier – for example, perceiving accurately and using coping self-talk – help people to manage rather than to avoid change.

Unchanged environmental circumstances

Lifeskills deficits are usually maintained both by how people think and also by how the environment constrains them. Most factors mentioned in the section on how people acquire lifeskills can help to maintain lifeskills deficits. People may continue to have insufficiently supportive relationships. They may still be exposed to examples of poor thinking and action skills. They may continue to receive inappropriate rewarding consequences. They may fail to receive or find adequate lifeskills instruction and also continue instructing themselves in their deficits. In addition, they may still be exposed to insufficient or faulty information and lack suitable opportunities to develop their skills and human potential.

PRACTICE
Goals

Lifeskills counselling has dual goals: developing the skills to cope with specific problems now and in future, and developing the skilled person. As such, lifeskills counselling goals can be overall or focused, elegant or inelegant. Focused goals entail helping clients acquire the processes of effective choosing in specific areas in which they have problems, for instance dealing with authority figures or speaking in public.

The skilled person

The overall goal of lifeskills counselling is to develop the skilled person who possesses the knowledge and skills to operate effectively in all the main areas of life. Terms like 'self-actualizing', 'self-realizing' and 'fully functioning person' are regarded as too vague and alien to the everyday language of most clients. Given time and client commitment, lifeskills counselling seeks to empower the skilled person rather than the person who is skilled in specific areas. The skilled person can make appropriate choices in a range of areas as well as confront new situations effectively. Below illustrative lifeskills required by the skilled person are grouped according to the five Rs of affirming psychological life.

• *Responsiveness*. Responsiveness skills include existential awareness, awareness of feelings, awareness of inner motivation and sensitivity to anxiety and guilt.

• *Realism*. Realism refers to the thinking skills listed earlier, such as coping self-talk and visualizing.

• *Relating*. Relating skills include: initiating, conversing, disclosing, listening, showing caring, cooperating, assertion, and managing anger and conflict.

• *Rewarding activity*. Rewarding activity skills include identifying interests, work skills, study skills, leisure skills, and looking after physical health skills.

• *Right-and-wrong*. Right-and-wrong skills include social interest that transcends one's immediate environment and ethical living.

Problem management and problematic skills goals

Lifeskills counselling goals encompass assisting clients both to manage problems and to alter the underlying problematic skills that sustain problems. Problem management models, such as those of Carkhuff (1987) and Egan (1994), are useful because clients frequently require help to manage immediate problems. However, a major drawback of such models is that they inadequately address the *repetition phenomenon,* i.e. the repetitive nature of many clients' problems. In the past clients may have repeated underlying self-defeating behaviours, or lifeskills deficits, and they are at risk of continuing to do so in future. An example of such repetition across time is that of people who keep losing jobs because of poor skills in relating to employers. Also clients may repeat self-defeating behaviours, or lifeskills deficits, across a range of current situations. For example, the same people may be non-assertive at home, at work, in leisure activities and so on. Clients require assistance in developing lifeskills strengths that last into the future and not just for managing specific current problems. In reality, practical considerations may limit how much attention counsellors can pay to underlying lifeskills deficits.

DASIE: The five stage model

The practice of lifeskills counselling is structured around DASIE, a systematic five stage model for helping clients both to manage problems and to alter problematic lifeskills. The model provides a framework or set of guidelines for counsellor choices. DASIE's five stages are:

D DEVELOP the relationship, identify and clarify problem(s)
A ASSESS problem(s) and redefine in skills terms
S STATE working goals and plan interventions
I INTERVENE to develop self-helping skills
E END and consolidate self-helping skills

Stage 1: Develop the relationship, identify and clarify problem(s)

Stage 1 starts with pre-helping contact with clients and either ends sometime in the initial interview or may take longer. It has two main overlapping functions: developing supportive counselling relationships and working with clients to identify and obtain fuller descriptions of problems. Supportive counselling relationships go beyond offering empathy, non-possessive warmth and genuineness to more actively fostering client self-support. The nature of the supportive relationships differs according to the stage of the model. In stage 1 counsellors use relating skills to provide emotional support as clients tell and elaborate their stories. In subsequent stages, counsellors use relating skills to support training interventions.

Many of the counsellor skills used in stage 1 are the same as those used in other approaches: for example, reflective responding, summarizing and confronting. Counsellors collaborate with clients to explore, clarify and understand problems. Together they act as detectives to 'sniff out' and discover what are clients' real problems and agendas. Then they break them down into their component parts. An analogy for the role of questioning in initial sessions is that of plants and their root system. For example, a client comes to counselling saying 'I am depressed. Help me.' This statement about depression represents the above ground part of the plant. However, by listening, observing and effective questioning, the counsellor starts identifying roots of the

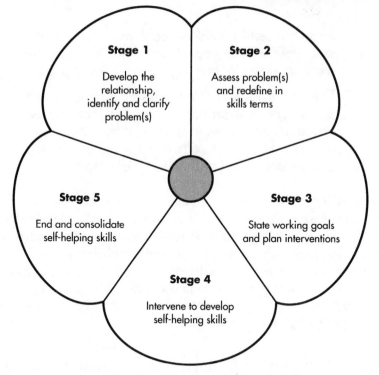

Figure 15.4 DASIE: the five stage lifeskills counselling model.

client's problem in five different areas: e.g. relates poorly to spouse, has a difficult parent, is short of friends, has few pleasant activities and gets little satisfaction from work. Now both counsellor and client have information about the overall problem's sub-structure so that they can develop hypotheses about how the client contributes to sustaining each problem area.

Counsellors can use skills language when structuring initial sessions. One possibility is to start the session by giving clients an open-ended permission to tell their stories. After they respond, the following statement might structure the remainder of the session.

> You've given me some idea of why you've come. Now I'd like to ask some more questions to help us to clarify your problem(s) (specify). Then, depending on what we find, I will suggest some skills to help you cope better. Once we agree on what skills might help you, then we can look at ways to develop them. Does this way of proceeding sound all right?

When structuring counsellors can briefly state reasons for adopting a lifeskills approach. Following are examples.

> It can be useful to think of problems in terms of the skills you need to cope better. This way you get some 'handles' or leverage to work for change.
>
> The approach I take assumes that most behaviour is learned. To work effectively on problems people need to look at how they think and act. Unhelpful skills of thinking and acting can be unlearned and helpful skills learned.

As early as stage 1, counsellors explore ways of enhancing their efficiency as psychological educators. A whiteboard is an essential tool for the lifeskills counsellor. Many clients understand problems better if their component parts are visually presented. Furthermore, clients can easily record what helpers write.

Homework is a feature of lifeskills counselling. Between-session learning is enhanced by clients listening at home to audiocassettes of their counselling sessions. In addition, counsellors may negotiate other homework assignments with clients, for instance completing self-monitoring logs.

Stage 2: Assess problem(s) and redefine in skills terms

The object of this stage is to build a bridge between *describing* and *actively working* on problems and their underlying skills deficits. In stage 1, problems were described, amplified and clarified largely in everyday language. The description of clients' problems represents an expansion of their internal viewpoints rather than providing them with different insights. In stage 2, counsellors build upon information collected in stage 1 to explore hypotheses about how clients think and act that sustain difficulties. Counsellors add to and go beyond clients' present perceptions to look for 'handles' on how to work for change. They collaborate to break down clients' problems into their component skills deficits. Whereas stage 1 might end with descriptive summaries of problems in everyday terms, stage 2 ends with a redefinition of at least either the main or the most pressing problem in skill terms.

In stage 2 the nature of the supportive relationship changes. In stage 1, counsellors support clients in telling their stories in their own terms. In stage 2 counsellors support clients in making sense of their stories. A critical ingredient of stage 2 is for counsellors to maintain a skills focus. Maintaining a skills focus does not mean that counsellors immediately translate everything clients say into skills language. However the question at the back of helpers' minds in stage 2 is always: 'What skills deficits sustain clients' problems?' Most clients do not think of their problems in skills language, so counsellors require sensitivity in when and how they convey that clients may have specific thinking and action skills deficits.

The emphasis in counsellors' questions differs in stage 2 from that in stage 1. In stage 1 counsellors ask questions to clarify clients' existing frames of reference. In stage 2 counsellors are likely to question as much from their own as from their clients' frames of reference. Much questioning is based on information wittingly or unwittingly provided by clients – clues, hunches, how things are said, what is left unsaid, and overt and subtle indications of underlying thought patterns. While the major focus is on pinpointing skills deficits, attention is also paid to identifying skills strengths and resources. Strength reviews both identify skills for coping with problems and also prevent assessments from becoming too negative. Following is an example where the counsellor attempts to help a middle-aged client Tania, who gave up an office management job in a university department, identify her strengths.

Counsellor: Uh-uhm. So, I'm first going to ask you something which may seem a little bit strange. But what do you think were your strengths in how you handled both the problems at the office and as a worker?

Client: Um. How I handled the problems? My strengths were . . . that's hard because I keep focusing on what I didn't do right.

If they have not already done so, counsellors can suggest the value of breaking problems down into the component skills that sustain them. Furthermore, they introduce clients to the distinction between thinking skills and action skills, often using the inner and outer game analogy. In the following excerpt, the counsellor lays the groundwork for identifying two of Tania's thinking skills deficits: an unrealistic rule about perfection and choosing not to perceive her strengths and others' positive feedback.

Counsellor: There was a little more of the negative, it sounds to me, than there should have been.

Client: That's true. And I think too that was based on the fact that I thought I should be able to do everything absolutely perfectly.

Counsellor: And that gets into a rule about perfection.

Client: Yes.

Counsellor: Yes.

Client: Cause I wouldn't have been happy with anything less than them saying she's the best office manager we've had.

Counsellor: Right, right, right.

Client: I mean, in fact, I met one of the staff members in the street the other day and he said 'You're an absolute legend and we keep saying we need another Tania.' And I keep saying, 'Oh dear.'

Counsellor: Right, so it's partly your rule about perfection, that you felt you may not have measured up to perfection, but it's also that you didn't perceive your strengths and the fact that the academic staff did think you were super.

Client: Yeah.

Counsellor: But Tania wasn't thinking she was super.

Counsellors need to develop good skills at redefining problems in skills terms and communicating these working definitions to clients. A good redefinition succinctly suggests clients' main skills deficits that sustain problems. Counsellors need to distinguish important from less important material. Redefinitions that are too comprehensive confuse. Often it helps to write redefinitions in skills terms on whiteboards. Visual communication makes it easier for clients to retain what you say and, if necessary, suggest alterations. Counsellors use a simple T diagram to present thinking and action skills weaknesses for sustaining each problem (see Figure 15.5). At the top of the T there are headings for 'Thinking skills deficits' and 'Action skills deficits'. These headings are divided by a long vertical line down the middle to allow specific deficits to be listed on either side.

Redefinitions of problems in skills terms, otherwise known as T redefinitions, need be negotiated with clients. Counsellors require good questioning and facilitation skills when checking redefinitions with clients. If counsellors, in stages 1 and 2, have competently gathered information, skills redefinitions should flow reasonably logically from this material. Clients who share their counsellors' conceptualizations of problems are more likely to commit themselves to developing self-helping skills than clients resisting counsellors' conceptualizations. Redefinitions of problems in skills terms are essentially hypotheses, based on careful analysis of available information, about clients' thinking and action skills deficits. As hypotheses they are open to modification in light of further or better information. Redefining problems in skills terms can be difficult. Mistakes in redefinition not only lead to time and effort being wasted, but may contribute to clients being even less able to manage problems.

Figure 15.5 is a redefinition of Tania's office management problem in skills terms. Even though she had given up this job, Tania wanted to understand the issues raised by it because they were undermining her confidence in getting another job.

Stage 3: State working goals and plan interventions

Stage 3 builds on counsellors' redefinitions in skills terms to focus on the question 'What is the best way to develop the required self-helping skills?' Stage 3 consists of two phases: stating working goals and planning interventions.

Thinking skills deficits	Action skills deficits
Insufficiently owning responsibility for being a chooser at work Unrealistic personal rules, for example, everyone must approve of me, I must be the perfect manager Inaccurately perceiving, for example, not acknowledging own strengths, discounting positive feedback Negative self-talk, for example, about confronting difficult colleagues	Giving instruction non-assertively (poor verbal, voice and body messages) Getting support skills, for example, from department head

Figure 15.5 T format redefinition of Tania's office management problem.

Stating working goals

Goals can be stated at different levels of specificity. First, goals can be stated in overall terms such as: 'I want to feel less depressed'; 'I want to improve my marriage', or 'I want to come to terms with my disability and get back into life'. Such overall goals statements give clients visions about what they want from counselling. However, overall statements refer more to ends than to means. Second, goals can be stated in terms of the skills required to attain ends. This level of specificity is required for stage three. Assuming counsellors succeed in redefining problems in skills terms, stating goals becomes a relatively simple matter. Working goals are the flip-side of redefinitions: positive statements of skills strengths to replace existing skills deficits. For instance, Tania's thinking skills goals are to develop her skills of: owning responsibility for being a chooser at work; possessing realistic personal rules about perfection and approval; accurately perceiving her strengths and others' feedback; and coping self-talk for confronting difficult colleagues. Tania's action skills goals are to develop her skills of giving instructions assertively and of getting support.

Third, goals can be stated still more precisely. For example, Tania's giving instructions assertively skills can be broken down still further into specific verbal, voice and body message goals for different target people. Each case requires being treated on its merits. Clients can only cope with so much information at any one time. A risk of getting into too much detail in an initial session is that clients retain little if anything. Usually detailed descriptions of skills goals are best left to later sessions. In stage 3 counsellors should state working goals clearly and succinctly. If using whiteboards, they can alter existing skills redefinitions to become working goals. Counsellors ensure that clients understand and agree with working goals.

Planning interventions

Statements of working goals provide bridges to choosing interventions. Counsellors not only hypothesize about goals but also about ways to attain them. An important distinction exists between interventions and plans. Interventions are intentional behaviours, on the part of either counsellors or clients, designed to help clients attain problem management and problematic skills goals. Plans are statements of how to combine and sequence interventions to attain working goals.

Clients come for counselling with a wide variety of problems, expectations, motivations, priorities, time constraints and lifeskills strengths and deficits. Counsellors tailor intervention plans to individual clients. In very focused helping, say anxiety about an imminent test, counsellors are likely to plan to manage the immediate problem with less emphasis on altering underlying problematic skills. With more time to alter problematic skills, counsellors may choose between structured plans and open plans.

Structured plans are step by step training and learning outlines of interventions for attaining specific goals. Sometimes structured plans involve using existing material, for instance developing relaxation skills using a programme based on Bernstein and Borkovec's (1973) *Progressive Relaxation Training: A Manual for the Helping Professions.*

Counsellors and clients can also design partially structured plans to attain working goals. For instance, in the case of a recently fired executive, certain sessions might be set aside for testing to assess interests and aptitudes and for attending a brief course to develop specific action skills, such as résumé writing and interview skills. Agendas for the remaining sessions are negotiated at the start of each session.

Open plans allow helpers and clients, without predetermined structure, to choose which interventions, to attain which working goals, when. Open plans have the great advantage of flexibility. Clients may be more motivated to work on skills and material relevant at any given time than run through predetermined programmes independent of current considerations. Furthermore, owing to the frequently repetitive nature of clients' skills deficits, work done in one session may be highly relevant to work done on the same or different problems in other sessions.

Stage 4: Intervene to develop self-helping skills

The interventions stage can have three objectives. First, to help clients manage their presenting problems better. Second, to assist clients in working on problematic skills and in developing skills strengths for preventing and coping with specific situations. Third, to help clients become more skilled persons. Counsellors are psychological educators or, in more colloquial terms, user-friendly coaches. To intervene effectively they require good relating skills and good training skills. It is insufficient to know *what* interventions to offer without also being skilled at *how* to offer them. Skilled counsellors strike appropriate balances between relationship and task orientations; less skilled helpers err in either direction.

Table 15.1 depicts methods of psychological education or training and methods of learning in lifeskills counselling. Counsellors work much of the time with the three training methods of 'tell', 'show' and 'do'. They require special training skills for each. 'Tell' entails giving clients clear instructions concerning the skills they wish to develop. 'Show' means providing demonstrations of how to implement skills. 'Do' means arranging for clients to perform structured activities and homework tasks.

Individual sessions in the intervention stage may be viewed in four, often overlapping, phases: preparatory, initial, working and ending. The preparatory phase entails counsellor thinking in advance how best to assist clients. Counsellors ensure that, if appropriate, they have available: session plans; training materials, for instance handouts; and audio-visual aids, for instance whiteboards and audiocassette-recorders. The initial phase consists of meeting, greeting and seating, then giving permission to talk. Though a skill not restricted to the initial phase, early on counsellors may wish to negotiate session agendas. For instance, counsellors may go from checking whether the client has any current pressing agendas, to reviewing the past week's homework, to focusing on one or more problematic skills and/or problems in clients' lives. As necessary, agendas may be altered during sessions.

Within a supportive relationship, the working phase focuses on specific thinking skills and action skills interventions designed to help clients manage problems and develop lifeskills strengths. Whenever appropriate, counsellors assist clients to use skills language. The ending phase lasts from towards the end of one session to the beginning

Table 15.1 Methods of psychological education or training and of learning

Psychological education or training method	Learning method
Facilitate	Learning from self-exploring and from experiencing self more fully
Assess	Learning from self-evaluating and from self-monitoring
Tell	Learning from hearing
Show	Learning from observing
Do	Learning from doing structured activities and homework tasks
Consolidate	Learning from developing self-helping skills in all the above modes

of the next. This phase focuses on summarizing the major session learnings, negotiating homework, strengthening commitment to between session work, and rehearsing and practising skills outside helping.

Thinking skills interventions vary according to which skill is targeted. Common themes are increasing awareness of weaknesses in the targeted skill, challenging faulty thinking and training in effective thinking. For example, a counsellor working with a client, one of whose working goals is to develop a more realistic rule about approval, can intervene in the following sequence: introduce and raise awareness of the skill of choosing realistic personal rules; identify the current unrealistic rule and its consequences; dispute the unrealistic rule; reform the unrealistic rule into a more realistic rule, for instance. 'Though I would prefer to be liked by my colleagues, what is more important is that I respect myself and do my job as well as I can': encourage the client to change his or her actions to accord with the changed rule, for instance, by being more assertive; and emphasize practice and self-helping.

Action skills interventions include developing clients' self-monitoring skills, sequencing graded tasks, conducting rehearsals and role-plays, timetabling activities, using exercises and games, using counsellors' aides, and assisting clients to identify supports in their home environments for their changed actions. Often lifeskills counsellors work with clients to set up personal experiments in which clients use new action skills in real-life settings on a try-out basis. Clients develop 'If . . . then . . .' statements. In the 'If' part of the statement they stipulate a specific situation and the targeted skills they will use in it. In the 'then' part of the statement they predict the consequences of using their changed behaviours. After a period of rehearsal and practice, clients try out their changed action skills in real life. Then, together with their counsellors, they evaluate the consequences.

Interventions for focusing on feelings emphasize developing clients' thinking skills and action skills. In redefining problems and stating working goals, counsellors need to distinguish between experiencing feelings, expressing feelings and managing unwanted feelings. Interventions for assisting clients to *experience* their feelings include legitimizing the importance of feelings, rewarding listening, using feelings questions, role-play methods, confronting inauthenticity, training in inner listening and developing appropriate thinking skills. Interventions for *expressing* feelings are the same as the interventions for developing action skills described above. Interventions for *managing* feelings vary according to the feeling to be managed. For instance, thinking skills interventions for managing depression can target negative predictions, unrealistic personal rules, unnecessarily negative views of self and attributing too much of the cause for negative events to oneself. Action skills interventions for managing depression can target relating, assertion and engaging in pleasant activities skills.

Consolidating learned skills as self-helping skills takes place at the end of and between each session. Frequently clients are asked to fill out homework sheets. Providing written homework instructions for clients serves the following purposes: giving a message that homework is important, clarifying and helping clients remember what is required and providing something in writing that can be posted as a reminder.

Stage 5: End and consolidate self-helping skills

Most often either counsellors or clients being up the topic of ending before the final session. This allows both parties to work through the various task and relationship issues connected with ending the contact. A useful option is to fade contact with some clients by seeing them progressively less often. Certain clients may appreciate the opportunity for booster sessions, say one, two, three or even six months later. Booster sessions provide both clients and counsellors with the chance to review progress and consolidate self-helping skills. Scheduling follow-up telephone calls can perform some of these functions too.

Lifeskills counselling seeks to avoid the 'train and hope' approach. For instance, prior to the ending stage, counsellors structure realistic expectations when discussing working definitions and goals with clients. The concept of lifeskills gets away from notions of magic and cure. Counsellors explicitly and repeatedly state that clients have to work and practise not only to acquire but to maintain the targeted lifeskills.

Counsellors attempt to build clients' self-observation and assessment skills. Transfer and maintenance of skills is encouraged by such means as developing clients' self-instructional abilities, working with real-life situations during helping, and using between-session time productively to listen to session cassettes and to rehearse and practise skills. Often counsellors make up short cassettes focused on the use of specific skills in specific situations: for instance, the use of coping self-talk to handle anxiety when waiting to drive off on the first tee in golf. Counsellors then encourage clients to make up similar coping self-talk cassettes for other situations: for instance, walking down the fairway on the first hole. Thus, not only do clients possess cassettes they can use to maintain skills in future, they have also acquired the skills of making new cassettes, if needed.

In addition, counsellors work with clients to anticipate difficulties and set-backs. Then together they develop and rehearse coping strategies for preventing and managing lapses and relapses. Sometimes clients require help identifying people to support their efforts to maintain skills. Counsellors also provide information about further skills building opportunities.

Applying the model

Counsellors, in the best interests of clients, need to apply the DASIE counselling model flexibly. Managing problems and altering problematic skills rarely proceed according to neatly ordered stages. The stages tend to overlap. Also, counsellors may revert to earlier stages as more information or new problems emerge.

DASIE is a model of central tendency. The model assumes that much counselling is relatively short-term, say 3 to 10 sessions, and tends to be focused on one or two main problems and problematic skills areas. However, counselling can also be very brief, say 1 or 2 sessions, or it may be extended to 10 to 20 sessions or more. Both in brief and extended counselling, counsellors adjust how person-oriented or task-oriented to be. For example, in brief counselling an early skills focus may be inappropriate with recently bereaved clients needing space to tell their stories and experience their grief. On the other hand, an immediate skills focus may be highly appropriate with clients anxious about upcoming job interviews. Since different reasons exist for extended helping, there are no simple answers for how best to go about it. Vulnerable clients may require more gentle and nurturing relationships than robust clients and take longer to attain insight into how they sustain problems. However, it is possible to overgeneralize. From the initial session some vulnerable clients may appreciate identifying and working on one or two specific skills deficits.

The DASIE counselling model requires counsellors to possess effective thinking skills as well as effective action skills. Counsellors step outside everyday language to conceptualize problems in skills terms. Counsellors should possess both good relating skills and good training skills. In addition, lifeskills counsellors require a range of specific interventions related to clients' problems and problematic skills. Building a repertoire of interventions takes time and effort. Proficiency in lifeskills helping is a lifetime challenge.

Other applications

Lifeskills counselling can be used to help clients confront existential concerns as well as immediate problems. Take the case of people suffering from terminal cancer. They may require assistance in at least four areas: confronting and coming to terms with death anxiety; dealing with problems that arise from the cancer experience, for instance, changes in physical appearance and declining health; coping with problems that they have independent of their cancer, for instance a stressful lifestyle or poor communication with a spouse; and finding genuine meaning for the remainder of their lives (Nelson-Jones & Cosolo, 1994b). A skilled lifeskills counsellor is alert to and prepared to work in all these areas.

Lifeskills counselling has group applications. First, lifeskills concepts can be interwoven with the work of interactional counselling groups. For example, counselling groups might use skills language to analyse either communication within the group or members' problems outside the group. Also, group counsellors can assist members in developing relevant thinking and action skills. Second, lifeskills counselling principles can be extended to lifeskills training groups, for instance training groups in listening skills or stress management skills. Key characteristics of such groups include using skills language, stipulating clear thinking skills and action skills goals, offering supportive relationships, using good training skills, and emphasizing consolidating trained skills as self-helping skills.

Above all, lifeskills counselling is a self-helping approach. Truly elegant use of it means that clients are able to apply it to both old and new problems. The DASIE counselling model can be adapted to become the CASIE self-helping model:

C CONFRONT, identify and clarify my problem
A ASSESS my problem and redefine it in skills terms
S STATE working goals and plan self-helping interventions
I IMPLEMENT my plan
E EVALUATE the consequences of implementing my plan.

If people are to affirm their psychological lives, they require the courage and skills to do it for themselves.

CHAPTER REVIEW AND SELF-REFERENT QUESTIONS

Chapter review questions

1. Why is lifeskills counselling a psychological education approach to counselling?

2. What are some differences between psychological life and biological life?

3. What are lifeskills?

4. Why does lifeskills counselling emphasize the importance of skills language?

5. Describe each of the three forms of self. How are they related?

6. What is the energizing drive?

7. What is survival anxiety?

8. Why is normal anxiety an inevitable part of life?

9. What does Nelson-Jones mean by personal responsibility?

10. What does Nelson-Jones means by courage?

11. What are the inner and outer games of lifeskills counselling?

12. Describe each of the five ways of sending action skills messages.

13. Why are supportive relationships important in helping children acquire lifeskills?

14. Apart from supportive relationships, what other processes are important in helping children acquire lifeskills strengths and avoid acquiring lifeskills deficits?

15. How do people maintain lifeskills deficits?

16. What is the skilled person and what are the five Rs for affirming psychological life?

17. What is the difference between a problem management goal and a problematic skills goal?

18. What is the role of the counsellor–client relationship in lifeskills counselling?

19. What are the goals of stage 1 of the DASIE model and what are some counsellor skills for attaining them?

20. How do lifeskills counsellors go about assessing clients' problems?

21. What are some important skills for redefining clients' problems in skills terms?

22. What are the different levels of specificity for stating clients' goals and which level applies to stating working goals?

23. What is the difference between an intervention and a plan and what are some different kinds of plans?

24. What are trainer skills and what is their role in lifeskills counselling?

25. What are some interventions for developing clients' thinking skills?

26. What are some interventions for developing clients' action skills?

27. What are some interventions for helping clients:
    (a) experience feelings
    (b) express feelings
    (c) manage unwanted feelings?

28. What skills do lifeskills counsellors use for consolidating clients' trained skills as self helping skills?

Self-referent questions

1. How do you react to applying skills language to your own problems and life?

2. Identify one of your lifeskills deficits and describe how you acquired it.

3. For the lifeskills deficit you identified above, how have you maintained it in the past and how are your currently maintaining it?

4. How skilled a person are you? Answer with respect to each of the 5 Rs.

5. Confront a problem in your life and redefine it in skills terms, identifying at least one thinking skills deficit and one action skills deficit.

6. Translate the thinking skills deficits and action skills deficits identified above into a statement of working goals and develop a plan to attain them.

7. Implement your plan and evaluate the consequences of doing so.

8. What relevance, if any, has the theory and practice of lifeskills counselling for how you counsel?

9. What relevance, if any, has the theory and practice of lifeskills counselling for how you live?

Annotated bibliography

Nelson-Jones, R. (1993). *Practical Counselling and Helping Skills: How to Use the Lifeskills Helping Model* (3rd ed.). London: Cassell.

Nelson-Jones, R. (1992). *Lifeskills Helping: A Textbook of Practical Counselling and Helping Skills* (3rd ed.). Sydney: Holt, Rinehart & Winston (Australian edition).

This book is aimed at people training either to be professional counsellors or for roles with a large counselling content. Part 1 provides a theoretical framework, overviews the lifeskills helping model, and reviews characteristics that people bring to helping either as students or counsellors. Part 2 presents the component skills for each of the five stages of the DASIE counselling process model.

Nelson-Jones, R. (1993). *You Can Help!: Introducing Lifeskills Helping*. London: Cassell.
This book is a beginners' text for non-professional helpers. The component skills for each of the five stages of the DASIE counselling process model are described in simple 'how-to' language. Learning points are highlighted and relevant case material and activities reinforce the book's practical, user-friendly approach.

Nelson-Jones, R. (1993). *Training Manual for Counselling and Helping Skills*. London: Cassell.
The training manual's purpose is to assist students and others learn practical counselling skills. It consists of 84 exercises and 16 experiments, mainly designed to build skills for each of the five stages of the DASIE model. The training manual can be used alongside either the advanced or the beginners' lifeskills helping texts.

Nelson-Jones, R. (1984). *Personal Responsibility Counselling and Therapy*. Milton Keynes: Open University Press.
The first part of this book reviews the concept of personal responsibility in the theory and practice of different counselling approaches. The second part develops the theory and practice of a counselling approach with personal responsibility as a central integrating concept. The book represents a developmental stage in what was to become lifeskills helping.

Further references

Nelson-Jones

Nelson-Jones, R. (1979). Goals for counselling, psychotherapy and psychological education: Responsibility as an integrating concept. *British Journal of Guidance and Counselling, 7*, 153–68.

Nelson-Jones, R. (1986). Toward a people-centred language of counselling psychology. *The Australian Counselling Psychologist, 2*, 18–23.

Nelson-Jones, R. (1987). DASIE: A five stage model for problem management counselling and helping. *Counselling, 61*, 2–10.

Nelson-Jones, R. (1988). The counselling psychologist as developmental educator. *The Australian Counselling Psychologist, 4*, 55–66.

Nelson-Jones R. (1989). *Effective Thinking Skills: Preventing and Managing Personal Problems*. London: Cassell.

Nelson-Jones, R. (1990). *Human Relationship Skills* (2nd ed.). London: Cassell.

Nelson-Jones, (1991b). *Lifeskills: A Handbook*. London: Cassell.

Nelson-Jones, R. (1992). In the counsellor's chair: Stephen Palmer interviews Richard Nelson-Jones. *Counselling, 3*, 203–206

Nelson-Jones, R. (1994a). Hello DASIE! Introducing the lifeskills helping model. *Counselling, 5*, 109–12.

Nelson-Jones, R. & Cosolo, W. (1994b). How to assess cancer patients' thinking skills. *Palliative Medicine, 8*, 115–21.

Others

Allport, G.W. (1955). *Becoming: Basic Considerations for a Psychology of Personality*. New Haven: Yale University Press.

Alpert, R. & Haber, R.N. (1960). Anxiety in academic achievement situations. *Journal of Abnormal and Social Psychology, 61*, 204–15.

Bandura, A. (1986). *Social Foundations of Thought and Action: A Social Cognitive Theory.* Englewood Cliffs, NJ: Prentice-Hall.

Beck, A.T. (1991). Cognitive therapy: A 10–year retrospective. *American Psychologist, 46*, 368–75.

Beck, A.T. & Weishaar, M.E. (1989). Cognitive therapy. In R.J. Corsini & D. Wedding (Eds.), *Current Psychotherapies* (4th ed., pp. 285–320). Itasca, IL: Peacock.

Bernstein, D.A. & Borkovec, T.D. (1973). *Progressive Relaxation Training: A Manual for the Helping Professions.* Champaign, IL: Research Press.

Bowlby, J. (1979). *The Making and Breaking of Affectional Bonds.* London: Tavistock.

Carkhuff, R.R. (1987). *The Art of Helping* (6th ed.). Amherst, MA: Human Resource Development Press.

Egan, G. (1994). *The Skilled Helper: A Systematic Approach of Effective Helping* (5th ed.). Pacific Grove, CA: Brooks/Cole.

Ellis, A. (1980). Overview of the clinical theory or rational-emotive therapy. In R. Grieger & J. Boyd (Eds.). *Rational-emotive Therapy: A Skills Based Approach* (pp. 1–31). New York: Van Nostrand.

Ellis, A. (1987). The impossibility of achieving consistently good mental health. *American Psychologist, 42*, 364–75.

Ellis, A. (1989). Rational-emotive therapy. In R.J. Corsini & D. Wedding (Eds.), *Current Psychotherapies* (4th ed., pp. 197–238). Itasca, IL: Peacock.

Frankl, V.E. (1959). *Man's Search for Meaning.* New York: Washington Square Press.

Freud, S. (1936). *The Problem of Anxiety.* New York: Norton.

Glasser, W. (1965). *Reality Therapy: A New Approach to Psychiatry.* New York: Harper & Row.

Lazarus, A.A. (1984). *In the Mind's Eye.* New York: Guilford Press.

Lazarus, A.A. (1989). Multimodal therapy. In R.J. Corsini & D. Wedding (Eds.), *Current Psychotherapies* (4th ed., pp. 503–44). Itasca, IL: Peacock.

Maslow, A.H. (1962). *Toward A Psychology of Being.* New York: Van Nostrand.

Maslow, A.H. (1970). *Motivation and Personality* (2nd ed.). New York: Harper & Row.

May, R. (1975). *The Courage to Create.* New York: Norton.

May, R. & Yalom, I.D. (1989). Existential psychotherapy. In R.J. Corsini & D. Wedding (Eds.) *Current Psychotherapies* (4th ed., pp. 363–402). Itasca, IL: Peacock.

Meichenbaum, D.H. (1986). Cognitive-behavior modification. In F.H. Kanfer & A. P. Goldstein (Eds.), *Helping People Change: A Textbook of Methods* (3rd ed., pp. 346–80). New York: Pergamon Press.

Meichenbaum, D.H. & Deffenbacher, J.L. (1988). Stress inoculation training. *The Counseling Psychologist, 16*, 69–90.

Mowrer, O.H. (1964). *The New Group Therapy.* Princeton, NJ: Van Nostrand.

Raskin, N.J. & Rogers, C.R. (1989). Person-centered therapy. In R.J. Corsini & D. Wedding (Eds.), *Current Psychotherapies* (4th ed., pp. 155–94). Itasca, IL: Peacock.

Rogers, C.R. (1951). *Client-centered Therapy.* Boston: Houghton Miflin.

Rogers, C.R. (1959). A theory of therapy, personality, and interpersonal relationships, as developed in the client-centered framework. In S. Koch (Ed.), *Psychology: A Study of Science* (Study 1, Volume 3, pp. 184–256). New York: McGraw-Hill.

Rogers, C.R. (1980). *A Way of Being.* Boston: Houghton Miflin

Sartre, J.P. (1956). *Being and Nothingness.* New York: Philosophical Library.

Skinner, B.F. (1971). *Beyond Freedom and Dignity.* Harmondsworth: Penguin.

Steiner, C.M. (1974). *Scripts People Live*. New York: Bantam Books.
Sullivan, H.S. (1953). *The Interpersonal Theory of Psychiatry*. New York: Norton.
Sullivan, H.S. (1954). *The Psychiatric Interview*. New York: Norton.
Tillich, P. (1952). *The Courage to Be*. New Haven: Yale University Press.
Yalom, I.D. (1980). *Existential Psychotherapy*. New York: Basic Books.

Name Index

Subject Index